THE GLORIES
OF
DIVINE GRACE

*"For the Spirit himself giveth testimony
to our spirit, that we are the sons of God.
And if sons, heirs also; heirs indeed of God,
and joint heirs with Christ: yet so, if we suffer with him, that we may be also glorified
with him. For I reckon that the sufferings of
this time are not worthy to be compared
with the glory to come, that shall be
revealed in us."*

—Romans 8:16-18

THE GLORIES

OF

DIVINE GRACE

A FERVENT EXHORTATION TO ALL
TO PRESERVE AND TO GROW
IN SANCTIFYING GRACE

By

Fr. Matthias Joseph Scheeben

(1835-1888)

Translated by

Patrick Shaughnessy, O.S.B.

*"By whom he hath given us most
great and precious promises: that by
these you may be made partakers of
the divine nature . . ."* —2 Peter 1:4

TAN Books
Charlotte, North Carolina

TAN Books
Charlotte, North Carolina
www.TANBooks.com
2000

FROM THE BOOK . . .

"Not only does grace surpass all natural things, it also surpasses all the miraculous works of God. . . . Thus the work of grace is the greatest wonder of God's omnipotence. It is even greater than His creation of the world out of nothing. It can be compared only with that unspeakable act of God the Father by which He begets from all eternity His own Son, equal to Himself, and in time unites Him with a human nature." —*Page* 12

Publisher's Preface

THE Glories of Divine Grace will very likely become the most influential book a Catholic will ever read—and one of the most insightful. For it is all about Sanctifying Grace, which is none other than the life of God imparted to our souls at Baptism. The entire purpose of this book is to show us what that fact should mean to us and how it should affect and alter our lives—indeed, how we who are baptized should therefore live. Few people, including most Catholics, ever give Sanctifying Grace a thought, other than to ask themselves whether they are in the state of grace. But the author of this book—an eminent German theologian of the 19th century—writes sixty chapters about the nature of Sanctifying Grace, how it brings about our union with God, how Sanctifying Grace works, the effects of it upon our souls, and how we can and should grow in it.

If anyone with even a modicum of faith can read the first two pages of this book and not continue on through the end, it would be surprising. For *The Glories of Divine Grace* is not an abstract thesis in theology, but rather a popular book written for *all* Catholics, to show them what an unbelievable gift God has given mankind in Sanctifying Grace. It is a book written with passion and for the salvation of souls, a book of rare understanding, and a book designed and written—with a pen on fire—to shock its readers into an understanding of what they have been for so long taking for granted, without ever really knowing what they possess, and which makes them vastly different in the elevation of their nature from those who do not possess this incomparable gift.

What is Sanctifying Grace? It is none other than the life of God Himself imparted to the soul, whereby man is raised, in a true sense, to the divine level and by which man becomes a friend and a child of God, an heir to Heaven, and is thereby and thereafter pleasing in His sight—so long as man remains in the state of Sanctifying Grace. Sanctifying Grace is our "ticket to Heaven," so to speak. When we die, we will ultimately go to Heaven or to Hell for all eternity, depending on whether or not we have Sanctifying Grace in our souls. The presence or absence of Sanctifying Grace in our souls at the moment of death will decide our eternal salvation or our everlasting damnation.

How do we receive this admirable gift? It is received through the Sacrament of the Catholic Church called Baptism. *And how can we lose it?* We lose it by committing mortal sins, which are those sins 1) of a grievous nature (in themselves, or which we think are grievous), 2) which we fully know to be mortally sinful, and yet 3) which we commit anyway, with the full consent of our will.

How do we gain back Sanctifying Grace? We gain it back through the Sacrament of Penance (Confession) when we confess our sins to a priest with true sorrow and a firm purpose of amendment. We can also gain back Sanctifying Grace by making an act of perfect contrition, which is a prayer of sorrow for having offended God *because He is infinitely good and worthy of all our love.* (But, having committed a mortal sin, we still have to go to Confession before receiving Communion, even though we have made an act of perfect contrition.)

Ezechiel the Prophet was speaking of Sanctifying Grace when he said: "But if the just man turn himself away from his justice, and do iniquity according to all the abominations which the wicked man useth to work, shall he live? [I.e., shall he be in the state of Sanctifying Grace?] All his justices which he has done shall not be remembered: in the prevarication by which he has prevaricated, and in his sin, which he hath committed, in them he shall die" [i.e., he will be in the state of mortal sin, with his soul dead to God's grace, and he will go to Hell if he dies in that state]. (*Ezechiel* 18:24). Again, Ezechiel has written: "And when the wicked turneth himself away from his wickedness, which he has wrought [mortal sin], and doeth judgment and justice, he shall save his soul alive." (*Ezechiel* 18:27). This is to say that, when a sinner turns away from his mortal sins and repents in accordance with God's law, he shall gain back Sanctifying Grace.

The term "Sanctifying Grace" is not used in Sacred Scripture, but Sanctifying Grace is referred to in Scripture time and again, and Fr. Scheeben points out to us in this marvelous treatise many of the passages from the Bible that refer to this precious gift of God. Some Scriptural terms for Sanctifying Grace and its effects are "living water," "born again," "wedding garment," "new creation," "children of God," "divine adoption," "life," "justice," "just," "charity," etc.

In *The Glories of Divine Grace*, the author speaks almost always simply about "grace," but by this term he means "Sanctifying Grace," which is *"life,"* spiritual life—the life of God imparted to the soul, which causes the soul to be (as we say) "in the state of grace." This is to distinguish it from "Actual Grace," which is a passing *"help"* from God to do a certain good thing or to avoid an evil thing. Indeed, the author speaks occasionally about Actual Grace, but for the most part in this book, when he speaks merely of "grace," he is speaking about Sanctifying Grace. And when he speaks about "the glories of divine grace," he is *always* speaking about Sanctifying Grace, the grace of God that gives life to the soul—supernatural life, the life of God.

He explains most clearly that this "life of God" (Sanctifying Grace) is so much above us that we cannot possibly acquire it on our own; that it is strictly a gift which God freely bestows upon us; and that without it, our "works" (good works) are dead, as far as meriting an eternal reward. But with it, the good or virtuous works that we do have merit in the sight of God and will forever redound to our spiritual credit in eternity. Those who deny the eternal value of good works (i.e., Protestants) are correct with regard to works performed when a person is *not in the state of grace*, for without Sanctifying Grace in his soul, a person merits by his good works nothing at all for eternity. But when a person is *in the state of grace* (has Sanctifying Grace in his soul), that person *does indeed* merit by his good works an eternal reward, because he is now no longer a mere "natural" human who performs these works, but a child of God who does them. Such deeds done while the life of God is in one's soul have merit for eternity, for they have been done by no mere natural man, but by an adopted son of God, by a living branch on the vine which is Christ.

We see in the parable of the five wise and five foolish virgins, who have lighted lamps in their hands and are awaiting the arrival of the bridegroom and his party (representing Christ coming at the death of an individual to judge him), that when he was late in coming, they slept, and the lamps of the foolish virgins burned out (they had lost Sanctifying Grace); whereas, the lamps of the five wise virgins had been replenished with the extra oil they had wisely brought with them, and thus they were ready, with their lamps burning (their souls in the state of Sanctifying Grace), to go forth to meet their Lord and enter into the marriage feast (representing Heaven). However, the foolish virgins were left outside (representing Hell). Although the term "Sanctifying Grace" is not mentioned, that is clearly what is referred to in this parable. And *The Glories of Divine Grace* again and again cites famous Scriptural passages that refer to Sanctifying Grace, which is the Catholic term for the life of God received into our souls at Baptism.

As St. Teresa of Avila could come back to earth and appear in vision to a certain person and state that she would gladly live her entire life over again, just to be able to say one more "Hail Mary" and thus enhance the level of her happiness in Heaven, then what should not we be doing to grow and grow in Sanctifying Grace while we can, and thereby gain a higher place in Heaven, where the level of our happiness will be that much greater? And this is why *The Glories of Divine Grace* is so influential: because it will motivate us to attempt at every turn in our lives—just as the Saints have done—to continue to grow in divine grace, uninterruptedly, right to the end of our lives. No other book we know of has such power to influence and persuade people to come to understand properly, to co-operate with, and to augment Almighty God's divine gift of Sanctifying Grace in our souls, so that we will desire ever to increase our store of it.

This is a book that should become a constant companion at one's bedside, even after a person has once read it, for it is a book that—read a chapter at a time, now and then—will keep before the mind of the Catholic striving for perfection a constant, continually fresh idea of the greatness of this gift of Sanctifying Grace, because, having been baptized in Christ, we need to live as *new men*, "newly created" men and women, people raised up to a level that the unbaptized have no dream even exists!

After reading a few chapters of this book, one will begin to realize why many of the greatest Saints were people who never committed a mortal sin, and why some were even so privileged as never to have committed so much as a purposeful venial sin. In these great Saints, grace built upon grace, and their souls grew in Sanctifying Grace unimpeded, so that their spiritual progress was never set back by their falling into mortal sin. Thus were they able ever to advance in the life of God, their unobstructed spiritual growth being the secret of their spiritual greatness. The lesson for us in this regard from *The Glories of Divine Grace* should be that we should *never* "experiment" with mortal sin, because even after having been forgiven mortal sin, there is left a spiritual debt to be paid because of it, and most likely an inclination to that sin, both of which can sometimes take a lifetime to efface by continual penance. No one would think of putting his hand upon a red-hot burner, even for a few seconds. This would leave a burn mark that would probably last the rest of that person's life. Such a foolhardy deed is somewhat analogous to the effect of mortal sin upon our souls, but with the added effect that-mortal sin also throws up a dam before the stream of God's life-giving grace, impeding it from continuing uninterruptedly its beneficial effect in our souls—until we should once again gain forgiveness.

In this book, the author marshalls before our minds all the reasons to abandon sin and to grow in divine grace, because mortal sin drives out Sanctifying Grace. "For grace, being of a divine nature and kind, can co-exist with sin as little as God Himself can." (Page 39). The author goes on to score point after point that most people have never ever thought about concerning the action of divine grace. As mentioned, few people ever think about Sanctifying Grace, but without it, we are doomed to Hell; and with it, we are destined for Heaven. Therefore, no study is more important than that which the present book contains. For this book demonstrates, over and over again, that there is no objective in life more important than preserving and growing in Sanctifying Grace. And therefore there is no book, other than the Bible, more important for Catholics to read and understand than *The Glories of Divine Grace*. It promises to be an absolute revelation to most Catholics. For, as Fr. Scheeben states:

"Let us not think that only the great Saints can and should lead a supernatural life. This life does not consist in those extraordinary revelations, ecstasies and miracles with which the Saints are favored by God, but rather in the intimate union with God which grace renders possible for us all and in that holy consecration which the unction of the Holy Ghost communicates to all the actions of true Christians. The common dignity and destiny of all Christians is the foundation upon which the Saints constructed the tall edifice of their virtues and graces; it is the root which in the Saints is developed in all its richness, in all its fullness. We have, then, the same foundation, the same root of sanctity [as the Saints], and if in us it does not attain such splendid development, usually this is because we do not sufficiently cooperate with the work of grace, or perhaps we even place many obstacles in its way." (Pages 354-355).

In another place the author says: "How is it possible that there are still so many men who are unmindful of their high calling and who rather cling to the earth than allow themselves to be borne to Heaven by God—Christians who prefer to move within the limits of their poor nature than to transcend these limits and with the Angels lead a heavenly life." A paragraph later, he continues:

"Be this far from you, dear Christian, if you know the meaning of the Christian name and glory in it! Embrace with your noble heart the grace of God, and as a true child of God, endeavor to become more and more like Christ, your Heavenly Model. Be not guided by the laws of a perverted world, but by the law of grace and of the Holy Ghost. By constant striving after every virtue, keep yourself on the lofty height to which grace has raised you. Soar above the earth and above your own nature through intimate communion with God, your Father. Keep yourself, as much as possible, through constant prayer, in the vestibule of Heaven. This [type of] life alone offers an occupation worthy of your high dignity; in it alone is the realization of the supernatural, divine life that the children of God should lead." (Pages 355-356).

Prepare yourself, dear Reader, for a book quite unlike any other you have ever read, for a book that will explain to you the real meaning of what it is to be a Catholic, a child of God and an heir to Heaven. You have been born again, this time to an exalted state which it is beyond the reckoning of man adequately to appreciate, but you are about to gain some idea of it as you peruse the pages of *The Glories of Divine Grace*.

Thomas A. Nelson, Publisher
August 30, 2000
St. Rose of Lima

A CAPSULE PREVIEW

"By reason of grace, we are living members of Christ. But every action of a member has the same value as if it proceeded from the head. Whatever the members suffer is considered the same as though suffered by the head. In view of this, every work that we perform in the state of grace is a work of Christ, who lives and acts in His Mystical Body. . . .

"Accordingly, the value and merit of our deeds is, according to St. Thomas (*S. Th.* 1-2, q. 114, a. 3), not to be measured according to our natural power and dignity, but according to the infinite power of the Holy Ghost, who is in us. This is also one of the reasons why the Apostle calls the Holy Ghost the 'Spirit of promise,' the 'pledge of our inheritance' (cf. *Eph.* 1:13-14), and us, the children of promise. (Cf. *Romans* 9:8).

"O incomprehensible dignity! O inexhaustible wealth of divine grace! It is not only a great good in itself, but it is a source of numberless supernatural, heavenly gifts. It weighs so much in God's scales that we miserable, earthly men can, with our insignificant works, balance the whole Heaven. 'For that which is at present momentary and light of our tribulation,' says St. Paul, 'worketh for us above measure exceedingly an eternal weight of glory.' (*2 Cor.* 4:17). What can give such an immense value to our troubles and sufferings, which are in themselves but trifles? . . .

" . . . where grace is concerned, nothing is unimportant, because all these works and sufferings are those of God's children. Dipped in grace, the chaff becomes gold; filled with its rays, the drop of water becomes the brightest pearl. Thus, every good work, though little in itself, becomes, through grace, of very great value, capable of purchasing for us the greatest treasure, Heaven and God Himself." —*Pages* 238-240

CONTENTS

—Part 1—
WHAT IS GRACE?

—Part 2—
UNION WITH GOD

—Part 3—
HOW GRACE WORKS

—Part 4—
THE EFFECTS OF GRACE

—Part 5—
HOW TO GROW IN GRACE

—Part 1—

WHAT IS GRACE?

Chapter 1

HOW DEPLORABLE IT IS THAT MEN SHOULD HAVE SO LITTLE REGARD FOR GRACE

THE GRACE of God which we are to consider here is a ray of divine beauty, infused by God into the soul of man. There it sheds such a bright and beautiful light that the soul delights the eye of God and is most tenderly loved by Him; it is adopted as His child and spouse and is elevated from earth to Heaven, above all the confines of nature. By grace the soul is received into the bosom of the Eternal Father and, together with the Divine Son, participates in the nature of the Father on this earth, and in His glory in the life to come.

Unfortunately, our intellect cannot keep pace with our tongue, which proclaims new wonders at every word that it utters. And how should we be able to understand these sublime heavenly gifts, when even the blessed spirits—who already possess and enjoy them—cannot fully comprehend and appreciate their value? They too, in beholding the throne of Divine Mercy, can only admire in deepest reverence His unbounded grace and goodness. But they must also marvel at our incredible, miserable blindness when we esteem the grace of God so little, seek it so negligently, and lose it so easily. They sorrow over our most unspeakable misfortune when we, by sin, cast ourselves from the throne of that heavenly sublimity to which grace had raised us, a position exceeding the natural dignity of the highest angels. From this height sin casts us into the deepest abyss, into the company of the brutes and of reprobate spirits. And we are not horrified, we do not shudder, we scarcely experience the slightest regret!

St. Thomas teaches that the whole world and all it con-

tains is of less value before God than the grace of a single
soul. (*S. Th.* 1-2, q. 113, art. 9, ad 2). And St. Augustine main-
tains that the whole Heaven, together with all the Angels,
cannot be compared to this grace. (*Ep.* 1 *ad Bonif.,* cap. 6). It
follows, then, that man ought to be more thankful to God for
the smallest share of grace than if he had received the perfections of the highest spirits; than if he were made king of
heaven and of the whole world, with full possession of all
power and dominion. How infinitely superior in value is
grace to all the riches of this earth! And yet the least of these
riches is often blindly preferred to grace. The most
detestable created good induces us to cast away grace sacrilegiously—in playful jest, as it were. There are always men
who wantonly surrender to the enemy of their soul this plenitude of gifts, including God Himself, for the mere indulgence of one sinful, unchaste look. More inconsiderate than
Esau, they lose an inheritance greater than the world for the
sake of a miserable momentary enjoyment!

"Be astonished, O ye heavens, at this, and ye gates
thereof, be very desolate." (*Jer.* 2:12). If one brief, sinful pleasure would cause the sun to disappear from the world, the
stars to fall from heaven, and all the elements to be disturbed, who would be so rash and insane, who would be so
mad as to sacrifice the whole world to his lust? But what is
the destruction of the universe compared to the loss of
grace? Yet this loss occurs so easily and frequently to many
people. It occurs every day, every moment. How few are
those who seek to prevent this loss in themselves or others,
or who at least mourn over such a loss!

We are awe-stricken at an hour's eclipse of the sun; at an
earthquake that buries a whole city; at a pestilential disease that swiftly carries off men and beasts in great number. Yet there is an occurrence far worse, far more terrible
and deplorable, which we behold thousands of times every
day without emotion: the neglect and loss of the precious
grace of God by so many men.

Elias could not bear the sight of the destruction of a
mountain (*3 Kings* 19); the prophet Jeremias was incon-
solably grieved at the desolation of the Holy City; Job's

friends mourned seven days in silence at his lost fortune. We may eternally grieve and weep, but our sorrow will not even in a slight degree equal the misfortune that befalls us when sin devastates the heavenly garden in our soul; when we cast off the image of Divine Nature; when we lose the queen of virtues, holy charity, and all her heavenly court; when we spurn the gifts of the Holy Spirit, and the Holy Spirit Himself; when we reject the sonship of God, the prerogatives of His friendship and the claim to His rich inheritance; when we squander the price and fruit of the Sacraments and our merits; in a word, when we lose God and all Heaven by the loss of grace.

The soul that loses grace may truly apply to itself the words of Jeremias in his *Lamentations*: "How hath the Lord covered with obscurity the daughter of Sion in his wrath! *how hath* he cast down from heaven to the earth the glorious one of Israel, and hath not remembered his footstool in the day of his anger! The Lord hath cast down headlong, and hath not spared, all that was beautiful in Jacob." (*Lam.* 2:1-2). But who considers this great misfortune? Who grieves over it? Who is restrained from new sins? "With desolation is all the land made desolate; because there is none that considereth in the heart." (*Jer.* 12:11).

How little we love our true fortune, our true advantage! How little we understand the infinite love with which God comes to offer us His most precious treasures! We act in the same manner as did the Israelites whom God desired to lead out of the slavery of Egypt and the barren desert into a land that flowed with milk and honey. They despised the inestimable gift that God offered them; they despised the manna that God gave them on their journey; they abandoned God, and longed again for the fleshpots of Egypt. Now the promised land was a figure of Heaven; the manna was a type of grace—a figure of our nourishment and source of strength on the road to Heaven. But if God "lifted up his hand over them ["who set at nought the desirable land"]: to overthrow them in the desert" (*Ps.* 105:24-26), how great a responsibility do we incur through our disregard for Heaven and grace!

We disregard grace because we permit ourselves to be too deeply impressed by our senses with transitory things and because we have but a superficial knowledge of lasting, heavenly riches. We must therefore endeavor to correct our error by deep and very careful reflection. Esteem for eternal things will increase in us in the same degree as that for the temporal diminishes. We must draw as near as possible to the overflowing and inexhaustible fountain of divine grace. The glory of its treasures will so delight us that we shall henceforth have contempt for earthly things. Thus we shall learn to admire and esteem grace; and he who admires and praises grace, says St. John Chrysostom, will zealously and carefully guard it. Let us then, with the divine assistance, begin "the praise of the glory of his grace." (*Eph.* 1:6).

And Thou, great and good God, Father of light and of mercy, from Whom cometh every perfect gift (cf. *James* 1:17), Who hast predestined us to be adopted through Jesus Christ as Thy sons, according to the purpose of Thy will (cf. *Eph.* 1:5), Who hast chosen us in Him before the foundation of the world, that we should be holy and unspotted in Thy sight in charity (cf. *Eph.* 1:4), grant us the spirit of wisdom and revelation in deep knowledge of Him, enlighten the eyes of our heart that we may know what is the hope of Thy calling and what are the riches of the glory of Thy inheritance in the Saints. (Cf. *Eph.* 1:17-18). Give me light and strength that my words will not be prejudicial to the gift of Thy grace, by which Thou dost raise men from the dust of their mortal origin and receivest them into Thy heavenly court.

Christ Jesus, our Saviour, Son of the living God, by Thy Precious Blood which Thou hast shed for us poor creatures and which Thou didst not consider too great a price for us, grant that I may in some measure reveal the inestimable value of grace to those whom Thou hast redeemed and restored to Thy favor.

And Thou, highest and holiest Spirit, Pledge and Seal of Divine Love, Sanctifier of our souls, by Whom the grace and love of God is infused into our hearts, by Whose Seven Gifts this grace and love is developed, Who gives us Thyself with grace, teach us what grace is and how precious it is.

Blessed Mother of God, and therefore Mother of Divine Grace, permit me to make known to those who have by grace become children of God and thine own children the treasures for the procuring of which thou hast offered thy Divine Son.

Holy Angels, ye spirits filled and glorified by the light and fire of divine grace, and ye holy souls who have already passed from this place of exile into the bosom of the heavenly Father and there enjoy the sweet fruit of grace, assist me by your prayers, that I may for myself and others dispel the deceptive cloud before our eyes and that I may reveal the sun of grace in its brightest and undimmed splendor, so as to kindle in our hearts a living and everlasting love and desire of that very grace.

Chapter 2

GRACE SHOULD BE PRIZED VERY HIGHLY BECAUSE IT IS INFINITELY SUPERIOR TO ALL NATURAL THINGS

WE BEGIN with the least prerogative of grace, namely, that it is infinitely above all natural things. St. Augustine says: "'Heaven and earth shall pass away,' according to the assurance of our Saviour, but the salvation and justice of the elect will remain; the former contain only the works of God; the latter reflect the image of God." (*In Joan.*, tr. 72). St. Thomas teaches that it is a greater work to bring a sinner back to grace, than to create Heaven and earth. (*S. Th.*, 1-2, q. 113, art. 9). For the heavens and the earth are transitory and temporal things; but to convert a sinner is to bring him to share in the immutable Divine Nature. In creation God erects a dwelling for Himself; in giving man a rational nature, He places His servants and creatures in this dwelling; but when He gives man His grace, He receives him into His bosom, makes him His child, and communicates to him His own eternal life. In a word, grace is altogether a supernatural gift; that is, it is a gift which no created nature can possess by itself or claim as rightfully due to itself. Properly, grace belongs only to the nature of God Himself. God cannot produce a created being that would by its nature possess grace; such a creature would not differ from God Himself.

Closely connected with this opinion is the reiterated and clear decision of the Church that neither man nor any other creature bears in his nature even the least germ of grace; further, that nature has the same relationship to grace as inanimate matter has to the principle of life. Lifeless matter cannot give itself life; it must receive life from a living being. Similarly, the rational creature has no grace of itself and cannot even acquire it by its own labor or merit. God alone can, out of pure love, give this grace by opening the abyss of His omnipotence, and by pouring out upon nature His divine power. How great must that good be which so eminently surpasses the nature, power and merit of even the highest Angels!

A learned and pious man says that all visible things are far inferior to man and would still be inferior even if they were infinite in number. (Lessius, *De Div. Perf.*, I. 1, cap. 1). St. John Chrysostom holds that there is nothing in this world that may be compared to man. (Serm. 15, *De Verb. Apost.*). But St. Thomas teaches that grace is worth more than the human soul.

We may well say that grace surpasses all natural things, just as God Himself does. Grace is like heavenly light which, from the depths of the Divinity, diffuses itself over the rational creature.

The sun and its light are inseparable. The sun and its light are far more precious and perfect than the earth, which of itself has no such light. Let us apply this to grace. Our nature is the earth which receives the rays of the Divine Sun. By these rays our nature is so elevated and glorified that it becomes divine itself. Just as God, whom we possess by grace, not only contains within Himself the perfection of all things, but is infinitely more perfect than all things together, so is grace more precious than all created things. Grace, as the Book of *Proverbs* says of wisdom, is "better than all the most precious things: and whatsoever may be desired cannot be compared to it." (*Prov.* 8:11).

Let us then raise our eyes to these treasures and decide whether they are to be despised or to be sought with all diligence. Were we ever so rich in natural goods, in gold and silver, in power and authority, in science and art, all this wealth vanishes into nothing before grace, as a heap of clay before a precious diamond. And if, on the other hand, we were ever so poor, by the grace of God alone we are richer than all the kings of the world; we possess the best that the great God, in His infinite liberality, could give us.

How grateful, therefore, ought we to be to God for such a gift; we thank Him that He has called us into existence out of nothing; that, as the Psalmist says (cf. *Ps*. 8:8-9), He has subjected all things under our feet, the sheep and the oxen, the birds of the air and the fishes of the sea, and we must for that reason exclaim with the Psalmist (*Ps.* 8:5): "What is man that thou art mindful of him? or the son of man that thou visitest him?" How much greater thanks must we render for the supernatural treasures of grace, and how carefully must we preserve them!

A learned theologian, Cardinal Cajetan, says we must not for one moment lose sight of the value of grace, lest we also forget the great punishment prepared for those who despise the great gifts offered them gratuitously by God with such tender love. Such a punishment awaits them as awaited those men in the Gospel who were invited by the king to his banquet, but who, on account of another trifling gain or pleasure, would not come. We frivolous and ungrateful men despise the invitation of God to His heavenly banquet in order to follow the invitation of the world and the devil, who delude us with their deceitful gifts and pleasures. The devil not only gives us nothing better than God, but something far inferior; and this he gives, not to make us happy but to ruin us for all eternity. God gives us gratuitously, with incredible love, a precious diamond; the devil, in a very miserly way, and with implacable hatred, gives us a bright but false coin. What criminal folly it is to give up the precious diamond and to purchase the counterfeit coin, thus perishing miserably and cruelly!

But the immeasurable distance between grace and the natural gifts should not only prevent us from losing grace by mortal sin, but should urge us on to a fervent practice of the virtues so that we may merit an increase of grace. Even if you lose no grace by not attending holy Mass on weekdays, or by neglecting an opportunity of prayer, a work of mercy, an act of mortification, or of self-humiliation, you nevertheless suffer an immense loss if you do not increase your capital when it can so easily be done. For the least degree of grace is worth more than all the riches of the world.

If a miser could, by a single day's fast or by a single prayer, secure a whole fleet laden with treasures from India, who could restrain him from the act or disturb him therein? Who could make any impression on him by pointing out the difficulty of his performance or the danger to his health? With what right, then, and with what prudence—or rather folly—do we pretend such a difficulty when we are certain of a reward the smallest share of which incomparably surpasses a thousand Indies—indeed, a thousand worlds! Yet we remain idle and will not labor to cultivate a field that immediately yields a golden harvest! We are not required to shed our blood in this labor. One sigh is sufficient, one tear, one earnest resolution, one pious wish, the one word *Jesus,* by which we express our love for Him or invoke His assistance. Who would not gladly invoke Jesus a thousand times a day if he could thereby obtain so many chests of gold? And yet this is nothing in comparison with what we in unshaken faith expect to receive from God. If we could only impress these glorious riches of grace deeply upon our hearts, we should then repeat, not thoughtlessly, but with deep and vivid conviction, the words of a pious teacher: "Grace is the mistress and queen of nature." (Gerson, *Serm. de Circumcis.*).

Chapter 3

GRACE IS MORE SUBLIME THAN MIRACLES

NOT ONLY does grace surpass all natural things, it also surpasses all the miraculous works of God. Thus St. Augustine understands that remarkable promise of Our Lord that the faithful would do greater things than He Himself had done on earth. (*In Joan.*, tr. 72). He says we might explain this promise by such an occurrence as St. Peter's healing of the sick by his mere shadow. We do not read a similar account of our Saviour. But it is more probable—he continues—that we are to understand here the work of justification in which we are able to cooperate. For although we do not produce grace in ourselves, we can, with divine assistance, prepare ourselves for grace and make ourselves worthy of it. We can encourage and induce others to do the same thing, and thus we can perform greater works than Christ did through His miracles.

Both on the divine and on the human plane, the working of grace is more sublime and glorious than the working of miracles. God usually works miracles only in visible things, as when in a supernatural way, He restores health to a man or raises the dead to life. But by grace He works in the soul and, in a manner, creates the soul anew, elevates it above its nature, plants in it the germ of supernatural life. He reproduces Himself in it—so to speak—impressing upon it the image of His own nature. Thus, the work of grace is the greatest wonder of God's omnipotence. It is even greater than His creation of the world out of nothing. It can be compared only with that unspeakable act of God the Father by which He begets from all eternity His own Son, equal to Himself, and in time unites Him with a human nature. Supernatural, sublime and full of mystery as is the genera-

12

tion of Christ, so supernatural and mysterious is the infusion of grace into our souls, because, in the words of St. Leo, we thereby participate in the generation of Christ. (*Serm.* 26, cap. 2.).

However, we must cooperate more in this work than the Saints could in the miracles worked through them by God. They could only suffer God to act through their mediation, without being able of their own power to contribute anything. But when grace is concerned, God wills that we ourselves, with His assistance, prepare our soul for it, receive it from His hand, preserve and cultivate it and merit its increase.

O wonderful greatness which God has given us, taking our soul to Himself as His spouse, that by the power received from Him she may produce in herself the image of God and become the child of God! O wonderful power which God has granted to His Church, to communicate His grace to her children by her teaching and her Sacraments! Can man desire anything greater? Can he cooperate in any greater work? Do you wish to perform a great and wonderful work, admirable not in the sight of foolish men but in the sight of the Angels of Heaven? Do you wish to be made a spectacle to the world and to the Angels? Behold, this is the greatest work: labor to acquire and to merit an increase of grace for yourself and your fellow creatures.

If men only knew what a great deed it is to abandon their past by sincere contrition for their sins and to begin a new life! In reality they perform a greater work than if they raised the dead to life or than if they created a man out of nothing. "If God has made you man," says St. Augustine, "and you make yourself a just man" (with God's help, of course), "your work is better than that of God." (*Serm.* 15, *De Verbis Apost.*).

If you could recall your deceased brother to life by contrition for your sins, would you be so full of hatred toward God or of cruelty toward your brother as not to do this! Now you may easily, by one act of [perfect] contrition, raise yourself from death—not of the body, but of the soul—from an eternal death to an eternally blissful life. And yet you hesitate, and you refuse that wonderful assistance which God offers you.

St. Chrysostom teaches that it is greater to revive a mortally wounded soul than a dead body. (T. 4, hom. 4, antiq. ed.). Who, in fact, that is not entirely blind, could esteem it greater to reinstate the body in a perishable life and the enjoyment of earthly, temporal pleasures, than to raise the soul to an eternal life and the enjoyment of heavenly gifts— to secure for it, and in it and by it also for the flesh, an eternal happy life? But if we ask miracles of God for the preservation of our bodily life, why do we not cooperate with *that miracle* which will restore to us the life of the soul?

Not only [perfect] contrition, which recovers lost grace, but all good supernatural actions performed in the state of grace are of great value and have a marvelous power. Every degree of grace that we acquire raises us higher above our nature, unites us more closely to God, and causes us to ascend ever more above all the heavens. Had we the power to work visible miracles, or at least to accomplish great things with ease, how zealously we should use this power, and what an honorable duty we should consider it to turn this capital to profitable advantage! With how much zeal do great artists and poets practice their art and continually produce new and more beautiful works!

If we only considered what power every good work possesses for the increase of grace and the gain of eternal happiness, we should let no moment pass without loving God, adoring Him, and praying to Him, and we should be ashamed to draw one breath without sighing to God; we should even rejoice with the Apostles to suffer something for God's sake. (Cf. *Acts* 5:41). If we knew how greatly we may enhance our dignity by a single act of virtue, we should purchase the opportunity at any price. We could not bear to lose one chance out of a hundred offered to us.

No man would be so cruel as not willingly to cure a sick person, or to enrich a poor one, if he could do so by one small act of charity, or by a short prayer. But are we not much more cruel to ourselves if we refuse to augment the heavenly beauty, glory and treasures of our soul at an equally insignificant cost? Why do we not season all our actions with the spirit of faith and of charity? For we should then acquire a higher degree of grace, which is nobler than all the things of nature and greater than miracles.

The infusion and communication of grace is itself a wonder of the highest order, and greater than all other wonders. But why does it not excite our wonder and admiration? It is only because it is invisible to our bodily vision and occurs, not rarely and exceptionally, but universally, and according to fixed laws. These two circumstances should make it more precious in our eyes.

It is not visible because it is a wonder wrought in the soul and not in the body. We cannot see it because we cannot see God, with whom we are united by it. As God would not be the infinitely great God if we could see Him with our bodily eyes, so grace would not be so great and admirable if it were visible to us.

If, moreover, grace is given according to a universal and fixed law, so that we may acquire it by our ordinary actions, this only reveals still more the infinite love and power of God. For God is so liberal that He accomplishes this great work, not at rare intervals, on extraordinary occasions, and through a few of His greatest servants only, as He does with other miracles; rather, He connects it with our most ordinary actions and lets it disappear, as it were, in the circle of our own daily activity. O Lord, should we esteem Thy gift less which makes us venerate Thee, the Donor, so much more? Or should we appreciate it less because Thou grantest it to all and at all times and with the greatest readiness? But if Thou wouldst grant it to one alone and only once, how could this one entertain the wicked thought of renouncing the possession of this most singular gift? Yes, O God, Thy bountiful liberality must induce us always to remember Thee, O most gracious Giver, and to exert all our power to preserve Thy gift in us and to hold it in highest honor.

Chapter 4

BY GRACE WE ARE ELEVATED
FAR ABOVE NATURE

HAVING SHOWN that grace is far superior to all natural things and even to miracles, we might add that, in a certain sense, it is more precious than even heavenly glory, which appears to be the highest good that God is able to give us. For the glory of Heaven, in which the blessed behold and enjoy God, is nothing else but the full development of the grace that we possess. Grace is the fountain, springing up into life everlasting; it is the root, of which the blossom and fruit is beatitude; it has, then, the special privilege that this beatitude depends upon it and is founded upon it. "The wages of sin is death. But the grace of God, life everlasting," says the Apostle. (*Rom.* 6:23). But if, according to St. Paul, grace is life eternal, then it must not only lead to that life, but already contain it in itself. As sin is a greater evil than its punishment, death, so grace must be a greater good than eternal happiness considered in itself, for by grace we merit it.

But of this we shall speak later. Let us now consider how grace is such a precious and excellent gift that it communicates its qualities and greatness to its possessor; how it is not only itself exalted above nature, but how it also elevates one far above nature.

"Place me," says an old philosopher (Seneca), "in a very rich house that abounds with gold and silver; I shall not, on account of these things, admire myself; for though they are with me, they are not within me. Such external treasures do not touch the nature of men; and though they dazzle the eye by their great splendor, they improve him neither in health nor in the form of his body, and least of all in the

16

qualities of his mind." That, however, is precisely the prerogative of grace: it raises its possessor to its own exalted
position; it penetrates the soul, the true interior man, and
unites itself so closely to the soul that it communicates to
all its own prerogatives. It weaves all its treasures together
into a golden vesture studded with diamonds, and envelopes the soul with that vesture. Just as it is itself the
greatest work of God, so it makes the soul receiving it in
rich inheritance appear as the greatest, noblest and most
glorious of God's creatures. Thus St. Cyril of Alexandria
says: "The grace of Christ clothes us, as it were, with gor-
geous purple and raises us to a dignity that surpasses all
knowledge." (*In Joan.*, cap. 1, v. 14).

What an unheard-of honor and liberality it is when a man
is lifted up from his native lowliness and obscurity and is
placed, not only—like another Adam—as lord over his visible earth, but is so far elevated above all the heavens to a
degree above that of the natural nobility of the highest
angels. For the Angels themselves do not by nature possess
the dignity that we acquire by grace; they also receive it as
a gift only from the gracious bounty of God. Without it they
would rank even further beneath us than we by nature are
inferior to them.

Who, then, can sufficiently lament the blindness by which
we exchange this pinnacle of greatness for a detestable
servitude! Meanwhile, we endeavor by mutual quarrel, dis-
pute and envy to ascend to a place blindly considered higher
than the other. If at our birth we were given the choice, we
should certainly always select the highest position. We
should not choose to be inferior even to the highest Angel.
What witchcraft, then, so blinds us, that when this honorable name and theme of grace is offered, or rather, is urged
upon us by God, we scarcely notice it; or, if we have accepted
it, we so easily and for such a small price give it up!

Recognize, O man, the splendor which you receive from
grace; remain true in life to the high position which your
soul occupies by grace. What have you in common with the
world, which is so far beneath your feet? You who by the dignity of your new condition have been transferred into

Heaven and have there erected your throne, why do you still wallow in the mire of this earth?

The ancient heathen philosophers were led to understand by natural reason that love for the things of earth is foolish if we think of the heavens and of the stars. "If," says one of them, "we should give human reason to ants, they would in the same manner divide their small fields into as many provinces as kings do with their countries. Above us are limitless distances, before which earthly space disappears as nothing." (Seneca, *Praef. in Quaest. Nat.*). Another remarks: "If one should look down from the sun or from the moon upon our earth, the whole earth would appear as a small disk. The largest kingdoms and fields would appear only as small points, hardly visible." (Lucian, *In Incarom.*).

How then shall we conduct ourselves—we who in reality, and not only through words or imagination, have been elevated above the heavens by grace? What shall we think of ourselves and of these earthly things? There is a far greater distance between grace and earthly things than between the sun and this earth of ours. Yet we allow ourselves, like very stupid people, to be misled by external appearances. Stupid people suppose the sun is very small in comparison with the earth. Likewise we foolishly cannot understand the invisible greatness and sublimity of grace. But if we can disprove appearances by the certain calculations of astronomers, why should we not let the far more certain principles of faith remove our ignorance in regard to grace?

Only a few, mindful of the high condition and dignity they have received by grace, despise the lust and desires of their inborn nature and, as a peasant suddenly made king, are ashamed of the character, pleasures and ways of their previous low conditions. St. Isidore of Alexandria wept because he was compelled, like the animals, to take bodily food; whereas, he was destined for the banquet of the blessed in Heaven. St. Paul considers it wrong to yield to flesh and blood and to appreciate anything else in us than the new creation which God has established in us by grace. He exhorts us to find pleasure only in things that are above, not the things that are on earth. (Cf. *Col.* 3:2). What madness, then, impels us to forget the delights of Heaven and to follow even brutish instincts and beastly pleasures! Let us direct our desires to that height to which we have been elevated. If we must desire anything on earth, let us desire crosses. For in this way we shall crucify ourselves to nature and to the world, and thus we shall show that we belong to another, higher world.

Chapter 5

GRACE IS A PARTICIPATION IN THE UNCREATED DIVINE NATURE[1]

IT IS CERTAINLY a great thing that man by grace should rise above all created nature, but it is something greater still that he should participate in the uncreated divine nature. To speak more precisely, man in the state of grace is so superior to all created things because he is so near to God. On account of this nearness, he partakes of the prerogatives of God, just as a body partakes of the light and heat of fire, in proportion to its being close to the fire.

This excellent union with God is taught us, according to the unanimous explanation of the holy Fathers, by St. Peter when he writes that, by the very great and precious promises God has made us by Jesus Christ, we may be make partakers of the Divine Nature. (Cf. *2 Ptr.* 1:4). In other words, St. Peter teaches that the prerogatives which are above all created nature and proper only to the divinity are, as far as possible, communicated to us creatures.

The Saints cannot find expressions sufficiently apt to describe this magnificent gift. One early ecclesiastical writer says: (Ps. Dionys., *Ep. 2 ad Caim.*) "Sanctity or sanctifying grace is a divine gift, an inexpressible copy of the highest Divinity and the highest Goodness, by means of which we enter a divine rank through a heavenly generation." (Cf. *Eccl. Hier.,* cap. 2). The holy martyr Maximus

---

1. What is said in the following chapters of the deification of the soul by participation in the Divine Nature will appear to some as exaggerated, novel, and dangerous. There is here question of a great mystery which cannot be passed over in silence, but must be considered with reverence and faith.

writes: "The divinity is given us when grace penetrates our nature by a heavenly light, raising it above its natural condition by the greatness of glory." (*Centur. Oecon.* 1, 76). These and most of the other holy Fathers teach—with St. Thomas—that by grace we are, in a manner, deified. They apply to this mystery the words quoted by our Saviour: "Is it not written in your law: *I said you are gods?*" ("and all of you the sons of the most High"). (*John* 10:34; *Ps.* 81:6). In a word, by grace we are elevated in some measure to the highest order of things, to the throne which God alone occupies in virtue of His nature. We thus ascend the highest Heaven.

If we consider the various classes of beings known to us, we perceive that each class differs in its nature from the others and is more perfect than others, so that all together they form a ladder of many rounds, the summit of which is occupied by God. Some things enjoy existence only: lifeless things—for example, stones and metals. Others have a certain kind of life, as the plant, which by its own innate power from the root produces the blossom and the fruit. Animals have, besides this life, the ability to feel and to move. Man, finally, has also a spiritual life, so that he may know and love even immaterial things. Above man there is an immeasurable gradation of pure spirits, invisible to us. Each spirit has its own peculiar high perfection. Infinitely above all these natures is that of God, for no other nature is so purely spiritual. No other nature is similarly able to behold God immediately or to unite itself so intimately to His own nature by love. All other natures are darkness compared to the Divine Sun. Other natures cannot, of themselves, adequately represent the peculiar perfections of this Sun.

This sublime Divine Nature, by the infinite power of its equally infinite love, draws our nature to itself, receives it into its Divine Bosom, immerses it into itself as iron is dipped into the furnace. Thus we belong to God's kind in the same manner as the palm tree belongs to the class of plants, and the lion to that of animals.

If, out of all the millions of men and Angels, God had selected a single soul and bestowed upon it this unheard-of dignity, such a soul would, if visible, darken the beauty of the sun, of all nature and of all the heavenly spirits. It would amaze mortal men. The Angels themselves would be inclined to adore it as God Himself. How then is it possible that we despise this same gift when it is so extravagantly lavished upon all? And how is it that our ingratitude increases even as God wills to be more liberal toward us?

Our ambition makes us purchase with immense trouble and large sums of money the society of the great. And yet we despise communing with the great God! If anyone is expelled from the council of a king, he can scarcely endure the ignominy. Should we not esteem it a bitter loss, an irreparable injury to our ambition, to be expelled by mortal sin, not only from the society of God, but from God's family and relationship? In fact, the man who despises this union with God's goodness and divinity hates God Himself; such a man is a deadly enemy to his own honor, his sound reason, his own person and to God. Worldly honors often consist in the opinion and esteem of men, rather than in the possession of intrinsic worth. A man may, at the bidding of his sovereign, occupy the highest position of honor, without being on that account more perfect and honorable in himself. But grace communicates to us a divine dignity. We receive not merely a high name, but a real perfection of the divine order, for grace likens our soul to God Himself.

"By the union with the Son and the Holy Ghost," says St. Cyril of Alexandria, "all of us who have believed and have been likened to God are partakers of the Divine Nature, and this not only in name, but in reality. For we have been glorified with a beauty surpassing all created beauty. For Christ is formed in us in an indescribable manner, not as one creature in another, but as God in created nature. Christ transforms us by the Holy Ghost into His image and elevates us to an uncreated dignity." (*De Trin.*, 1. 4.).

"What is essential and substantial in God," says St. Thomas, "exists as a quality superadded to nature in the soul which participates by grace in the divine love." (*S. Th.* 1-2, q. 110, art. 2, ad 2.).

This beautiful and sublime mystery is illustrated by the holy Fathers in various ways. St. Athanasius compares the

Divinity to a precious perfume which communicates its fragrance to the objects that come into contact with it. (*Lib. ad Serap. de Spir. Sancto.*) He also compares it to a seal which leaves its own form impressed in the soft wax. St. Gregory Nazianzen says our nature is so intimately united to God and so partakes of His perfections that it may be symbolized by a drop of water falling into and absorbed by a cup of wine. St. Thomas, following St. Basil, gives us the figure of unrefined iron, which is cold, black, hard and without beauty. He says that when such iron is put into fire and penetrated by its heat, it appears bright, warm, flexible and liquid, without losing its own nature. If we remember now that God is the purest spiritual light and the fire of eternal love itself, we can in some measure understand how God, descending with His full glory to His creature, or receiving it into His bosom, can, without destroying its nature, penetrate it with the full glow of His light and warmth, so that its natural lowliness and weakness disappear, and it is seemingly altogether absorbed in God.

If we could acquire the brilliant mental activity of the Angels as easily as we can merit an increase of grace, we should certainly not neglect the opportunity. But why do I speak of the perfection of angels? Even those of a lower nature attract us: the swiftness of the deer, the strength of the lion, the flight of the eagle. How gladly we should seize such perfections if they were within our easy reach! But the perfection and glories of the Divine Nature, perfections which not only enrich our nature but ennoble it throughout and raise it up to the divine, these perfections are not great enough in our eyes to call forth a little exertion on our part! Where is our reason, our Christian faith?

Let us suppose that God had wonderfully united in a single man all the perfections to be found in creatures: that this man was stronger than the lion, more beautiful than the flowers of the fields or than the dawn of day, brighter than the sun, more enlightened than the Cherubim. Let us further suppose that this man hazarded all these gifts on one cast of the dice. Who would not shudder at the folly and meanness of such criminal ingratitude? Thus, the folly of

Samson was so much greater by reason of his very great strength, which he betrayed to the hypocritical tears of a deceitful woman. And we surrender our relationship with God! We surrender the splendor of the Divine Sun, the might of the divine virtues. All this we surrender to our miserable flesh, which is the daughter of corruption, the sister and mother of worms! Here the pen itself is shocked at the mention of such a pitiable and yet common spectacle. Weep, you Angels of peace, over this cruel madness that makes your brothers on earth turn against themselves and unworthily desecrate so many and such great gifts!

May those of us, however, whose eye is clearer, and whose condition of soul is more normal, esteem and admire our own dignity and embrace with the whole love of our heart its Author, the Father of all light. If the planets enjoyed the knowledge of their beauty, they would certainly be inflamed with grateful love toward the sun, whose light gives them their brightness and whose reflection makes them so lovely and wonderful. The prince loves his distinguished ancestry; the son, his father; everything loves its kind. Should not a similar sense of relationship and likeness draw us from this earth to God?

Would that we Christians were not less impressed with our dignity than heathen philosophers are with the dignity of man! Heathen philosophers have called man a miracle, the marrow and the heart of the world, the most beautiful being, the king of all creatures. But if man appears so great in the light of reason, how much greater should he not appear in the light of faith! Let us open the eyes of our soul and heed the warning of St. Chrysostom: "I beg and beseech you, do not suffer that the extraordinary gifts of God" (which we have received through the grace of Christ) "increase your guilt and the punishment of your negligence by their infinite greatness."

Chapter 6

THE PARTICIPATION IN THE DIVINE NATURE EFFECTS A SUPERNATURAL SIMILARITY TO THIS NATURE

THE PARTICIPATION in the Divine Nature is so sublime a mystery that we must explain more thoroughly the manner in which it takes place. A certain participation in the divine perfections is found in all the things that God has created. All things resemble God, more or less, in their existence, their life, their force and activity. In all things God reveals His glory, so that according to the Apostle, the invisible glory of God may be seen and considered in created things. But their similarity is of a very different nature. In material things we find only a slight impression of God's glory—the footprint, as it were, that one leaves when walking over soft earth. The print shows where a man has been, but it contains only an image of his foot, not of his whole form and nature. Now since God is a spirit, material things reveal themselves as the work of His hands and bespeak His wisdom and power, but they do not represent His nature. Our souls, however, and all pure spirits, are by their very nature a certain image of the Divine Nature; they are, like God, spiritual, rational, endowed with free will. Yet their nature is finite, created out of nothing, and therefore very different from the Divine Nature. They are similar to the picture of a man which a painter has painted on a canvas in various colors. This picture reveals to us the form, the features, and the complexion of the person represented, but it always remains far inferior to the likeness that a mirror reflects. For in a mirror the person appears by his own light and not by that of another. He appears in his whole natural beauty, freshness and life. In like manner the rational creature then only becomes perfectly similar to God when it has become a true mirror of the Divinity, reflecting It in Its own peculiar beauty. The rational creature becomes perfectly similar to God when it has been penetrated and glorified by the divine fire; when, in a manner, it has been transformed into God, as a bright crystal globe that collects the rays of the sun appears like the sun itself.

The participation in the Divine Nature, then, which we enjoy by grace, consists in this: our nature assumes a condition peculiar to the divine nature and becomes so similar to the Deity that, according to the holy Fathers, we may truly say it is deified, or made deiform. "Deification," says Ps. Dionysius, "is the greatest possible likening and union with God." (*Eccl. Hier.,* cap. 1). St. Basil likewise teaches: "From the Holy Spirit springs an unending joy, the likening to God; to be made God, however, is the highest that man can wish and desire." (*De Spir. Sancto,* cap. 9). We do not speak of a dissolution of our substance in the Divine Substance, or even of a personal union with it, as in the Incarnation. We speak only of a glorification of our substance into the image of the Divine Nature. Neither shall we become new gods, pretending independence of the true God, but in truth we are made, by the power and grace of God, something which God alone is by nature; we are made like Him in a supernatural way. Our soul receives a reflection of that glory which is peculiar to Him and above all creatures.

If we wish to understand better this likeness with God, we must examine in order the different prerogatives which distinguish the Divinity from created natures.

Let us first consider the external existence and life of God. God alone exists by His own power. He is eternal and immutable, and depends on no one. But creatures are of themselves nothing; they exist only because God has created them and permits them to exist. For that reason they are, even after their creation by God, as nothing when compared with Him. "I am Who am," says the Lord. "All nations are before Him as if they had no being at all, and are counted to Him as nothing, and vanity." (*Is.* 40:17). For all creatures, even the immortal spirits, would, by reason of their nature, sink back again into their nothingness if God's goodness did not sustain them.

But grace is, according to St. Paul, a new creation and the foundation of a new, immovable kingdom. (Cf. *Eph.* 2:10; Cf. *Heb.* 12:28). By it we are received into the bosom of the eternal God, into the side of the eternal Word, through whom the Father has created all, and who is coeternal with Him. We are called to eternal life. We are called to dwell in the tabernacle of God's eternity, at the very fountain and source of all being and life. Here our eternal existence is as secure as that of God Himself; here we need fear neither death nor destruction, and when heaven and earth pass away and the stars fall from heaven, we shall not be affected because we shall rest in the bosom of the Creator, far above all creatures.

Hence the Book of Wisdom says: "The just shall live for evermore: and their reward is with the Lord; . . . therefore shall they receive a kingdom of glory, and a crown of beauty at the hand of the Lord: for with his right hand he will cover them, and with his holy arm he will defend them." (*Wis.* 5:16-17). Of those, however, who separated themselves from God and esteemed the transitory goods higher than the treasures of His grace, the same book says: "What hath pride profited us, or what advantage hath the boasting of riches brought us? All those things are passed away like a shadow, and like a post that runneth on, and as a ship that passeth through the waves: . . . so we also being born, forthwith ceased to be and . . . are consumed in our wickedness." (*Wis.* 5:8-13). If then we wish really to exist, to exist eternally and as something really great, why do we not go to the fountain of all being? Why do we rely on our own nothingness and pursue other things which are as vain and transitory as our life here below? Why do we wish to be great in a cheap and gaudy garment? Why do we seek to immortalize ourselves in the mouths of men, and not rather in ourselves and in the bosom of God?

The sinner desires—as did our first parents, and the devil himself—"to be as God." In all truth, God Himself wills that we should be as He, but not without Him, not outside Him, not in opposition to Him. He does not will that we should make ourselves as other gods, to adore ourselves and to be adored. He wills that we should be as He, but in His bosom, at His heart. He wills it to be through Himself and in union with Him, as in the case of His own Divine Son, who is not another God, but the same God with the Father. How great, then, is the folly of the sinner, who instead of desiring to be one with God as His child, rejects this infinite love of God, and chooses rather to be His enemy!

Chapter 7

GRACE CONFERS UPON US THE
HIGHEST PERFECTION

"I WILL BE like the Most High," said Lucifer, when he
considered the beauty and glory with which God had
adorned him. (*Is.* 14:14). He blasphemed God by speaking
thus, because he wished to possess this glory independently
of God. But we cannot praise God more, or render Him more
acceptable thanks, than by confessing that He will make us
similar to Himself by His grace. Our Saviour Himself says:
"Be you therefore perfect, as also your heavenly Father is
perfect." (*Matt.* 5:48). This is to be understood primarily of
moral perfection, but from all that we have said, it may be
interpreted to mean also that we shall participate in the
other perfections of God.

Consider then, Christian soul, called to communion with
God, the riches of His glory. Admire His perfect nature,
which, because it is the purest being, contains all imaginable glory and happiness. Admire His infinite Majesty, shining forth as many rays as the beauties and perfections we
behold within us, about us and above us. See how the
Almighty has by one word created this wide world, so beautifully diversified; not exhausted by this one labor, He could
create a thousand worlds besides with the same ease. See
how He called into existence and ordered so harmoniously
the countless heavenly bodies, some of which are a thousand or a million times greater than this earth. See how He
who moves all things is not moved Himself; how He ordains
the different causes, arranges the elements; how He produces from His treasury all perfections and forces; how He
produces treasures of metals, of springs, of plants and animals, of the science of men and angels. And if now, in the

face of such a multitude of riches and glories, you fall on your knees in adoring admiration and imagine yourself annihilated as a poor worm before the splendor of the sun, then, O Christian soul, be amazed also at yourself, who have been surrounded and clothed with beautiful gold and purple by a wonderfully loving God in His grace.

All created natures have different perfections, and no one enjoys all those that are found in others. The elephant has the strength of the lion, but not his swiftness; the lion has the strength of the elephant, but not his size. Animals surpass plants in the possession of senses, but are not adorned by such beautiful blossoming. Man is far superior to irrational animals because of his rational soul, yet the irrational animals possess many corporeal advantages in which man is wanting. But God, in the simplicity of His being, contains in an eminent manner all the perfections of all creatures together, as the sun in its simple light contains all the diversified beauty of the seven colors of the rainbow. The various natures of creatures are like different rays—refractions of the one great ray of the sun. The nature of our souls and of angels, being spiritual, is incomparably more perfect than that of material things, yet it is only as one refracted ray of the Divine Sun, and it does not contain the perfection of all others, although it is the most beautiful of them all. But in grace, the light of divine glory is reflected by the soul pure and entire, and the soul is made so sublime an image of God that all the perfection of creatures are gathered in it.

Though, O Christian, you are ever so poor in natural gifts, envy no one. If you are ever so rich in treasures, power, influence and knowledge, behold: the poorest of your brothers is by grace far more perfect and happy than you; he possesses in his heart the most glorious and beautiful of kingdoms, the kingdom of God.

"But," you object, "of all these glories I see nothing. What does a treasure profit me, if I cannot enjoy it?"

True, you do not see your glory, and yet it is within you. If you have an unpolished diamond, you do not yet see how precious and beautiful it is, though it has the same value now as when it is polished. When you hold the seed of a tree

in your hand you may not suspect that a great and beautiful tree is contained in it. Likewise the beautiful and divine
perfection, which grace communicates to you, is within you,
hidden and concealed. We are now sons of God, says St.
John (*1 John* 3:2), but it has not yet appeared what we shall
be when we shall see God as He is.

As long as you do not see God face to face, you cannot see
the image of His Divine Nature in you. Grace is, so to speak,
the dawn of the light of the Divine Sun; you must only wait
till this Sun rises, until it develops in you its whole splendor, until it penetrates and glorifies you with the glow of its
heat. Your glory will delight you the more, the longer it has
remained hidden from you. Until then, you must, according
to the words of St. Paul, walk by faith and not by sight,
believing the unfailing promise of God. For St. Peter tells us
that "by the power of God" you "are kept by faith unto salvation, ready to be revealed in the last time," and through
Christ we have the lively hope of an incorruptible inheritance—undefiled and unfading, reserved for you in heaven.
(Cf. *1 Ptr.* 1:4-5).

In grace you have the pledge—indeed, the root—of your
future glorification in soul and body. If you still sigh in the
servitude of the flesh, if you feel depressed by suffering and
frailty, sigh with the Apostle after the freedom and glory of
the children of God, when even your flesh will partake in
the spiritual qualities of the glorified soul. Then, with the
fullness of perfection, free from all suffering and fear of
death, beautiful as the sun and swift as the eagle, you will
feel the power of grace and possess in the fullest abundance
all those perfections which you perceive in visible things.

Chapter 8

GRACE MAKES MAN PARTICIPATE IN THE DIVINE COGNITION

THAT YOU MAY learn at this point what glory and happiness is hidden in grace, I will now show it to you in all its greatness, in that condition wherein the light of grace passes over the light of glory. From this you will understand how truly and perfectly we partake of the Divine Nature by grace.

Every nature is best known by its peculiar force and activity. Thus, plants are distinguished from minerals by their growth, their blossom and their fruit; animals differ from plants by their sensation and motion; man differs from animals by his reason and free will.

By his reason, man is in some degree like God, but there still remains an immense distance between the divine and the human nature. For man's intellect, and even that of the highest Angels, can know directly only creatures, finite and created beings; it cannot behold face to face the great and infinite God. God, the Creator and Lord, may be known by rational creatures, but only from a distance, for the glory of God is more removed from the creature than the sun is from the earth. The creatures only see, as it were, the hem of His garment—the reflection of His own glory in His great, glorious Creation. He Himself, however, the invisible "King of kings . . . whom no man has seen, nor can see," "inhabits," as the Apostle says, "light inaccessible." (*1 Tim.* 6:15-16). His light is too bright, His glory too great, His greatness too extensive for creatures to fix their weak eyes upon Him without being dazzled. Even the Cherubim cover their faces and sink into the dust before Him to adore Him with the deepest reverence. God alone can by His nature behold His being; only "the only begotten Son, who is in the bosom of the Father" (*John* 1:18) and is of the same nature with Him, beholds Him face to face; only the Holy Spirit, who is in God, penetrates and fathoms His innermost nature, very much as—in man—only the spirit that is in him knows and penetrates his inner nature. (Cf. *1 Cor.* 2:11). To behold God, we must either be God or participate in the divine nature.

Well then, my good Christian, your spiritual eye must also become divine, as it were, and your soul must partake of the divine nature, if you are to see God face to face. The veil which covers your weak eyes must be removed; the light of the Divine Sun must transform your sight, must make it sunlike, that you may boldly gaze at it. And this the Holy Spirit effects in you when, by grace, He makes you partake of the divine nature. St. Paul describes this in beautiful words: "But we all beholding the glory of the Lord with open face, are transformed into the same image from glory to glory, as by the Spirit of the Lord." (*2 Cor.* 3:18). St. John likewise says: "We shall be like to him [God] because we shall see him as he is." (*1 John* 3:2). And the Son of God Himself says to His Father: "the glory which thou hast given me, I have given to them; that they may be one, as we also are one." (*John* 17:22).

In Heaven we shall know God as He knows Himself and as He knows us. "Then I shall know even as I am known," says the Apostle. (*1 Cor.* 13:12). But we could not have knowledge like that which is peculiar to the Divine Nature unless we were really made to participate in that nature. And if, on the other hand, we are in reality to partake of the Divine Nature and are really to be deified, that must be verified by our being called to partake of the divine cognition.

What a marvel, dear Christian, what a grace! Must we not exclaim here with St. Peter: "Into his marvelous light" God has called us (*1 Ptr.* 2:9)? Have you ever reflected upon the sublime greatness of this grace? We must thank God already for giving us our bodily sight, by which we may behold the whole visible creation with all its beauty and magnificence. But this we have in common with the brutes. It can and ought to be the subject of our pride and boast that we possess another infinitely superior light within us, the light of reason, by which we perceive not only the exterior qualities of things visible, their color, odor, and taste, but also their substance, beauty, harmony and their mutual relations. By the light of reason we also know spiritual things, our immortal soul, truth, virtue and finally, God Himself in the image of His creation. How proud we should be if we possessed all the science that has ever been discovered by human genius and application, or if we enjoyed the natural knowledge of the Angels! But this would not give us an immediate knowledge of the infinite truth and beauty of God. Thus, we may conclude how inferior our nature is to the Divine Nature and how no created eye can peer into the depths of the mysteries of God. It would be godless temerity to desire to approach the unapproachable light of God; His glory would overwhelm us and death would be the penalty for our rashness: "Man shall not see me [God] and live," says Holy Scripture (*Ex.* 33:20), and again; "He that is a searcher of [God's] majesty, shall be overwhelmed by glory." (*Prov.* 25:27).

But "the things that are impossible with men," says St. Irenaeus (*Contra Haer.,* 1, 4, cap. 20, al. 37), in explanation of this, "are possible with God." (*Luke* 18:27). He descends to us in His infinite power and goodness to elevate us to Himself; He Himself introduces us into His admirable light; He fills us with own light, that we may behold His light. "In thy light we shall see light," says the Psalmist. (*Ps.* 35:10). Only in His own light and not in our light can we see God.

What is all natural light of creatures compared with this divine light? It is as the weak, dim light of a lamp that illumines but poorly the narrow space of a human dwelling, compared with the glorious, heavenly light of the sun which fills the whole world. The eye of our reason, compared to the divinely glorified eye of the Saints is as the eye of the bat in comparison with the clear eye of the eagle fearlessly directing its gaze to the sun, undazzled by its light.

If then we experience a natural and inexpressible desire for the perception of truth and the enjoyment of the beautiful, why do we not seek to satisfy it at the only source where it can be entirely satisfied? If we seek with so much labor to acquire science, why do we not search after the source of eternal light? All our natural knowledge is pitiably imperfect, and we can never do more than merely scratch the surface. But the light of grace introduces us at once to the light of God and gives us not only the shadow but the substance and the highest source of truth. And if created beauty delights us so much, why do we not, with the royal poet, always seek the countenance of Him who is the fountain and ideal of all transient beauty?

In the Beatific Vision grace makes us share in the divine happiness by raising us up to the immediate enjoyment of the infinite and highest good. As much as the Divine Nature is above ours, so much the divine beatitude must surpass that which is attainable by and suitable to our nature. The animal is not capable of the same enjoyment as man; it can only delight in the things of the senses. Man takes delight in spiritual things, in order, harmony and beauty, especially as these are found in truth and virtue. In like manner, the joy and beatitude of God has an object accessible only to Himself, whose beauty and loveliness eye has not seen, nor ear heard and which has not entered into the heart of man, but is evident only to God Himself, to His own infinitely good, glorious, beautiful being. But while God makes us, through His Holy Spirit, partakers of His Divine Nature, He opens to us also the mystery of His happiness. He calls us to the enjoyment of that happiness, and makes us His associates in it. As He possesses Himself by His nature, so He wills to give Himself to us through grace. And as He, by our participation in His nature, places us upon His throne and introduces us into His light, so He wills also to let us feast at His table. By reason of our nature, He might have left us standing at a respectful distance before His door. There we might have admiringly contemplated the greatness of His works, the beauty of His mansion, and this would have been for us a joy and an honor as great as our poor hearts might desire. But He wills to manifest to us His own beauty, in the enjoyment of which He, with the Son and the Holy Spirit, is eternally happy; that beauty which unites in itself the real and possible beauties of His works, with all their wonderful diversity; that beauty which angels desire to behold, one ray of which is sufficient to inebriate all created spirits with joy.

In truth, not even the highest creature could have imagined or desired—much less claimed—such happiness. How much more should we be thankful to God for this inestimable grace! And what else can God demand of us than that we have a great and burning desire for the gift which He dispenses so liberally! Then we should always think and exclaim with the Psalmist: "My face hath sought thee; thy face, O Lord, will I still seek." (*Ps.* 26:8). If we love Him as He loves us, then we shall, as the Apostle says, know Him as He knows us. (Cf. *1 Cor.* 13:12).

"I cannot express, O my God," says St. Anselm (*Proslog.* [sub finem]), "how happy Thy elect will be; certainly they will rejoice according to the measure of their love, and they will love after the measure of their knowledge. But how great will be their knowledge, and how great their love? Certainly no eye has seen, nor ear heard, nor has it entered, in this life, into the heart of man, how much they will know and love You in the life to come. I beseech Thee, O God, that I may know Thee, love Thee, rejoice in Thee; and if I cannot do this perfectly in this life, that I may at least progress from day to day, until I arrive at this perfection. Let my knowledge of Thee progress here and become perfect there; let my love increase here and be perfect there: that my joy may be great in hope here and perfect in possession there. O Lord, through Thy Son Thou biddest and counselest us to ask and dost promise to grant that our joy shall be complete; I beseech Thee then, O true and faithful God, grant that my joy may be complete. In the meantime, may my soul consider it, my tongue speak of it, my heart love it. May my spirit hunger for it, my flesh thirst for it, my whole being desire it, until I enter into the joy of the Lord, and may He, as the Triune God, be blessed forever. Amen."

Chapter 9

GRACE MAKES US PARTAKE OF DIVINE SANCTITY

ALTHOUGH the glories already mentioned are so exalted and divine, yet it would seem that there is another glory which surpasses all others. It is indeed a great thing to behold all nature and all miracles far beneath ourselves; to possess, next to God, in virtue of His love, the same glory which He Himself possesses; to obtain the beginning and the root of heavenly happiness and immortality. But since nothing is more eminent in God than His sanctity, it is a still greater privilege to participate in this.

The two remarkable images in which the prophet Isaias (*Is.* 6) and the Apostle St. John (*Apoc.* 4) have represented the majesty of God are thus explained by St. Cyril: the exalted throne of God signifies His highest glory; the jasper, His immutability; the rainbow, His eternity; the seats of the twenty-four ancients, His wisdom; the seven lamps, His all-seeing and all-governing Providence; the thunder and lightning, the omnipotence of His Will; the crystal sea of glass, His immensity; the covering of His head and feet by the wings of the Seraphim, His incomprehensible infinity. But in this fullness of glory the Seraphim, who look on with a thousand eyes, are impressed by nothing so much as by the sanctity of God; this fascinates them, this they praise incessantly by the continual repetition of the song of glory: "Holy, holy, holy, art Thou, Lord God of Sabaoth." Therefore God is very frequently called the "Holy One of Israel," because this name includes all others. When the Psalmist describes the glorious, eternal generation of the Son of God, he says but this one word, that in the splendor of His sanctity (note the Hebrew text: *"In splendoribus sanctitatum."*) He is begotten

37

by the Father (*Ps.* 109:3), for by this sanctity all other perfections are heightened and hallowed.

Sanctity, indeed, signifies the highest quality of divine goodness, namely, singular and august eminence, purity, and rectitude. A creature may be good in virtue of its nature, and indeed every creature is good as it proceeds from the hand of God. Thus the rational creatures also would be good in their nature even without supernatural grace, as long as they did not contradict this natural goodness by sin. But this is a very limited and finite goodness, connected with many imperfections, as with so many stains, a goodness which may coexist with sin and be possessed even though one is separated from the highest good. But the divine goodness is the purest and most perfect that can be imagined, a light without any darkness or shadow of darkness, a light that can never be dimmed by the smallest spot. God is essentially the highest good, and can be separated from it as little as He can annihilate Himself. Hence we call God the only Holy One, the Thrice Holy, thereby expressing the highest prerogative of His nature.

We shall therefore be perfect partakers of the Divine Nature only when, by the grace of the Holy Spirit, we participate also in its sanctity. The holy Fathers identify this partaking of the holiness of the Divine Nature with a great and potent fire which seizes our imperfect nature, penetrates it, transforms it and cleanses it from all dross and stain, so that our goodness is, as far as possible, as pure and perfect as the divine. "Even the princes and powers of Heaven," says St. Basil, "are not by nature holy. The iron lying in the furnace does not lose the nature of iron; and yet, by intimate union with the fire, the iron becomes fiery itself, is penetrated by the whole nature of fire, and even assumes its color, warmth and power. In the same way, by their union with God, the Angels and souls of men have this sanctity inoculated and implanted into their whole being. There is only this difference: the Holy Ghost is by nature holiness, but the holiness of angels and men is a participation in His natural sanctity." (*Contra Eunom.*, 1, 3).

Do you understand now, dear Christian, with what deep

significance we call grace "sanctifying"? Grace is sanctifying not only insofar as that through it we obtain forgiveness of sin and the strength to observe the commandments of God, but also that through it our soul is made a most beautiful image of the divine goodness and holiness. It further signifies that grace is irreconcilable with sin and cannot coexist with it in the same soul. If you commit a mortal sin, you do not annihilate your nature, your natural faculties and the light of reason. But you do destroy grace. Its accompanying supernatural faculties and virtues immediately depart from your soul. For grace, being of a Divine Nature and kind, can coexist with sin as little as God Himself can. When grace has led to the light of glory and has perfectly united your soul with God and made it like Him, then you will lose even the capacity of sinning. By the inherent divine power of grace you will be as incapable of sinning as is God Himself.

Yet how little do we consider the great value of this gift and the superhuman dignity granted by it! "If man alone had received sanctity from the Holy Ghost," says St. Ambrose, "we should doubtless be raised above all angels, even the highest." (*De Spir. Sancto* 1, 1, cap. 7). The Seraphim, who so solemnly praise God as the Thrice Holy, would very properly regard us with the deepest reverence. Shall we alone seek our honor in godlessness and impurity?

Even the most wicked and impious of sinners, cannot in the depth of his degradation, sincerely refuse admiration for that splendor of sanctity which shines forth in so many members of Christ's holy Church. But why have the Saints become so great and so glorious if not because they have cooperated with, and in their whole life expressed the image of, that grace which we all may acquire? All true Christians who are in the state of grace, are called saints by the Apostle, because they have been sanctified in the waters of regeneration by the power of the Holy Ghost, and possess, so to speak, the substance of holiness. We all may and ought to become saintly as they, if not in the same degree, yet no less really and truly, because we are brethren and children of the Saints; we are, in truth, of the Thrice Holy God. What criminal folly it is, then, to soil by voluntary venial sin this garb of innocence, which we have received in Baptism! But what detestable wickedness it would be to rend it, to cast it from us, and to trample it underfoot by mortal sin!

Though not annihilated by mortal sin, our nature is already averse to this great injustice offered to God, because it has been created by Him for His service. But supernaturally considered, what a monstrous thing sin is, when we commit it after God has separated us from it and has so equipped us against it by a new nature, that to become capable of sinning, we must divest ourselves of this new nature and destroy the seed of God in our soul! Have pity on your sublime condition and dignity! Be moved by the jubilant chant of the Seraphim singing "Hosanna," and if you consider it a small matter to offend the sanctity of God, which you cannot injure, spare at least your own sanctity, which you ruin by sin.

Chapter 10

GRACE GIVES US A NEW, HIGHER NATURE

YOU HAVE seen how high the grace of God elevates human nature. You ascend by it into the bosom of God, to partake of His nature and of His knowledge and happiness, His goodness and holiness, His eternity and infinite perfection. But if you participate in His nature, you receive a new nature yourself; you are changed and "transformed," as the Apostle says, "into the same image from glory to glory" (*2 Cor.* 3:18), you are, as it were, created anew; you receive a new being of which your own nature had previously contained not even a germ.

St. Cyril of Alexandria teaches us this in the following words: "If we have once quit the sensual life, is it not evident that, by surrendering our life, so to speak, and by uniting ourselves to the Holy Spirit, we are changed into a heavenly image and transformed, to a certain extent, into another nature? Are we not justly called children of God, men of Heaven, since we share in the Divine Nature?" (*In Joan.,* 1, 11, cap. 12, al. 27).

What we here say of a transformation of our nature does not mean that our natural substance is destroyed or is absorbed into the Divine Substance; this would be an impious error. We speak here only of a transmutation, a transformation and glorification of our nature. You would, however, esteem this change entirely too little, if you supposed that grace makes us new men only in the sense in which a change of disposition or the acquiring of new habits makes us new men.

The change wrought by grace comes from God, not from the will or power of the creature; it is a marvel of divine omnipotence; it lifts us up out of the limits of nature and so

41

elevates and transforms us that we are not only made other men, but more than men; we appear as beings of a Divine Nature and kind.

That we do not lose our natural substance in this transformation the Holy Fathers very often explain by the simile of fire already mentioned. Iron does not cease to be iron when it is aglow with heat, as we may see from the fact that, when it loses this heat, it appears the same as it was before. But in its glowing condition it has no longer its natural hardness, inflexibility, coldness, and dark color, but it partakes of the brightness, warmth, and force of fire, consequently entering into a condition natural only to the fire. Thus, when we say that fire consumes iron, we do not mean that it destroys the iron, but only that it consumes the defects and imperfections of the iron. In a similar manner, as St. Cyril teaches, we do not put off the substance of our nature, but only its lowliness and imperfection. "Those," he says, "who are called by the faith of Christ to the sonship of God, have put off the lowliness of their own nature; glorified by the grace of God and adorned with it as with a precious garment, they are raised to a supernatural dignity." (*In Joan.* 1. 1, 14). Our nature is not changed into another nature by grace so that we lose what we have possessed, but it rather receives what it has not possessed, as St. Paul tells us: ". . . we would not be unclothed, but clothed upon, that that which is mortal may be swallowed up by life." (*2 Cor.* 5:4).

The garb of grace, however, is not merely superadded to the soul from without as is bodily raiment. As fire penetrates iron, so grace invests and penetrates the soul. Grace communicates a new quality to the soul by which it is transformed into the image of God. This new quality is called the new, higher nature of the soul. The nature of a being is nothing else but the innate quality by which it is distinguished from other things, has its peculiar forces and activities, and occupies its peculiar place among other beings. Thus we say that plants have a nature different from that of minerals, animals a nature differing from the nature of plants, and man a nature different from that of brutes. Man is distinguished from brutes by the rationality and spirituality of his soul. But in grace the soul receives a new, heavenly, divine quality, a quality which is as different and as superior as human nature is above the brute nature. By nature a servant of God, man becomes a child of God through grace. By nature man is just above the brute; grace raises him above his own nature, and even above that of the Angels. By nature man possesses the light of reason; by grace he receives the light of God—now in faith, hereafter in glory. By nature he is good, but by grace he becomes a holy creature. He ascends a new step on the ladder of beings; he is placed in a new relation to God, to his fellow men and to corporeal things; finally, he enters a new sphere of life, which is more heavenly than earthly.

This new quality is the germ and root of a higher life. An ordinary tree, by having the branch of a superior type of tree grafted onto it, takes the nature of this branch and brings forth its blossom and fruit. In a similar way, our soul is in the highest manner ennobled by the communication of God's grace, which is called in Holy Scripture the seed of God. (1 John 3:9). Thus, man is raised from his natural, abject position and is transplanted into the bosom of God as into a garden of paradise. There in heavenly sunlight the soul blossoms into a new life which it never knew or imagined before. Or rather, to speak more appropriately with the Apostle of the Gentiles and with our Saviour Himself, the soul, as a wild olive branch, is grafted upon a good olive tree (Rom. 11:24); it becomes a branch of the true vine (John 15:1), the Incarnate Son of God, in order to partake of His Divine Life, which is watered and nourished by the dew of the Holy Spirit.

But if grace confers upon us a new and heavenly nature, what pains we ought to take to acquire and preserve this nature and to live in a way worthy of such a nature! How little esteem does he show for the dignity of human nature who conducts himself as a brute and who gives himself over to beastly lusts and pleasures! How utterly mean and abominable would any act be which would cause one to cease to be a rational creature and which would lower him to the level of the brute! That cannot happen because the likeness of God is indelibly imprinted on our soul. But man may, by the stupidity of intoxication and by the still greater corruption of impurity, reduce himself to a condition in which he is more like brute than like man. We involuntarily shudder at such unnatural conduct. How much more should we shudder at every mortal sin, which not only casts a passing cloud over our heavenly nature, but altogether destroys and eradicates it! Man in his natural state is composed, as it were, of two natures, a corporeal and a spiritual; in him there are two men—an "outer" and an "inner" man, says the Apostle (Cf. *2 Cor.* 4:16)—a mortal and an immortal man. Since we cannot serve both natures at the same time, we must subject the corporeal to the spiritual. But as the flesh should serve the spirit, so should our spirit serve God and His grace, for as the spirit is superior to the flesh, so is grace superior to the spirit. If the spirit subjects itself to the flesh, it is drawn down from its eminence to the level of the flesh and becomes carnal itself; but if it gives itself up to grace and is penetrated and moved by it, it is carried up to God and becomes itself divine. "He who loves the earth," says St. Augustine, "is of the earth; he who loves the world is of the world; he who loves God—what shall I say, brethren; not I, but the Word of God tells you—he who loves God becomes God; 'I said you are gods.' " (Cf. *John* 10:34). In the same measure in which we cooperate with grace and tend toward the Author of grace, the Father of Light, we are filled with His light and glory; we are carried up to Him by His grace and partake of His nature. How detestable it is, then, to allow oneself to be dragged down to the mire of sensual lust when we may elevate ourselves so high on the wings of heavenly love.

We have far more reason to glory in grace than to disregard it. For what enthusiasm must animate our heart when we consider the heavenly race to which we belong! As true as this is, it is likewise true that the sublime nature which we possess is not ours in virtue of our human nature. We are not originally of the divine race, and we can obtain this sublime nature only by the grace of God. Lucifer forgot this when he beheld himself in the splendor of his heavenly light; Eve also forgot this when she was misled by him through that same temptation. That we also may not forget it, God has not again given to us those gifts which made the life of our first parents so happy and peaceful in the flesh, as if they possessed no carnal nature. He lets us feel very clearly that we are of the slime of the earth so that we may not become conceited. Because we have, so to say, been caught up with St. Paul into the third heaven, He has given us the sting of the flesh for our chastisement, our confusion, and our wholesome humiliation. (*2 Cor.* 12:7).

But even this confusion should not rob us of the sense of our heavenly dignity. For precisely therein is the power of our higher nature of grace manifested; for grace descends to our weakness and hereafter consumes it in the heavenly glory. Therefore, we may say with the Apostle: ". . . therefore will I glory in my infirmities, that the power of Christ may dwell in me. For which cause I please myself in my infirmities . . . for Christ. . . . For when I am weak, then am I powerful." (*2 Cor.* 12:9-10).

Chapter 11

GRACE IS IN A CERTAIN SENSE INFINITE

THE NEW NATURE which grace confers upon us has, above all other created natures, the sublime prerogative of participation in the infinite, Divine Nature. In the first place, all other natures—as has already been explained—are only single rays of the Divine Sun, refracted in different colors; grace, however, is a pure, unbroken reflection of the infinite light of the Divine Sun.

Moreover, grace enables the soul to raise itself above the limits of its nature and its surroundings, to behold the infinite God in His infinite nature, to possess and enjoy Him. How could the soul do this if it did not contain something of the infinite power of God? And if it does accomplish this wonderful thing, must we not attribute to the soul a merit and value corresponding, in some degree, to the greatness of that infinite good which we possess by grace?

Besides this, all created natures have a limited and definitely determined sphere of perfection beyond which they cannot of themselves pass. If gold is pure from all foreign composite, it cannot become more perfect or purer gold than it already is. Every species of plant can attain to a certain height and size, no more. The different kinds of animals reach only a definite size and perfection, and then they can progress no further. They have run their course and necessarily succumb to an incessant retrogression and final dissolution. Rational creatures, with the nature they have, cannot improve indefinitely. Their progress lasts just so long as the development of their natural faculties will last. But since their natural faculties are finite, the development of rational creatures must also have a determined and limited end.

Grace alone knows no such restriction; it alone is enclosed by no limits. Since it is a ray of the Divine Nature, grace has its measure and end only in the infinity of God. It can increase daily, hourly—always growing richer, greater, nobler. It never passes its appointed limits, for it has no limits. It always remains grace; it is always a participation in the Divine Nature; it always becomes more and more what it is destined to be. "What could place a limit on supernatural love," says St. Thomas, "since it has its origin in the infinite and eternal power of God and is itself nothing else but a participation in the infinite sanctity of God?" (*S. Th.* 2-2, q. 24, art. 7). The vessel of our nature which receives grace is indeed narrow and limited. But grace, when received by our nature, makes the capacity of our nature ever greater. Every measure of grace received qualifies our nature for a still greater measure.

Every degree of grace is in itself infinitely valuable; it is a treasure more precious than all created things in Heaven or on earth. With St. Paul we should count all things as loss (*Phil.* 3:8), that we may gain Christ and His grace. But this treasure is a thousand times more precious because it is, at the same time, a capital which may easily be increased and multiplied to an infinite degree. Every supernatural action performed in the state of grace, every moment in which the grace given is used and made to bear fruit, merits another increase of grace from God. And so it rests with man to double this grace again in a short time. The greater this increased grace is, the greater also is the merit of our works and the easier and greater is a new increase and multiplying of our capital.

Today the world directs all its aims to an easy and certain increase of fortune by a shrewd manipulation of stocks and bonds. Often, in a very short time, a poor man has acquired a fortune. But if the children of this world are so shrewd in acquiring temporal treasures, which do not render the possessor truly happy, and in the gain of paper, which the smallest spark may destroy, ought not the children of God to feel ashamed that they are, in their field, not only less wise, but incomparably more foolish? For with them there is a question of acquiring—even more easily—true, eternal, heavenly treasures and bonds which no banker, no king, but the infinitely mighty God will redeem with the fullness of His immense wealth and eternal happiness.

Grace gives an immense scope to our aims and desires and leaves them the freest possible play. At the same time grace has this great advantage: we need only to desire it in order to find it; to receive grace, we need only to love its Donor. By this ardent desire for grace and for heavenly happiness, and by a sincere love for the Father, we acquire and merit all good gifts, and that according to the measure of our love and desire. Why do we not manifest here a holy greediness and importunity? Why do we not, like St. Paul, forget the things that are behind and stretch forth our hand to those that are before us? (*Phil.* 3:13). We should measure the soul's profit and advantage not by the treasures already in our possession, but by those which are to be acquired. The Apostle ran the course of perfection with rapid stride, but we do not hurry (*Phil.* 3:12f.); we often pause in our course, as though the smallest part of the eternal and highest good were already sufficient. The Apostle considers himself as not yet perfect; and yet in his good works, in his countless sufferings and glorious miracles, he has the best pledge and evidence of extraordinary perfection; still, he always seeks something higher and more perfect. That which we still lack is without limit; that which we already possess is little and insignificant. But God, who is most liberal in dispensing His gifts and Himself, ceases to increase our small fortune only when we tire of our progress. Why do we commit such an injustice against God and His grace, and against ourselves? Let us remember the wife of Lot, who instead of looking forward, looked behind her and was turned into a statue of salt. Let this example serve to make us prudent and to spur us on to a holy zeal.

The miser is not so much delighted by all he has, as he is annoyed by the least thing that he does not possess. About what he has he is quiet and secure; that which he does not have he pursues with a zeal that knows no bounds or rest. Would that we were at least equally zealous in the pursuit of the heavenly treasures of grace! How soon we should obtain them in the greatest abundance! What can excuse our indolence? Perhaps the fear that we should also become unhappy as the miser by such restless activity. The miser indeed becomes unhappy by his insatiable desire because he never enjoys his acquisition and must lose all in the end. A holy desire for grace, however, leads us to an eternal rest in God, and He will satisfy us more and more, in proportion to our desire and hunger for Him. Grace, moreover, permits us to enjoy what we already have, even as we make progress toward our goal; because the reason our desire constantly increases is, that at every step, we experience more and more how sweet and pleasant the Lord is to those who serve Him.

Chapter 12

GRACE AND THE INCARNATION OF THE SON OF GOD

THE GLORIES of grace described up to now are so great, superb and divine, that it would seem that outside of God and next to Him there is nothing sublimer in Heaven or on earth. Indeed, because grace is in a certain sense infinite, we could not, without a special divine revelation, discover by reason or faith anything greater. Now God has revealed to us two other mysteries which are doubtless greater and more glorious than that of grace: the mystery of the Incarnation of the Word and the mystery of the divine maternity of Mary. But the more we consider these ineffable mysteries in the whole depth of their significance and importance, the more we will understand that, although grace is not superior or equal to them, yet it is placed in its true light by them and receives from them a very special beauty and glory.

By the Incarnation the human nature of Christ was united with the Divine Word in one and the same Person, so that henceforth God is truly man, and one Man is truly God. The human nature is not changed into the divine, but it does not have its individual independence; it is so implanted and ingrafted into the second Person of the Holy Trinity that it belongs to the Divinity and enjoys a really divine dignity. By grace, however, we are not truly made God; we retain not only our own nature but also our own personalities; we are deified only insofar as we are made similar to the Divine Nature by a god-like quality. Thus, the elevation of the human nature of Christ to the infinite dignity of the true God is certainly incomparably superior to our union with God by grace.

But if we consider carefully, we see that this elevation of the human nature of Christ is not an honor accorded to a human person, because there is no such person in Christ. It is rather an infinite condescension of God, who steps down from His eminence to appropriate to Himself a created nature. Therefore, we do not say that a man was made God, but we say God was made man. By grace, however, a created person—man—shares in the Divine Nature; this he does, even though he is not God, nor is he made God. And so we admire grace almost more than the Incarnation.

"Which is the more adorable mystery," asks St. Peter Chrysologus, "that God gave Himself to the earth, or that He gives you to Heaven; that He Himself enters into such intimate union with our flesh, or that He introduces us to companionship with the Godhead; that He is born, like us, to servitude, or that He begets us as His freeborn children; that He adopts our poverty, or that He makes us His heirs and the co-heirs with His only-begotten Son? Certainly it is more adorably wonderful that earth should be changed into Heaven, that man should be transformed by the Deity, and that the condition of slavery should receive the rights of dominion." (*Hom.* 67). In another place the same Saint says: "So great is the divine condescension towards us that the creature knows not which to admire more: that God has descended to our servitude or that He has transported us to His divine dignity." (*Hom.* 72).

The elevation of man by grace balances, as it were, the condescension of God in the Incarnation. God matches the depth of His descent by the height to which He elevates man. Between God and man a wonderful exchange takes place: He adopts our nature to make us partakers of His Divine Nature. Therefore Holy Church directs the priest to say at the Offertory in Holy Mass: "O God, grant that we may be made partakers of His divinity who vouchsafed to become partaker of our humanity, Jesus Christ, Thy Son, our Lord."

And this equalization, this balance between the humiliation of God and the elevation of man by grace, has so profound a reason that the holy Fathers teach that the Son of

God was made man on account of grace, to elevate us by grace. "God was made man, that man might be made God," says St. Augustine. (Serm. 13 de temp., *et al passim*. Cf. Petavius, *De Incarn. Verbi,* 1, 2, cap. 8). And another Father says: "The Son of God was made the son of man that the children of man might be made children of God." (St. Athanasius, *Cit. apud Petavium, 1, c.*). Many other Fathers teach the same things as St. Augustine, thus only repeating that sublime saying of the Apostle: "God sent his Son, made of a woman . . . that we might receive the adoption of sons." (*Gal.* 4:4, 5).

We find in the writings of St. Fulgentius a beautiful explanation of this passage: "God was born of man that man might be born of God. The first birth of Christ, as the Son of God, was of God; the second, of man. Our first birth is of man; our second, of God. And because God, to be born of a woman, adopted the reality of the flesh, He has given us at our regeneration in Baptism, the spirit of sonship. What Christ was not by nature at His first birth, that He was made at His second birth by grace, that we might also be made by the grace of the second birth what we were not by nature of the first. God, however, brought us grace when He was born of man; we, on the other hand, receive grace gratuitously, that by the donation of the incarnate God, we might partake of the Divine Nature." (Ep. 17, *sive lib. ad Petrum diac.* cap. 7, nn. 14-15). As truly, then, as God is born of man in adopting our nature, so truly is the Divine Nature communicated to us. There is only this difference: the Son of God adopted not merely the qualities, but the substance of human nature; we, however, share in the Divine Nature only through a god-like quality.

If, then, the condescension and humiliation of God in His Incarnation are so great, must not the elevation of man to God likewise appear infinitely and incomprehensibly great?

But the humanity of Christ may be considered not only in its personal union with the Son of God, but also in the condition and qualities which it received on account of its divine dignity. Here again the inestimable greatness of grace is made manifest. God, in all His wisdom and power, could give the human soul of His Divine Son no more worthy adornment than that which our soul receives through grace. This is the sublimist that can be found in a creature, for it deifies the creature and makes it, in the highest sense, a participant of the Divine Nature. But there is a difference between the soul of Christ and our own souls: the soul of the Son of God has every claim and right to grace; His soul does not receive grace as a gratuitous gift, but merits it; moreover, the soul of the Son of God receives grace directly, and in exceeding abundance; finally, the soul of Christ cannot, in any way, lose grace. Our souls, on the other hand, receive grace as a gratuitous gift through Christ, and in a limited measure; in addition, our souls easily lose grace by sin.

And so it cannot be denied that the Incarnation, in all its circumstances, is an infinitely greater and more sublime mystery than grace. However, since there exists between the Incarnation and grace such an intimate union and similarity, grace does not suffer from the comparison, but is rather placed by it in a still brighter light.

But besides this, grace, as we obtain it through Christ, receives from the Incarnation an additional and indescribable, a new and ineffable splendor.

The divine dignity, which the humanity of Christ receives through its personal union with the Eternal Word, is reflected upon all the members of our race. As that humanity was made the true body of Christ, so all regenerated mankind was made the Mystical Body of Christ. Christ is indeed, as much and more than Adam, the head of mankind, and we are His members. Since Christ had a right to grace, we acquire a right to grace through Christ. By Him, mankind appropriates grace and possesses it as something which is due to man for the reason that man's Head is Christ. Christ is the heavenly vine through which streams the fullness of divine life; we are branches into which this life is poured forth.

"O Christian soul," exclaims St. Leo (Serm. 1, *De Nativitate Domini*), "recognize your dignity! Know that as a Christian you surpass the Angels, not only in nature but also in grace! For the Angels are kindred to God only by one tie, namely, that they partake of His Divine Nature; but you are kindred to God in a twofold way, because God has only adopted your nature. If, therefore, these pure and holy spirits were capable of envy, they would envy us, because God has taken upon Himself the nature, not of angels or of archangels, but of the seed of Abraham." (*Heb.* 2:16). We may, then, account God as one of our own and call Him our brother, that which is not permitted to the Angels. "Very foolish are they," says the venerable monk Job, "who would rather be angels than men." (Lib. 3, *De Incarn.*). For although the Angels are not subject to pain, suffering and death, yet they do not have God as their brother. Even if we are exposed to much suffering and tribulation, we are consoled by that supreme honor. Only abysmally wicked and foolish pride would not appreciate and be satisfied with such an honor. But if you are able to appreciate in some measure this honor, then beware of desecrating this divine dignity by any unbecoming conduct. We ought to belong in thought, word and deed to none but Him who, entering into relationship with us, has adopted us as His own. "Let us esteem our Head," St. Chrysostom tells us, "and always remember of what an adorable Head we are members. It is certainly proper that we should surpass even the Angels and Archangels in virtue, since God, by assuming human nature, has placed all things beneath the feet of human nature." The Saint finally concludes with the sorrowful but just complaint: "Is it possible that the body of such a Head is cast before the devils to be abused or trodden under foot by them and that we do not shudder at such a horrible crime?" (Hom. 3, *Ad Eph.*, 1).

By holy Baptism, we are incorporated into the Mystical Body of Christ. In token and pledge of this union with Christ, we receive the sacramental character. This character shows that we are Christ's, and that He is ours; by this character we are really Christians; we are, as it were, Christ Himself, insofar as we, the body, form one whole with the Head. The character is indelible in the soul and gives us a right to the grace of God as long as we live, for the body of Christ must also be filled with Christ's life of glory. But the character leaves us this right only so long as we live up to His command.

If it is a great crime to banish grace from our nature, how much greater is the sin when we deprive a member of the body of Christ of its own heavenly life! And if it is criminal neglect to permit ourselves to be robbed of grace, how much more criminal is it to cast grace away! Now that we have Christ Himself as a pledge that no power in Heaven or on earth can wrest grace away from us, it would be criminal to give this grace and ourselves to the devil. St. Gregory Nazianzen teaches us how to meet the attacks of the devil: "If he tempts you to avarice and at any time represents to your eye all the kingdoms of the world as belonging to him and offers them as a reward to you for adoring him, despise him as a poor beggar; in view of the holy seal of your soul, say to him: 'I also am the image of God and am not cast down from the glories of Heaven through pride, as you have been cast down. I have put on the Lord Jesus Christ; you ought rather to adore me.' Believe me that these words will conquer him and will make him retire with confusion into darkness." (Or. 40, *In S. Lumina*).

Remember that however high and exalted the dignity may be which you possess as a member of the body of Christ, this dignity becomes truly precious for you by grace alone; without grace it will profit you nothing, but will rather bring you greater perdition. Only insomuch as you partake also of the spirit and life of Christ will it be profitable to you to belong to the body of Christ through the seal of Baptism. To be a member of Christ is certainly a great, a very great honor; but the dishonor of being a dead member is all the greater. As a dead member you will be cut off entirely from the body. Even when thus cut off, you will not lose the mark impressed upon you by the seal of Baptism, but it will then be a mark of malediction and damnation for you.

Grace, however, makes you a living member of Christ; it gives you a participation in the Divine Nature. It can be a sign only of blessing, not of malediction. It effects that you not only take part in the sufferings and death of Christ while you are on earth, but that you will also be glorified with Him hereafter. You will be united with Him for all eternity, and you will live—with Him and through Him—the blessed life of Heaven. With grace you gain Christ entirely; without grace you lose Him entirely.

You should be willing to suffer everything, to sacrifice everything, in order that Christ, the God-man, the King, Father, and Brother, the Head, the Crown, the Delight, the Joy of mankind, be not taken from the world. All this, however, is lost for us if we lose grace. Let our fear be only the fear of separation from Christ; let our desire be only the desire of union with Christ by grace. In comparison with grace we should count all things as shadows, vanity and dreams.

Chapter 13

GRACE AND THE DIGNITY OF THE MOTHER OF GOD

IN THE mystery of the Incarnation there is elevated to the divine dignity not a human person, but only a human nature. The divine maternity, however, is a supernatural dignity which has been communicated to a human person; it is therefore more easily compared with the dignity granted us by grace.

To prevent any misunderstanding, we must above all faithfully hold that in Mary grace cannot be separated from her divine maternity. Such is the deep meaning of the dogma of the Immaculate Conception so solemnly proclaimed by the Church, namely, that the Mother of God cannot be supposed to have been despoiled of God's grace for even a moment. Because she communicated her human nature to the Son of God, she has a right beyond any other person to share in Christ's Divine Nature by grace. As Mother, she forms one person, as it were, with her Son. His rights are her rights; His gifts are hers; His sanctity is her sanctity. She is that woman whom St. John beheld in his revelation, who does not receive the light of the Divine Sun from afar, but who is rather completely surrounded and enveloped by this Sun. Therefore the grace which fills her soul has this excellent prerogative above the grace of all other creatures, that it is especially due to her; it is so necessarily due to her that she can never lose it or be without it; it is so plentifully due that we may all draw from it. Christ is spoken of as full of grace and truth; likewise, she is called by the Angel, not only *blessed* with grace, but *full* of grace. As He is the only-begotten Son of the Father, so Mary is the firstborn daughter of the Father.

If we consider the sublime dignity of Mary, we may not venture to compare with it our heavenly dignity which we receive through grace. But if, for a moment, we abstract from this union, and if we consider the maternal dignity of Mary in itself alone, then we may safely assert, without fear of prejudice to her, that grace is a greater gift and that it confers a higher dignity than the divine maternity.

As mother of God according to the flesh, Mary ranks high above all creatures; she deserves the love and respect of her Son, the reverence of the Angels, the service of men. But, rather than lose grace, she would gladly choose to give up the privileges and honor of being Mother of God. She would rather be a daughter of God by grace, than the Mother of God according to the flesh; for she well knows that Jesus, although He embraces her with an incomparable love, would nevertheless love another soul more, if this other soul were richer in grace. Christ Himself wished to intimate this when He said: "'Who is my mother and who are my brethren.' And stretching forth his hand toward his disciples, he said: 'Behold my mother and my brethren! For whosoever shall do the will of my Father, that is in heaven, he is my brother and sister and mother.'" (*Matt.* 12:48-51). On another occasion, when a certain woman from the crowd called His Mother blessed, saying: "Blessed is the womb that bore thee, and the breasts that nursed thee," He answered with deep meaning: "Yea rather, blessed are they who hear the word of God, and keep it." (*Luke* 11:27-28).

He certainly did not wish on these two occasions to deny His Mother, or to do her an injustice. He intended rather to say that His Mother is worthy of Him only for the reason that she performs the will of His Father in the most perfect manner. She hears His word and keeps it, and so she possesses in the fullest measure the grace of God. If another soul—which cannot for a moment be supposed—were more perfect in this respect than His Mother, He would honor such a soul more than His Mother.

As Mother of our Saviour in the flesh, she had given birth to Him only according to the flesh. She received the Eternal Word into her bosom to invest Him with a human nature;

she thus enjoyed a natural relationship with Him. But by receiving the Word of God into her soul, she also conceived and brought forth her Son spiritually; she was clothed with the splendor of His Divine Nature and thus entered also into a heavenly relationship with Him. Certainly this latter relationship cannot be separated from the former and is necessarily connected with it. But the words of St. Augustine remain true: "The maternity would have profited the Virgin nothing if she had not borne Christ still more happily in spirit than she bore Him in the flesh." (*De Sancta Virgin.* III). From this it by no means follows that the maternity of Mary according to the flesh is of little or no value to her. Rather, its highest privilege and its sublimest significance consist in its being inseparably connected with grace and in its having grace as a necessary consequence.

But if the divine maternity of Mary would have been profitless without grace, and if Mary would have preferred to possess grace than to have the divine motherhood without grace, can we dare to compare and prefer any other purely human dignity to grace? How can we love fame among men more than the honor of standing in grace with God! How can we cherish to appear great in the eyes of men, rather than to know that our names are written in the Book of Life! How can we boast of possessing a temporal advantage over our fellow men, when they may surpass us in grace of God, which almost makes souls the equals of our Saviour's own Mother!

By grace we are in a wonderful manner rendered similar to the Mother of God. It was impossible for the Son of God to adorn the soul of His Mother, or His own human soul, with a perfection of a higher kind than grace confers. Indeed, He had to grant her this grace in a much larger measure and higher degree than to us; but by the reception of grace we imitate in ourselves the maternity of Mary. The same Holy Spirit that descended into the bosom of Mary to endow her with a holy fertility, also descends into our souls to beget in a spiritual manner the Son of God. As the Blessed Virgin, by lending a willing ear to the word of the Angel and by fulfilling the Will of the heavenly Father, was made the Mother of the Son of God in the flesh and in spirit, so must our souls give birth spiritually to the Son of God by faithfully receiving the Word of God, and by corresponding to the command of God, who will give us His grace. Yes, even according to the flesh the Son of God comes to us in order to dwell in us, as He dwelt in Mary's bosom. He wills to be one with us in the flesh, as He is with His Mother. Can we be surprised, then, that our Saviour says that whoever does the Will of His Father is His mother, brother and sister? And must not we, in thanksgiving for the similar grace that God has given us, intone the same hymn with Mary and exclaim: "My soul doth magnify the Lord. And my spirit hath rejoiced in God my Saviour . . . . Because he that is mighty, hath done great things to me . . ." (*Luke* 1:46 ff.).

But if it was necessary that on account of her maternity Mary should be so pure and holy as never to suffer the stain of the slightest sin, if we shudder at the thought of her having been able to offend, even by the least fault, the Son whom she bore in her bosom, must we not also, in view of our intimate union with Christ, regard the least sin as a terrible and atrocious crime?

There is another consideration that we must not pass over at this point. Mary is greater and more exalted than we because she is the Mother of God and at the same time our mother. But how can the Mother of God be our mother also? She is not our mother according to our human nature. That we have received from Eve, not from Mary. She is our mother insofar as we are living members of His body. She is our mother according to grace, by which we receive a new, heavenly nature and partake of the Divine Nature of her Son. As God alone can be our Father by grace, so our Mother by grace can be no one else than the Mother of God.

What delight ought to fill our soul at this thought! How our heart should thrill with joy in the sublime conviction that we are so closely related to the Mother of God, and that we may rightly call the Queen of Heaven and Earth our mother! And how highly we should esteem the inheritance she bequeaths to us, the pledge of her maternal love, the image she impresses on our soul, to make it like herself and like her Divine Son! How tenderly we should love and honor her and, in token of our gratitude, endeavor to guard and protect the great gift of grace which she grants us through her Son! How we should be on our guard, lest by the loss of grace we should show ourselves unworthy of such a great mother and should lose the dignity which belongs to her children!

Chapter 14

HOW MUCH GOD HIMSELF ESTEEMS GRACE

AFTER ALL that has been said, you will believe and clearly see the fact that grace, which includes so many and such incomparable privileges and gifts, is inestimably precious. But if all this leaves no impression on your heart—either because you do not see these glories with your bodily eyes, or because the visible and transitory riches of the world fascinate you too much with their charms—then learn the value of grace from the infinite value of the price that God Himself has paid for it. If you cannot rightly esteem it yourself, see how much God has valued it. If you cannot understand it, submit your intellect to the obedience of faith by making the infallible judgement of God your own. Weigh the value of grace in the infallible balance of God.

And what do you behold? What more could the great God do, with all His infinite wisdom, power and goodness, than He has already done in order to procure grace for us? What greater things could He sacrifice for it than He has actually sacrificed? He has not spared His own Son, His own Blood, His own life of infinite value.

Even the human life of the Son of God is a divine life on account of the infinite dignity of His Person; it can be sacrificed only for the sake of another divine life. Neither Heaven nor earth, with all their splendor and the countless number of beings they contain, was worthy to be bought and saved by the life of the Son of God, or even by a tear, or by a drop of His Blood. On the other hand, theologians say that even if the Son of God had to acquire grace for one soul only, His Incarnation and death would not have been in vain. By sacrificing His life for us, the Son of God wished to indicate that He had to purchase for us the life of the children of God, and that the grace which adorns our soul possesses a value as infinite as the precious Blood of His holy Body. For if His human life is of infinite dignity because it belongs to a Divine Person, the life of grace is of infinite value because it makes us partakers of the Divine Nature.

A disgraceful treason had irretrievably lost the grace which God in His infinite love had originally bestowed upon man. Then, with even greater love, God wished to acquire it again for man. To that end He made every effort that His infinite wisdom could invent and permit. He therefore conceived a plan, which, by its unheard-of novelty, amazed the heavenly host. He Himself would become man to restore to mankind the dignity of His children and to bring them back to His paternal bosom. Behold the Son of God, as He leaves the throne of His Father to seek one of His servants in the most remote corner of His Kingdom, and to enclose Himself within the bosom of a human being in a poor cottage at Nazareth! Behold how low He descends, going beneath the Angels! See with what zeal He takes upon Himself all the trials and sufferings of human nature! Would it not seem that, at such a price, He intended to purchase His own salvation, His own life, His own happiness, His own glory and Divinity?

But He wanted nothing else than to acquire grace, which the world estimates so cheaply. He did not believe such a price too high. Moreover, He bought it not for Himself, but for us.

If, then, the Son of God, who in His infinite wisdom estimates all things according to their true value, willed to purchase grace for us at such a price, how ashamed we ought to be that we bear the loss of grace so easily! Every moment that we are without grace ought to be more terrible for us than Hell itself; and yet in the state of sin, we are able to let days, weeks, and months elapse and all the while we quietly and calmly sleep and eat, we play, and we enjoy ourselves! The great God humbles and annihilates Himself to restore lost grace to us; and we, who are the special subjects of this grace and stand in so great need of it, we faithless mortals destroy it by our sins and crimes. How can we esteem so lightly that which God considers of such value?

For Christ it was not enough merely to come down from Heaven to earth; He willed to labor and suffer for thirty-three years in His human nature. For even in His humanity He was the true Son of God, and all His actions had infinite merit. By one drop of His precious Blood He might have obtained pardon of our sins for us; by one act of love to His heavenly Father. By one act of glorifying God, He might have easily merited grace for us. But no: To make us fully aware of the infinite value of grace, He willed to show that not even a God-man can do and suffer too much for it. Therefore He has suffered all that man can suffer. He fasted forty days in order to satisfy our hunger by the bread of grace; He had His Body torn with scourges that we might be clothed with the robe of grace; He allowed His hands and His feet to be pierced by sharp nails and to shed precious Blood, so that he might pour out into our souls the heavenly waters of grace; finally, He sacrificed His divine life on the ignominious instrument of the Cross to raise us to the throne of grace and to fill us with divine life.

Can that be so very unimportant which the Son of God willed to acquire in such a laborious manner? We so easily believe men who promise liberty, blessing and happiness and who proclaim themselves true saviours of the world. But as soon as it would become necessary to buy our happiness by their sacrifices, they are not in the least prepared to fulfill their promises. From this we should learn how insincere their good wishes are, how little they really love us and how little they esteem the goods they promise us. Why do we not believe our Saviour, who makes so many and such great sacrifices for us? If He would tell us that we must suffer all that He has suffered to merit grace, we should be obliged to believe Him, the Eternal Truth; we should have to believe that the meriting of grace deserves such efforts. How much more readily must we believe that grace is a treasure to be gained at any price since He has proven by deeds that even the God-man, whose dignity is infinite, cannot suffer too much for grace. If you believe this, then you will also understand that all those little sufferings which man may undergo for the sake of grace are nothing compared to its infinite value. If you suffer all that Christ suffered, you could not [by yourself] merit even the least degree of grace. Thank your Saviour, then, with your whole heart for having suffered so much for your sake. Endeavor to be made conformable to Him in His sufferings, as far as possible, for then you will have learned to esteem grace as it should be esteemed.

Certainly that is a great good for the winning of which the Son of God gave His life. But even this, Christ did not deem a sufficient price for grace. He went still further. In order to propagate grace among men, He instituted a Sacrament and a Sacrifice which contain nothing else than His own Body and Blood. It was not enough for Him to be born only once, to die once, to be buried once. He willed to be born again in a mysterious manner in the hands of the priest, a thousand, a million times, at every hour and all over the world. He willed to renew the Sacrifice of the Cross upon the altars of holy Church and to be buried again in the hearts of the faithful. How much insult and dishonor must He always suffer in this Holy Sacrament when the defiled hands of a wicked priest come into contact with Him, when poor and unadorned altars shelter Him, or when a heart defiled with sin receives Him! What impels Him in this infinite zeal to give us grace, when we, in dreadful blindness, scarcely move a step to obtain it, and on the contrary, pursue that which may despoil us of grace? God has done many and great works for the sake of grace; we labor and suffer very little for it, or perhaps not at all.

Even if the intrinsic value of grace were not so great in itself, yet that which was actually paid for it ought to give it an infinite value in our eyes. For we hold a thing in higher honor if we have obtained it with great labor and many sacrifices; its great cost increases its worth in our eyes. When David while on a military expedition was suffering very much from thirst, a few of his brave warriors had, with great labor and danger, brought him some water; but he considered it too precious to be drunk by himself because of the great danger undergone by those who had procured it. Accordingly, he offered it to the Lord instead of drinking it. (*2 Kings* 23:14-17). Yet his soldiers had not actually sacrificed their lives, but had only exposed themselves to danger. Must not the sacrifices which Christ has made for grace render it doubly precious to us?

Yes, grace is as precious as its price, the Blood and life of Christ. He who despises grace despises not only the eternal and infinite treasures contained in its bosom, but also the price with which Christ has purchased it. St. Eusebius of Emisa (Hom. 9, *De Pasch.*) says very significantly: "I feel that I am something great, that I am a work of God; but I am conscious of being something far greater, incomparably greater, because I am redeemed at such a great, such a superabundant price that I appear to be equal to God in value." And in another place the same Saint remarks: "Not gold, nor an angel, but the Author of our salvation Himself was laid in the balance, so that man might, from the great price with which he was bought, learn the greatness of his dignity." (Hom. 2, *De Symb.*).

As often, then, as you exchange grace for sin, so often do you, in the most insolent and shameful manner, trifle with the life, the Blood and death of the great and terrible Lord and God! All the labor of many years of His ardent love, a love that did not spare itself, is destroyed in a moment; the inheritance that He acquired with so much trouble is cast into the abyss of sin.

God created light, the joy of the whole world, with four words. With the same ease He produced the stars, the plants and the animals. He gave life to the Angels by a mere movement of His Will and to man by the light breath of His nostrils. He worked the greatest miracles by a word, a touch, a sign, by His mere Will. By the three words He spoke to Lazarus in the sepulchre, He might have raised all the dead to life. But to restore grace to you, who so audaciously despise it and cast it away, Almighty God undertook a work that cost Him labor, an unspeakable labor of very many years. He gave up His own life. He did so with joy, because

He knew grace was worthy of such a price. But you do not tire of the ways of sin. You often remain in sin for weeks and months, and you do not consider your repentance worth even a slight effort! You think to redeem your sins by a hasty Confession, and soon after you are as careless, as gay and as merry as though nothing had happened. Perhaps you even forget your good resolution. How miserable! See where your blindness and the intoxicating habit of sin are leading you. If you would only, as true servants of God, consider most attentively the great price of your redemption, certainly you would—like them—approach the Sacrament of reconciliation with bitter compunction and holy zeal. You would shield yourself with a strong resolution of amendment. You would preserve with greatest care the recovered grace. You would henceforth always remember the words of the Apostle: "Or know you not, that your members are the temple of the Holy Ghost, who is in you, whom you have from God; and you are not your own? For you are bought with a great price. Glorify and bear God in your body." (*1 Cor.* 6:19-20).

Finally, grace is held in such high regard by God that, rather than permit the loss of grace, He would elect to have all other evils descend upon man. Do you see the great wars and the terrible epidemics that in a short time change whole countries into deserts? Do you see the many evils that happen to individual human beings? Have you observed the countless persecutions that sinners wage against the just, and in which the sinners often seem to triumph? All these evils are permitted by God because men are thereby induced to seek their salvation and happiness not upon earth but in grace. All these evils—for which many men blame Divine Providence—are permitted by God because they are as nothing compared with [the loss of] grace. These very evils are intended to convey grace to man and preserve it for him. If God gave His only-begotten Son for man, why should He not rather destroy the whole creation than suffer mankind to be without His grace?

Why should not we also learn from this divine lesson to esteem grace and its price? May we lose honor and a good name, if only grace does not fail us! May we lose our riches, our parents, children, friends, our health and our life, may we lose all, may heaven and earth pass away, if only we can retain grace! Christ rightly teaches us to sell all that we possess and to give the price to the poor. For the sake of grace, Christ teaches us to sever all, even the dearest human ties. For the sake of grace, Christ teaches us to despise and sacrifice our own lives. His own bright and cheerful example has shown the way. Happy is the soul who has found the pearl of grace. For whoever possesses grace is able to purchase God and Heaven and all other good things.

—Part 2—

UNION WITH GOD

Chapter 15

THROUGH GRACE WE RECEIVE INTO OUR SOUL THE PERSON OF THE HOLY GHOST

IN THE FIRST part we considered the nature of Sanctifying Grace. We saw that it is a most sublime, supernatural creation, infused into the soul by God in a marvelous way. Through this grace our nature is made partaker of the Divine Nature and becomes like it in its holiness.

Since our nature is thus raised so high and is made so much like the Divine Nature, it follows that we enter into a most intimate union with God Himself. Through this union, the splendor and value of grace is evidently raised still higher. This mysterious union with God, which is effected by grace, will constitute the matter of this second part.

In the language of the Holy Scripture and of the Fathers, the Holy Ghost is usually designated as that Divine Person with whom we are especially united through grace. For the distribution of Sanctifying Grace pertains to Him, as the Spirit of holiness, and for this reason the union of God with the creature and of the creature with God is appropriated to Him. Moreover, He is the personal expression of divine love. Since, on the one hand, the union of God with the creature is effected through His love, and on the other hand, our union with God in this life is shown especially through our love for Him, it is very natural that we think especially of the Holy Ghost and name Him first of all when there is question of the relation to the Holy Trinity which we acquire through grace. This is so much the more justified since revelation teaches that through grace the Holy Ghost is given to us and comes with grace in order to dwell in our soul.

Thus, following the Fathers and the theologians, it would

be against faith to hold that the Divine Spirit is in us by reason of His gifts only, and not by His very being.

Accordingly, we must believe that He gives Himself to us with His gifts, from which He is inseparable. St. Augustine does not hesitate to affirm that the Holy Ghost is His own gift. Theology has, as a result, given to the Holy Ghost the name "Gift" as a proper designation of Him.

Various explanations of this are given. According to the Apostle, it is the Spirit of God who transforms us by His power into the image of God. (Cf. *2 Cor.* 3:18). But He does this, not merely as the sun, which from afar and from without, changes a crystal into its image by its rays. Rather, the Holy Ghost must, as any other being, be present in the place where He works, and accordingly, He illuminates our soul as a light that is inside a crystal, or as a fire that penetrates most intimately the body that it makes bright and glowing.

According to the same Apostle, the Holy Ghost is also the seal by which God impresses on our soul the image of His Divine Nature and holiness. Now, although the seal imprints into the wax only its form, and yet in order to do this, must be brought into the closest union with the wax, likewise, the Holy Ghost, when He imprints on us His image, enters into a most intimate union with our soul.

Again, St. Paul says of the Holy Ghost that God has placed Him in our heart as a pledge in order that we may have no doubt whatever that He is earnest in His intention of giving to us the full splendor and the entire inheritance of the children of God.

It was not enough for God merely to have the Holy Spirit work in us with His sanctifying power and to place in our hearts the gifts of that Divine Person. In order that we may be certain that this power will not fail and that these gifts will not be taken away, He has enclosed in our hearts the Giver of the gifts and the very Principle of supernatural power. Moreover, He has reserved our heart to Himself, sealing it with the same Holy Ghost. Therefore, the Apostle says: "The charity of God [which with grace is His highest gift] is poured forth in our hearts by the Holy Ghost, who is given to us." (*Rom.* 5:5).

But as the Holy Ghost must Himself come to us to bring us grace, so, on the other hand, grace leads us to Him, unites us to Him and makes us possess Him.

"Through Sanctifying Grace," says St. Thomas, "the rational creature is so perfected that he may not only use created goods but may also enjoy the Uncreated Good. Therefore, the invisible sending of the Holy Ghost takes place in the gift of Sanctifying Grace, and the Divine Person Himself is given to us." (*S. Th.* 1, q. 43, a. 3, ad 1).

As is evident from these words, St. Thomas is far from affirming that by grace we are merely enabled to enjoy the Holy Ghost in knowledge and love, as we know and love things that do not belong to us and remain distant from us. He teaches rather that we possess and enjoy the Holy Ghost Himself in the same manner as things that we not only see but also hold, embrace, and take into ourselves. Or, to express this mystery as far as possible in all its depth: through grace we are enabled not only to know and love God from afar, through the beauty and the goodness of creatures, but also to possess Him immediately in our souls.

Thus the Divine Nature is not simply the object of our enjoyment in some indefinite way. With grace It becomes most intimately present in a new and more perfect way than It is in all things by reason of Its omnipresence. For, as theologians unanimously teach that the Beatific Vision in the life to come cannot be imagined without a true, efficacious, and thoroughly intimate presence of God and union of our soul with Him, so we must also say that in this life we cannot love Him supernaturally unless the Divine Object of our love is present in our soul in the most intimate way. As object of the Beatific Vision, God is at the same time truly the food of our soul and is as intimately united with the soul as bodily food is with the body. Likewise, the supernatural love of God is at the same time a true, spiritual embracing of God, by means of which we take Him into the very center of our soul and there hold Him fast.

In a twofold way and for a twofold reason, we are really and truly united with the Holy Ghost through grace. First, insofar as He, the source of grace, comes to us with it and unites Himself with us; and again, insofar as grace leads us to Him and unites us with Him.

The Holy Ghost draws near to us in an inexpressible, intimate way in order to give us grace and love as a participation of the Divine Nature and sanctity, as an outflowing from the bosom, from the all-holy heart of God. And we draw wonderfully near to Him through the same grace, since as a sharing of the Divine Nature it makes us capable of the Divine Being and of the Divine Persons.

The Holy Ghost—and therefore God—is indeed present also to created things, not only by His activity, but also by His essence, for it is through this that He acts. But by grace His presence becomes much more intimate and of an entirely different type. In the ordinary created thing, God is present only as its maker and conserver. Without His presence in this way, things could not exist. But in the soul having grace He is present as sanctifier, giving Himself to the creature and sharing with him the holiness of His own being. That recalls the way in which God the Father is in His only-begotten Son, namely, through the substantial sharing of His nature. The Holy Ghost is in us by reason of the gracious sharing of the holiness which is proper to the Divine Nature. Thus, as the presence of the Father in His Son is different from His presence in creatures, similarly the presence of the Holy Ghost in the souls of the just is different from His ordinary manner of dwelling in creatures.

Although the Holy Ghost is present to all creatures, although He dwells in all created nature as in a huge temple, so that Holy Scripture says of Him: "The spirit of the Lord hath filled the whole world" (Wis. 1:7), yet He dwells in a very special way in the soul that is adorned with grace. So true is this that theologians do not hesitate to affirm that if God would cease being present to other creatures—supposing for a moment the impossible—He would still dwell in the souls of the just.

In comparison therefore with the just soul, one can hardly call Creation a temple of God. But if it is considered as such, then the soul must be the altar, the tabernacle of the same. If the universe is the house of God, such a soul is His favorite room. We shall do better to follow the Holy Scripture and call all Creation the footstool of God, on which the hem of His garment falls, while we call the soul of the just the throne of God, being filled with the divine splendor. And even that is not enough. If one wants to be exact, we must say that in the soul of the just the Holy Ghost is present as the soul itself is in the heart, enlivening, moving and ruling it.

This sacred presence of the Holy Ghost in our soul endures as long as we retain Sanctifying Grace. The Holy Ghost does not come to us merely as a transient guest wishing to remain with us for a short time only and then to pass on. Our Saviour has asked the Father that He send us the Consoler, the Spirit of truth, that He might remain with us always. (Cf. *John* 14:16). This exalted Guest wishes to dwell with us forever, never to leave us again, but to lead us to our eternal home.

O wonderful greatness of grace which brings such an exalted, enjoyable, and holy Guest to our soul and unites Him so intimately and so inseparably with us!

If Zachaeus considered himself happy to be able to receive into his house for a short time the Son of Man in His human nature, how much more fortunate must we consider ourselves, since we can give lodging to the Holy Ghost, not simply in our house, but in the very center of our heart! Let others regard it as a great honor when they can receive an earthly king into their house. We must consider as nothing all insults and dishonor coming from men as long as we keep the Holy Ghost in our heart. We should rather oppose all the insults and hate which the world renders us, and we should do so with a holy pride in the knowledge that no one can drive this exalted Guest from our soul. "If you be reproached for the name of Christ," says the prince of the Apostles, "you shall be blessed: for that which is of the honour, glory, and power of God, and that which is his Spirit, resteth upon you." (*1 Ptr.* 4:14).

Now this sublime Guest does not come to honor us with His presence only; He brings to us a priceless treasure. This treasure is again the Holy Ghost Himself. Or rather, He is not only a treasure but also the pledge of a still greater treasure. We are now able to taste the Holy Ghost in the sweetness of His love. But in the future we are to enjoy the Father and the Son and the Holy Ghost and their entire Divine Being and splendor. He is, as the Apostle tells us, the pledge of our inheritance (cf. *Eph.* 1:14), the inheritance which is none other than Himself. Since this inheritance is nothing else than God Himself, the pledge for it could be no other than God Himself. For only a divine pledge can be to us security for a divine inheritance and give to us a foretaste of the enjoyment of God.

How differently should we not consider the pricelessness of this treasure and the consolation of hope which this pledge guarantees to us! But one can enjoy the Holy Ghost, the Spirit of divine love, only in the measure in which one loves; for one enjoys love only by loving. Accordingly, the more we seek to love this source of holy love, the deeper He will sink the treasure of His holiness and love into our soul. Moreover, this will intensify our desire and trust to be able once to enjoy this treasure, not only as hidden behind a veil, but in all its fullness and splendor. And if we do not always feel its sweetness, our love is still shown by the pain which the fear of separation from Him causes us. When out of indifference we do not foster this love in us, the Holy Guest hides Himself in order to instill into us salutary fear through the thought of being deserted by Him.

But no, let that be far from you, dear Christian, to be indifferent to the purpose that the Holy Ghost has when He comes into your heart. He comes to you in order to give Himself to you and thus to make you happy. But He comes at the same time as your Lord and God to take possession of you as His temple. "Or know you not," says the Apostle, "that your members are the temple of the Holy Ghost, who is in you, whom you have from God; and you are not your own?" (*1 Cor.* 6:19).

Since, therefore, you have received the Holy Ghost, you have been consecrated as His temple and you belong to Him. All that you do should be for His honor and glory. Besides Him you should serve no false gods, which would be to desecrate the temple of the true God. "And," says the

Apostle in another place, "what agreement hath the temple of God with idols? For you are the temple of the living God." (*2 Cor.* 6:16).

What an awful crime it would be to desecrate the temple of God! This we know from the greatness of the punishment that the Apostle attaches to such an act: "But if any man violate the temple of God, him shall God destroy." (*1 Cor.* 3:17). Now through grave sin this temple of God is not only harmed, it is destroyed and annihilated. For mortal sin destroys in us the grace from which it is built.

O frightful, unwholesome deed, by which we in a moment, as Samson, tear away the pillars of this splendid building to bury ourselves under its ruins and thus rob God of His sanctuary! The atheistic Antiochus did not dare to destroy the temple of Jerusalem. He desecrated it only and robbed it of its treasures. And yet he soon felt on himself the frightful, avenging hand of God. Worms grew out of his body, rotting flesh fell in pieces from his limbs; and he died amidst inexpressible pain in the greatest despair. And you who damage the sanctuary of the Holy Ghost and destroy His temple, what have you to expect?

May we mortals then realize how terrible grave sin is, by which divine grace is cast away. It would be preferable that the whole world be destroyed than that one mortal sin be committed. The destruction of the whole world would be the ruin of only a stone of God's temple, but the destruction of the temple itself by grave sin desecrates the very sanctuary and drives God out of His own holy dwelling.

The Holy Ghost dwells not only in our soul but also in our body, since this latter is united to the soul and forms one with it. And thus our body is a temple of the Holy Ghost, blessed and sanctified by His presence. It is a holy vessel, still holier than the ark of the covenant of the Old Testament, because we bear in it, not only the tables of the law, but the Lawgiver Himself. Hence the Apostle says to us: "For this is the will of God, your sanctification; that you should abstain from fornication; that every one of you should know how to possess his vessel in sanctification and honour: not in the passion of lust, like the Gentiles that know not God: . . . For God hath not called us unto unclean-ness, but unto sanctification." (*1 Thess.* 4:3-5, 7).

Surely these are words worthy of deep consideration. We can hardly think highly enough of the dignity and reverence that belong to our body because the Holy Ghost dwells in it.

The body is matter for admiration already as a simple instrument, as a dwelling, as the external expression of our soul. For a higher spirit spiritualizes and clarifies the body, a noble heart elevates its behavior and movement and effects so that a mere glance charms and enchants us. One word makes us enthusiastic for the hardest work and pierces us through as a glowing arrow because it comes out of a living, spiritual soul. Often we ourselves can give no account of the impression which a man makes on us, seeing that his exterior has no proportion to this effect. But we remain, never-theless, under the spell of the spirit that speaks out to him.

Now then, should we not esteem, love and honor the Christians in whom the Holy Ghost has established His dwelling! What dignity and purity, what recollection and devotion, what warmth and enthusiasm should be ex-pressed by our features, our words and our behavior, that we may thus give witness of the excellence of the heavenly Spirit whom we house!

And how holily should we not esteem our fellow man as a worthy temple of the Holy Ghost! How can we treat him as something of little worth and injure him without considera-tion if we are able to serve this sanctuary of the Holy Ghost. If we were as enlightened as the Saints we would kneel down, as they did, before the sick and the helpless and per-form for them the most menial services with great rever-ence, knowing well that even the smallest service to the temple of God is exalted and holy. Holy Scripture says that God Himself treats us with kindly deference (cf. *Wis.* 12:18), as a precious vessel, and certainly for no other reason than that He sees in us His own Spirit. Let us love, then, through the Holy Ghost the temple of God in our neighbor that we also may be worthy to be temples of God and to be filled with His Divine Majesty!

Chapter 16

THE ENTIRE HOLY TRINITY IS INTRODUCED INTO OUR SOUL BY GRACE

W E CAN EASILY prove the indwelling of the Holy Trinity from what has been said heretofore. The Holy Ghost is Himself God, and *one* God with the Father and the Son. Because of the unity of their essence, all three Persons are inseparably bound together with one another. Therefore, where one is, the two others must also be. Hence, our Saviour Himself says: "If anyone love me, he will keep my word, and my Father will love him, and we will come to him and make our abode with him." (*John* 14:23).

Origen (*In Levit.* 4, 4) rightly refers to this mystery that word concerning the fellowship with the Father and His Son Jesus Christ which St. John wishes to the faithful, in order that that they may rejoice with Him and that their joy may be full. (Cf. *1 John* 1:3-4). St. Augustine refers to the same mystery. (*Sermo Domini in Monte* 1. 2, c. 6, n. 20-24). He asks how we in the Lord's Prayer can say to the Father: *Who art in Heaven*, when He is present everywhere. To this he answers that by *Heaven* is to be understood the just on earth and the Angels above, since the Father, with the Son and the Holy Ghost, dwells in them as in a royal palace, as an inseparable companion of His grace.

Grace is indeed a sharing of the holiness of God. But His holiness flows out of His nature and is accordingly inseparable from it. Whoever receives grace receives consequently the triune God in his soul.

In this we see the wonderful power of grace, drawing down the entire Holy Trinity from Heaven into our soul, or rather changing the soul itself into Heaven. With St. Chrysostom (*In Ep. ad Hebr.* 27.4), we may well note how insignificant appears the power that Jesus had of commanding the sun to stand still. For it is something much greater to draw down upon earth the Lord of Heaven Himself.

O holy grace, builder of a new Heaven, of a new temple, of a new palace and throne for the King of Heaven and earth! Who would not open his heart to Thee with joy that Thou mayest prepare there a worthy dwelling place for the Triune God?

And who shall dare to drive Thee, O great God, out of this place of rest! Indeed, such a one would be worse than Herod, who drove the child Jesus out of the stable of Bethlehem. For there the Son of God had a place that was not worthy of Him, but through grace our soul is so splendidly ornamented that God dwells in it as willingly as in Heaven. Who would dare then to destroy this heaven? And if someone dares to do it, shall not all Creation avenge the grievance thus offered to its Lord? The more honorable and condescendingly the Holy Trinity comes down to me, the more worthy of condemnation is this wrong. "What is a man," we must cry out with the pious Job, "that thou shouldst magnify him? or why dost thou set thy heart upon him?" (*Job* 7:17). Yes, that is the correct expression. In grace God turns His heart towards us, lays His heart on our heart, or rather, in our heart. He does not come as to servants, to receive from us the faithful homage of a free and blessed servitude. This in itself would be no small honor. But He comes rather as to friends, to live with us in intimate and trustful fellowship.

It was, indeed, a great honor for Joseph in Egypt, for Daniel and Mardochai, that they stood so near to earthly kings. But such honor is not even a shadow in comparison with the honor accorded us when the omnipotent God comes into our heart through grace and unites Himself so intimately to us.

For this fellowship is, according to the expression of the blessed and deeply learned Carthusian Dionysius (*Com. in 1 Joan.* 1, 9), so intimate that we have in common with God conversation, mysteries, occupations, sentiments, desires and interests.

And in fact, who besides the Christian united with his God can speak those sublime words: "It is good for me to adhere to my God, to put my hope in the Lord God"? (*Ps.* 72:28). Such a one speaks continually with God in prayer and converses with Him in meditation, having his ear ever attentive to the sweet tone of the divine voice. Such a soul eagerly grasps all His holy inspirations and impulses. It considers separation from God worse than death. And when it occasionally happens that it no longer feels the friendly signs of the usual familiarity, the soul sighs bitterly out of fear that it may have been the cause of God's withdrawing Himself from it.

On the other hand, God opens His heart to such a soul, gives to it His grace, takes it under His special protection, gives it a taste for His mysteries, and that peace which surpasses understanding. God Himself has said: "My delights were to be with the children of men." (*Prov.* 8:31). If it were a case of men speaking, we would have to shake our head in doubt at such a statement. For who would not consider it as an exaggeration that God should find His joy in being with us? But when it is God who speaks, we must believe, and we must acknowledge that our heart acquires through the indwelling of God a splendor great enough to fill God Himself with delight.

We human beings find pleasure in dealing with pure, noble souls. We read in the lives of the Saints that great crowds came from afar to enjoy consolation from them, to see them and to hear a word from their mouth. Even the relics of the bodies of Saints are the object of our veneration. But are not we ourselves a still greater sanctuary, a living shrine of the Divinity in which dwell, not the dead ashes of the Saints, but all three Persons of the most Holy Trinity?

If you knew yourself, Christian soul, how you would treasure and esteem yourself! If you but knew yourself, O saintly soul, loved and dwelt in by God, honored and admired by the Angels! Oh, if you but knew yourself, lovely paradise of your Creator, splendid tabernacle of the Holy Trinity, beautiful bridal chamber of the heavenly King! If you but knew yourself, golden ark of the covenant, not of the

Old, but of the New Covenant, altar of the Divine Majesty, treasury of the gifts of the Holy Ghost, temple of the living throne of the Divinity, broad Heaven in which glitter resplendently, not material stars but rather the Divine Persons! If you knew yourself, daughter of the Father, sister of the Son, bride of the Holy Ghost, associate and companion of the whole Blessed Trinity! If you only knew yourself, how highly you would prize yourself, not because of what you are of yourself, but because of the dignity that grace brings to you! How you would hold in honor yourself and grace, and guard against its loss!

Rightly do we praise St. Frances of Rome, who always saw an angel beside her as her companion. How we should marvel if the Archangels and the Thrones, yes if all the blessed spirits would stand beside and encircle a man! But what is that in comparison with the company of God—of all three Divine Persons—who is united with every soul that possesses Sanctifying Grace!

If it is hardly thinkable that a soul that knows it is surrounded by angels could dare to drive them away by an unbecoming act, or to desert them in order to associate itself with the devils and reprobates, how awful and incredible must it appear that our soul can behave thus towards God! Who can believe that this happens often; yea, that nothing happens more frequently?

Let us hold fast to the high dignity that has come to us at the time of our justification through Baptism and Penance. Let us be more assiduous in honoring the Divine Majesty which dwells in us by walking worthy of God and concerning ourselves more with Him and with heavenly things!

Chapter 17

THROUGH GRACE THE HOLY GHOST BREATHES HIS OWN LIFE INTO US

IF THE entire Holy Trinity is united to our soul through grace, if the Holy Ghost especially, the Spirit of counsel and of light, of fortitude and piety, dwells in us, this presence cannot be fruitless in our soul. The Father works continually and the Son does likewise, but the Holy Ghost is given to us in order to renew, continue, and perfect in us what our divine Saviour taught and left with us.

God is a living God, and the Holy Ghost is the breath of the divine life. He must, accordingly, dwell in our soul as the breath of divine life, as the soul of our soul, in order to breathe into it a new, higher life—His own holy, divine life.

Our soul has its natural life. Thereby we understand, not that life by which it gives movement and sensation to the body, but especially its own spiritual life, consisting in the use of reason and free will, by which it can know and love spiritual things—the true, the beautiful and the good. The soul is, according to its nature, an image of God by reason of this higher life only. But as this natural image is to the living God only like a lifeless picture in comparison with its living model, so is our natural life only a shadow of the divine life. Hence it is that we speak of the death of a soul which, robbed of supernatural grace, lives only a natural life—which in this case is, of course, marred by defects.

The lifeless body of Adam, which God formed with His own hands, was a marvelous piece of work. Through the infusion of that divine breath which gave to this work of art life and motion, thought and speech, man was raised up to a new degree of being, which no other earthly creature attains. If now even this excellent life is death when compared to grace, we may draw from this a slight idea of what the supernatural life must be.

God infused His breath, or as Holy Scripture says, His own spirit into our soul, that was heretofore only a faint lifeless image of Him, and He enlivened it with the breath of His holy life. This divine breath of life is grace. Through it the Holy Ghost unites Himself with us. Through it He fructifies the earth of our soul with the seed of a higher, heavenly life. This He does in a far higher way than when, hovering over the waters at the time of Creation, He fructified the earth with the seeds of plants; even in a far higher way than through that breath with which He made the lifeless Adam into the living lord of Creation.

Through grace, the Holy Ghost comes into our soul in a way like to that in which He once came down into the womb of the Virgin in order to make the root of Jesse, the Son of God, spring up as a heavenly flower.

One of the most sublime and most beautiful miracles narrated in Holy Scripture is the one told of the prophet Eliseus, who brought back to life the son of the Sunamite woman. The Prophet, says Holy Scripture (*4 Kings* 4:34), bent over the child. He put his mouth on the child's mouth, his eyes on the child's eyes, his hands on the child's hands. Then he let himself down upon the child, and the warmth of life returned to the lifeless flesh. This miracle is a beautiful type of that far greater wonder that takes place in our soul when grace is infused. Here it is not a man being brought back to human life by another man, but God awakening our soul to divine life.

With inexpressible love and tenderness, God bends over His image, our soul. He puts His mouth on its mouth in order to breathe into us the breath of His life and the Spirit of His love. He joins His eyes to the eyes of our soul, that is, to our reason. He unites His hands with ours, and His divine power with the natural life of our soul, thus giving us a new life, by which the soul lives in God and God in it forever.

Then, after God has breathed His life into our soul, He cannot leave it, as Eliseus did after he had restored life to the boy. Our soul cannot live separated from Him, as the seed lives on after it has been separated from the tree that has fructified it. No, God remains in our soul, as the soul remains in the body that it enlivens. He breathes His Spirit into it in order that He may remain in it and effect there what the soul does in the body. He remains that He may move and guide the soul and continually awaken and support in it the light of divine knowledge and the flame of divine love.

In a certain sense He grafts His life onto the weak little tree of our soul in order to change its natural life into a divine one and to raise it up to a heavenly life, in order that it may henceforth, filled with divine power, bring forth heavenly blossoms and fruits that will never fade away.

The soul adorned with grace becomes then in reality a new, ennobled tree which is always green, always in bloom, and always bearing fruit. For it is always given to drink of that heavenly water, which, as our Saviour said, springs up to life everlasting because it flows out of the bosom of the living God. (*John* 4:14). This water is, indeed, the Holy Ghost Himself.

That is the sense of the Apostle's words: "For the wages of sin is death. But the grace of God" . . . which is poured into our hearts by the Holy Ghost who is given to us . . . "is life everlasting." (*Rom.* 6:23).

Now behold, O Christian, have you understood; have you heretofore appreciated the worth of this divine and heavenly life—or better, will you ever be able to appreciate it?

Indeed, life is of itself something so precious that each one, even the least living thing, belongs to a higher class of creatures than all those things, even the greatest and most beautiful, that have no life. But the life of man, which is the crown of God's work here below, is without doubt something more precious and more sublime than the whole earthly creation. Whoever takes the life of a man does a greater wrong than one who annihilates the whole material world. And whoever saves such a life acts in the eyes of God as though he created a new world.

This is true even in regard to natural life. Even this life is priceless, more so than all other things on earth. But, as we said before, the field of that activity which man can carry on through his natural powers is very limited. The soul can know only created things. Only mediately and from afar can it know God, insofar as created things reveal traces of Him.

But through grace an entirely new world is opened to it, and an entirely different activity is made possible. Through it the spirit is made capable of knowing God Himself, not only in His external works, but in His infinite holiness—nay more, in His own inner life. By grace the soul is put in position to love God and to deal with Him, not only as the creature with the Creator, as the subject with the king, as the servant with his master, but as the child with its father, as the full-fledged member of the family with the head of the family. Through grace, the old man is clothed with the new man, "who according to God is created in justice and holiness of truth." (*Eph.* 4:24). From this we can easily conclude that all natural life cannot be compared to the supernatural life that grace gives the soul.

The life of any being manifests itself especially through the activity or movement that takes place in it. Thus water, even though it be lifeless, is called living when it does not remain still but when it flows and bubbles in a lively manner. Plants are living because they raise themselves up and develop themselves from the root through their own inherent power. That is a higher type of activity and therefore of life, so that compared with plants even the flowing water appears as dead. A yet higher form of life is had by the animal, for it can move about and its activity is not limited to one place. Man moves himself more perfectly, piercing even the interior things with his intellect, searching out not only sensible things but also spiritual things. He even raises his eyes in wondrous anticipation to the heights above where the Almighty is enthroned. Therefore, the natural life of man is as far above that of other creatures as his activity is above that of which they are capable.

But this activity is also limited, for it cannot go beyond the realm of that which is purely natural. As long as the Spirit of God does not come to us with His grace, our soul lies on the ground as the body of Adam before it was given life. Without grace, our soul cannot raise itself above created things to be able to receive and enjoy the light of the true Sun. It cleaves as a worm to the earth, that is, to creatures, to the shadow of the glory of God. But it cannot fly up to Him with the bold flight of the eagle, to look upon Him and to unite itself to Him.

Just as water is lifeless if compared with plants, as the worm may be called dead if compared to the eagle, so may our soul be considered as dead as long as the Holy Ghost does not pervade it with mighty breath and share with it His own life.

If now the natural life of the creature is to be valued so much, and if everyone who knows how to treasure the works of God takes care not even to trample on a worm without necessity or reason, how priceless must the divine life be! And if the body loves the soul so much, how much more should not our soul sigh after the Holy Ghost, who fills us with divine life.

Oh, that we might treasure that heavenly life of the soul at least as much as the short, miserable life of the body! This latter is at most a continual dying and daily and hourly draws nearer to its dissolution and bears within itself from its beginning the seed of its corruption. To what lengths do we not go to hold on to this life! What sacrifice is too great to avoid death, which we consider as the last and greatest of all evils! And yet we know that we cannot keep death away, once its hour has come.

Our soul, on the other hand, bears within itself, through the grace of the Holy Ghost, the seed of life everlasting, which rejuvenates itself from day to day. "Though our outward man is corrupted, yet the inward man is renewed day by day." (*2 Cor.* 4:16). Moreover, the grace of the Holy Ghost is eternal life, not only for the soul, but also for the body. But, says the same Apostle in another place, "If the Spirit of him that raised up Jesus from the dead, dwell in you; he . . . shall quicken also your mortal bodies, because of his Spirit that dwelleth in you." (*Rom.* 8:11).

Therefore, we should take more care for the life of the

soul and be more concerned for its welfare than for the good of the poor flesh. What do we gain when we spare our body so anxiously and give it so much artificial care? "If you live according to the flesh," says the Apostle, "you shall die" (*Rom.* 8:13), die in the flesh and die in the soul. But when through the Holy Ghost you deny and mortify the flesh, you will live forever, not only in the soul but also in the glorified body. How true and apparent, then, is the teaching of our Divine Saviour: ". . . He that loveth his life shall lose it; and he that hateth his life in this world, keepeth it unto life eternal." (*John* 12:25).

But how few there are who wish to understand this; how few who weigh the true worth of the life of their soul and body according to these words; how few think of the words: "What doth it profit a man, if he gain the whole world, and suffer the loss of his own soul?" (*Matt.* 16:26). Of what use are all the joys and pleasures of this earth, of what use is your indolent and comfortable life, your great expense in nursing and gratifying the flesh? All that is loss and poison, death and destruction.

And if perhaps you do not entirely destroy yourself, it is bad enough that you make yourself tender and soft, that you become a burden to yourself and others, and that you prepare for yourself the painful accusation in eternity that you neglected thousands of opportunities for merit which you could easily have used. Take only half as much care for your soul and lay out only a very small expense for it, and it will bring you life everlasting and eternal happiness and will be for you an incalculable gain.

As the heavenly life of the soul is infinitely better and more precious than the earthly life of the body, or the soul's natural life, so also is its loss the most terrible and frightful death. Here, if anywhere, the Proverb holds: "The most noble thing becomes in its ruin the most ignoble." Nothing is more loathsome, repugnant and detestable than a human body from which life has gone out. As it was while alive more beautiful and glorious than all lifeless things, so when it has lost its life, it becomes far more ugly than they. A corpse that is decaying is considered as something loath-

some, driving away all by its terrible appearance and sick-
ening odor. Must not then the loss of supernatural life,
which you bring about by awful suicide, be much more
frightful and draw after it worse consequences? Indeed, as
the life of a single soul is far more precious than the bodily
life of all men, so is the soul that has died through mortal
sin much more gruesome than a whole acre of dead bodies.
If you could see your soul in this condition, as God and your
Guardian Angel see it, and as it was permitted to several
Saints, you would tremble and fear and be restless until you
had gotten rid of this abomination.

St. Antoninus (*Summa Theol*. IV, t. 14, c. 6, 1, 3.) tells of a
monk who, being one day on a journey, came upon a corpse.
When passing, he carefully covered his nose with his mantle. The Angel who accompanied him in the figure of a man
did not appear to notice the unpleasant odor. Afterward,
they met a well-dressed young man. Then the Angel held
his hand before his face as he passed. When the monk wondered about this, the Angel explained that the natural odor
of a decaying corpse did not bother him, but the unnatural
and unbearable smell of a soul in the state of sin was
enough to drive away the whole heavenly court. St. Basil (*In
Ps*. 22 n. 5) pertinently says: "As smoke drives away bees
and a carcass the doves, so does sin drive away the Angels."

We meet something similar in the life of St. Catherine of
Siena. While she was at Siena many miles from Rome, she
was annoyed by the evil odor of one who was living at Rome
in the state of sin. And when once a very well-dressed
woman came to her to speak to her, the Saint could not be
brought to answer even a word because—as she later
explained to her confessor—of the frightful odor coming
from the woman's soul.

Only those who bear such a stain in their soul do not
notice its ugliness nor its offensive odor. But precisely this
is a sign of their death, for the dead lose sensation when
they lose life. And this insensibility is yet worse than death
itself, for it robs one even of the desire of life. It leaves one
indisposed to receive life again and surrenders one, who
otherwise might be saved, to a more terrible, eternal death!

May the merciful God preserve all the just from this awful death. And may He fill all who have had the misfortune to fall with that salutary fear concerning their condition, without which it is impossible to be brought back to life.

Chapter 18

GRACE MAKES US CHILDEN OF GOD BY ADOPTION

W E COME NOW to a property of grace which contains the sum of all its aforementioned glories and reveals them in their nature and importance with very great clarity.

Since grace makes us partakers of the Divine Nature, we are taken into the very family of God. God becomes our Father, His only-begotten Son our brother, and we ourselves children of God.

"Whoever are led by the Spirit of God, they are the sons of God," says St. Paul. (*Rom.* 8:14). And he adds: "Because you are sons, God hath sent the Spirit of his Son into your hearts, crying, 'Abba, Father.'" (*Gal.* 4:6). "The Spirit himself giveth testimony to our spirit that we are sons of God. And if sons, heirs also: heirs indeed of God and joint heirs with Christ." (*Rom.* 8:16-17). And again: "Who hath predestinated us unto the adoption of children through Jesus Christ unto himself: according to the purpose of his will: unto the praise of the glory of his grace, in which he hath graced us in his beloved Son." (*Eph.* 1:5-6).

Indeed, we can say that nothing shows so well the glory of divine grace than the fact that, according to its very nature and activity, it makes us children of God. On the other hand, nothing makes us marvel more at the love of God than the fact that He has received us as His children. "Behold," says the beloved disciple, "what manner of charity the Father hath bestowed upon us, that we should be called, and should be the sons of God. (*1 John* 3:1).

We recall this wonderful, consoling truth to our mind when we say in *The Lord's Prayer,* taught to us by the Son of God Himself, "Our Father, who art in Heaven." By calling

91

God our Father, we show that we are His children. But whether it is that custom has made us indifferent to the meaning of that word, or whether it is that we have never grasped it with genuine, living and illuminating faith, the truth is we remain cold and we do not consider how high above all creatures we should soar to the bosom and heart of the all-powerful God.

Imagine that we are to learn the Lord's Prayer today for the first time, and let us listen to the words of the great St. Peter Chrysologus with which he explains the *Our Father* to those who are being prepared for Baptism.

"What I shall now say with fear and trembling, what you are to hear with dread and awe and to speak with reverence and fear, is a matter of astonishment for the Angels and of wonderment for the powers of Heaven. What then can be expected of the weak spirit of man? Having seen it once in a mysterious way, Paul expressed it, without, however, taking away the veil. 'That eye hath not seen, nor ear heard, neither hath it entered into the heart of man, what things God hath prepared for them that love him.' (*1 Cor.* 2:9). Our human misery, our earthly make-up, our mortal being, our misery-plagued nature, subject to suffering and corruption, cannot grasp, is not able to appreciate, and fears to believe what today it is forced to acknowledge. Human frailty does not know how to merit such a plenitude of gifts, such exceedingly great promises, such a treasury of gifts. That, I believe, the Prophet Habacuc foresaw when, full of great fear, he said: 'Lord, I have heard thy word and was afraid.' (*Hab.* 3:2. This and the following texts follow the Septuagint version). He was afraid of that which he heard, not because he as prophet heard God, his Lord and Master, speak, but because he, the servant, realized how God had become father to him. 'I have considered thy works and have trembled.' Hear what the Prophet says further. 'I was on my guard and my inner being shuddered at the voice of the prayer of my lips.' After he had realized the greatness of the divine gift, he was on his guard, that he might not, as Adam in Paradise, change from a child of God to an enemy and an outcast. He became an earnest and careful watchman over himself now that he realized, after the loss of so great a good, in how fragile a vessel he kept the heavenly treasure. 'And my inner being shuddered at the voice of the prayer of my lips.' If the sentiments of his heart had prompted his tongue to speak, why did he tremble in view of his wishes, of his desires, of the object of his prayer? Because it had not come from himself, but from the inspiration of the Holy Ghost. Listen to St. Paul saying: 'God hath sent the Spirit of his Son into your hearts, crying *Abba, Father.' [Gal.* 4:6]. When the Prophet heard this voice of the Holy Ghost in his heart, he wondered that he had merited something so great, and his whole interior trembled. Rightly, then, he added: 'And trembling seized my limbs and beneath me my power was shaken.' What is the meaning of the expression *beneath me?* It shows that the same man who is raised so high by grace formerly lay prostrate by reason of his nature, and that the earthly power was not able to support the divine. Mount Sinai fumed and shook when God descended to give the law. What then should our weak flesh do when God descends into it to give His grace to us? He comes as Father because men cannot support God, because the slave cannot bear the Lord. And because He is faithful to the words He has spoken: 'Open thy mouth wide, and I will fill it' *[Ps.* 80:11], so now you, His faithful ones, open your mouth so He Himself may fill it with this cry: 'Our Father, who art in Heaven.' He Himself teaches us to pray; He encourages and commands us to do so. Let us follow, then, the grace that calls us, the love that draws us, the tenderness that invites us. May our soul feel that God is our Father; may our soul recognize Him as such, our tongue proclaim Him, and all that is in us follow after grace and not fear. For He who has changed Himself from Judge to Father wishes to be loved, not feared." This is the language of St. Peter Chrysologus. (*Hom.* 68, 72).

See how much the Saints esteemed the dignity of the children of God and how much they marveled at it. It might almost appear to you that they spoke in exaggerated terms. But if you consider all that our holy Faith teaches on this point, you will see that they have scarcely grasped and taught the whole truth.

By reason of our nature we are not, properly speaking, children of God, but only His servants and bondsmen, and the least of these. We are far below the Angels, who themselves are by nature only servants of God. For we are, as they, only creatures of God and the works of His hands. Therefore, we are entirely subject to Him with all that we are and all that we have, and we are obliged, as subjects, to serve Him as our highest King and Lord and to glorify Him as our ultimate end. If we had remained in this, our natural condition, God would not be, strictly speaking, our Father.

But since, even in this case, He would have given us being, would have showered us with natural benefits, would have watched over us with great care and would have treated us not as a tyrant but as a good and gentle Lord, He would have been a Father to us in a figurative sense, and more a father than the one who begot us.

But we would by no means have had a natural relationship to God, much less that of a child to its father. As much as we are like Him, by reason of our intellectual soul, being even His image, we are nevertheless not thereby related to Him in the strict sense, because we were not begotten by Him, but were created by His Will, and consequently we have not received His own Divine Nature.

Only the Eternal Word—which was not created, but rather created us and all other things—only He is by nature the Son of God in the strict sense. Only this Son is truly one with the Father and receives from Him the same divine nature that He Himself possesses. He alone is truly begotten by the Father—in a most sublime way—since He, as the image of His essence, the imprint of His substance, the pure reflex of His splendor, the expression of the word of His knowledge, proceeds from the Father as light from light, as God from God, being Himself God, and one same God with the Father. For this reason He is called Son of the living God (cf. *Matt.* 16:16) because He is not begotten by the Father through the free condescension of His gracious Will, as in the case with us (cf. *Jas.* 1:18), but from the very bosom of

God (*Ps.* 109:3), that is, out of the proper, innermost, personal life of the Father Himself.

If we had been left in the condition which is ours by nature, what would this Son have in common with these works of God, with these poor creatures that were made through the Son? In the same degree in which the Son stands near the Father and rests in His bosom, so do creatures stand outside of God and far from Him. In the same degree in which He is like to the Father and bears His image, perfect and entire, in Himself, so are creatures unlike Him and have in themselves only a dark and feeble outline of His image. In the same degree in which He is heir of the Father, and as His heir receives His whole kingdom, all the treasures of His omnipotence, wisdom and knowledge, so must the creature be excluded from this inheritance, since the servant cannot claim the same rights as the Son. In the same degree in which He sees the Father face-to-face and is one with Him in the most intimate, inexpressible love, and is united with Him through the Holy Ghost as the bond of the incomprehensible embrace of this love, so must the creature humbly remain at a distance. The creature can and should love his Creator, as the good servant loves his master. But to receive a kiss from the father's mouth and to be able to embrace the father with the liberty of a child, that the servant may neither hope for nor desire. He may not even dare to kiss the father's hand—he who ventures to press forward only for a kiss of his feet.

Now then, if man had remained what he was by nature, would he have dared to risk greeting as his Father the King of Heaven and of earth, the King of immortal life, who dwells in light inaccessible? Would it not be to encroach sacrilegiously on the rights of the only-begotten Son of God, who alone was begotten from eternity in an inexpressible way in the bosom of the Father? Would it not be putting on an even plane with Him a creature who was called out of nothingness by this same Son, a creature that would fall back into nothingness if it were not supported by the power of the Son's Will? Still less would a creature call God his Father, since putting a man alongside the Son would imply that he was to receive the same love and inheritance of the eternal Father and that he was to become one with the Father as the Son is one with Him.

Nevertheless, Christian Soul, you have nothing to fear. What is impossible with me is possible with God. What we cannot claim by right, the infinite liberality of God gives us in grace. Although we are not by nature children of God, we become such through grace, and so true is this that, as adopted children, we are put on a par with the natural Son of God. We become by grace what He is by nature. What He has in Himself, that we obtain through participation in His nature.

A similar thing happens among men when a father takes the son of another man and places him alongside his own son, giving to him the same love, the same dignity, the same rights that he gives to his natural son. Thus, God the Father shows to us poor creatures the same love which He bears to the only-begotten Son of His bosom, though we have done nothing to deserve it. He loves us, as Holy Scripture says, in His only-begotten Son with the same love with which He embraces Him. He associates Him with us as our brother, shares His dignity with us and gives us the right to His inheritance. (*S. Th.* 3, q. 23, art. 1, 2).

But the Son of God Himself is so far from wishing to possess alone His rights with the Father and to rule us as His servants that He Himself took over the great task of purchasing with His Blood the life of the children of God. Therefore, He became man to give to all who received Him the power of becoming sons of God. (*John* 1:12). For this reason He became our brother in His humanity in order to make us His brothers in His divine splendor. He seeks His glory in this, to be not merely the only-begotten, but also "the firstborn amongst many brethren." (*Rom.* 8:29). Therefore, He called His Father also our Father: "I ascend to my Father and to your Father." (*John* 20:17). Therefore He teaches us to pray: "Our Father who art in Heaven." Therefore, He explains to us that He came into the world to give us the same life that He asks the Father for us, that we may be one with Him as He is one with Him. (Cf. *John* 17:21 ff.).

Therefore He wills that we become His coheirs in that glory
which He asked for Himself at the Last Supper, in that
divine glory that He had with the Father from the beginning of the world, when before the morning star He went
forth from His mouth in the splendor of sanctity as His
Word and as the image of His infinite glory and blessedness.

Consider now how inexpressibly great the love and grace
of your Creator is, one so great that He wanted to be to you,
not Lord, but Father, that He adopted you as His child and
as the brother of His only-begotten Son. If a king would take
the least of his subjects, one who was poor and sick and
lived in misery, have him cured and then adopt him as the
coheir of his son and make him his successor in his kingdom, with the command that all should obey him as the
king's son—who would be able to grasp the graciousness of
this prince? But we are by nature much further distant
from God than a subject from his earthly king. Moreover,
the misery from which God has freed us is incomparably
greater than that of such a poor man, and the glory that
God gives us is as much above that of an earthly king as
Heaven is above the earth. Finally, the favor and grace that
God gives to us is so much the greater insofar as He makes
us, who are strangers, to be His children.

He cannot, of course, make us His successors in His kingdom, because He is eternal. Therefore, He allows us to participate in His never-ending dominion, and what is more,
He Himself is our inheritance and our kingdom. "I," He
says, "am thy protector, and thy reward exceeding great."
(*Gen.* 15:1). He gives us Himself, the highest and infinite
Good, that contains in Itself all other goods.

As He alone is worthy of Himself, and the whole world
with all its goods could not make Him happy, so He alone is
worthy of those whom He makes His children. As His only-
begotten Son cannot inherit anything greater from Him
than that He see Him face-to-face and be ever one with
Him, so the Father gives to His adopted children the highest good that He can give—Himself—in order that they may
be able to see and enjoy Him for all eternity in undisturbed
possession of Him.

As God is infinite, as our inheritance is infinite, so likewise the dignity of the children of God is infinite, at least insofar as God is concerned. But it was not enough for His fatherly love to give Himself as a reward and inheritance while we did nothing to deserve this gift. Therefore, He gave His only-begotten Son in order that He might purchase this inheritance for us with His infinitely precious Blood.

In the world, the one who is adopted as a child and heir must perform at least some service and thus be of some value. But we of ourselves cannot do the least thing towards becoming children of God. "What is a man," says Job, "that thou shouldst magnify him? or why dost thou set thy heart [thy fatherly love] upon him?" (*Job* 7:17). If we should exert all the powers of our soul and body and do all possible good for years in God's service, if we should suffer innumerable trials and not cease to work and to suffer till the end of the world, we should still not be worthy to be taken as children of God and to possess God Himself.

And if only that were all—namely, that we are not worthy! But in reality, what have we done? We have only debts and sins to show, and we have committed these only too often, even after having become children of God. These make us unworthy of the eternal inheritance and subject to eternal damnation. So the natural Son of God had to give us Himself and to offer Himself for us in order, through His satisfaction, to make us worthy of God's sonship. Where has one ever seen such love of a father and his natural son that they adopted a stranger as child and brother?

How shall we repay such love from God?

"Turn back to God," says St. Peter Chrysologus, "by whom you are loved so much; give yourself entirely to His honor, who for your sake gave Himself entirely to dishonor, and recognize and love Him as Father, as you recognize and feel from His love that He is your Father." (*Serm.* 70).

Chapter 19

DIVINE GRACE MAKES US SONS OF GOD

WHILE WE represent our relation to God as that of an adopted child, we must take care that its perfection and intimacy be not diminished as a result, for the ordinary idea of adoption does not express the entire greatness of the favor that is done to us.

When an earthly father, out of love, takes someone as his child, he can give to such a one only his name and the rights of his natural son. But through the love that the Heavenly Father gives to us, it is brought about that we are not merely called children of God, but that we are such. "Behold," says St. John, "what manner of charity the Father hath bestowed upon us, that we should be called, and should be the sons of God." (*1 John* 3:1).

Divine grace consists not merely in the fact that God directs His affection to us, but above all in this, that He gives us a supernatural beauty and goodness, so that we consider His favor as the fruit of this and remain worthy of it. Likewise, we must say that God loves us not only as His children, in His Son and through His Son, but that He impresses on us the image of His Son and makes us like Him, that we may be truly His children. "For whom," says the Apostle, "he foreknew, he also predestinated to be made conformable to the image of his Son; that he might be the firstborn amongst many brethren." (*Rom.* 8:29).

God wills that we put on His only-begotten Son, that is, that clothed with His divine holiness, we take to ourselves His features and imitate His divine life. And in order that we may do this, He makes us, through the power of the Holy Ghost in the bath of regeneration, to be His children, like to His Son in all details.

99

What is born of flesh, the Saviour answered to Nicode-
mus, is flesh and cannot be born again in the flesh. (Cf. *John*
3:4-6). But it can and should be born again out of water and
the Holy Ghost, in order that it may become spiritual and
arise to a new spiritual life.

Thus, the Apostle James says: "Every best gift, and every
perfect gift, is from above, coming down from the Father of
lights. . . . For of his own will hath he begotten us by the
word of truth, that we might be some beginning of his creature." (*James* 1:17-18). "Being born again," says St. Peter,
"not of corruptible seed, but incorruptible, by the word of
God who liveth and remaineth for ever." (*1 Ptr.* 1:23). At our
rebirth, this eternal God places in our nature a seed from
which a new, everlasting life springs up. "Whosoever is born
of God, committeth not sin: for his seed abideth in him," says
St. John. (*1 John* 3:9).

This rebirth can be easily explained by what has been
said in our first book on the nature of grace. Every child
that is born receives its nature from its father. Therefore,
the Second Person of the Holy Trinity is called Son and the
First is called Father, because the Latter has shared His
own Divine Nature of being with the Former. When Holy
Scripture says we are born of God, nothing else is meant
than that through God's grace we are made partakers of His
own nature. Conversely, when through grace we receive a
sharing of the Divine Nature and of the divine life, it is then
true in a strict sense that we are born of God.

Now the only-begotten Son has the Divine Nature
entirely in His being; we, on the other hand, have it only in
those perfections that can be communicated to creatures.
Our supernatural birth is exceedingly different from the
divine because, as St. Athanasius says, first we are born and
then only reborn of God; whereas, the only-begotten Son
through His divine birth receives His being and the same
substance as the Father. (*Or. 2 contra Arianos* n. 59).

At any rate, as children of God, we have a far more intimate relation with God than adopted children have to their
father. We are children of God, not only because we have
been accepted and considered as children, but also because

He shares His Divine Nature and life with us and because He fills and enlivens us with His own Spirit. We are His heirs and we have a right to the inheritance. This right is based on our rebirth, as St. Peter teaches: "Blessed be the God and Father of our Lord Jesus Christ, who according to his great mercy hath regenerated us unto a lively hope, by the resurrection of Jesus Christ from the dead, unto an inheritance incorruptible, and undefiled, and that can not fade, reserved in heaven for you." (*1 Ptr.* 1:3-4).

In short, God makes those whom He adopts into new men, forms them according to His own image and that of His Son and seals them with the Holy Ghost as the seal of their dignity and the pledge of their inheritance.

Here again, we must let the Holy Fathers speak in order that their sublime words may impress on us the splendor of our rebirth as children of God and to excite in us feelings of gratitude and astonishment, as well as sublime sentiments, which will correspond to our rebirth. After St. Gregory of Nyssa has described the poverty of man and the infinite perfection of the Divine Nature, he continues: "And yet man, who is accounted as nothing in the universe, who is but ashes and straw and vanity, is united to and received as a child of this sublime and glorious Being, so sublime, that It cannot be seen, nor heard, nor investigated by reason. What word of thanks is in place here in sight of such a benefit? What word, what expression, what thought is excellent enough to sing the praise of such an incomparable favor? Man climbs above his own nature, changing from a mortal to an immortal being, from a weak and perishable to a perfect and everlasting, from a temporary to an eternal being, in short, from a man to God. For since he was made worthy to become a child of God, he will certainly have the dignity of his God and be the heir of all the paternal possessions." (*Or. 7 de Beat.*).

"Great," says St. Leo, "great is the mystery of this grace, and this gift surpasses all graces, that God names man His *son* and all call God *Father*. Through these names let us learn what sentiments correspond to such a sublime state. For if children through vices and bad behavior cast a shadow on the human lineage of illustrious ancestors and the unworthy posterity is shamed by the splendor of its ancestry, to what end will they come who do not fear, out of love for the world, to lose their share in the generation of Christ? If among men it is a matter of praise that the splendor of ancestry should be reflected in posterity, how much more glorious will it not be if those who are born of God let the image of their Father shine in them and allow Him who begot them to be recognized in them, as the Lord has said: 'Let your light shine before men, that they may see your good works and glorify your Father who is in heaven.' [*Matt.* 5:16]." (*Serm.* 26, *De Nativ. Dom.* 6, c.4). Let that chosen and kingly generation correspond to the dignity of its rebirth, and love what the Father loves, so that the Lord will not have to cry out again as He once did, complaining through the prophet, "I have brought up children, and exalted them: but they have despised me. The ox knoweth his owner, and the ass his master's crib: but Israel hath not known me, and my people hath not understood." (*Is.* 1:2-3).

"When we pray 'Our Father, who art in Heaven,'" says St. Peter Chrysologus, "we do not wish to say that God is not on earth, but that we, as His children, belong with Him in heaven" (*Hom. in Orat. Dom.* 67, 71, 72), that is, that we are a heavenly race, whose Father reigns in Heaven, and that a heavenly seed has been placed in us which will spring us into heavenly life. To what heights, O man, has grace suddenly raised you? To what heights has the heavenly nature borne you up, that you, still in the flesh and tarrying on the earth, forget already the flesh and the earth and say: 'Our Father, who art in Heaven'? He who recognizes and believes himself to be son of so great a Father should show his worthiness in his life. He should make manifest his Father through his manners and preserve by his sentiments and behavior what he has received through the Divine Nature.

"Since we are of divine race, the name of God becomes ours. The name of God and of His Son is also our name, insofar as we are called children of God and brothers of Christ. And when we say 'hallowed be Thy name,' we ask that the name of God, which in itself and by itself is holy, should also be hallowed and glorified in us, His children, by our deeds. For when we behave well, the name of our Father is praised, but when we do evil, the name of God is blasphemed and the word of the Apostle is fulfilled, 'The name of God through you is blasphemed among the Gentiles.' [*Rom.* 2:24]. Let us take care, therefore, that a heavenly life and godly manners be in us and that the image of the Divinity may be expressed in our whole behavior, because the heavenly Father rewards His worthy children with divine gifts; the degenerate, however, He casts down into a miserable slavery."

The Son of God Himself reminds us of our sublime dignity and of our destination when he says: "Be you therefore perfect, as also your heavenly Father is perfect." (*Matt.* 5:48). Because we are children of God, we must not content ourselves with ordinary, human perfection, but conscious of our high dignity, we must seek to imitate the great God Himself.

There is some truth in the words of one of the ancient pagans (Varro, cited by St. Augustine, *De Civ. Dei*, 1, 3 c. 4), affirming that it is useful to the state if strong men believe, even though falsely, that they are descended from the gods, so that the human spirit, trusting in its divine origin, may undertake great deeds with much boldness and carry them through more energetically. In fact Alexander, moved by the impious flattery of venal friends, who ascribed to him a divine origin, felt himself urged on not a little to undertake the deeds through which he astonished the world.

How then should we, who not only in appearance but in reality have become through the grace of God a divine and heavenly race, how should we direct our efforts to the highest good! We should seek to become like God Himself and to do and suffer great things for Him!

One of the most enlightened spiritual directors, Baltasar Alvarez, used to say to his novices, "Do not relinquish the high and sublime sentiments of children of God!" These words burned into their hearts and made them heroes. Some of them, having gone to Brazil to preach the gospel to the Indians, were attacked by pagans. When about to die for the Faith amidst the most frightful torture, one of them shouted to his confreres the words of their instructor: "Do not relinquish the high and sublime sentiments of children of God!" All then went joyfully to their death. May this beautiful sentence be our watchword also! Let us say it to one another; let us say it to ourselves when we are in danger of dishonoring our high dignity or when there is question of showing ourselves worthy of our great Father by some heroic act of virtue. It belongs especially to this sublime sentiment of God's children that we raise ourselves above earthly things and despise the world.

If we are truly children of God, then God is with us. "If God be for us, who is against us? . . . Who then shall separate us from the love of Christ? Shall tribulation? or distress? or famine? or nakedness? or danger? or persecution? or the sword? . . . But in all these things we overcome, because of him that hath loved us." (*Rom.* 8:31, 35, 37). Hence our confidence. For we are certain "that neither death, nor life, nor angels, nor principalities, nor powers . . . nor any other creature, shall be able to separate us from the love of God, which is in Christ Jesus our Lord." (*Rom.* 8:38-39).

Accordingly, we should despise the world because it cannot hurt us, and we should despise it because it cannot help us. Moreover, we should despise it also because the whole world, with all its treasures and good, is not worthy of the children of God. "He will never admire the doings of men too much," says St. Cyprian, "who recognizes himself as a son of God. He who admires anything else besides God casts himself down from the summit of his dignity." (*De Spectac.* c. 9).

Far be it from the children of God, whose inheritance is God Himself, to find satisfaction in earthly riches, in pleasures of sense, or in human honors. They must rather consider all these as nothing, as a burden, and direct all their desires and wishes irretrievably toward heavenly goods. To them we must apply the words of the Apostle: "If you be risen with Christ, seek the things that are above, where Christ is sitting at the right hand of God. Mind the things that are above, not the things that are upon the earth." (*Col.* 3:1-2). Where Christ is, there His brothers belong, there is their fatherland! Everywhere we are citizens, and everywhere we are strangers. Every home is strange to us, every strange place a home. (cf. *Epist. ad Diog.* 5).

In the world we should consider ourselves as strangers that are making a pilgrimage toward their heavenly fatherland. Hence, our life should already be in Heaven, according to the exhortation of St. Paul. (Cf. *Phil.* 3:20). Far be it from us to attach our heart to the world and to seek our happiness in it! We should rather sigh and weep that we are still so far from the face of our heavenly Father and that we have not yet been perfectly reborn. But here also we must not be pusillanimous. For the same Holy Ghost, through whom we are now reborn from the servitude of sin, will one day give to us rebirth from the slavery of the flesh, suffering and death.

Now we already have the Spirit of our Father as the pledge of our inheritance and of our future glory, that Spirit through whom we remain in God and God remains in us. The Spirit who binds God the Father with the Son and the Son with the Father in the unity of inexpressible love, the same Spirit has been sent into our heart through Sanctifying Grace. He comes to teach us to stammer the name of the Father, to impart to us a childlike trust of Him, and to give testimony of His love, to console us in our needs and sufferings and to bind us now already with our heavenly Father in most intimate love.

It is the same Spirit who draws back to God through an unintelligible restlessness and dissatisfaction when we begin to estrange ourselves from Him through love of the world and its distractions. It is the same Spirit who always rouses us up when we have been unfaithful to our good resolutions, the same Spirit who rewards us with great consolation for the least efforts we make in the service of God, to give us a foretaste of the peace and happiness with which He will one day reward us.

From this activity of the Spirit of God, we can and should realize that He dwells in our heart and also that we are children of God. For the Apostle says: "Whosoever are led by the Spirit of God, they are the sons of God." (*Rom.* 8:14). And likewise St. John: "And in this we know that he abideth in us, by the Spirit which he hath given us." (*1 John* 3:24).

Rightly does the great Pope Saint Leo exhort us to hold this gift in honor and to be thankful to the good God. "Let us, dearly beloved," he says, "thank God the Father through His Son in the Holy Ghost, who, because of the great love with which He loved us, had mercy on us, and when we were dead in sin, He enlivened us in and with Christ [*Eph.* 2:4-5], in order that we may be a new creature and a new creation. Let us put away the old man with his doings, and having been made partakers of the birth of Christ, let us reject the works of the flesh. Recognize, O Christian, thy dignity, and having been made partaker of the divine nature, beware lest you return to your former baseness through unbecoming behavior. Think of what Head and Body you are a member. Remember how you were torn away from the powers of darkness and taken into the light and Kingdom of God. Through the Sacrament of Baptism you have become a temple of the Holy Ghost. Beware lest you drive away so great a God by evil deeds and subject yourself again to the slavery of the devil. For you have been bought by the Blood of Christ, and He who redeemed you out of mercy will judge you in justice." (*Sermo 21, De Nativ. Dom.* 1, c. 3).

Chapter 20

THE WONDERFUL NOURISHMENT
OF THE CHILDREN OF GOD

"GOD," says St. Peter Chrysologus, "who has given Himself to us as Father and has taken us as His children, who has made us heirs of His possessions, who has distinguished us with His name and honored us with His glory and with His kingdom, desires also that we seek our daily bread from Him. But what Bread this is! The heavenly Father can only demand that His children ask for heavenly Bread, and this is the Son of God Himself, who said: 'I am the living bread which came down from heaven.' [*John* 6:41]. He Himself is that bread, which, sown in the Virgin, leavened in the flesh, prepared in suffering, baked in the oven of the grave, seasoned in the Church, laid on the altar, is daily offered to the Faithful as a heavenly food." (*Hom.* 67).

Indeed, the first obligation of fathers is to nourish their children, and our heavenly Father does not neglect this duty. But what a difference between the nourishment which earthly fathers give and that which God gives! The former can offer only what the earth produces; the latter gives us Him whom Heaven and earth has brought forth.

Here again we catch a glimpse of the greatness of divine love. What thought of mortals, what sagacity of immortals, O Lord, can realize Thy generous love towards Thy children! Didst Thou have nothing else with which Thine omnipotence could nourish them besides the most holy Body and precious Blood of Thy Son? O more than fatherly heart of my God! O Love that was never felt or imagined, even by a mother! O happy we, who as the Prophet says, have been made "an everlasting glory" since we are "nursed with the breasts of kings." (*Is.* 60:15-16).

107

Nature, of course, could not give this nourishment. But if God is greater than men, and if His children belong to Him more perfectly than the children of men belong to them, it seems only right that something greater should be prepared for us that would correspond to the majesty of the Father and the dignity of His children. Hence, God wished to place no limits on His love, He wished to pour out on us all the treasures of His omnipotence, and that which He found there most precious, namely, Himself, He wished to give to His children as food. "For what is the good thing of him, and what is his beautiful thing, but the corn of the elect, and wine springing forth virgins?" (*Zach*. 9:17).

Who can compare with this the love of a mother? Many mothers give their children to other women that they may be nursed by them. And even the best and most loving mothers, who nourish their own children, give to them only their milk, which is the superfluous part of their blood and flows spontaneously from their breast. But Christ gives to us all the Blood of His Body and of His heart, which was forced from Him, as it were, with a press through the power of His infinite love and in the midst of inexpressible suffering. He nourishes us with His whole Body, so that, according to the words of the Psalmist, the mouths of the infants and sucklings praise His love. (*Ps*. 8:3).

The extravagant wantonness of ancient times discovered the art of dissolving a precious pearl in the drink at a banquet and thus a whole fortune was consumed at one swallow. But if the expense of such a banquet was even equal to the value of all the goods of the world, what would it be in comparison with the meal that God has prepared for His children? For here God gives, as St. Thomas says, Himself and all created goods: "All that He is and has, He gives in the fullest measure. For there is nothing outside of the material, spiritual and divine natures. The material nature includes all that can be perceived by the five senses; the spiritual comprises the Angels, the souls of men, and all spiritual gifts and virtues; the Divine Nature has of itself all that is best. Accordingly, since God the Father gives us the Body and Blood of His Son, He gives us the most precious of corporeal substances. In giving us the soul of the same Son, the grace of which was more perfect than that of all angels and holy souls, He gives us the most sublime of spiritual substances. Besides this, He gives us the complete Divine Nature." (*Opusc.* 63. *De Beat.*, c. 2, 3). But since this nourishment is so worthy of esteem, we may rightly conclude how precious is the life of grace that is fostered by it, and how great the dignity that we attain by it.

When the divine Blood of God is taken into our body, let us remember that it flows also in our soul, by reason of the soul's rebirth through grace, giving us a certain godly dignity. When our body is united with the substance of the Body of Christ, it is for us a pledge that through grace we have been made partakers of the Divine Nature.

If we would but recognize and often consider these truths with lively faith, how high we should esteem the life of grace that is worthy of such nourishment. And with what longing, what love and fervor should we approach this heavenly meal, that makes us sharers of the Divine Nature and fills us with divine life. Our wonderment and love for this nourishment of God's children and likewise for grace, for the sake of which this food is given to us, must become even greater when we consider how it was prepared for us and how it is given to us.

God chose material bread and wine in order to prepare for us, by a wonderful change, heavenly bread and heavenly drink. The substance of bread is changed entirely into the Body of the Son of God, and the substance of wine into His Blood. That is a sign that our nature also, when it partakes of this food and drink, is changed in a wonderful and mysterious way. As the ordinary bread becomes heavenly bread, so should grace, which flows to us from the Sacrament, change our earthly nature and, without destroying its essence, make it heavenly and a sharer in the Divine Nature. In a similar way as we, after the Consecration, no longer recognize bread but honor the Body of the Son of God, we should likewise, having received grace, no longer recognize ourselves as merely natural men, but as children of God, and we should be correspondingly holy.

It is true that we cannot see this wonderful change with our eyes nor witness it with our other senses. But the change of the bread also remains hidden from our senses, since the external appearance is not altered. So also, our transformation through grace is hidden from our eyes because it takes place in the depth of our soul. Outwardly, the children of God are like other men. They are subject to the same sufferings and defects. With them all the outer man is decaying, according to the words of St. Paul (*2 Cor.* 4:16), yet the inner man is being renewed day by day and changed through the Spirit of God, until finally death will be swallowed up by life and a divine splendor and happiness will clothe—yes, fill—the whole man.

Let us then not err, either through incredulity or pusillanimity, but let us recognize with staunch faith the wonder that God works in our soul through grace. His omnipotence works on our soul through the mouth of the priest, just as well at Baptism and in Confession as it does on the bread at Holy Mass. It will support us in changing our sinful and carnal life into a holy and spiritual life. It will also break the strongest bonds that fasten us to the earth and to ourselves, in order that we who are of flesh live not according to the flesh. Although the body still burdens our soul, God's omnipotence can lift us up to Heaven in prayer and love.

The changing of bread and wine into the substance of the Body and Blood of Jesus Christ is not the only wonder that God works to prepare this heavenly food for His children. This one wonder is attended by a countless number of others, in which God suspends the laws of nature and breaks through their limits to prove to His children the greatness of His love and fatherly care.

What is more wonderful than that the appearances of bread and wine are retained without the substance, that one and the same Body is present at the same time on thousands of altars and tabernacles, that Christ remains really and substantially present, whole and undivided, under every smallest particle? Must we not conclude that the grace of sonship, for the sake of which God works so great a wonder, must also be one of the greatest marvels of His omnipotence?

But if God, for the sake of grace, suspends the laws of nature, which He Himself has established, must we not be ashamed that we do so little to overthrow the dominating laws of sin in our members and in our flesh, and that we are so remiss in bringing under control with a strong hand the evil inclinations that draw us away from God? Do we dare do less to gain, strengthen and retain the life of grace than God undertakes for us? Oh, our ungrateful and miserable indolence! God transgresses the boundaries of His ordinary providence to give us this precious means of grace, and we do not wish to deviate an inch from the path of our indolent, comfort-seeking nature! Yes, we even throw ourselves in the arms of our enemy, who wishes to make mockery of the inventive love of God!

I solemnly appeal to you, Children of God, through the Body and Blood of Christ with which you have been nourished, that your sentiments and dealings with so holy a food be not unworthy, that you do not so wantonly sell your life that has been sustained with such a wonderful and precious nourishment. Rather, let all true children of God hear the warning of St. Peter (Cf. *1 Peter* 2:2): Crave, as newborn babes, pure spiritual milk; as children in the unspotted purity of life, in holy simplicity of manner, in neglect of earthly things; as children far from the prudence of the world, from false cunning, from anger and concupiscence; as industrious children, docile, and desirous of learning; as children who grow continually until they reach perfect manhood, when, weaned from the milk of the mother, they are fed at the table of the father.

There is this distinction, as St. Augustine notes (*Conf.* 7, 10, 16), between Christ as our food and earthly food. This latter is changed into the substance of the one who consumes it; Christ, on the other hand, is a food that changes those consuming it into His substance, insofar as He makes us sharers in His own nature. He wishes, as heavenly food, to unite us to Him and Himself to us still more closely, in order that we may, according to His own promise, live by Him and in Him, as He lives by the Father.

Thus, the natural Son of God is the Food of eternal life for the adopted children of God, a food for the little ones here on earth and a food for the great ones in Heaven above. For the little ones, He is food with His Flesh, which He took from the womb of His Mother; for the great ones, He is food with His divinity, that He possesses in the bosom of the Father. There above He shares with His grown-up brothers the same nourishment, the same bread, which He receives from His heavenly Father and feeds them, as He Himself promised, at the table which His Father prepared for Him. (*Luke* 22:30). His food, however, is the Divinity Itself, the infinite Being of the Father. By reason of this food, the Son is like the Father, through the immediate, beatifying vision of whom He enjoys with the Father the most perfect happiness. As brothers of the only-begotten Son of God, we also shall be admitted to the enjoyment of the divine splendor, and in this enjoyment it will be truly a food for us, because the hunger and thirst of the children of God cannot be satisfied by anything less than God Himself.

St. Francis de Sales explains this sublime mystery very clearly in the following words: "When we look at an object, it does not unite itself with our eyes but is seen by us only through an image that is reflected in our eye. And when we know a thing with our intellect, the object is not joined immediately to this faculty, but only through a spiritual image or picture, which is called the intellectual form. But in Heaven—what a grace—the very Divinity is united with our intellect, without any intermediate picture or image. The Divinity Itself is united to our intellect and enters into it, becoming so present that it makes any image superfluous.

"What sweetness for the human intellect, to be thus always united with the most sublime object, so that it possesses, not an image, but the real presence, not a reflection or a representation, but the actual majesty of the Divinity!

"O infinite happiness, of which we have not only the promise but also the pledge in the Holy Eucharist, the perpetual banquet of divine grace! For here we receive the Blood of the Saviour in His Flesh and His Flesh in His Blood. Here His Blood is placed in our mouth through His Flesh, His Divinity through His humanity, that we may know that He will also give to us His divine Being at the banquet of His glory. In the Holy Eucharist we receive the substance of God, hidden, however, under the sacramental appearances; in Heaven the Divinity will be given to us unveiled, and then we shall see God face-to-face as He is." (*Treatise on the Love of God,* Book 3, Chap. 11).

According to this excellent explanation of St. Francis de Sales, the Divine Essence is as intimately united to our soul through grace, as corporeal food and the Body of Christ is united with our body in the holy Sacrament of the altar.

The Divine Being is spiritual food to us, but precisely because it is spiritual, it is the truest and most perfect food, furnishing more to our soul for life everlasting than the material bread does to the life of our body. It is in the fullest sense the "supersubstantial bread" for which our Saviour taught us to pray. It is a food that possesses in itself the marrow of divine life, and at the same time a drink that fills us with the fullness of divine happiness. It is a food, for it really makes us strong and big; it is a drink, for it floods us with the stream of divine bliss.

O wonderful, heavenly, godly Bread, that God has promised to and destined for the children of His grace! Even the highest Angels are not, according to their nature, worthy of such food; how much less we earthly and sinful men! How great must the dignity be, O God, which Thou hast given us through the grace of sonship, since it brings such Bread to us! Give us therefore also this grace, that we, conscious of this high, divine dignity, desire no other bread and seek only the one Bread that Thou art and that nourishes our soul in Thy bosom forever. "Grant unto us," thus we pray with St. Bonaventure, "that we continually hunger for Thee, the bread of angels, the refreshment of holy souls, our daily supernatural bread, in which is all sweetness, all loveliness and delight. Let my soul ever hunger after Thee on Whom the Angels desire to look. Let my soul enjoy It and be filled with the sweetness of this heavenly Food. May it thirst for Thee unceasingly, fountain of eternal life, source of never-failing light, stream of joy and overflowing of the house of God."

Chapter 21

GRACE ESTABLISHES A TRUE FRIENDSHIP BETWEEN GOD AND MAN

THE SONSHIP of God possesses another special advantage in this, that grace makes us true friends of God.

Among men, children do not always have the friendship of their father. They can cause him sorrow, and he on his part can be in bad spirit or conceited. In short, they can lose their love without thereby ceasing to be children. The grace of God, on the other hand, makes us children of God in such a way that, as long as we remain children [i.e., in the state of grace], we remain at the same time His friends.

Among men, moreover, adoption does not bring with it the perfect intimacy of mutual love. There remains a certain reverential fear of the adoptive father that hinders free and trustful relations with him. Grace, on the other hand, brings us so near to God that we can appear before His face, not only with the reverence of a child, but also with the freedom and trustfulness of a friend.

Insofar as grace implies divine sonship, it raises us high above the state of servitude. It removes the condition of estrangement, the relation of slavery and the immeasurable inequality that exists between God and us by nature, and places us in a condition of freedom as members of God's family, and thus gives us a certain equality with God. But grace does this yet more perfectly, insofar as it effects friendship with God, friendship in the strict sense of the word.

The word "friendship" designates a trustfulness and union of heart so intimate that theology finds it necessary to investigate thoroughly whether or not this term may be used to designate the relation between God and man. But there is no doubt that it may. (*S. Th.* 2, 2, q. 23, a. 1). That this word is the correct one we see in the expression "friend of God" that is given so often to Abraham ["Abraham thy friend forever"]. (*2 Par.* 20:7; *Is.* 41:8). And our divine Saviour Himself shows us this, saying, "I will not now call you servants . . . but I have called you friends." (*John* 15:15).

"What is greater," comments St. Cyril of Alexandria (*In Joan.* 1, 10, c. 2), "what is more glorious than to be and to be named a friend of Christ? This dignity surpasses the limits of human nature. For all things serve the Creator, as the Psalmist says, and there is nothing that is not subject to the yoke of His servitude. Unmindful of this, the Lord raises His servants who keep His commandments to a supernatural height and glory, calling them, not servants but friends, and treating them in all things as friends."

O most sweet and lovable God, Lord of so many useless servants! Thou didst think it too little that we should dwell in Thy house as workmen and servants; whereas, it would have been honor enough for us if we could but serve an Angel.

Marvel, O Christian soul, at God's condescension toward you! He has given you dominion over all irrational creatures, the earth and all that is in it. He could have placed as a condition for this that you serve some creature of a higher order, a seraph, for example. But no! God has not demanded this service of you. The great privilege of your position is to recognize nothing created above you. For God alone wishes to be your Lord. And even He does not wish to consider you as a servant, but rather to have you as His friend. For He has sent His own Spirit, to whom the Apostle says: "Where the Spirit of the Lord is, there is liberty." (*2 Cor.* 3:17).

Truly, it is a holy, ineffable freedom to be not servants but friends of the Lord. It is a holy freedom to see the great God Himself coming to us with the tenderness of a friend, just as though we were His equals. It is a holy freedom that we may approach Him with the ease and familiarity of a friend. St. Gregory the Great, full of wonderment, could well cry out: "O how great is the mercy of our Creator! We are not worthy to be His servants, and now we are called His friends!" (*Hom. In Evang.* 1. 2, hom. 26, n. 4).

One considers it a great honor to be able to serve a noble king of this world. But to serve God, the King of kings, is incomparably more honorable than even to be an earthly king or to govern extensive empires. How highly then, must we not treasure the friendship of God, which unites us intimately with Him in love and trustfulness? And how highly must we prize grace, which alone is capable of fitting us for this friendship!

But grace gives us, not only the freedom necessary for true friendship with God, but also the other condition of friendship, equality. True friendship finds equals or makes equals, according to an old proverb. (St. Jerome, *In. Mich.*, 1. 2, 7, 5-7). A friend is in a certain sense the other self of his friend. Everyone honors and loves his friend as himself and wants to be honored the same way.

By reason of our nature, God loves us as His creatures and servants. But the distance between Him and us is infinite and is therefore too great to allow us to be called His true friends. Consequently, it is understandable that the pagan philosophers said that a true friendship between God and man is impossible. (Arist., *Magna Moralia* 2, 11, 6).

Only grace raises man to such a high degree of similarity—even to a certain equality with God—that the distance between God and man is spanned, and friendship between them no longer appears unbecoming. This splendor of grace was before the eye of the royal Psalmist when he sang: "To me thy friends, O God, are made exceedingly honourable: their principality is exceedingly strengthened." (*Ps.* 138:17).

Grace actually raises us to a kingly dignity, which is honorable in the sight of all Heaven. And thus we are made equal in a sense with God and worthy of His most intimate trust. Yes, grace makes our nature so much like God that henceforth He sees Himself in us and can embrace us with the same love with which He loves Himself.

We would hardly believe that God could or would wish to unite Himself to us in so close a friendship if He had not shown by another wonderful deed how earnest He is with regard to our friendship and how perfect He proposes to make it. To show us that He wishes to make us as much as possible like Himself in His glory, He first became like unto us. He became man and, as one of us, lived several years in our midst and called Himself with special preference, "Son of man." He even invited all sufferings and miseries of our nature in order to share them with us as our brother and friend and thus really to feel with us. If He thus came down so low in His friendship for man, can we doubt that He made Himself like us except for the purpose of making us like Himself? Can we doubt that He will take us as His friends, as His equals, into His house, and share with us all His glory and happiness?

How foolishly and ungratefully we should act if we should belittle the friendship of so great a Lord or reject it disdainfully! The world would consider one a fool who would despise the friendship proffered him by a powerful king. So many men go to the greatest trouble to receive merely a gracious smile or a friendly word from a prince. And yet the favor of kings is so unstable that it can be lost through some slight accident. God, on the other hand, offers us His friendship freely, so that we need only accept it in order to possess it for all eternity.

In his *Confessions* (*Conf.* 8, 6, 15), St. Augustine tells a story that was related to him by an eyewitness, a story that helped to bring about his conversion. Two friends, who served in the court of the Emperor at Trier and courted his friendship, retired one day to an outlying garden house. There on the table they found a copy of the life of St. Anthony. One of them read it, was touched by its contents and said to the other: "Tell me, I pray thee, just what do we wish to attain with all these efforts? What are we seeking? Why do we serve in the army? Can we have any greater goal in the palace than to become friends of the Emperor? And then what is there that is not perishable and full of danger? And through how many dangers must we ascend to a greater danger? And when shall we attain it? But if I wish to be a friend of God, behold, I can do so in a moment." These words, spoken out of the depth of his soul, made a great impression on the other, and both immediately resolved to leave the court and seek in quiet retirement the friendship of the highest Lord, which lasts forever.

Let us imitate these wise men. And if we do not leave the world entirely, as they did, let us trouble ourselves at least to prize the friendship of God more highly than the friendship of the world. Let us strive, according to the fundamental law of friendship, to unite ourselves with God, as He unites Himself with us, to become like Him, as He has made Himself like us and wishes to make us like Himself. He has united Himself to us so intimately only that we may be, as true friends, of one mind, one will, one heart, and one spirit with Him.

"To will the same things and to reject the same things, that is true friendship," according to an ancient philosopher. (Sallust. *Catil.* 20). Let our aim be to will only what God wills and to love only what He loves. For we can repay His love in no other way since we cannot raise Him up and enrich Him, as He has exalted and enriched His friends.

Friendship is one of the greatest needs and one of the most exalted blessings of the human heart; to love and to be loved is man's desire and happiness. The heart of man is so lonely that it must seek another heart outside of itself, to which it may attach itself and in which it may confide. It cannot rest until it has found another heart that will share its sentiments and have compassion on its sufferings. It becomes then one with such a heart, so that they both seem to beat with one pulsation. Therefore we esteem ourselves fortunate when we have found such a heart. Holy Scripture itself says: "Blessed is he that findeth a true friend." (*Ecclus.* 25:12).

And yet we never find perfect contentment here. The heart of our fellow man, no matter now noble and lovable, is always weak and imperfect, and it likewise seeks its consolation and happiness in our own heart. Though the two give mutual support to one another, yet they are too narrow to be sufficient to themselves and therefore too weak to weather all storms.

What a happiness for us if we should find a heart that, itself infinitely noble and lovable, could penetrate our own and make it one with itself, a heart that could give us along with itself all that we desire!

Such a heart you find, Christian soul, in your Lord and God, when you are united to Him by grace. His divine heart comes so near to yours that it penetrates it and the two are melted into one, which then only one soul, one spirit vivifies. And this heart is at the same time the highest good, containing in itself every good, every beauty, everything amiable. All the love, all the sweetness that is in all the hearts in Heaven and on earth is found united in this heart—and infinitely more.

Of this heart alone is that entirely true which Holy Scripture says of true friends: "A faithful friend is a strong defence: and he that hath found him, hath found a treasure. Nothing can be compared to a faithful friend and no weight of gold and silver is able to countervail the goodness of his fidelity. A faithful friend is the medicine of life and immortality." (*Ecclus.* 6:14-16).

God is a friend who is present to you, not merely from time to time, but who remains with you always, if you do not drive Him from you [by committing mortal sin]. God is a friend, not merely that you can press to your heart at times, but whom you have dwelling in your heart continually. God is a friend to whom you do not have to express your sentiments by words; He understands and feels every beat of your heart. You can reveal yourself entirely to Him, even more so than to yourself. He understands and fathoms all your needs, your wishes and your feelings, better than you yourself. He is a friend who has no faults, but He does have all perfection; a friend whose nearness to you is so much the more lovable and delightful the longer you enjoy His friendship. His conversation hath no bitterness, nor His company any tediousness. (Cf. *Wis.* 8:16). And do you prize so little this one Friend and His friendship, to which grace introduces you, that you seek refuge in strangers rather than in Him? Will you not attach yourself and give your heart to this great and only Friend, as He has given His to you? How cruel you are to yourself, not to mention ungrateful toward Him!

Take to heart the words of the blessed Thomas à Kempis: "What can the world give thee without Jesus? To be without Jesus is a grievous hell; to be with Jesus a sweet paradise. If Jesus be with thee, no foe can harm thee. Whoever findeth Jesus findeth a good treasure—yea, a good above every good. And he that loseth Jesus loseth much—yea, more than the whole world. He that liveth without Jesus is in wretched poverty; and he who is with Jesus is most rich. It is a great art to know how to converse with Jesus, and to know how to keep Jesus is great wisdom. Be humble and peaceable, and Jesus will abide with thee. Thou mayest soon drive away Jesus and lose His grace, if thou wilt turn aside after outward things. And if thou drive Him from thee and lose Him, to whom wilt thou fly? And whom, then, wilt thou seek for thy friend? Without a friend, thou canst not live happily; and if Jesus be not a friend to thee above all, thou wilt indeed be sad and desolate." (*Imit. of Christ,* Book 2, Chap. 8, 2-3).

It is a great misfortune when one rejects the friendship of God. Then God is changed from a tender friend to a bitter enemy. The greater His love was for you, the greater will be His hatred. "For mercy and wrath are with him. He is mighty to forgive, and to pour out indignation." (*Ecclus.* 16:12).

But what does that mean, to have God as an enemy? No one can fathom the awfulness of this word. The greater the power of God and the sweetness of divine friendship (surpassing that of all men)—the more terrible also is His animosity—more terrible than that which all men together could have toward us.

Imagine a man whom everyone hates and persecutes, whom no one wishes either to see or to hear, who, as an outcast of all mankind, is rejected from their midst, who wanders about as one despised or as the fratricide Cain. Do you think such a one could eat and sleep in peace, or that he could live at all in view of the anxiety and torture of his state? Do you not think that in his despair he would prefer sudden death to such a deathlike life?

But how much more unfortunate is the one who has made

God his enemy and always sees the sword of so powerful a Knight suspended above his head! The former can still hope to withdraw himself through death from his miserable lot, but the latter through death really falls into the hands of his terrible enemy, never more to escape. How can a sinner, being an enemy of God, be light-hearted and joyful? How can he have any delight that is not made bitter through the terrible thought of his fearful enemy?

On the other hand, imagine a man whom all love and honor, whom all greet with a friendly smile, whom all bear in their hearts and shower with presents and favors, to whom they joyfully show all imaginable services, because they think that he is the intimate friend of the prince and that his affection for them is a pledge of the king's favor— truly we would praise such a one and envy him his happy lot.

But what would be the good fortune of this man in comparison with the one who has God as his friend: God, whose infinite love surpasses that of all men and angels; God, who enriches His friends with all the treasures of His omnipotence; God, who bestows grace on everyone and does good to all!

If it were simply a question of choosing the friendship of an earthly prince, and with it the friendship of all men, certainly no one would hesitate long. How then can we hesitate to make every effort to gain the friendship of God, which assures us at the same time of the friendship of all good men? Why do we not rather give up all else than lose such a friendship? The more disinterested the friendship of God is, so much the more is it pure and noble and therefore the more genuine and precious.

Human friendship is seldom or never entirely disinterested. If one does not love his friend simply for the sake of utility, still one does not exclude the possibility that he can be of benefit. At least one expects compassion and consolation from his friend and needs to be loved by him in return.

But God does not need our friendship in any way. He can expect no utility, no increase of His happiness therefrom, since He is of Himself infinitely happy. We receive from Him all that He has (*1 Cor.* 3:22), for He deals with the soul according to the principle that among friends all things should be possessed in common. But He does not desire our possessions for Himself, since He has no need of them. (*Ps.* 15:2). Even the reciprocal love that He desires from us is not for Him a need and cannot make Him happier than He is. As with everything else through which God makes us His friends and enriches us, our very love for God serves only to make us happy and content. God has only the glory and the joy of having made us His friends and thus of having made us happy.

But, you will say, did not God make all things for His own sake, and does He not then love His friends also for His own sake? Indeed, He does love you for His own sake, for only in this way can He love you truly and perfectly. Do you wish that He love you only for *your own* sake? Then His love for you could not be infinite, because you are not an infinite good and consequently you cannot be the object of infinite love. But He loves you because of His own goodness, which is wonderfully reflected in you through grace, and therefore He loves you, too, in Himself. He loves you because of His Divine Nature, which He has also shared with you through grace, and for that reason His love for you is infinite.

This is what is so admirable in God's love for us, namely, that the reason and the measure of His love is not our nothingness, but His own splendor. The fact that God loves you, not for your sake, but for His own, makes this love so much the more noble and genuine. Therefore, you should rejoice and be thankful.

Confide then with your whole soul in this so disinterested divine friend. You need not fear that He will withdraw Himself out of selfish motives. He is your friend only to enrich you and to make you happy. Be also unselfish toward Him. Love Him as He has loved you; love yourself only in Him. Give yourself to Him entirely, as He has given Himself to you; and as He has given you His grace and favor, give to Him the tribute of His honor and glory. Thus the holy bonds of friendship between Him and you will be drawn ever closer. Thus you will become worthy to bear them for all eternity for your honor and happiness and to be united inseparably with your Divine Friend in Heaven through glory, as on this earth through love.

Chapter 22

THE INEFFABLE LOVE GOD BEARS TOWARD US WHEN WE ARE IN THE STATE OF GRACE

THE MYSTERY of love that God bears toward us when through grace we have become His children and friends is so delightful and unfathomable that we must give more attention to it.

"What is a man that thou shouldst magnify him? or why dost thou set thy heart upon him?" (*Job* 7:17). We cannot repeat these words of wonderment often enough in our present consideration. "What is man? asks St. Bernard. "Without doubt he is vanity and nothingness. And yet he is something. How can he be nothing whom God has honored so much? Let us take courage, dear brethren! Even though in ourselves we are nothing, in the heart of God there may be something of us hidden. O Father of mercy! O God of the poor! Why dost Thou set Thy heart upon us? Since Thou Thyself hast said: 'Where thy treasure is, there is thy heart also.' (*Matt.* 6:21), must not then we be Thy treasure, since Thy heart is in us? How then can we be nothing at all if we are Thy treasures?" (St. Bernard, *Serm. in Dedid. Eccl.* 5, n. 3, 4).

Truly we have nothing in our nature that would justify the love of God being directed toward us in all tenderness. We can be the treasure of God only insofar as we receive the treasure of grace from His heart.

How great must be the beauty of grace that we bear in our fragile vessel; how glorious its splendor that it delights and enraptures the heart of God and makes Him have a very particular and extraordinary love for us.

There are various types of love. One and the same person can sincerely love another in various ways: with an ordinary and general, or with a particular and eminent love, that draws the heart out of the lover and attaches it to the object of his love.

In this latter love, which is called *ecstatic*, the renowned spiritual writer, Richard of St. Victor, distinguishes various degrees. The first is that in which the heart can no longer control its love; the second, that in which the heart cannot forget it; the third, that in which it can take pleasure in nothing else; the fourth and last is that in which it can no longer be satisfied even with the greatness of its love. The first degree he calls *insuperable* love, because no other affection can suppress it; the second is *inseparable*, because it is so firmly impressed on the memory that it cannot be effaced; the third degree is *exclusive*, because it can bear no rival; the fourth degree is *insatiable*, because it cannot be satisfied with any nourishment whatsoever.

It can surprise no one that man in such enraptured love can be drawn to God, the highest and most lovable Good, in whom man finds perfect satisfaction. But that God be drawn by such love to man—to man, whom He has formed with His hand of the slime of the earth—such a thing could not happen unless God had planted in man through grace something wonderful and precious, the ineffable splendor of which transports Him and overwhelms Him with the most fervent love. In fact, this love is so strong that it has moved the Son of God, the all-powerful King, to become our servant and has disarmed the anger of the just judge.

"The nature of the divinity is such," says Basil of Seleucia, "that having conquered all, it is conquered by the love of man." "God can never be satiated with the love of men. See in how many ways He tries to find one who will let himself be saved!" (*Or. in Genes.* 4, 1, 5, 2).

Therefore, the Divine Spouse in the *Canticle of Canticles* calls the soul that is adorned with grace, terrible as an army set in array. He begs her to turn away her eyes, lest she completely captivate Him.

Yes, divine love effects that God go out of Himself, as it were, and be immersed in the beloved. When the love of men for God does that, it is called ecstatic love. Though we may say of men that by love they go out of themselves and place their heart in the heart of their beloved, yet they can do this only in affection and sentiment. But God, whose being is the same as His love and perfectly one with it, enters substantially into the soul which He has made worthy of love through grace and unites Himself so intimately with such a soul that it seems He wills it to be a part of His being. St. Augustine says that half of the soul of one who loves dwells in his beloved. (*Conf.* 4, 6, 11). But the love of God is incomparably more powerful, since He places, not only half of His Spirit, but the whole in the hearts of His beloved friends. So strong and invincible is the love of God which grace gains for us.

Friendship, according to Aristotle, must be true and stable. (*Moral. Eudem.* 7, 2, 39-40; 53, 3). God Himself tells us that He is faithful in His love for His friends. "Can a woman forget her infant, so as not to have pity on the son of her womb? And if she should forget, yet will not I forget thee. Behold I have graven thee in my hands." (*Is.* 49: 15-16).

As the goodness of God, being infinite, surpasses all other good, so the care of His fatherly heart for His children far surpasses the care of every father and mother. Parents can lose, forget or cast off their children; and once at least, when death calls, they must leave them. But God can never do such a thing to His children. When children are forsaken by their parents, precisely then God is most ready to receive them. "My father and my mother have left me: but the Lord hath taken me up," says the Psalmist. (*Ps.* 26:10).

Conquered by His love, God comes to us really and in His very essence. The same love holds Him bound to us. It effects not only that we remember Him, but that He remain essentially present with us and in us. As long as we have grace, God cannot withdraw His affection from us. Neither can He withdraw His mysterious presence, because where His love is, there He is also, for He is love. Therefore He says, as though He could find His rest and happiness only with us: "My delights were to be with the children of men." (*Prov.* 8:31).

The third degree of love, says Richard of St. Victor, is had when one wishes to exclude all other lovers. How exclusive the divine love for us is appears from the fact that no one without grace can be admitted to His heart.

God indeed embraces all creatures with the arms of His merciful love, but He does not take all into His heart. He looks with complacency and mercy on them; that is, He loves them insofar as He sees something good in them. But He loves Himself with an entirely different love, with His whole heart. And precisely in this love do those share who through His grace have received His nature. For since He has shared His nature with those whom He has glorified with grace, so does He love them with the same love which He has for Himself.

Precisely because God has made all things for Himself, there is such a great difference in His love for them. He does not seek His glory in receiving something from them—for what shall a creature give to Him?—but in giving something to them. His love for creatures increases in the same degree in which He shares Himself with them. Now, it is impossible to give to a mere creature more than that which is given to the children of God through grace.

Thus we understand why God embraces them with an exclusive love and why He calls Himself a jealous God. (Cf. *Ex.* 20:5). He has given them all that He can, for even God cannot give more than Himself. Therefore His love for them embraces all that He can love. For the same reason, He loves His children as though He loved nothing else in the whole world. His eye rests on them with ineffable complacency. He looks at the rest of creatures, one may think, only insofar as they are for the good and the glorification of His children. And in reality He has subjected all these to the elect; all are destined to serve for the perfecting of the children of God, in order that these may cling to God without hindrance.

Finally, the love of God for the souls having grace is so insatiable, that after it should have more than satisfied itself here on earth with 33 years of suffering and pain, it still finds more new ways to show itself, as fire that always seeks new material to burn. Hast Thou, ever good and bounteous

God, so entirely forgotten Thy former blessings! Dost Thou no longer think of the expense of Thine omnipotence at the time of Creation to our benefit; dost Thou no longer think about this most incomprehensible of mysteries, Thy having become man; and dost Thou not think of the long and toilsome years of Thine earthly life? Dost Thou still cry to us: "I thirst!"? Hast Thou still not yet satisfied Thy love? No, good Jesus, all that was not enough for Thy love. After all the tiring trips through Judea, Galilee and Samaria, which exhausted Thy Body, Thy love was not yet made tired. Thou didst burn with the glowing desire, as sweet as it was bitter, to drink to the dregs the chalice of suffering. Thou didst desire not single drops but a whole ocean of sufferings, just as Thou didst will to pour out, not merely some drops of Thy Blood, but all of it. But even this immeasurable ocean could not contain the fullness of Thy love. Thou wouldst have gladly suffered far more, if it had been necessary for our salvation. Then finally, Thou hast sent Thy Holy Spirit as consoler from Heaven; Thou dost give Thyself to us in the Most Holy Sacrament; Thou dost give us Thy Father and makest Him to be ours.

What remains to thee that Thou canst still give to us to satisfy Thine ever restless love? Nothing else but Thyself. Nothing else but that Thou mayest live and work in us and fight and suffer with us in all the sacrifices and purifications that we need in order to become like Thee. Yes, this was the only thing that Thy power and wisdom could think of in order to satisfy Thine insatiable love. And Thou hast really so given Thyself to us by giving us Thy grace.

O happy soul adorned with the grace of God! Thou that hast become a partaker of this love of God! If grace brought with it only this one good, could it be balanced by all treasures and pleasures? It is always a joy to be loved. But to be loved by such a Lord and with such a love—such bliss is so delightful that it seems unbelievable that a man can despise it. What a hideous thing sin must be, that it conquers the invincible love of the invincible God! And how rash must that soul be that goes so far as to reject this love and to trample it underfoot by giving up grace!

God bestows His love on you wholly and entirely, and you insult Him and His love by dividing your meager love between Him and a thousand unworthy things, or rather by squandering it through your vain attachment to transitory things! God never tires of loving and embracing you and of showering benefits on you, and you weary if you must move a finger for so lavish and devoted a friend! O come, you friends, you lovers and beloved of God, and with your tears wash away the shameful insults offered to this Eternal Love!

In the same degree that we have despised this love in the past, let us be the more grateful now. Let us give to God, our most constant Lover, a love that can be overcome by no assault. Let us be jealous and see that no one surpass us in love, as He has taken care that no other creature should have a place closer to His heart. Let us repay His continual care for us with a lively and joyful remembrance, keeping Him always before our eyes. For His very special love, let us give our whole heart to Him alone, leaving no room therein for other affections. Let us correspond to His insatiable desire to do good to us by striving unwearyingly to love Him more and more and to give Him ever greater honor. One need only to begin to love, and having once tasted its sweetness, one will never cease from it. Though love does all it can, it longs to do more, for it is proper to sweetness that it never satisfies, but always causes greater thirst.

Chapter 23

THE HEAVENLY BEAUTY THAT GRACE
GIVES TO THE SOUL

BEAUTY IS the principal object of pure love. Even the perishable beauty of the body enkindles the heart to love. But the higher qualities of the heart and of the spirit can so captivate a soul that the will of the beloved becomes powerless, and it stands blindly, ready to serve at the beck of the one loved.

From God's ineffable love of our soul, we can only conclude that the soul must have a wonderful, heavenly beauty. And this is so much the more, since the divine love is able not only to estimate things at their true worth, but is also powerful enough to make them worthy of itself.

Human love presupposes beauty in the object. Man must find real beauty already present; otherwise, he cannot become enthusiastic enough to love. But he cannot give the beauty. Divine love, however, is the cause of beauty. For all things have of themselves nothing, having received their whole being from God. Thus, God can love a thing only insofar as He makes it partaker of His own goodness and beauty.

That holds in general for all of God's love and for all beauty and goodness of created things. But it holds in a very special way for the supernatural love of God and the supernatural beauty of the spirit. When God stoops down to our soul with supernatural love, He adorns it with a supernatural beauty, and precisely because of this beauty, which He Himself has given us, His loving eye rests on us with unspeakable complacency. But since, through grace, the love of God becomes active in us and abides with us, grace must contain God's beauty in itself and bestow it upon us.

130

Therefore, St. Augustine says, speaking of the elevation of man through grace: "When human nature, distinguished above all others, is cleansed from injustice, it is changed from hideousness to beauty." (*De Trin.* 1. 15, c. 8, n. 14). Still more appropriately St. Cyril of Alexandria teaches that, when we remain holy, we form Christ in ourselves and bear His features and His behavior. (*Contra Anthrop.* c. 6).

Indeed, the image of the Divine Nature and holiness is impressed on our soul through grace. It becomes a mirror of beauty, that is, of the holiness in God, and reflects, though not in all its purity and clarity, this holiness. It becomes a child of God, an adopted child, clothed as it were with a mantle, with the royal ornaments of God's own Son, that is, with His virtues. It becomes a newborn child, because the heavenly Father, who had impressed on him at his creation only a shadow of the Divine Nature, now shares His divine life, not only in figure, but in reality and impresses on the soul His divine features, just as on His natural son. The soul is made deiform, godlike, according to the holy Fathers and mystics; it is made like God's holiness and thereby becomes partaker of God's own beauty.

Whoever wishes to imagine the beauty of a soul having grace must have seen the infinite beauty of God, that beauty which the Angels long to see, that beauty which contains all created beauty in itself, that beauty which is the pattern, the measure, and the unattainable ideal of all that man considers splendid, of all the beauty that God can create.

Moreover, through grace our soul becomes a temple—the true throne—of the Holy Ghost and of the Holy Trinity, of which the Temple and the Holy of Holies in Jerusalem were only a type. But if that temple of stone was, by command of God, decorated so splendidly that it was rightly reckoned among the wonders of the world, what will God not offer to decorate this living temple as befits His majesty!

If God covers the earth, which is but His footstool, with the richest and most diversified tapestry of beautiful verdure, crowns it with wreaths of the loveliest flowers, encircles it with silvery threads of streams and rivers and places the twinkling stars as diamonds above it, what heavenly treasures, what precious pearls, what magnificent splendor will He bestow on the temple of our soul, in which He, with all the love of His Divine Heart, dwells and will continue to dwell forever?

And if men seek to make their temple of stone grand and magnificent with all the resources of wealth and art, how much more will God adorn and glorify the sanctuary of our soul, where He is adored in spirit and truth?

"To the just soul," says St. Ambrose, "God speaks as He once did to Jerusalem: 'Behold Jerusalem, I have painted thy walls.' The painting of the soul consists in this, that with the help of grace it reflects in its activity a beautiful image of the divine activity and holiness."

Hence, Solomon, in *The Canticle of Canticles,* praises so enthusiastically this divine beauty of the just soul. How great this beauty is and of what kind—that no mortal can express or understand. If the natural beauty of a great and noble soul surpasses all corporeal beauty, how much more true is this of the supernatural beauty that is had through grace? For there is a greater distance between grace and the natural being of the soul than between the soul and all the beauty of the visible world. That the heavenly beauty of grace is invisible for our bodily eye—and even for the eye of our soul—does not lessen its greatness. This is rather a sign of its sublimity, since all that we can see or attain through reason has only a limited and earthly beauty. Indeed, if the splendor of a soul adorned with grace could be seen, those looking on would be enraptured and transported with wonder and delight.

When God once revealed this beauty to St. Catherine of Siena, she covered with kisses the footsteps of those who were engaged in bringing sinners back to the grace of God. Transported with joy, she said to her confessor: "If you, my father, could behold the beauty of one soul adorned with grace, you would gladly suffer death a thousand times for the sake of one such soul."

Christ Himself, who was drawn down to earth by this splendor of holy souls, or rather with the purpose of imparting this splendor to souls, said to St. Bridget that if she would see this beauty she would be blinded and overcome and would faint away as though lifeless.

Indeed, just as our eyes can be blinded, not only by the sun itself, but also by its reflection in a crystal, so the human soul cannot bear the reflection of the divine light that is given out by the soul having grace. If gazing at the bright sun causes all around us to become dark, what would the beholding of a soul in the splendor of its supernatural glory effect? When St. Frances of Rome saw her Angel near her, the light of the sun was darkened by his brightness.

Even the Angels, who are accustomed to heavenly sights, are enraptured by this beauty. It is they who in *The Canticle of Canticles* cry out at the sight of the soul joined to God through grace: "Who is this that cometh up from the desert, flowing with delights, leaning upon her beloved?" (*Cant.* 8:5).

Indeed, the glory to which God raises the soul through grace is so great that even the natural beauty of the Angels is as nothing compared with it. The Angels themselves wonder how a soul that was sunk in the desert of this sinful earth and robbed of all natural beauty can be clothed with such a wonderful splendor. But this wonder of the Angels will not surprise us when we see and hear that God Himself considers the beauty of grace with astonishment and rapture. For how otherwise can we explain what He says in *The Canticle of Canticles* to the soul: "How beautiful art thou, my love, how beautiful art thou!" (*Cant.* 4:1).

God is not concerned with the beauty of bodies, which He by His word brought out of nothingness. He can be astonished at nothing that is not divine. As He considers throughout eternity His infinite beauty with the same endless delight, His eye also rests with unspeakable satisfaction upon the image of His Divine Nature, which the Holy Ghost impresses as a seal upon our soul. He is astonished, as it were, at the wonderful power of His love, which is able to adorn with such beauty a poor, miserable creature and to make it so much like Himself. He is astonished with the gold of His grace. He is astonished with the beautiful and lovely garden, with never-fading bloom, which His love has planted, refreshed by the breath of His Holy Spirit as by a mild, vernal breeze, and in which He dwells with unspeakable delight. And thus He cries out repeatedly: "How beautiful art thou, my love, how beautiful art thou!" (*Cant.* 4:1).

Does not this twofold exclamation indicate a twofold beauty of the soul? The soul has, first, a created beauty, effected by the splendor of grace, that clothes and surrounds it and covers it with the precious, golden robe of all the supernatural and divine virtues. Again, the soul is doubly beautiful, having also an uncreated beauty, that of the Holy Spirit, who has erected His throne within it. For as the royal palace must first be splendidly furnished to receive the king in a becoming manner, but receives its greatest ornament in the king himself, so the Holy Ghost first forms our soul into a magnificent and glorious temple and then confers upon it its highest adornment and most excellent glory by dwelling personally in it.

The soul adorned with grace is but a golden setting in which the most precious jewel, the Holy Ghost, God Himself, is enclosed. As in a ring, the gold is distinct from the jewel, and yet they are so closely united that they form but one whole and one beauty, so likewise the Divinity is distinct from the just soul, but is so intimately united with it through love that the beauty of both appears to be one and the same.

The same adorable truth was revealed by our Saviour Himself to St. Teresa by another beautiful image. He showed her the soul as a crystal globe that was not merely illuminated from without by the divine sun of grace, but bore this sun in its center. From this center the sun filled with divine splendor the different parts of the globe, representing the different faculties of the daughter and bride of God: "All the glory of the king's daughter is within." (*Ps.* 44:14).

If God then considers the beauty and loveliness of your soul with such delight, ought not you, Christian soul, gladly conform your judgment to that of the highest and infallible Judge of art, even though that beauty be invisible to you? Do you dare to esteem any other beauty, compare it, or even prefer it to this?

Compare, then, this beauty of grace with all others that

delight you. In this way you will see [by] how much grace surpasses all these. For all that you admire in every other beauty is found here in a far higher degree and without any imperfection.

Lifeless things please you by reason of their exterior perfections, by the harmonious composition of their parts, by their pleasing colors and the splendor with which they are decorated. Grace, however, effects a heavenly harmony among the faculties of your soul, sheds over it a divine luster, and glorifies it with eternal and imperishable beauty. More beautiful than lifeless objects are living things. Their beauty is in their inner perfections, the bloom of their youth, their manifold activity, the fullness of their vital power. But there is a higher, a purer, a more perfect life—that of the soul through grace—a life that never grows old but is always being rejuvenated, a life that ever brings forth heavenly blossoms and diffuses the fragrance of divine bliss.

Every unspoiled heart is delighted by the beauty of virtue, purity of heart, the order of the moral law actually realized in the soul. But all these receive a far higher splendor through grace, by which the Holy Ghost Himself impresses on our soul the law of God, unites it most intimately with the archetype of all justice, adorns it with the supernatural and divine virtues and invests it with justice and the true sanctity of the Son of God.

Grace, accordingly, as the image of the Divine Nature, gives to the soul a truly heavenly beauty, because it is a sharing of the Divine Nature, that is, an outflowing of its holiness. The Holy Ghost, who wishes to dwell in the soul, cannot choose a dwelling that is unworthy of His majesty. If Heaven is hardly sufficient for Him, therefore, how much less worthy of a human soul! He must adorn the soul in such a way that it may become at least an earthly image of Heaven.

Here we may get a glance of the awful disorder that sin causes in us by robbing us of grace. Sin places itself as a dark storm cloud between the divine Sun and the soul, and in a moment the splendor of its heavenly beauty is extinct, the supernatural life is killed, the virtues are destroyed and the splendid robe of the children of God is tattered. From a fragrant and lovely garden of God, the soul is transformed into an abominable and pestilential abyss, where reptiles, serpents and the hellish dragon himself dwell. From an image of the lovable God you are made an image of Hell and of the devil.

The devil is so hideous that Our Lord told St. Bridget that, if she could see him in his deformity, she would either sink lifeless to the ground, or if she did not die, she would experience unspeakable pain. Into such a monster is one changed by sin, who in grace had shone as a mirror of divine glory.

Your soul is disfigured in the same way when sin drives out the divine Sun. This also was shown to St. Teresa by the above-mentioned image of the crystal globe, for after Christ had withdrawn Himself from its center, there remained nothing but frightful darkness. Who would not be frightened by the thought of that eternal night, of that incomprehensible hate, of the deformation of the once so beautiful features, all of which can be caused by one sin! And who should not tremble at the thought of how little is necessary to destroy so delicate a beauty lent to you by God and beware not only of its loss but of the least stain that might disfigure it.

What pains and time, what expense does one undergo to keep or increase the perishable beauty of the body? Hours are not enough; one uses days and anxious care to put the hair or some piece of clothing in order and to add grace and dignity to the deportment of the body.

And should one hour be too much for us to put the soul in order? Should we be unwilling to bestow upon the beauty of soul, which secures for us the friendship of God and Heaven, that care which we bestow on the hair or dress?

The world hopes by such trifles to gain the empty admiration of men. We know, on the other hand, from God Himself, that every—even the least—effort we make in preserving the purity or enhancing the beauty of the heavenly figure of our soul secures for us a greater measure of His love.

In *The Canticle of Canticles* He says: "Thou hast wounded my heart, my sister, my spouse, thou hast wounded my heart with one of thy eyes, and with one hair of thy neck." (*Cant.* 4:9).

Every glance toward God, every virtuous act performed in grace and every sigh of the soul that loves God, even though so light as a hair, becomes an arrow that wounds, not the unstable heart of man, but the eternal and constant heart of God. Every step that you take in the pathway of grace is so beautiful and lovely that God, beholding you, exclaims: "How beautiful are thy steps in shoes, O prince's daughter!" (*Cant.* 7:1). Every word that you address to God is so dear and precious that it brings down upon you His richest blessing, as the Psalmist sings: "Grace is poured abroad in thy lips; therefore hath God blessed thee forever." (*Ps.* 44:3).

Nothing in the beloved is insignificant to the lover; nothing in the beloved soul is insignificant to the loving God. Here each and every thing is great because it gains God's love for us. What a motive for us to gain the love of God!

Chapter 24

GRACE MAKES THE SOUL A
TRUE SPOUSE OF GOD

WE HAVE SEEN how God has become, through grace, our Father, our Brother, our Friend and consequently has approached as near to us as one man can to another. But God is so intent on being all in all to us and the fountain of His grace is so copious and inexhaustable that, as long as we can find among men a more intimate union, we must not rest satisfied without referring this also to the relation of our soul to God.

The union between bride and groom, between man and wife, is the most intimate that can be had among men, both according to nature and according to God's command: "A man shall leave his father and mother, and shall cleave to his wife, and they shall be two in one flesh." (*Eph.* 5:31; *Gen.* 2:24).

The ineffable love which God bears a soul in the state of grace and the supernatural beauty which He gives to it, already intimate to us that this relation of husband and wife also exists between God and the soul in the highest and most perfect manner. Matrimony, according to the teaching of the Apostle, is a great Sacrament; it is a sacred sign of sublime significance because it represents the union of Christ with the Church and consequently also that of God with the soul.

Therefore, St. Paul represents the relation of Christ to Christians under the image of a marriage and considers it his task to see that Christ takes possession of the soul of a Christian as a pure, unspotted bride. (*2 Cor.* 11:2).

But as the reality and prototype is more perfect than the image and representation, the union of God with the soul

138

through grace must be more intimate than that of man and wife. These are merely one in one flesh; God and the soul are one spirit. "But he who is joined to the Lord, is one spirit," says St. Paul. (*1 Cor.* 6:17).

As spirit is far above flesh, as God is far above created things, so is the union of God with the soul far above the union of man and wife. Indeed, this union of God with the soul is so real and intimate that in all created nature its like is not to be found. God embraces the soul with the arms of His love and fills, yes, penetrates it, with His spirit and thereby holds it so close to Himself that no power in Heaven, on earth or under the earth can tear it from Him. Only the soul itself can break this bond when, in the perversion of the will, it refuses fidelity to God.

It is indeed something great to have God as Father, as Brother and [as] Friend; but all these delightful names— and far more—is contained in the term *spouse,* which He applies to the just soul. This He does in *The Canticle of Canticles.* Similarly, in the *Psalms* He calls the soul His sister, His friend and His daughter. But that name which penetrates most deeply into our soul is "spouse." "As among men," says St. Bernard, "the name of 'mother,' 'sister' and 'friend' does not signify as much as the name 'spouse,' in like manner, the mutual, gracious affections of God and the soul could find no more delightful expression than in the name of 'betrothed' and 'spouse.' For these have everything in common; nothing is special to one, nothing separated. Both have but one inheritance, one house, one table, one bridal chamber, and finally, one flesh." (St. Bern., *In Cant. Serm. 7,* n. 2).

Accordingly, here is best seen the ineffable grandeur of grace. It is grace that makes us be children of God the Father and gives us a divine dignity that makes our soul be of equal birth with the Son of God and worthy of His espousal. It is grace that gives our soul a heavenly beauty and loveliness, which so fascinates the Son of God that He descends from His divine throne to embrace it and lead it back to His heavenly Father. Grace introduces the Holy Ghost into our soul, where, as the bond of divine love, He is at the same time the bridegroom, the pledge and the wedding-ring of its espousals with the Son of God. It is grace that makes the soul be one spirit with God, so that it learns—or at least strives—to will the same things that the just, holy God Himself wills, as it is fitting for a friend to do.

An earthly king who brings a bride home with him shows his love first of all by splendid wedding gifts. Then, through his union with her, he makes all his possessions and rights common between them. Finally, he raises her to a participation in his kingly dignity.

To the soul that God makes His spouse through grace, He gives this threefold distinction in full measure. The wedding gifts, the virtues and gifts of the Holy Ghost, surpass in value all the treasures that the earth can offer. The common possession of goods that an earthly prince may grant to his spouse may make her rich according to earthly estimation, but what is this in comparison with that to which the Lord of Heaven refers in the words of the kind father: "All I have is thine"? (*Lk.* 15:31). The participation in the kingly dignity which is granted to God's spouse is so sublime that the majesty of an earthly king appears as a shadow beside it.

Among all earthly sentiments, there are none more powerful than those that bring about and sustain marriage. Must not then our soul be moved with much greater force and power to embrace its heavenly Spouse, who has become all for it, who does no injury to the blossom of its purity, but rather sanctifies it through the union, who loves it with eternal love, who has suffered death to purchase it with His Blood, out of whose side it has been born, through whose Blood it has been washed of its sins and adorned with divine holiness?

With what care must the soul strive to please Him alone and thus to be as He wishes it, holy, unspotted and glorious, without stain or blemish or anything of the sort. (*Eph.* 5:27). How it must make every effort to belong to Him entirely, as He has given Himself entirely to it; to love Him as He has loved it and to cling to Him with unfailing fidelity! How it must strive to make itself worthy in this mortal life, where it first celebrates the espousals, that it may one day be admitted to the marriage of the Lamb and enjoy the vision of the divine countenance.

We read, considering it a great thing, that Esther, a woman of low condition, is chosen to be the bride of an earthly king. But that king is only a human being like her, who lives but a short time and cannot satisfy all the longing of her heart. He can give her only an empty name and supply her with earthly treasures and external ornaments. But he cannot give her internal nobility nor beauty of soul. Yet such an espousal is considered by men as the best fortune imaginable!

Learn from this, Christian soul, how highly you should treasure your heavenly Spouse, the King of Heaven and earth. The whole world would accuse of foolishness and ingratitude the bride of an earthly spouse if she would reject his hand, or deceive him unworthily, or become entirely unfaithful to him and throw herself into the arms of his most bitter enemy. But would you not act much more foolishly and shamefully if you would reject the hand of your divine Spouse and desecrate His heavenly bridal chamber, which you yourself are, by admitting His most hateful enemy, sin, and by giving yourself to the unclean seducer? Must not the whole heavenly court weep, must not all the elements rise up to avenge this insult to their King! Only too often must we witness such shameful frivolity, and perhaps even be guilty of the same thing ourselves.

If the union between God and the soul that is effected by grace has its faint image in earthly marriage, the qualities of a true marriage must also be found in the bond of grace. We must therefore consider these more in detail to learn what obligations toward God grace imposes on us.

St. Thomas, following St. Augustine, names three blessings of Matrimony which constitute its charm and happiness: fidelity, the Sacrament or the blessing, and the offspring. Fidelity indicates the indivisible unity of Matrimony by which husband and wife belong exclusively to each other. The Sacrament or blessing signifies the indissolubility of the tie formed by God. Indeed this is demanded even by nature, as our Saviour says: "What therefore God hath joined together, let no man put asunder." (*Matt.* 19:6). But as Sacrament, marriage implies a much closer union. The child, finally, represents the fruit of Matrimony, its crown and seal, since it lets the married couple enjoy the ineffable pleasures of father and mother, uniting them still more closely.

All these blessings of Matrimony are found in a far greater measure in the union which grace effects between God and the soul. The latter must only acquire, preserve and enjoy them; for God, on His part, leaves nothing undone to promote their attainment and increase.

Of fidelity, God Himself says by the prophet Osee: "I will espouse thee to me in faith: and thou shalt know that I am the Lord." (*Os.* 2:20). The Apostle Paul holds up to me as a model the fidelity of God to His spouse: "Husbands, love your wives, as Christ also loved the Church, and delivered himself up for it." (*Eph.* 5:25).

God gives Himself to His spouse whole and undivided. True, He has countless spouses besides you, but He does not thereby cease to belong entirely to you, and His love for you is not lessened on that account. For He is not a limited being, as man, who does not have in his heart enough love and spirit of sacrifice for even one of his fellow men. He is rather as the sun, which, though united by its rays with a thousand eyes, is nevertheless seen and enjoyed in its entirety by each one. He is wisdom and truth, which need not divide themselves, but are given entirely to each one, even when they are announced simultaneously to thousands of men.

For this reason, O Christian soul, rejoice that the greatness and power of your beloved can make so many souls happy. Far from envying others, you should consider all as your brothers, love them in your Spouse, and thus their happiness will greatly increase yours.

The heart of the Spouse is unlimited in its greatness and therefore can embrace all creatures. But your heart is exceedingly small and narrow; you are not in a condition to embrace Him, even to a small extent. How then can you divide this heart and with it cling to a thousand different things? Even when you give your heart entirely to your

Spouse, you do nothing that could worthily repay His love.

Therefore, He is so jealous of your fidelity, as He Himself says, "I am the Lord thy God, mighty, jealous." (*Ex.* 20:5). He desires for Himself every beat of your heart, every moment, every sentiment, and He is rightly angry with you when, besides Him, you tolerate something else in your heart that you love, contrary to His Will.

But even when you have offended His holy zeal, He does not cease to be faithful to you. His jealousy spurs Him on to make greater effort to win your heart again for Himself, and His planting all outlets and bypaths with sharp thorns to leave you no other way than that which leads to Himself is only a sign of His ineffable love. Where do you find among men such a faithful and undivided love? And if there you do not find it, why will you deprive yourself by your culpable levity of enjoying it in God?

The bond of union between God and the soul is, on God's part at least, eternal and indissoluble, as the eternity and unchangeableness of the Divinity demand. The same Spouse who has said, "I will espouse thee to me in faith" (*Os.* 2:20) has also said: "I have loved thee with an everlasting love." (*Jer.* 31:3).

Your Spouse, who has loved you with an everlasting love, also gives Himself to you forever. He can neither die nor withdraw from you out of disgust. Only you, through your own fault, can die the death of sin, or feel disgust toward your Spouse, and thus with your own hand break the heavenly bond that binds you to Him. Sometimes, it is true, He seems to withdraw from you for a short time. But this He does only in wholesome chastisement of your neglect of Him or to try your fidelity, only to return to you with greater love and friendliness. Despise then all other enjoyments and pleasures, avoid all idle distractions, devote all your time to His service. Thus, your union with Him will become more intimate from day to day, until finally, He Himself will come to take you into the eternal mansions of His Father. There, no power in Heaven or on earth, not even you yourself, will be able to separate you from Him.

The third blessing of Matrimony, fecundity, is found here

also in the highest degree. It is a heavenly and wonderful fecundity, with which that of Matrimony can hardly be compared. It is a fecundity so much greater and more glorious because it does not violate the purity and virginity of the spouse. On the other hand, it rather exalts her and produces a fruit that is not separated from the bosom in which it has been begotten, but remains there as the blossom in a tree. This fecundity is the splendor of the purity of the spouse and her most beautiful adornment.

We stand here before a series of mysteries, which only a soul practiced in the life of grace can imagine; to understand them is reserved for eternity.

As the dew falling from Heaven fructifies the plant, the Son of God fructifies the soul adorned with grace. As the sun by its light penetrates into the clear eye and is mirrored in it, the Son of God begets first in the soul the image of His own Divine Essence and is Himself reborn in it in order to exercise with the soul a new fruitful activity.

The soul receives its heavenly Spouse first of all through grace. Through Him it is reborn, is made His child and is consequently made like Him. Accordingly, every degree of virtue and piety through which the soul grows in grace is the fruitfulness expected by Christ and brought forth by Him, for with grace He also grows in the soul.

What a wonderful fecundity, in which the Son of God, who was begotten from the bosom of the eternal Father, is born anew in the soul through grace! What a wonderful fecundity, in which the mother does not sacrifice her own life for the child, but is herself reborn to new life! What a wonderful fecundity, which does not cause the blossoms of virginity to wither and yet produces the most perfect fruit; yes, where the blossom itself is at the same time the fruit! In short, it is a fecundity that may be considered as an example, or rather as an image, of the virginal fecundity of the most blessed Mother of God.

If now the soul is born anew through the coming to it of its Spouse and receives His power in itself, it strives henceforth to bring forth fruit on its part in order to show its gratitude. It can do this in a twofold manner.

Above all, it must show its fecundity in good works. This offspring of virtue far surpasses the longed-for blessing of carnal posterity. The natural progeny is limited to a very small number of children; the spiritual knows no number nor measure, for virtuous deeds and services can be multiplied every day, and since they do not perish in eternity, they do not trouble the parent with the fear of an untimely death. They rather give the soul a certain prospect for eternal life in Heaven. The natural fecundity produces a posterity that inherits and takes to itself the wealth of the father and mother; the spiritual children, however, give the mother the right to an eternal, heavenly inheritance, and in place of dividing and using up the parents' riches, they increase them without limit.

The more the soul tries to fill the treasury of its divine Spouse with the fruit of its gifts, the more it must feel that its accomplishments are very small. Hence, the appearance that all who truly love God are never content with what they do, but driven by an inner force, they always seek to gain others for the service of God and to make them fruitful in salutary works.

But God gladly shows His love to them by sending, as a reward for their fidelity, souls whose salvation or perfection is the fruit of their prayer and sacrifice.

Happy the soul espoused to God when it brings forth a rich harvest of good works and virtues and gives to its Spouse, as the fruit of an unspotted and faithfully preserved union with Him, a large number of saved souls. Such a soul is to be acclaimed happy because it may thus offer to God compensation for His love, a compensation that, even in His eyes, is of immeasurable value.

Again, such a soul is happy because, by all its fruitful activity, grace and its love for its Spouse are increased in it; it is happy because, with every new fruit, the love of the Spouse for the soul and thereby also its security increases. A mother considers every new child as a support of her marriage, as the honor of her motherhood and as a pledge of the love and favor of her husband. This is far more the case in the union of the soul with God, since the soul is not worn out by its fruitfulness and loses neither beauty nor strength, but becomes stronger through the birth of good works, more fruitful through the number of its children, more powerful, fresh, and pleasing to God through their care. For the prophet Isaias says: "Then shall thy light break forth as the morning, and thy health shall speedily arise, and thy justice shall go before thy face, and the glory of the Lord shall gather thee up. . . . and thou shalt be like a watered garden, and like a fountain of water whose waters shall not fail." (*Is.* 58:8, 11).

But if the soul is espoused to its heavenly Beloved, not only by grace, but also by its own fruitfulness, it makes itself worthy of Him and clings to Him ever more closely. Then, already in this life, He unites Himself intimately with it, fills the mind with His light and allows the heart to experience His delightful presence, so that all its powers enjoy the goodness and sweetness of God, and the soul itself feels that holy confidence in grace and the fidelity of its Spouse, which is said to drive out fear. (Cf. *1 John.* 4:18).

This does not mean that the soul loses its childlike reverence before its Lord and God. It does not mean that, as long as it lives upon this earth, the soul is ever given absolute certainty of its salvation or that the fear of its own weakness is ever entirely taken away. It knows well enough from experience that the words of the Apostle are justified: "He that thinketh himself to stand, let him take heed lest he fall." (*1 Cor.* 10:12). But the knowledge of the fruitfulness that its Spouse has given to its weakness consoles it with the assurance that He who has worked so much through it will never destroy His work in it nor His union with it.

Do not hesitate a moment, then, Christian soul, to give yourself entirely to your heavenly Spouse. "Hearken, O daughter," says the Psalmist, "and see, and incline thy ear: and forget thy people and thy father's house. And the king shall greatly desire thy beauty; for he is the Lord thy God." (*Ps.* 44:11-12). Yes, it is the Lord thy God, who comes down to you, to lead you to His Heaven, who knocks on [the door of] your heart with ardent desire and is so condescending as to beg of you to open your heart to Him. Do not withdraw from Him, lest at the same time you withdraw from your greatest honor and happiness. Strive to be His pride and joy and He will make you a ruler in Heaven for all eternity.

In order to retain holy fidelity to your heavenly Spouse, consider frequently the beautiful words spoken to her intended seducers by St. Agnes, the spouse of Jesus, faithful unto death: "Another lover has already taken possession of me: I am espoused to Him whom the angels serve, whose beauty the sun and moon admire, whose Mother is a virgin, whose Father knows no wife. My right hand and my neck He has encircled with precious stones; my ears He has adorned with priceless pearls. He has joined Himself to me with the ring of His fidelity and adorned me with innumerable jewels. His body is already united to my body; milk and honey I have received from His mouth, and His blood has reddened my cheeks. When I love Him, I am chaste; when I touch Him, I am pure; when I accept Him, I am a virgin. To Him I shall remain faithful; to Him I give myself with all the fervor of my heart."

Chapter 25

GRACE MAKES US MEMBERS OF THE KINGDOM OF GOD AND PARTICIPANTS OF HIS DOMINION OVER ALL THINGS

A S GRACE makes our soul a spouse of God, the King of Heaven and earth, it also elevates the same to be queen over all things. "He that spared not even his own Son," says St. Paul, "but delivered him up for us all, how hath he not also, with him, given us all things?" (*Rom.* 8:32). With still more right can we say: If God through grace has made us partakers of His Divine Nature, will He not subject all other things to us? The dignity of God's spouse gives to our soul the clearest right to sovereignty over all things.

The spouse of the king is queen. She has the same throne, the same crown and is honored by all the subjects, just as the king himself. Accordingly, that must also hold of the spouse, which the father [in the Gospel parable] said to his first-born son—who, however was not his only son: "All I have is thine." (*Lk.* 15:31). For the spouse obtains through marriage a greater right to participation in the dignity and honor of the husband than the son to that of the father.

Moreover, grace makes us true friends of God, and the first law of friendship is that friends share everything with one another and possess all in common. The fact that this is seldom or never carried out among men is a sign that their friendship is imperfect, enclosed within narrow limits. The friendship of God, on the other hand, knows no limits and ceases to give only when there is nothing more to give and nothing more to share.

We are through grace children of God, consequently His heirs and co-heirs with Christ. (*Rom.* 8:17). As St. Anselm asks: What is there in Heaven or on earth or beneath the

148

earth that must not obey and be subject to those whom the Lord of all things has chosen as His friends and adopted as His children?

All other creatures have been created for the use of man, who by nature bears in his soul the image of God. How much more so should they be subject to him when he has become partaker of the Divine Nature!

As man is the crown and glory of the earth, the soul adorned with grace is the crown and glory of Heaven and earth, in short, of all Creation. Our faith teaches that all things were created for the only-begotten Son of God and all things in Heaven and earth are destined for His honor and glory. But the adopted children of God are one with Him. They reign with Him and all His love rests on them. They are, then, together with the Son of God, the highest end and destiny of Creation.

Through the supernatural power of grace, they should despise all created things and trample underfoot whatever appeals to their pride and to their senses and courageously bear the anger and enmity of those who would frighten them away from the service of God. This is conquering the world; this is putting on the perfect spirit of which David speaks. (*Ps.* 50:14). To him who has come thus far is to be applied the words of Our Lord: "To him that shall overcome, I will give to sit with me in my throne: as I also have overcome, and am set down with my Father in his throne." (*Apoc.* 3:21). And ". . . To him that overcometh, I will give the hidden manna . . . and . . . a new name. . ." (*Apoc.* 2:17).

True, in this life the just do not have the full enjoyment of their dominion and often seem to be the poorest and most desolate.

But who would have recognized the King of all things in the poor, rejected Christ Child in Bethlehem? Who would have recognized in the poor, indigent Virgin of Nazareth the Queen of all creation? Who would have considered the sick beggar, Lazarus, greater and richer than King Herod or the Emperor Tiberius?

Truth is often veiled from our eyes. We must therefore, through the light of faith, seek to esteem that which is truly great and noble. "As long as the heir is a child," says St. Paul (that is, as long as he lives in this land of exile), "he differeth nothing from a servant, though he be lord of all." (*Gal.* 4:1). He is neither conscious himself of his rights and riches, nor is he recognized as their possessor by men. But when he has entered into the kingdom of his father, his greatness appears, and the world is astounded that the one who is despised takes possession of all his goods, to enjoy them forever.

Therefore, it is by no means necessary that God's children enjoy earthly things and worldly honors. They can call nothing their own and yet, like their divine Brother, Christ, have all things under their feet.

And precisely then they show that they are above the world, when they despise all things, seeking primarily the kingdom of God, in the firm hope that, according to the words of our Saviour, all things will be added to them. Besides, the things of this earth are too poor and miserable to be worthy of the love and desire of the children of God. Then only, when all Creation, in the words of the Apostle, shall be delivered from the servitude of corruption and glorified by a heavenly light, when the new Heaven shall have descended upon earth and transformed it into a new Heaven and glorious city of God, then only will Creation be a worthy dwelling-place of the children of God; then shall they possess it and in it enjoy the glory of God.

But even now, no barrier of proprietary rights can prohibit the children of God from the highest and truest enjoyment of Creation. Though the rich accumulate lifeless gold and shining silks in their palaces and wardrobes, though they alone be able to purchase works of art for large sums of money, though they call fields and meadows their own and reap the fruits therefrom to convert them into money or to feed and delight their bodies, they can never withhold grand and glorious nature from even the poorest child. Even the poorest may step forth from his poor cottage, and everything great and beautiful that his eye beholds about him he may call his own. It is his because it is the work of his heavenly Father. In every flower of the field, in every tree, he sees an image of the beauty and goodness of his God, who through these things gives pledges of His love. All the living beings, which inhabit the earth in such manifold variety, announce to him the omnipotence and love of his heavenly Father. The more he enjoys that inner peace which the assurance of being a child of God gives to him and the better he understands the true loveliness of all beauty, the more joyful he finds the loveliness and wisdom which fills the smallest creature and the most ordinary of God's actions. And thus he can call all his own, and for a twofold reason. First, because it is the property of his Father, and secondly, because, while needing nothing, he nevertheless gets enjoyment from it, perhaps more than does the one who owns it.

The wealth of a child of God is not limited to the earth; it can look up even to Heaven, consider the splendor of the sun and the stars, lose itself in that immense space and then call out with St. Ignatius: "How miserable the earth seems to me when I consider the heavens!"

What consolation must fill the heart of God's child when he considers that all these bodies of light, in view of which the whole earth (to say nothing of the wealth of a prince) appears as nothing, serve *him* as well as the most powerful men on the earth. He realizes, moreover, that his throne shall once be set above all these; whereas, all the riches of this earth are limited to a small earthly space.

Besides, earthly riches give no man the power to rule nature arbitrarily and to make it serve him at a given sign. But in the lives of the Saints—His especially loved children—God has shown that grace can give an unconditional dominion over living as well as lifeless things, when it serves our good and the honor of God. The poor St. Francis called the birds of the air and commanded them, as long as it pleased him, to sing the praise of God and to delight Him with their melodies. When the people were unwilling to listen to his sermons, St. Anthony of Padua called the fish, and they obeyed his command and came from all sides to listen to his words.

We would all have this dominion, as Adam had in Paradise, if we had not lost original grace in him. We shall regain it only in the life to come, where there will be no effects of Original Sin. Since it is grace through which we earn our heavenly glorification and all the blessings that go with it, it always remains true that we have it to thank if we are once made lords of all things.

Even the privations that we have to put up with in this life become for us, through grace, a heavenly fortune. "To them that love God," says the Apostle, "all things work together unto good . . ." (*Rom.* 8:28). All that we give up or do without for God's sake, will, according to the promise of our Saviour, be given back a hundredfold. As often as it happens that we give up something, either freely or according to God's plan, we renounce the right that belongs to us as children of God, and God accepts it as though we had given something to Him that belonged to us.

Thus, earthly goods belong to us in the fullest sense when we renounce them or, according to God's wise providence, when we do not possess or enjoy them. For then we dispose of them as God Himself does. We give them to God when we acknowledge the property of other men according to His law.

Oh, how rich we would feel in all our poverty, how happy in all misery, if with lively faith we considered ourselves as kings of this world! Far from coveting our neighbor's goods, we would gladly be content with the little we have, and even with poverty, saying to ourselves that in time all will be given to us and that now no one can possess and enjoy as much as his heart desires. Yes, we would renounce joyfully the temporary enjoyment and possession, that our hearts might not be too attached to these and thus make us unworthy of their eternal possession.

Chapter 26

THE INTIMATE UNION WHICH GRACE EFFECTS BETWEEN GOD AND US

HERETOFORE, we have tried to explain the wonderful, mysterious union which grace effects between God and us by comparing it to the various unions that we find among men. We have found that all these human bonds and relationships are far less perfect than that brought about by grace. But we would conceal the most admirable and sublime mystery if we did not add that grace unites us to God by a very special type of union, causing us, in a true and profound sense, to grow together into one being, one body, one spirit with Him.

The relationship of father and son, husband and wife, are of kinship and mutual alliance only; they are not a real, permanent union of the body. The relation existing between friends is one of mutual love and sentiment, not a real union of spirits. In fact, the union of two created human persons is necessarily imperfect, since human beings are limited and finite and cannot interpenetrate one another. But God, in His infinite perfection, can unite Himself to Angels and to men as fire is united to an object, heating and illuminating it. God can unite Himself to us in a somewhat similar way as the soul is united to the body which it vivifies. Though it remains distinct from God, the soul is, at the same time, made one with Him in a singular manner, in a way that may be compared to that in which a man, soul and body, or his head and members, are one. This is the complete meaning of the Apostle's words: "But he who is joined to the Lord, is one spirit [with him]" (*1 Cor.* 6:17)—one spirit not merely in the unity of sentiment and affection, but in the unity of life and being. It is this sublime unity to which the Son of God

153

referred when He prayed to His Father after the Last Supper: "And the glory which thou hast given me, I have given to them; that they may be one, as we also are one: I in them, and thou in me; that they may be made perfect in one . . ." (*John* 17:22-23). A moment before, Christ had prayed to the Father for the same unity, saying: "And not for them only do I pray, but for them also who through their word shall believe in me; that they all may be one, as thou, Father, in me, and I in thee; that they also may be one in us, that the world may believe that thou hast sent me." (*John* 17:20-21). The ineffable unity of nature which God the Son has with the Father is, according to His express and oft-repeated teaching, the true type and foundation of our union with God. But the Son is not only kindred or similar to the Father, He is one with Him as the branch is one with the tree, the ray of light with the light, the brook with the fountain. So too, grace makes us one with God, not in the same perfect manner, but in a similar way. And yet it is not a question of a mere relationship or similarity, but of an intimate union which makes us, as it were, one being with God.

Concerning this union, St. Cyril of Alexandria teaches that, imitating the unity of the Blessed Trinity, we may enjoy a twofold real union with God, namely, union of the soul with the Son of God in His Divine Nature and union of body with Him in His human nature. (*In Joan*. l. 11, c. 11, 12). The latter union represents and brings with it the former. Considering the Son of God in His human nature, we know that He unites us, not only in imagination or affection, but in truth and reality, in one Mystical Body, of which He is the Head. Moreover, He unites our soul to His divinity to form with it one spirit.

Let us consider first our union with the sacred humanity of Christ. Of this we read in St. Chrysostom the following: " 'We, though many, are one body,' says the Apostle. [*1 Cor.* 10:17]. Why do I still speak of participation and union? We are ourselves the body of Christ. For what is the bread upon the altar? The Body of Christ. And what do they become who receive it? The body of Christ; not many bodies, but one body. As the bread is one whole, comprised of many grains, which however cannot be seen as individual grains, and though they continue to exist, their distinction cannot be perceived in the unity of the whole, so we also are united with one another and with Christ. For you are not nourished by *one* body and your neighbor by *another*, but all are nourished by the same body. Thus St. Paul says: 'We, though many, are one body, all of us who partake of the one bread.' [*1 Cor.* 10:17]."—(St. Jn. Chr., *1 Cor. Homily*, 24, 2).

St. Cyril expresses himself in the following way: "Let someone tell us of the virtue and significance of the mystical sacrament. Why is it given to us? Is it not that it may cause Christ really to live in us through our reception and communion of His sacred Body? For St. Paul writes: 'The Gentiles are joint heirs, are fellow-members of the same body, and joint partakers of the promise in Christ Jesus through the Gospel.' [*Eph.* 3:6]. But how are they of the same body? By being honored with the reception of the Holy Sacrament, they are made one body with Him, as each of the holy Apostles. For why otherwise has the Apostle called his own members, or rather those of all Christians, members of Christ? 'Do you not know that your bodies are members of Christ? Shall I then take the members of Christ and make them members of a harlot?' [*1 Cor.* 6:15]. And our Saviour Himself says: 'He who eats my flesh, and drinks my blood, abides in me and I in him.' [*John* 6:57]. Here it is important to note that Christ will be in us, according to His own words, not merely by a certain relation of love or by a certain feeling, but by a real union. For as two pieces of wax when melted and placed together form one whole, so are we united to Christ and He to us through our reception of His Body and Blood." (*In Joan*. 1. 10, c. 2).

Ordinary bread is also united with the body of the one who partakes of it. But since it is lifeless and perishable bread, it cannot convert one's body into its own substance, thus forming one body. But the Body of Christ is living, undivided, imperishable Bread, and therefore it unites to itself the bodies of those who receive it; it makes them its members and fills them with divine life. It nourishes us as the vine feeds, penetrates and vivifies the branches with its own vitality. Thus our mystical and supernatural union with Christ is well represented by the union of the branches with the trunk of the vine.

The union of our body with the Body of Christ is only the means and the figure of that union effected by grace between our soul and the Divinity. We are made one spirit with God as really and truly as the body, of which Christ is the Head, must be vivified by the same spirit in whom the Son of God lives.

Here again let us listen to St. Cyril. "Of the spiritual unity we must explain that we are all united in the certain, definite way with one another and with God by receiving the same Holy Spirit. For although we are many—considered individually—and Christ puts into the heart of each of us the Spirit of Himself and His Father, and because this Spirit is one and indivisible, He unites the spirits of men so that they all appear as one in Him. For as the power of the body of Christ renders all those who receive it one body, so likewise the Spirit of God, by His indwelling, leads all to this spiritual unity. St. Paul, therefore, tells us: 'Bearing with one another in love, careful to preserve the unity of the spirit in the bond of peace: one body and one spirit, even as you were called in one hope of your calling; one Lord, one faith, one Baptism; one God and Father of all, who is above all and throughout all, and in us all.' [*Eph.* 4:2-6]. For if the one spirit dwells in us, the Father of all will be in us, and God will unite through His Son those that partake of the same Holy Spirit." (*In Joan.* 1. 11, c. 11).

We are then truly made one spirit with God. This does not mean that the substance of our soul ceases to exist, but it is so intimately united with God that in a certain manner there results from the union one whole. In the human body, also, the members are essentially distinct from the head and the soul from the body. Yet they are really one because they form one whole, and thus it is between our soul and God because, in the words of our Saviour, we abide in Him and He in us. (*John* 6:57). As the iron is in the fire and the fire in it, absorbing and consuming it entirely, so that they no longer appear to be distinct, so the fire of the Divinity penetrates our soul and takes it to Himself, making it seem identical with God Himself.

This explains more fully and throws more light on what was said in the first Part concerning the deification of the soul. There it was said that the soul is deified, that is, made similar to God; here we add our mystical union with God, which is inseparable from the supernatural similarity. Thus, the deification of the creature implies, not only the greatest possible similarity with God, but also an intimate union with Him. As the creature, raised above itself and deified, loses its imperfections, so in its supernatural union with God it casts off its natural, solitary condition and its dependence on self, to exist no longer in itself and for itself, but in God and for God. Thus we distinguish in the sacred humanity of Christ a twofold deification. The one consists in its personal union with the Eternal Word, the other in its glorification by divine grace. True, we are not so intimately united to God as is the humanity of Christ, but we do really exist in God and for God, and this union finds its best illustration in the union that exists between the Divinity and humanity of Christ.

The deification of the soul by grace presupposes union with the divine Persons and is caused by this union. Just as the branch is similar to the vine and partakes of its life only because it is of the vine and forms one whole with it, so we are made similar to God and partakers of His life only by being received supernaturally by Him and being made one with Him. And as the branch does not exist in itself or for itself but belongs to the tree, so we exist, no longer in and for ourselves, but in God and for Him. It is no longer we who live, but God who exists and lives in us. Thus that great mystery is begun and prepared in us which, according to St. Paul, will form the highest perfection of created nature, that God, namely, will be all in all. (*Col.* 3:11). God is all in us, not only because He has created us, not only because our whole being is dependent on Him, not only because we, as the work of His hands, are His possession and reveal His glory, but because He has drawn us entirely to Himself and has poured Himself out in us, because He absorbs us and unites Himself to us as a drop of water is dissolved by a stream of wine, because, finally, He has grafted us into Himself, as it were, and bears us in His bosom as members of His only-begotten Son, with whom He is perfectly one.

Let us not fear to lose ourselves in this ineffable union with God. We are lost in an unfathomable abyss, an abyss, not of annihilation and darkness, but one of the greatest glory and happiness. We lose ourselves only to find ourselves again in God, or to find God Himself with His whole glory and beatitude. For the more we belong to God, the more He belongs to us; the more we live in Him and for Him, the more He lives in us and for us. Is a branch lost when it is grafted onto a more excellent tree and begins to receive its life from this superior tree? Left to itself, it would have a much less perfect life, but now it can boast not only of the life which it draws from the tree, but also of the life and perfection which the root and the trunk possess for themselves. Thus, when we are united to God by grace, we not only obtain and direct into our soul a ray of divine glory, a small stream of divine life, but we may also consider as our own the divine Sun Itself, the fountain of divine life, and we may rejoice at God's perfections as though they were ours. Hence, by the very fact that we are deified in a twofold manner, we also partake in a twofold manner of the divine beatitude: first, by beholding the beauty and bliss of God as He Himself beholds and enjoys it; secondly, by possessing through grace this glory and bliss and calling it our own.

Is not this the most sublime dignity to which the almighty grace of God can elevate man? Can human reason comprehend the honor conferred on us when we are made one body with Christ, one spirit with God? Can the human heart bear the transporting delight when it learns that its members are members of Christ; that its spirit is made one with the Divine Spirit? With what great love should we be inflamed toward God when we see ourselves so intimately united to Him! Though the love which is based on likeness of character or kinship is great, that love is undoubtedly greater and more intimate which unites indissolubly the various parts of a whole, as the head and the members, or the soul and the body. For in such a case there exists, as St. Paul so beautifully explains, the most intimate unity and communion: "That there might be no schism in the body; but the members might be mutually careful one for another. And if one member suffer any thing, all the members suffer with it; or if one member glory, all the members rejoice with it." (*1 Cor.* 12:25-26). Each member loves himself in others and others in himself. Should we not then love Christ, whose body and members we are, who is the Head, infinitely more dignified and beatifying than the physical head of our body? How greatly we ought to love the Holy Ghost who vivifies our soul more excellently than the soul vivifies the body!

The soul is rendered so dear to the body by its intimate and living union with it, that only with the greatest pains does separation take place in death. And this in spite of the fact that the soul does not raise the body above the defects of its nature. But since union with God deifies the soul, immersing it in the ocean of divine glory and happiness— and this being a union of spirit with spirit, it is far more intimate than that of the body and the soul—must it not bind us to God with the strongest ties? Must we not take the greatest care to preserve it and be unspeakably grieved if this union is destroyed, not by external violence, but by our own will, by the sword of sin?

If a spirit, created outside of the body and perfect in every respect, would of its own accord and out of pure compassion unite itself to a body that lay lifeless and exposed to decay, in order to be made one with it, to give it life and motion and to preserve it from impending dissolution, how much love and gratitude ought this body return to the spirit if it were able to do so? And yet the condescension of this spirit could not be compared to the mercy God shows us when He enters our naked, helpless and miserable soul, and speaking the blessed word "live," produces immediately blissful beauty and immortality? And yet where is the gratitude that we ought to show, where is the love we ought to give Him? Where may we find a thousand hearts and tongues to praise and love so merciful a Father?

Since we are one body with Christ and one spirit with God, and since we abide in God and He in us, we should also live in Him and let Him live and act in us, that we may say with the Apostle: "And I live, now not I; but Christ liveth in me." (*Gal.* 2:20). For all the members of the body live by the life of the head, and the heart lives by the life of the soul that is one with it. The divine heart of Jesus Christ—from which courses the vivifying sap of the Precious Blood through His sacred Body and which contains in itself the plenitude of the Holy Spirit and of divine life—is the heart and the fountain likewise for His whole Mystical Body, that we may all be one heart and one soul with Him. As the individual members of the body do not each have a heart of their own, but all draw the vital fluid from one heart, so we should give up our own heart, immerse it in the divine heart of Jesus and fasten it to Him, that it may seek its nourishment in Him, beat and act only in Him and live by Him and in Him.

What a heavenly life will then be developed in our heart when it dies to itself and is absorbed in the divine heart of Jesus and feels no longer its own pulsations and impulses, but rather those of God! How heavenly will our life be when our Saviour takes our heart out of our breast and places His own in its stead!

We esteem ourselves happy when we possess and may preserve the heart of a dear friend or of a saint who has departed from this life. If we could carry with us such a heart, not dead but alive, and receive it into our breast, into our own heart, our joy would be full. Should we not then ardently desire to take the divine heart of Jesus into our own, where it will communicate its own life to us and take the place of our poor and miserable heart, which is exhausting itself by beating and must soon fall to dust? How can our heart object to this union and transformation and prefer its own miserable life to the divine life? O Jesus, tear my heart away from itself with holy force, though it suffer and bleed ever so much, that it may not hate Thee by perverse love of itself, but may rather love itself truly and recover itself in Thee! Soften its hardness by the fire of Thy divine heart and melt it so that it may receive the impress of Thy image, as molten wax receives the seal.

Union with God and Christ has, moreover, the sublime advantage that we are made one body and one spirit, not only with Christ and God Himself, but with the Saints in Heaven and the just on earth. These are all likewise one body with Christ and one spirit with God. With them we form one great body, of which Christ is the Head and which is vivified by the spirit of God.

". . . One body and one Spirit," says the Apostle! (*Eph.* 4:4), And again "So we being many, are one body in Christ, and every one members one of another." (*Rom.* 12:5). "There is neither Jew nor Greek; there is neither bond nor free; there is neither male nor female. For you are all one in Christ Jesus." (*Gal.* 3:28). Here all distinctions of persons that exist among men disappear, for all are melted together into one great whole, very much as many grains of wheat go to make one loaf of bread. Even the great distinction of nature, which separates us from the Angels, is lost sight of, for we, as well as they, are made one spirit with God. And in our body, by reason of which we are inferior to them, we are made one body with Christ.

Thus united in God, we should also imitate among ourselves the exceedingly intimate union of the Father with the Son in the Holy Spirit. The same Holy Spirit, who, according to St. Augustine, is the bond of union between the Father and the Son, also embraces us all and unites us most intimately with each other, as the soul unites the different members of the body. As a golden chain, He links us to God and Christ and likewise to all the choirs of the blessed spirits, to the Apostles, martyrs, confessors and virgins. In Him we are all joined together and belong to one another.

What joy to belong to this immense, intimate Communion of Saints and in it to possess, together with the countless number of saints, their glory and happiness! For although each member of a body has its peculiar qualities, nevertheless, these same belong likewise to the whole body and to all the other members by reason of the union of all the members of the body. Thus, we may rejoice at the wisdom of the

Cherubim, the burning love of the Seraphim, the dignity of the Apostles, the fortitude of the martyrs, the gift of fore-knowledge possessed by the prophets, the miracles of the confessors, the purity of virgins—we may boast of all these as though they were our own because all proceed from the same Spirit, who dwells also in us and belongs to us as members of the same body. If then the possession of the body of one Saint is so dear to us, how we ought to cherish this living, intimate union and association in the Spirit of God!

How much they are to be pitied who, through blind and perverse passion, suffer themselves to be separated from this most honorable, dignified and amiable society and to be united with the enemies of God, the outcasts of mankind and the inhabitants of Hell! O great and unhappy fall! They were gracious rings on the hand of God, and from this hand they derived their dignity and splendor, and now they have cast themselves into the deepest filth and mire. They were artistically and divinely wrought links in the golden chain of Saints, and by their union with the other members their own beauty and value were enhanced, and now they are fettered to the same chain with the fratricidal Cain and the traitor Judas. They were precious jewels in the crown that adorns the head of God, and now they are the prey of the devil, who has defiled and polluted them and inserted them into this terrible crown of victory.

Let us not be so cruel as to sever our soul from grace and from the Communion of Saints by mortal sin, but let us rather endeavor to maintain this union at any price. Let us make every endeavor to "keep the unity of the Spirit in the bond of peace," as St. Paul exhorts us. (*Eph.* 4:3). Let us thus imitate among us that sublime unity of the Father and Son. Let us unite ourselves ever more closely with God and His saints, that we may become more worthy of their society and that the tie which binds them to us may be drawn closer each day. Let us love our neighbor as ourself, in God and in Christ, united to the Holy Spirit, and thus also to ourselves. In this manner we shall cooperate in the great work which is the end of all Creation so that God may be All in all and we may enjoy that unspeakable happiness that can flow only from perfect union with God and the Saints.

For by this union, the joy we shall experience in the Beatific Vision is multiplied manifold. Here how St. Anselm, in holy ecstasy, describes this: "Human heart," he says, "poor heart that suffers so many tribulations and is immersed in sufferings, how you would rejoice if you possessed all things that are prepared for you in Heaven! Ask your soul if it could comprehend its joy at such great happiness. And if another, whom you loved as yourself, possessed the same happiness as you, your joy would be doubled, as you rejoice no less at his good fortune than at your own. Moreover, if many others enjoyed the same good fortune, you would rejoice for each individually as much as for yourself, if you loved each of them as yourself. In that perfect love of numberless Angels and Saints, in which one loves another no less than himself, each will rejoice for all the others, as much as for himself. If the heart of man cannot comprehend the joy of so great a good, how will it be large enough for so many and such great joys? And since each rejoices at the fortune of another in proportion to the love he has for him, all those in Heaven, loving God incomparably more than themselves or others, will rejoice more at the happiness of God than at their own and that of all the others. . . . My Lord and my God, my Hope and the Joy of my heart, tell my soul whether this is the joy of which Thou didst say through Thy Son: 'Ask and you shall receive; that your joy may be filled.' For I have found a joy that is full, and more than full. For if the heart, the mind, the soul, and the whole man is filled, a super-abundance of joy will still remain. That joy, then, will not fully enter into the rejoicing, but the rejoicing will fully enter into the joy." (*Pros.* c. 25-26).

Christian Soul, if you read and consider these enchanting words, must not your heart kindle with a burning desire to enter into the communion of God and His Saints? Must it not be filled with an ardent gratitude to God, who by His glorious grace, has destined you to such intimate and sublime union with Himself and His Saints? Oh, consider this sweet truth very frequently, meditate upon it unceasingly, and you will certainly not lose—so frivolously—the treasure of grace.

—Part 3—

HOW GRACE WORKS

Chapter 27

LIGHT AS A SYMBOL OF GRACE

IN THE preceding Part, we considered the supernatural, mysterious union with God which grace effects in us. We saw how it makes us living temples of the Holy Ghost and of the entire Holy Trinity and begets divine life in our soul. We saw how it procures for our soul the ineffable dignity of a child, of a friend, of a spouse of God, clothing it with all the privileges and qualities befitting such a position. We saw, finally, how it makes us one body and one spirit with Christ and God.

Now we must examine more carefully the activity and fruits of grace in the soul. Every glance that we have cast at grace has revealed to us new wonders and glories. But we may be certain that its treasury is inexhaustible and that it will continue to excite our admiration and wonder in what is yet to be seen.

We wish to make clearer all that has preceded and all that is to come by representing light as a symbol of grace. In this we are following Holy Scripture and the Fathers.

As light has been called the grace of the sun, so has grace been called by the holy Fathers the light of God. For the sun is indeed the most sublime image of God, who is for the spiritual world what it is for the material world. God is the Sun of justice and of eternal truth, of the highest beauty and of infinite love, of pure glory and perfect blessedness. "God is light, and in him there is no darkness," says St. John. (*1 John* 1:5).

The Divine Nature itself is the purest light. Accordingly, if we become partakers of it through grace, this latter must also be a light—a light that, streaming forth from the innermost being of God, illumines our soul and transforms it

167

from glory to glory into the image of God. (Cf. *2 Cor.* 3:18). And if God Himself is light, and moreover, according to the words of St. James, "the Father of lights," from whom comes "every best gift and every perfect gift" (*James* 1:17), grace, as His best and perfect gift, is also the purest and most sublime light, the father of which is God. It is by that light that we in this life of darkness are at least so far enlightened that we can find the way to our goal. When we have attained this, we shall be introduced to the eternal light of God, which manifests to us the divine splendor in all its depth and allows us to gaze upon it unveiled, face to face.

Through grace we are born of the light of God and the fire of the Holy Ghost. As the children of God, we become "children of the light" (*Eph.* 5:8) and hence are called, as God, *light* itself. Therefore the Apostle says: "For you were heretofore darkness, but now light in the Lord." (*Eph.* 5:8). Similarly, St. Peter says to those having grace: "But you are a chosen generation . . . that you may declare his virtues, who hath called you out of darkness into his marvelous light." (*1 Ptr.* 2:9).

The image of light is so fitting and so beautiful that we cannot speak of grace without speaking of the light of grace. Hence, this image is used regularly in the language of the Church. The Roman Catechism thinks it cannot describe grace to us better than by saying that it is a certain brightness, and a light that washes away all our stains and makes the soul beautiful and resplendent. The holy Fathers call Baptism, by which we are reborn to light through grace, the Sacrament of illumination, or simply *illumination.*

Of all the things that we perceive with our senses, light is indeed the most pure, beautiful, lovely and sublime. Although we see other things through light, yet it is in its nature and being so mysterious that no one has yet discovered exactly what it is, and we know better what it is not than what it is. Although it is in material things, yet it has something spiritual about it because—bound to no particular place, but diffused throughout all space—it penetrates material things and enlivens all nature.

In a similar way grace, itself created, is in the created

spirit a quality making the soul Godlike, yet it is something divine, an outflowing of the Divine Nature and glory. Just as the Divine Nature cannot be perceived in itself—though present in all things and revealing itself in all things—so also is grace an inscrutable source of beauty and glory.

If, now, material light is so rich in its qualities and splendor that we cannot find words to express this, how much more inestimable and unintelligible must be grace in all its richness?

Light is considered with astonishment by all, investigated by scientists, praised by poets. It is called the bloom of colors, the beauty of the world, the smile of Heaven, the joy of nature, the delight of the eye, the quickening of the soul, the image of God, the life of all things, the bond of the universe. But its outstanding praise consists in the fact that it was at the time of Creation the first charm of the world; that it drove away the chaotic darkness from the earth and was first praised by the Creator Himself as good.

And yet, all that is splendid and glorious in material light, and excites our love and admiration, is found in a more excellent and more wonderful way in the light of grace. Material light gives colors to life. Without light, they would be lifeless and vain. Without light, pearls would not be distinguishable from ordinary pebbles, nor velvet from common wool. Precisely so, all created spirits, the souls of men as well as the Angels of Heaven, are by nature shrouded in deathlike darkness. Without grace, they would be, according to St. Augustine, without form or figure, they would count as nothing in God's sight, they would be as though they were not. (*De. Civ. Dei,* 1, 11, c. 11). Only through grace do they appear in that glorious ornament of light that ever charms the eye of God.

If material light is an emanation from the most perfect body, namely, the sun, so is grace an emanation from the most perfect Spirit, the Divine Spiritual Sun, who has established the sun as a weak image of His own splendor. If the material sun makes dark planets become shining stars, grace makes souls to be spiritual stars in the spiritual Heaven, as the Prophet Daniel says: "The light will shine as stars in all eternity." (Cf. *Daniel* 12:3). If material light changes an unspotted mirror or a clear crystal into an image of the material sun, so that one thinks he sees in it the sun itself and can hardly bear its brightness, so grace casts upon the soul the rays of the Divine Sun, clothes the soul with it as with a royal mantle and introduces it into the soul's center as a light into a lamp.

What is brighter than a mirror when it suddenly reflects the full glare of the sun? Although being now accustomed to it, we consider lightly the splendor of this spectacle, it would certainly enrapture our mind and understanding were we to see it now for the first time. But the brightness of this mirror is not even a shadow of the majesty of the soul that receives with grace, not only the image of God, but God Himself, and is filled with all that is most beautiful and glorious in God.

Ancient philosophy spoke of seven operations of light. It penetrates, enlightens, warms and inflames, enlivens, expands, elevates and pictures. Grace also produces all these effects, but in a higher way and in a greater measure.

Light penetrates and brightens the transparent bodies with which it shares itself. Other ornaments, colors, gold and precious stones can adorn bodies only from without. They cannnot give to them an inner beauty. The same is to be said of riches, honors, bodily beauty and even of the natural spiritual qualities which distinguish one man from another, such as learning and culture. All these are merely an external adornment which touches only the surface, not the interior of the soul. But grace, as a divine light, penetrates the soul in all directions, in all its parts and faculties, to the innermost root of its being, transforming it with heavenly beauty and divine splendor.

Light illumines the eye and fills it with images of material things, regardless of whether they are near or distant. It alone shows us the figure and the nature of things whose activity we perceive through the other senses. It carries our perception farther than any other sense, far beyond the limits of the earth, into the most distant stars of the firmament.

Grace does likewise. It enlightens the eye of our soul, or rather, gives us a new eye, enabling us to see a new world. By reason we can have only an external view of truth. We perceive by it only a reflection of eternal truth in the created world, only its efforts and rays, but not this eternal truth itself in its inner nature. The light of grace, however, causes us to see—now by faith and its accompanying wisdom, but hereafter by vision—the visible world and the eternal cause of all things visible and invisible, temporal and eternal, namely, the love of God. It leads us even to the bosom of God, into His never-fading light, making possible to us a glance into the deepest mysteries of His Heart, which by right only the eternal Father and His only-begotten Son, as well as the Holy Ghost, may contemplate. For through grace, "God, who commanded the light to shine out of darkness, hath shined in our hearts, to give the light of the knowledge of the glory of God, in the face of Christ Jesus." (*2 Cor.* 4:6).

Light warms and inflames bodies, for it is related to heat. In the divine Sun, more yet than in the material sun, air and heat are inseparably united. Out of the light of the Father and the Son proceeds the fire of the Holy Ghost, the divine flame of love. And so God through grace enkindles in our hearts, not only the light of faith, but also the lovable and beatifying fire of His divine love.

The light of the sun calls forth and preserves life in the whole of nature. When, during the night, the sun disappears for a short time, all life on earth goes to sleep: the petals of the flowers close; the songs of the birds are silenced; all faculties grow tired, and all living things longingly await the coming day. When the sun withdraws somewhat in winter, bestowing its blessings only in half measure, the life of plants is extinguished, field and meadow are changed into bleak desert—until the returning spring, with the full blessing of the sun, brings back new life.

The light of grace works yet more powerfully in the soul. Without grace, the soul does not have even the seed of that heavenly life to which God has called us. But through grace it becomes a glorious paradise that blooms in a perpetual springtime, and knowing neither night nor winter, constantly brings forth new blooms, though the old ones do not wither. It enraptures the eye and the heart of God by the brilliancy of its colors and the fragrance of its flowers. We alone are at fault if sometimes, because of our laziness, it becomes night, or if a cold wind takes away the warmth of divine love.

Through heat, its inseparable companion, light expands gold and all metals. To air it does the same thing, making it elastic. Grace expands still more the narrow vessel of our soul. For insofar as it not only illumines but also fills with warmth and power, it enables the soul to gain new and greater treasures of grace. The more we use grace, the greater becomes our capacity for receiving it. It increases the elasticity of our soul, extending its activity far beyond the limits of its natural abilities and inducing it to magnanimously desire and undertake even greater things, until the whole world itself is too narrow a field for its activity and God alone in His infinite perfection can fully satisfy it.

Through the power of light, warm air rises from the earth towards Heaven, plants come out of the earth's bosom and turn toward the source of light in order to sun themselves in the light and to drink in its blissful rays. Grace, likewise, raises our soul to the Divine Sun and causes it to turn with ardent desire towards It, so that it rises upward and grows until it is united with God. All spiritual growth proceeds from It.

Light, finally, pictures things as they really are. This long-known property we grasp now fully for the first time, for we form the truest and most faithful pictures with light. Human art can with all its instruments form no more perfect picture than that which we are able to make light itself bring forth on an artificially prepared plate. Under the influence of the sun plants unfold in that form which they must take on according to their nature and the plan of their Creator. There is no truer picture of a man than that which light forms of him in a mirror.

In a similar way, God cannot produce in us a more perfect image of Himself than through the light of grace. He has

painted in nature various images of His goodness, His justice, His fruitfulness, but only according to a certain measure, and therefore they are by no means a perfect representation of Him. But through grace He allows the light of
His nature to flow into us as into a mirror, that it may work
in the fullness of its power and thus produce, not merely an
outline, but a full, true and living picture of His sanctity.

We should continue to consider the glories of grace under
the image of material light, for it is the symbol of all that is
good and beautiful, of all that is lovable, mild, friendly, gentle, stimulating, beatifying, pure, holy, perfect, strengthening, radiant and glorious. The more we rejoice at its advantages, the more we will be delighted by its excellence, invisible to the bodily eye, but visible to the eye of faith, especially when we see that the symbol and figure is far inferior
to the reality.

Now if material light is so dear and valuable to us that we
would consider the privation of it to be almost as terrible as
death itself, must we not treasure the light of grace in an
infinitely greater degree? To be in darkness and no longer
able to see the light of heaven was a hard blow for Tobias,
and took from him, as he himself said, all the joy in life. (Cf.
Tobias 5:12). But is he not far more miserable who, deprived
of the light of God by grievous sin and cast down into the
deep night of the spirit, taps his way around without light,
stumbles and falls over everything, is cast into the most
frightful abyss and thrust away from the face of God,
nowhere finding rest or joy?

Tobias preserved, in his bodily blindness, the light of grace.
He could, therefore, bear patiently the material darkness
because he was certain that for the sight he had lost on earth
an eternal light would be given him in Heaven. The sinner,
however, if he does not convert, has no hope ever to regain
the light of grace and must fear that in the darkness of Hell
even the light of reason that is left to him will show him
nothing else except what will add to his fright and misery.

It is said that as St. Francis Borgia was once celebrating
Holy Mass in a certain city of Portugal, it became suddenly
so dark that the stars could be seen at noonday. The inhab-

itants there were so shocked, thinking that the Last Judgment was about to take place, that they filled the city with weeping and lamenting, and leaving their houses, they hastened to the churches as the best place of refuge. There they hoped to find safety under the protection of the holy man. But when their crying and lamenting was not lessened there, St. Francis energetically called their attention to the zeal and care they should take lest the rays of the Divine Sun go down upon them forever, seeing that they were so troubled by the present momentary darkness. He reminded them that they were deprived of this true heavenly light by every mortal sin and that the consequent evils were indeed inestimable and indescribable.

We ourselves see, on the occasion of an eclipse of the sun, how gloomy nature becomes. The birds flutter about anxiously, animals seek a safe retreat, and we also would be terrified if we did not know that the light of the sun was not extinguished, but only covered, and soon to reappear in full splendor. May we be likewise terrified at the mere thought of closing our heart by a mortal sin to the sun of grace and perhaps of extinguishing its light in us forever. In order that we may always keep the heavenly light of grace in us, we must cleanse our hearts from all stain and filth.

As a light cannot be reflected from a mirror that is not smooth and pure or penetrate a body that is not clear and transparent, so grace cannot penetrate a soul that is not free from the filth of sin. We see material light with the eyes, spiritual light with the heart. In order to enjoy material light, the eye must be clear; for the enjoyment of the spiritual light, the heart must be pure. The less we stain our souls with the dust of venial sins, the less we soil it by clinging to earthly or even sinful things, the more grace pours its heavenly light into the soul and reveals its divine splendor. Hence our Saviour says, "Blessed are the clean of heart, for they shall see God." (*Matt.* 5:8).

We are told how to keep the light of grace from being extinguished in our soul by St. John Chrysostom (*In 1 Thess. Hom.* 11. n. 1), commenting on the words of the Apostle, "Extinguish not the spirit" (*1 Thess.* 5:19): "Heavy darkness," he says, "night and dark clouds cover the earth. That is what St. Paul expresses in the words, 'You were once darkness.' (*Eph.* 5:8). Accordingly, since dark night surrounds us in which no moon shines and we wander about in this night, God has given us a splendid lamp by enkindling in our hearts the grace of the Holy Spirit. Some, as Peter and Paul and all the Saints, have made this light more splendid, joyous, and friendly; others have extinguished it after the example of the foolish virgins, as those who suffered shipwreck in the faith, as the one guilty of incest at Corinth and the apostate Galatians. Hence, St. Paul says: '*Extinguish not the spirit,*' (*1 Thess.* 5:19), for thus he is accustomed to call grace. But grace is extinguished by a sinful life. For as one extinguishes a lamp by throwing water or earth upon it, or by taking the oil out of it, so does it also happen with grace. When you cast upon it superfluous care for earthly and perishable things, you extinguish the Spirit. Likewise, when like a strong wind a powerful temptation comes, all is lost if the flame is not strong enough, or does not have enough oil, or if the cover is removed from the lamp, or the door of the house left open. What is this door? What the door is to the house, that our eyes and our ears are to us. Do not permit a strong wind of temptation to come through and extinguish the lamp, but close the door with the fear of God. The mouth also is a door which you must lock and fasten. Then the light can enter, but every dangerous draft from without is excluded. For example, if someone has insulted or cursed you, close your mouth. For if you open it, you only increase the storm. Do you not see that the strong draft that blows through when two opposite doors in a house are open becomes powerless as soon as one of the doors is shut? So also here: The two doors are your mouth and that of the one who insults you. If you close yours and allow no wind to go through, you weaken the storm; but if you leave yours open, the storm cannot be checked. Therefore, let us not extinguish the Spirit.

"It often happens, however, that the flame dies out even when there is no storm. When the oil is used up, that is, when we do not give alms, the Spirit is extinguished. For this same Spirit comes to you as an alms from God, and if He does not see in you the fruit of alms, He departs again, for He cannot remain in an unmerciful soul.

"If the Spirit is extinguished, the consequences are known to everyone who has ever sought his way on a moonless night. It is difficult to travel at night from one part of the earth to another, how can it be safe to climb at night the steep way that leads from earth to Heaven? Do you not know how many enemies are found between these two places, how many wild animals, how many spirits of wickedness? If we have the light of grace, they will not be able to hurt us; but if we have extinguished it, they will catch us and take away all our goods. Thieves themselves begin to steal only after they have extinguished the lights. They see in the dark because they do the works of darkness; whereas, we are not accustomed to the light of darkness."

Chapter 28

THE WONDERFUL POWER WHICH GRACE HAS TO DESTROY MORTAL SIN

THE FIRST effect of the light of grace is the removal of the awful night of grave sin. This is done as soon as grace is infused into the soul, that is, at the moment of justification.

Grace is not only inexhaustibly fruitful in heavenly goods and blessings, it is also powerful and strong in driving out evil. Hence, the soul adorned with grace is compared in the *Canticle of Canticles* with a well-arranged line of battle and with the horsemen of Pharaoh. (Cf. *Canticle of Canticles* 1:8, 6:3, 9).

Bodily medicines have special value, not in their expense, their odor, their taste or appearance—for they are of ugly appearance, of bitter taste and of disagreeable odor—but in their power of healing. For this reason they are sought in the bowels of the earth and in the depths of the sea and are brought from the most distant countries.

The medicine of grace, on the other hand, is doubly precious. First of all, its value lies in this, that it not only gives to us none of those diseases that require so much medicine, but is even lovable in the highest degree and pleasant to use. Moreover, it contains unlimited heavenly powers and such a wonderful virtue of healing that it overcomes death and every sickness of the soul and wipes away the greatest of evils—that evil which alone is worthy of the name and can be done away with by no other power in Heaven or on earth.

Here one may, with the Psalmist, call on mankind: "Understand, ye senseless among the people: and, you fools, be wise at last." (*Ps.* 93:8). Your sensuality, your anger, your concupiscence deceive you when, contrary to the words of the Holy Ghost, they tell you that poverty, sickness, pain, insults, and death itself are true evils.

Sin alone is the true evil. Sin alone cannot be good. All else can be good for us and can give honor to God. Sin alone cannot be caused by God; whereas, He loves and treasures everything else. When the Son of God, who certainly knows how to distinguish genuine good from evil, came into this world to take away evil and to give us good things, He took to Himself everything else: He bore all sufferings and every insult; He became like us in all things, sin excepted. Sin alone He most definitely avoided. To destroy it, He gave His life and His Blood and wished to bear all other evils in order to drive from us this one alone. We do not wish in any way to hurt those who suffer. We agree with them when they say that things which take away our life or other earthly goods are painfully evil. Admitting this, sin is still the greatest of evils, or better, it is the only true evil of all; it alone deserves the name *evil* without any qualification. It is the only evil that God has not made.* It robs us of the highest, infinite Good, God Himself. It is also a monster, so frightful and terrible that all other evils draw back from it.

Sin is, moreover, the source of all other evils which ever have covered or ever will cover the earth with misery. All the wars that have slaughtered millions of men, all the epidemics, which have laid waste whole countries, in short, all the misfortunes that have taken place on the earth since the fall of Adam—all these are the sad fruit of sin. The one

---

*Strictly speaking, God does not create *any* evil. "For God made not death, neither hath he pleasure in the destruction of the living. For he created all things that they might be: and he made the nations of the earth for health: and there is no poison of destruction in them, nor kingdom of hell upon the earth." (*Wis.* 1:13-14). Philosophically considered, evil is "the absence of the proper good" in a thing. Through earthly causes, evil, or the absence of good, can result. God allows this for a higher good: "And we know that to them that love God, all things work together unto good . . ." (*Rom.* 8:28). But moral evil consciously done, called sin, is done by man and not in any respect by God. For God, being Goodness itself, cannot be the author of evil. —*Publisher*, 2000.

cruel drop of poison of that one sin has infected and poisoned the whole human race with all evils.

Against this fruitful poison there is no other remedy but the Blood of the God-man, together with its power and fruit—divine grace. An infinite evil demands a remedy that is infinitely powerful. We must drink the Blood of Christ as medicine; by this Blood we must cleanse ourselves from our leprosy. We do this when we receive into ourselves that stream of grace which flows out of the side of Christ, in which we wash away our sins and from which we receive new life.

As soon as we receive grace, we are changed from enemies into children of God, and then we may appear before God with confidence and placate His anger. We have thus put on Christ, and in His justice and true sanctity, we are exceedingly pleasing to the heavenly Father. Just as God cannot hate His only-begotten Son, neither can He hate those who, through grace, have become the living members of His Son and bear in themselves His image.

A man can hate his own child, continuing to hold against it a fault committed, without the child thereby ceasing to be his. But God cannot hate His children, because they are at the same time His friends and His spouses, because He sees Himself in them, and finally, because He has received them into intimate union with Himself.

The great evil of sin consists in man's turning his love away from God and God's turning His love away from man, so that an enormous and frightful chasm is formed between them. Conversely, the wonderful power of grace in destroying this evil consists in this, that it alone removes that double chasm, reuniting man with God and God with man. Man cannot by his own power so change his evil will and raise it again to God as to be enabled to embrace Him with supernatural love. Much less can he thus draw God down into his soul, so as to be again taken into God's arms as His child.

Only grace effects both of these things. It pours into our souls the supernatural love of the Holy Ghost through which we again cling to God. At the same time it draws down on us all the love of the heavenly Father, so that He forgets our sins and considers our soul as His friend and spouse. Oh, how great and wonderful is the power of grace, which, as heavenly medicine, destroys that evil against which no created power on earth or in Heaven can prevail, against which only the God-man and the omnipotence of God is effective. This will appear still more wonderful if we consider the way in which grace effects its task.

Grace is not only strong enough to wipe out one sickness; for it takes no account whatever of the number or greatness of the diseases. Even if one had committed all the sins and crimes from the fratricide of Cain to the devilish exaltation of the Antichrist at the End of Time, the smallest ray of Sanctifying Grace coming into the soul would so destroy them all that they would disappear at once, for the least degree of this divine holiness overcomes even the greatest wickedness.

We may also add that, when grace sanctifies our soul, it does not leave the least trace of mortal sin. It does not, indeed, always destroy the inclinations to sin which flow from natural perverseness or previous evil habits, but it always removes from the soul all that is really wicked and deserving of condemnation. Accordingly, St. Paul says: "There is now therefore no condemnation to them that are in Christ Jesus" (*Rom.* 8:1) through grace. And the holy Council of Trent teaches that God no longer hates anything in those reborn in Baptism. (*Conc. Trid. sess.* 5, c. 5).

If our sins are as scarlet, they will be made, as God assures us through His prophet, white as snow (*Is.* 1:18); and if they are as red as crimson, they will be as clean wool. The same idea is expressed even more clearly by another Prophet (cf. *Mich.* 7:19), who promises us that God will plunge our sins into the depths of the ocean, in order to bury them so deep that they may never again return, even though we commit other sins.

It is yet more wonderful that no matter how great or numerous our sins may be, grace heals them in a moment without trouble or delay. It does not need to struggle with them for a long time; the beginning of the fight is also the victorious end. Just as God at the time of Creation commanded that there be light, and immediately there was light, so grace needs but to come and to command and the night of sin disappears.

Scarcely had David acknowledged to the Lord that he had sinned, when he heard that his sin was taken away. Scarcely had he brought himself to admit his injustice, when he saw his wickedness forgiven and God again reconciled with him. Such a definite, sudden and perfect cure is called in the visible world a miracle. Shall we then wonder less at this triumph of grace over the most powerful and frightful enemy, whom no other power can force, because it is not visible? Or shall we refrain from considering such a wonderful healing simply because it does not happen exceptionally, as is the case with miracles, but through the mercy of God is repeated time and again?

It appears to us superfluous that the Divine Saviour should have warned the man whom He had miraculously healed to avoid sin lest something worse happen to him. (Cf. *John* 5:14). For a man will do all he can to avoid a relapse into such a sickness. But we must be ashamed when we think of all that we do to avoid bodily sickness. We do and suffer so much that the rigor of the most zealous penitent can hardly be greater. If the sick person wants to drink, it is not permitted to him; if he wishes to eat, he is told to wait. If the doctors wish to open an artery or to cut and cauterize the wound, the sick person surrenders his limb or body. He does not get up, he does not go out without the permission of the doctor. He remains shut in and lying by himself; he denies himself the most desirable pleasures, offers money and property—all this in the uncertain and often deceptive hope of a brief enjoyment of health, which, even if regained, is soon lost again.

On the other hand, what is more negligently sought and treated with less esteem than grace, the easy and only remedy for the deadly diseases of the soul—grace which frees the soul together with the body from eternal death, grace which leads us infallibly to immortal life! O thoughts of men, how clever you are in indifferent and worthless things and how blind in those things that are of the greatest value to you! Let us consider what an ineffable grace God has shown us by forgiving our sins, in order that we may so much the more carefully avoid relapse into sin, mindful of the sacrifice and the penitential works that our Divine Saviour has offered for us, and of the goodness with which the heavenly Father has accepted this as a substitute for our incapacity.

Let us also remember that we are obliged, according to the measure of our weakness, to do for the perfect cure of our spiritual sickness at least some of that which we so readily do to restore our weakened bodily powers. Even reasonable self-love must teach us that without penance and self-denial we can never be fully healed. If that be difficult for us, it will be sweetened not a little by love, which enables us to say with the Apostle: I now "rejoice in my sufferings for you, and fill up those things that are wanting of the sufferings of Christ, in my flesh, for his body, which is the Church." (*Col.* 1:24).

Chapter 29

GRACE INFUSES INTO OUR SOULS THE SUPERNATURAL DIVINE VIRTUES

INSOFAR AS grace wipes out sin, it effects at the same time our justification. According to the teaching of the Council of Trent (Sess. 6 c. 7), the forgiving of sin, the sanctification and renewal of the inner man and the infusion of the three theological virtues, Faith, Hope and Charity, are one and the same thing. We have seen before how grace plants in our soul a supernatural, heavenly and divine life, the life of the children of God, reborn of the Holy Ghost. Here we learn in what this life consists, in what faculties it exists and in what activity it reveals itself.

We can perceive life only in its effects, but from these we can draw conclusions regarding its nature. Following this method, the philosophers as well as spiritual writers affirm that life is that inner power which enables a being to rule and move itself from within. Now the natural life of the soul, that by which man is distinguished from the animals, shows itself above all in the activities of the natural powers of the soul, especially in the acts of the intellect and will. Supernatural life, therefore, shows itself in the activity of the intellect and will enlightened and moved by grace.

As grace perfects the essence of the soul and makes it partaker of the Divine Nature, that is, of the sanctity of God, so it also perfects the faculties of the soul, that they may produce actions as high and sublime as is necessary to correspond with the divine holiness. It gives to them, accordingly, a new, higher capability, by which they can produce acts of virtue which, by right, only God can perform. These supernatural capabilities, which are infused into us by grace and through which grace produces its effect by means of our cooperation, are called by the theologians *supernatural infused virtues.*

There is a great difference between the infused virtues and the so-called acquired virtues, those, namely, that we can appropriate to ourselves by our own activity. These consist in a certain readiness, acquired by our own practice and effort, by which we are enabled to perform with greater facility, decision, quickness and ease acts that are naturally possible. They may be compared with the fruitfulness which may be imparted to a tree through care, irrigation and watchful protection from all evil influences. By such efforts, one does not seek to have the tree produce fruit of a different species, but only that it produces its own fruit with more certainty, of improved quality and of greater quantity.

The infused virtues, on the other hand, are like the fruitfulness that we can implant in a tree by grafting on it a branch from another, more excellent tree. Their principal activity consists in this, that our souls bring forth fruits of a far more noble and excellent kind, for which nature has not even placed in man a seed.

At the same time, the infused virtues give to the soul a certain ease in the exercise of supernatural acts. However, they do not root out at once all evil inclinations and weaknesses of our nature. We must, therefore, with God's help, remove the impediments to the divine life in us, and by cooperating with the supernatural power infused by God, acquire facility in its exercise.

Another image will help to show the difference between the natural and the supernatural virtues. Iron is tempered by fire and is magnetized by being rubbed upon a magnet. The tempered iron is harder and better than ordinary iron, but its nature is not changed. But magnetized iron seems to be an entirely different material. As if by magic, it loses its inertia and immovability, acquires a new power of attraction and is in a mysterious way drawn by the poles of the earth.

The natural virtues do nothing else but temper our spiritual faculties and strengthen them, that by frequent practice and the help of God, they may do that which by nature is good. Grace, on the other hand, magnetizes our faculties by a mysterious contact with the Divinity, which communicates to them Its own divine power. Thus, they are changed into new divine faculties; they feel themselves attracted by higher, undreamed-of objects and raised up into mysterious regions, as by an invisible hand. God Himself becomes the pole, the center and the source of our life: the pole for which it strives, the center around which it revolves, the source from which it draws its nourishment. That is what is meant when it is said that we share in the inner life of God.

The participation in the divine life which is effected in us by the infused supernatural virtues consists principally in the fact that we imitate in ourselves the divine activity or holiness, that we unite ours with it, and through it unite ourselves to God, as far as possible. This we do by knowledge, love and trust, in a similar way as the three Divine Persons are one in their unity of thought, love and action. Grace is given to us that we may be holy, and sanctity is the goal of grace. When we accept grace, we oblige ourselves to strive after supernatural perfection and holiness, which consists in becoming like God. Grace would fail to attain its goal if it did not lead us to holiness. But that is holy which leads to God and thus makes us like God, or which unites us with God because it is like Him.

In Christian faith we attain a supernatural knowledge insofar as our knowledge follows Divine Revelation, by which we are enabled to know God as He knows Himself.

In Christian charity there is infused into our souls by the Holy Ghost a love similar to that by which God loves Himself, so that we love Him, not merely because of His benefits toward us, but because of His own goodness. Hence, we pray: "I love Thee, O my God, because Thou art in Thyself the highest, most perfect, and most lovable Good."

In Christian hope, finally, we support ourselves immediately on the infinite power of God, as though it were our own. Thus, we experience that sublime trust, not only to obtain God's help for all our needs in this life, but to be able to possess and enjoy God Himself in all His greatness and for all eternity.

Christian faith is accordingly a supernatural and divine

knowledge; Christian charity is a supernatural and divine love; Christian hope is a supernatural and divine trust. Hence these three virtues are called the divine or Theological Virtues. They are thus called, not because they are especially related to God, but because they unite us more intimately and immediately, in a divine way, we may say, with God. The other virtues have their own proper activity and their special objects, and only through these do they attain God. The Theological Virtues have God Himself as their primary and exclusive object and at the same time as an immediate motive, and therefore they can be produced in us only by a communication of the Divine Nature.

It is with these divine virtues that God equips His children that they may be able to lead a life worthy of their new condition and may, already in this land of exile here on earth, be united with Him as their Father and the object of their happiness. It is also especially through these virtues that we may prepare ourselves for life everlasting, that life which we are one day to enjoy with our heavenly Father. For the life that we, as children of God, should lead already here on earth must be of the same kind as that which awaits us in Heaven. But in Heaven we shall know God as He knows Himself and enjoy Him as He enjoys Himself.

According to the explicit teaching of Holy Church, the light of glory is necessary for such a knowledge and enjoyment. This light strengthens the faculties of our soul and makes them God-like. Therefore, in this life also the faculties of our soul must be elevated and made God-like, that we may be able to know and love God in a way that is similar—though not in the same degree—to the way in which we shall know and love Him forever in Heaven. This also serves as a basis for our confident hope that this perfect knowledge and love will be ours.

It is certain that God has through grace made us His children and heirs of Heaven. It is also certain that He gives every being the means necessary to attain its end. Finally, it is just as certain that, through grace, God equips His children with those divine virtues without which they cannot be united to Him in a supernatural way. The more we investigate the riches of nature, the more clearly do we see how God has so equipped even the lowest of creatures that they can preserve their being and fulfill their purpose. The higher the kingdom of grace is, the more certain we can be that here, too, all has been carefully provided for in favor of the children of God.

Consider the plants. They have roots that go deep into the ground in order to seek there the necessary moisture to support and strengthen the whole. They have their stems, that unceasingly tend toward the light, from which they receive warmth and life. They possess certain powers of attraction and production in order to draw up and assimilate the matter suitable for their maintenance and the development of their life.

But what is the soul that is adorned with grace? It also is a plant, a wild olive branch, grafted onto Jesus Christ as onto a noble olive tree. (Cf. *Rom.* 11:24). It has its roots in faith, which penetrate into the depths of the Godhead, to draw thence the nourishment of divine life. Hope is its trunk, by which it is lifted up to the Sun of Justice, to find there light and warmth. Love is the drawing power with which it takes hold of God, to receive His own life into itself, or rather, to bury itself in Him.

The bird, that God has destined to move in the air, has received from Him feathers and wings that enable it to soar on high; and each one, according to its manner of flying, is so formed that it can remain in the thin air and perform incredible feats of strength. This is an image of the children of God. Out of the depth of their nature, by reason of which they belong to the earth, they rise to God on the wings of faith, hope and love; they feel at home in regions of which the earthly-minded can hardly think without dizziness. When they cooperate faithfully with grace, they perform incredible things, the accounts of which are placed in the category of fables or deceit by the backward wisdom of man.

Indeed, grace does not do this alone. Even the greatest gifts of God remain without effect if there be no corresponding fidelity in their use. But when a man directs his own efforts according to the quantity of supernatural power received, he can do things that otherwise would appear to him as legends or, at most, as miracles that God permits only to those whom He loves in a special way. No matter how artistically a ship may have been built, it does not sail of itself. But as soon as strong arms have taken hold of its rudder and the sails are unfurled or the fire enkindled, developing a mighty steam power, the ship begins to move, launches out into the deep, cuts through the waves with great speed and in a few days reaches a distant part of the earth where it is laden with treasures and then begins its return journey.

In a similar way, the Christian is cast out on the stormy waves of this world to seek the harbor of Heaven. His natural powers may be sufficient to sail a small boat from one bank to the other on a narrow river or lake. But on the wide ocean that separates the finite from the infinite, he needs an entirely different means and other powers to reach the distant shore. These powers God gives in the divine virtues. Faith is our compass that directs us infallibly to our heavenly home, which of ourselves we cannot see. Hope takes the place of rudder and sails, giving us a supernatural trust that we shall reach so distant a goal. It increases our courage and assures us of the all-powerful help of God. Love, finally, is the principle of motion, a holy and mighty propelling power that brings us more surely and more quickly to God than steam bears a ship over the ocean. By the power of these virtues, we sail forward courageously, combat the storms, overcome the billows, avoid the rocks and shoals and arrive safely at the port of eternity.

Oh, how great is the goodness of God, how great the splendor of His grace, which raises so high and transforms all the powers of our spiritual nature, which introduces into our soul all these three virtues in order to infuse into it a heavenly and divine life! May all Christians consider often the sublimity of these divine virtues and really feel their delightfulness and lovableness through the fervent use of them. Then they will certainly not make so light of them and of their source, grace, but will take pride in being allowed to possess and foster a divine life in their soul.

Chapter 30

SUPERNATURAL DIVINE FAITH

THE FIRST of these three divine virtues is faith. The subject or seat of faith is our intellect, which illumines and strengthens, enabling it to partake of the knowledge of God and to know with certainty the mysteries which naturally are hidden from every created eye, being known to God alone. It places a new eye in our soul; or better, it allows us to look through the eye of God and thus makes us partakers of the divine knowledge. If through grace we are made to share in the Divine Nature, we must also take part in the knowledge that is proper to this nature. We must, as St. Paul says, know God as He knows us. (Cf. *1 Cor.* 13:12).

This, of course, will take place perfectly only when grace has become perfect in us, that is, in the light of glory; and when in the bosom of the Father, on the side of His only-begotten Son, by the power of His light, we see Him as He is, face to face. But neither does God forget His children in this land of exile. Even now, they should know Him, their crown and inheritance; and since no one knows the Father except Himself and His Son, with the Holy Ghost, He must reveal Himself to us through His own Word. But since we cannot with our natural powers grasp this Divine Word in a fitting way, He must make us capable of believing it by giving us supernatural strength and light.

There is something uncommonly wonderful about this divine faith. If the world does not consider it as something great, it is because, according to the teaching of St. Ambrose, the narrow heart of the earthly-minded cannot grasp the greatness of faith. The world thinks that faith is something only for the weak and uneducated, that it is a sign of littleness and weakness of mind. On the contrary, as

189

St. Leo says, faith is the only vital force of great souls. (*Sermo 43 de Quad*, 5, c. 2).

All the Faithful know, adds the holy Pope, that God's Providence watches over all men and all things. But as soon as evil tongues begin to move against us, as soon as the opposition of the worldly-minded knocks at our hearts, as soon as the lust of the world works on our passions, our understanding is darkened, our heart is taken captive and God is forgotten. Only a few are strong enough not to be shaken by that which so easily constitutes a danger for the ordinary Christian.

Indeed, strong faith is necessary to form strong souls. But stronger souls are also needed in order to build up a stronger faith. It is true that a frivolous human faith—by which one believes other men without sufficient reason and without valid proof—is a sign of weakness and littleness of mind. Divine faith, on the other hand, is the most excellent and dignified act of a rational creature, because by it man submits himself to the highest, infallible intellect, which has revealed itself to him through clear and undeceiving signs.

Rather than see in faith a sign of weakness and limitation, we must say that all human power and wisdom, yes, even that of the Angels, is not enough to make an act of faith as God requires, unless help be had from on high. The most that a created spirit in its greatest natural perfection can do is to subject itself to God's word in deep reverence and unconditional obedience as a rational creature, and to submit its own judgment to Him who is the Supreme Wisdom. But, by its own power, the creature cannot raise itself to God nor unite its judgment with His. Neither can it embrace supernatural truths with the same firmness of will and conviction of mind as it grasps natural truths, but it holds these supernatural truths with even greater firmness because it does not accept them by reason of its own knowledge, but by reason of its subjection to the truthfulness of God, which excludes every possibility of error. The result of casting oneself thus on God is that the knowledge of man takes on the firmness, if not the clearness, of divine knowledge and partakes of its infallibility.

This presupposes faith, of which one is capable only through supernatural grace. This alone gives one the power to ascend high enough to receive the word of God as though it actually came from His mouth—which, indeed, is really the case. (Cf. *1 Thess.* 2:13). It is only through faith that a man supports himself on God as on a solid rock and finds in Him unfailing security and certainty, a far greater firmness than is given by any human experience, knowledge or support.

From this we easily see that we are far from divine faith when we accept a truth because we think that we understand its sense or the reason on which it is based. That may be human faith, which is based on one's own view or on the assurance of others; it is not divine faith. This always has as its ultimate motive divine truth. Even in cases where the human mind can penetrate more or less the object of faith, we may not hold that we accept it because we understand it or insofar as we can explain it; but here also, the final and deepest reason of our faith must be our subjection to God and the veracity of Him who can neither deceive nor be deceived. If we overlook this fact, we may easily deceive ourselves and imagine that we have divine faith when it is only human. Hence, our Divine Saviour says that no one can come to Him by faith unless he be drawn by the Father. (Cf. *John* 6:44).

The act of faith surpasses all natural power; it is supernatural in the full sense of the word. We do not wish to say that it is impossible for man to make an act of faith. It is a human act, freely made and reasonable. But no one can make such an act unless supernatural grace—which is denied to no one—be given him by God. That is what is meant when revelation teaches that faith is a supernatural gift. This it is because the ability to make an act of faith must be given by God.

But it is not to be said that faith is to be found in him into whom God infuses it in such a way that the recipient has nothing at all to do about it. Indeed, it is for this very reason that faith is something so great and wonderful, because, on the one hand, it is so great a grace, and on the other, it demands of the human spirit so great and heroic an effort. He who practices faith is not weak, but strong beyond imagination. His power of understanding is not little, but is almost unlimited. Faithful souls are truly great and strong spirits—far greater and stronger than all the worldly wise. For these latter are supported only by the vacillating need of their natural reason, which is tossed about by the winds of their humors and passions. (Cf. *Eph.* 4:14). The souls of the faithful are, however, truly manly and strong, since by faith they sink anchor into divine truth. With supernatural security they defy all storms, and with unshaken conviction they hold to the principles of the highest truths.

But grace gives us not only such supernatural strength as is necessary for divine faith, it is also a supernatural light that enlightens us in coming to faith and enabling us to believe, not blindly, but with open eyes. To be able to believe, we must know that God Himself speaks to us. This we can know by natural reason, if we consider attentively the external signs that accompany revelation. But if God did not enlighten us internally in a mysterious way and place a new inner ear into our heart, we could not recognize and accept His word in the way necessary for the act of faith.

It is with good reason that grace is described in the language of the Holy Scripture and the Church as a *light*. It never works on the heart and will alone, but also enlightens the intellect, and through the enlightened intellect, operates in the soul.

The same thing holds for faith. One speaks of the obscurity of faith, and rightly so, for the mysteries that we embrace through faith are so deep and so sublime that reason is not only unable to understand them, even when they are revealed, but the nearer it approaches them, the more it is blinded by their splendor. Nevertheless, this obscurity is still brighter and allows us to know more than does reason. Therefore, one speaks rightly of the *light* of faith. Faith compared with reason is as the morning twilight compared with the semi-darkness of dusk, wherein one can hardly distinguish the outlines of things. This twilight is already an effect of the full light that awaits us when day breaks. And if our eyes were not strengthened by grace, we could not bear these first rays any more than the owl, which sees well enough in the dark but cannot find its way about when the first rays of dawn appear.

The supernatural attraction of grace is not a blind and obscure attraction, but a bright and enlightening one that represents to us our supernatural destiny in all its divine splendor and draws us toward it. Grace is like a heavenly ether whose vibrations communicate to us the voice of God far better than the earthly atmosphere of our senses and reason. By grace we perceive the Divine Word immediately, as it proceeds from God's mouth; we feel its divine power and, precisely because of this, we are moved to accept it. Therefore, the Apostle teaches that God enlightens the eyes of our heart through grace and opens its ear that we may know—and know supernaturally—whom we believe. (Cf. *Eph.* 1:18).

After we have thus, by the light and strength of grace, grasped and received into us the word of God, we must by the same supernatural light learn to understand, at least to some extent, the truths which God reveals to us. For these truths are so sublime that the light of reason is as incapable of understanding them as it is of revealing them to us. Though a man born blind may hear a very accurate and detailed description of the objects we see, he will nevertheless always have a very imperfect knowledge of them. The same would apply to us in regard to supernatural truths if God, who reveals them to us by His Word, did not at the same time infuse into us the supernatural light of grace, which little by little gives us some understanding of them. How thorough this understanding will be will depend on our cooperation with grace.

For here also, grace does not work alone, but we must cooperate with it. As without the light of faith we can neither discover nor penetrate supernatural truths, neither do we arrive at a clearer understanding of them without making an effort ourselves. Just as we do not accept the faith as a rational conclusion that cannot be refuted, neither does it grow in us without our cooperation. Faith is more an affair of the free, well-disposed will than of pure reason. Therefore, we must not think that mere study and research are sufficient. Those who have time and talent are indeed obliged to study, but it is prayer and meditation that will lead them, as well as all the Faithful, to a deeper knowledge of God. A pure heart gives more light concerning the eternal truths than a keen intellect; and true piety, together with earnest striving after virtue, brings God nearer to the simple than science brings Him to the learned. Hence, we have the sad possibility that one may spend his whole life studying the most sublime truths, and at the same time grow less fervent in faith, or even lose it.

Of course, we never attain in this world an immediate vision of the mysteries that would do away with faith. Nevertheless, they can become as clear and understandable as conditions in this dark world permit. Indeed, it is not difficult to penetrate the mysteries of faith. How deeply many souls are penetrated with their truth—to say *convinced* is not enough—and yet they may have only mediocre intellectual abilities! But they have a clean heart and deep piety and live conscientiously according to their knowledge. To these the Holy Ghost daily opens new sources of light through which they put the wise to shame. How foolish are they who see nothing else in faith but darkness and oppression of reason!

Our reason, though very powerful if considered in itself, is, when compared to the knowledge of faith, only an earthly light, illuminating creatures with its feeble rays and obscurely pointing out the Creator in the distance.

Faith, on the other hand, raises us above all created things to God. Taking God, the ultimate cause and source of all things, as a starting point, faith shows us in its true light everything in the whole visible and invisible world. It discloses to us the depths of the Divinity, revealing to us how, from all eternity, the Son proceeds from the Father and the Holy Ghost from both, as the bond of their mutual love. It discloses how the Son goes forth in time from the bosom of the Father to pour out onto His creatures the plenitude of His divine glory and happiness and to unite in intimate communion all creatures with Himself and the Father in the Holy Ghost. It shows us the final, supernatural end of all things, where the temporal passes over into the eternal, the transitory into the immutable, and is joined to God so that God is All in all. Should such a light as this appear to us as mere darkness and obscurity? And should we fear to submit our reason obediently to faith, and not rather glory in it, thanking God with St. Peter that He has called us into His admirable light? (Cf. *1 Ptr.* 2:9).

Indeed, we repeat, there is a holy darkness in this light, but it is a darkness similar to the twilight that indicates the dawn and announces the approaching splendor of the sun. It is a darkness that ought to be dearer to us than all the lamps burning in the night, a darkness like that of a starry night which reveals greater mysteries to us and gives far greater scope to our vision than even the brightest day. The day permits us to see only a small part of the earth's surface, a mere speck in the great world: night, however, carries our vision to the greatest and most distant stars, through the immeasurable space which the sun had hidden from our view.

There is darkness in faith, but it is of such a kind as to render palpable for us that which we cannot see. "Faith," says St. Paul, "is the substance of things to be hoped for, the evidence of things that appear not." (*Heb.* 11:1). "Do you hear," cries St. Bernard to a heretic who said that faith was mere opinion, "do you hear: *substance!* Not a fickle opinion, not an idle fancy! Here all is solid, all is secure, admitting no doubt, no hesitation." (*De error. Abelardi,* c. 4, n. 9). Indeed, faith grounds us in divine truth so firmly and immovably that we recognize with infallible certitude that our conviction of the truth of Divine Revelation can no more be false than the truth of God Himself, on whom our faith is based. Faith is darkness because here we do not see with our own eyes. But instead, we see with the luminous eye of God, before which there can be no darkness.

Faith is a night, but a night that enlightens us with a heavenly reflection. It is night in comparison with the day of eternal glory, but it is a bright day if compared to all the light of reason and of the senses. These, when compared with faith, are but dark night. The more we appreciate and love reason, the more highly we will prize faith.

We rightly esteem and treasure reason as a gift of God because through it the light of God's countenance is impressed on our soul as a seal, and by it we are raised far above irrational creation. We rightly consider it as the greatest misfortune when one loses the use of reason, and we think it much more to be lamented than when one loses the use of an eye. With far more reason the light of faith should be holy and dear to us because it raises us, not merely above the animals, but above all rational creatures, and because it is the worst of misfortunes if, through our own fault, we rob ourselves for all eternity of this light.

How terrible and gruesome it would be if a person in a fit of madness would tear out both of his eyes, or if someone would knowingly and willingly rob himself of the use of his reason! Yet it would be still more cruel, as well as a heinous crime, if one would refuse, as so many unfortunately do, to accept the heavenly and divinely offered light of faith, or if, after having received it, one would, by frivolous doubt or stubborn pride, extinguish it in his soul and thus cast himself into utter darkness.

But how few there are who understand this misfortune! How many, on the other hand, who go about proud and boastful in their self-willed blindness! There are so many who plague themselves during their whole life with restless striving, with countless sacrifices of money and health in order to acquire human knowledge and to learn to know the most insignificant things. These never stop to consider that one spark of this heavenly light contains incomparably more truth than all the natural knowledge of men and angels together.

All human knowledge is, according to the words of St. Augustine (*Enarr. in Ps.* 135, n. 8), like the moon, giving us light during the night of this life on earth; whereas, divine wisdom is to be compared to the great stars that illumine the day of eternity and already here below send out their rays through the light of faith. (St. Aug., *Conf.* 1, 13, c. 18, n. 23).

Human knowledge is like the light of evening, which grows less and less. The deeper reason tries to penetrate into the nature of things, the more it must recognize its weakness. Finally, it sees dark night before it, where truth really begins. Here, precisely, the light of faith, as the growing light of dawn, reveals to us a new supernatural world and places in our soul the seed of a heavenly knowledge of immeasurable fruitfulness, a seed that will not die, except through our fault, a seed that will blossom with unfading splendor in the light of glory.

We should make more effort and sacrifice to correspond with the grace of faith and to increase the spirit of faith in us, to attach ourselves to God's word, and to receive His light more and more. If we would only go to half the trouble that the learned take to acquire human wisdom! How we would bask in this heavenly light! With what delight we would absorb its glorious rays! How quickly all earthly things would appear to us vain and colorless! Heaven would take on a charm for us and urge us on to the practice of every virtue. We would be so proud of our faith that, with the Apostle, we would glory in knowing only Christ and Him crucified. (Cf. *1 Cor.* 2:2). All the wisdom of this world would be filled with holy gratitude toward God, who has freed us from the power of darkness and has called us into His admirable light.

Chapter 31

THE SUPERNATURAL, DIVINE VIRTUE OF HOPE

THE SECOND of the Theological Virtues infused into us by grace is Christian Hope. Like Charity, Hope also is in the will. This faculty has two different acts. The first is to love the good and to take delight in it. The second is to pursue the good with earnest activity and firm confidence. As faith gives to our intellect a supernatural power of understanding, hope endows the will with a divine power and a supernatural confidence, that it may effectively strive after the infinite Good and securely attain it. Hope also raises us above all creatures, letting us rest in the bosom of God, strengthening us and supporting us upon His omnipotence as upon an unshakable rock.

Its greatness proceeds from two facts. First, it makes us confident of possessing God, the highest Good, for all eternity. Secondly, it bases this confidence upon nothing less than the infinite power of God Himself, who alone by nature possesses Himself and can therefore grant this possession to creatures.

Hope, or confidence, says St. Thomas (*S. Th.* 1, 2, q. 25, a. 1), is that elevation of the soul by which it confidently pursues a sublime and arduous good, despising and overcoming all the obstacles encountered.

It is an elevating sentiment, filling the soul with joyous courage through the consciousness of having supernatural power and enlivening it with very special confidence. The more sublime the good for which we strive and the greater the power by which we are supported, so much the stronger is the feeling of joy that hope gives to us.

How strong, then, must Christian hope be which God

infuses into our soul through grace! Through it we enjoy the consoling thought that we are called by God to the dignity of His children; that we are able to be His heirs and co-heirs with His Son; that the whole world is subject to us; and that God Himself with all His glory, treasures, and happiness is to belong to us.

Through hope we are supported, not by the fragile reed of created power, but by the power of God Himself, who, according to the words of the Apostle, fills us with the fullness of His Divinity and works in us more abundantly than we ask or conceive. (Cf. *Eph.* 3:19-20).

Through hope, we are enabled to consider as our own the omnipotence, wisdom, and goodness of God and to rest in possession of them as though they belonged to us.

For insofar as God makes us His children, He belongs to us. Insofar as He embraces us with the ineffable love of a father, He takes us in His bosom, strengthens us with His divine power, so that we may cry out with the Apostle: "If God be for us, who is against us? He that spared not even his own Son, but delivered him up for us all, how hath he not also, with him, given us all things?" (*Rom.* 8:31-32).

From this consciousness, the children of God draw their peculiar character, unintelligible to the world: that triumphant confidence, which, without being forward, braves all persecutions, all human fear, all impediments to progress; that steadfastness in suffering that cannot be shaken by any created power, nor can it be given by such a power; that holy indifference which men of the world regard as our insensibility, but which does not spare us from fighting and from feeling pain; that trust in God which does not fail, even when the soul is given over in trial to all dryness and want of consolation, apparently deserted as Christ on the Cross; that joy of heart that makes us certain of the attainment of our goal, in spite of the fact that we are convinced of our incapability and shall never be without a holy fear for our salvation.

Hence the Apostle says: "Who then shall separate us from the love of Christ? Shall tribulation? or distress? or famine? or nakedness? or danger? or persecution? or the sword?

(As it is written: For thy sake we are put to death all the day long. We are accounted as sheep for the slaughter.) But in all these things we overcome, because of him that hath loved us. For I am sure that neither death, nor life, nor angels, nor principalities, nor powers, nor things present, nor things to come, nor might, nor height, nor depth, nor any other creature, shall be able to separate us from the love of God, which is in Christ Jesus our Lord." (*Rom.* 8:35-39).

Indeed, we feel our own weakness and sigh under its weight. Likewise, we are certain—and infallibly certain—that no hostile power, either in the other world or in this, nor our own great weakness can prevent us from attaining our high goal—if we ourselves do not cast God's grace from us, despise this virtue of hope and thus withdraw ourselves from God.

God's power will never desert us, provided we never desert it. It remains with us as long as we remain with it, completing and solidifying the heavenly building on the weak foundation of our soul. Only we ourselves can destroy this building by tearing away the foundation.

O Lord, how can our weak and miserable heart grasp this powerful trust, triumphing over all things and even over ourselves! Certainly we cannot produce it ourselves; only Thy powerful grace can infuse it into us. Divine hope can stand only on the ground of supernatural faith. Our limited understanding, left to itself, would consider such trust as foolishness and presumption. Our heart would collapse at the sight of so many trials that hope must overcome, if Thy grace did not give it strength to support itself by resting on Thee and on the service of Thy Son, forgetting its own helplessness and worthlessness. How greatly they err who say that the Catholic Faith leads men to self-complacency and to canonization of self!

Truly those who speak thus know neither the faith nor the hope of Christians. No, it is not our justice or sanctity that gives us confidence in living and dying; it is only the mercy of God and the merits of Jesus Christ. Let the Jews trust in the works of the law, and the world in its cleverness; we trust, with the Psalmist, only in the name of the

Lord. (Cf. *Ps.* 19:8). By that we do not mean to say that we leave it entirely to God to care for our salvation. Only the one who does what he can has a right to expect help and salvation from God. Otherwise, our trust would not be hope, but presumption.

We have a right to base our hope on the little that we do, with the help of God's grace, because, on the one hand, God is the true basis of our hope, and on the other hand, we, by our activity, are cooperators with God in the work of our salvation.

Therefore, St. Paul says that we "glory in the hope of the glory of the sons of God" (*Rom.* 5:2), and further, that we "glory also in tribulations knowing that tribulation worketh patience; and patience trial; and trial hope; and hope confoundeth not." (*Rom.* 5:3-5).

If we always understood rightly how to base our hope on God and on His only-begotten Son, in whom is all our sanctity and salvation, and if we sought to purchase the right to cast ourselves upon Him by inciting ourselves, according to the warning of the Apostle, to make certain our calling by good works (cf. *2 Ptr.* 1:10), we should not fall so easily into a state of hesitancy and pusillanimity. But we tremble at the sight of every danger; we lie down in the face of the least pain; we cleave to the earth and do not dare to take a step on the road to Heaven.

If we should consider only our natural powers, we would indeed find reason to hesitate. But how can we justify ourselves here, since God fills us up with such might that we can overcome all the powers of Hell?

Let us therefore hold to this grace with confidence and make it our strength in order that our heart may be freed from all fear and anxiety. Usually, we are very much inclined to trust in our own strength and to boast of it, in spite of its limitations. Why do we do this incalculable harm to ourselves and this great injustice to God by not trusting in Him? Strengthened by Him, let us do our best and despise all our enemies. For all creatures must serve and work together for the welfare of those who love God, and all the treasures and riches of God are at their disposal.

We must hold this grace of heavenly hope in high esteem. We must appreciate the hope of heavenly glory more than all earthly riches and power, awaiting with unshaken confidence the possession of the highest good, which will crown our hope with the unspeakably happy assurance that we can never again be deprived of it.

Chapter 32

DIVINE CHARITY

THE THIRD and greatest of the Theological Virtues is love of God and neighbor. "And now there remain faith, hope, and charity, these three," says the Apostle, "but the greatest of these is charity." (*1 Cor.* 13:13). Charity is the greatest virtue because it perfects faith and hope. By faith we know the highest Good only from afar, by love we embrace It and unite ourselves already here on earth with that which we hope to possess in Heaven. Faith and hope may be *dead;* they may be in us without joining us in a perfect, living union with God. Love, on the other hand, cannot be *dead,* because it unites us with God, who is life itself. Hence, faith and hope are made living when charity is joined to them.

We may have the faith and hope of children of God without being God's children, that is, without having Sanctifying Grace. Love, however, is inseparable from faith and hope and from Sanctifying Grace, because we cannot love God as our Father unless we are children of God and unless He looks down on us with fatherly love.

When God gives us faith and hope, He does not come Himself but merely send His gifts, that they may prepare a place for Him. But when love is poured out into our hearts, the Holy Ghost Himself is given to us. He comes to us with grace to dwell in our souls. This supernatural love is, therefore, as great a gift as grace itself; indeed, according to the opinion of St. Augustine, even as great as the Holy Ghost Himself, who through it and in it is given to us.

As God unites Himself to us through grace in a supernatural and ineffable way, so we unite ourselves with God through supernatural love in a mysterious way. Thus, we complete or close that wonderful circle, that golden ring, that image of the divine bond which unites God the Father with His only-begotten Son and the Son with the Father in the Holy Ghost.

With ineffable love the eternal Father begets the Son of His love, the splendor of His glory; the Son is united to the Father and returns to Him with the same infinite love, and both in this love breathe the Holy Ghost as the bond of their union. In like manner, God bestows upon us the same love that He has for His own Son by making us participate in the Divine Nature; and we return to our heavenly Father by filial love, as we have proceeded from Him; and the same Holy Ghost, who proceeds from Father and Son, becomes also the bond and seal of our union with God.

That can be better understood if one considers the nature of grace and the relation of grace to love. Through grace, God draws near to us with the fullness of His goodness and holiness. Therefore, grace must fill our soul with a divine magnetism that draws it to God in a supernatural way and immerses it in Him. Through grace we participate in the Divine Nature; and just as we are called to know God as He knows Himself, so we must be enabled to love Him as He loves Himself.

As grace is a participation in the Divine Nature, the love proceeding from grace is a participation in the divine love. Hence, some theologians thought that love as a virtue is not distinct from God, but is the person of the Holy Ghost Himself. This is not true. Created love is something that, according to the words of the Apostle, is poured into our hearts by the Uncreated Love, that is, the Holy Ghost. (Cf. *Rom.* 5:5). It is a flame which His holy fire enkindles in our soul, an image of that divine love from which He Himself proceeds, as the immediate vision of God in Heaven is a participation in that divine intelligence from which the Eternal Word proceeds. For this reason, love is so closely connected with the innermost life of God that one can say with St. Augustine that, when it is given to us, God Himself is given. (*Sermo 156,* n. 5; *epist. 186,* n. 7).

This is divine, not simply because God is its object and it joins us with God, but because by it we love God as only He can love Himself by reason of His Divine Nature. As the love that God has for Himself is a holy love—because its object is the purest and highest Good, and it loves this Good as it deserves to be loved—so must our love for God, which proceeds from grace, be a holy love, because it is like God's.

Through grace, we are adopted children of God; we are made, as it were, of equal birth with God and draw as near to Him as children to a father. Being thus so closely related to God, our love for Him must be like His love for us: it must be of the same kind and therefore divine.

Through grace, God loves us in His only-begotten Son with a fatherly love, for it is because of His Son that He bestows upon us supernatural love, and therefore He can love us thus only to the extent to which He sees the image of His Son in us. We must, correspondingly, love Him with the love of His Son. Indeed, man's supernatural love of God is nothing else but the love of our Saviour and Brother for our common Father. Therefore, St. Paul says: "For the charity of Christ presseth us." (2 Cor. 5:14).

It stands to reason that this divine love is entirely supernatural. Considering our natural power only, we can and should love God as our Creator and Lord, for we are the natural image of Him. But this natural love is as far from the divine as the creature is from the Creator, or as the natural knowledge of God in the mirror of created things is from the immediate vision of His being. This natural love is also related to God as to its object. But this relation is of an altogether different kind from that of divine love. The slave and the child may love the same person—the one as his master, the other as his father—as being of one nature with them. Thus natural love remains far away from God; it is not able to elevate itself and join itself to God.

But supernatural love climbs up to God and loves God for His own sake, as He loves us and as the eternal Son loves Him. This love buries itself in God as though we were of the same nature and one with Him. See how great and wonderful, how splendid and rich in blessing is grace, which makes you capable of such a sublime, supernatural, holy and divine love.

Love is the most delightful and lovable thing in creatures or in God. Yes, it is delight and lovableness itself, as its name shows. Our heart has been made for love; in it the soul finds its joy and happiness; it encloses its innermost being in love in order to give itself entirely to it and to live and flourish in it. It desires nothing more than to find a worthy object of its love with which it may intimately unite itself and into which it can pour itself. Hence we consider ourselves fortunate if we can love a creature who charms us by his beauty or who is bound to us by ties of relationship or friendship.

It should be incomparably more delightful and joyous to be able, in any way at all, to love and enjoy God Himself, the highest and infinite Good, our gracious Creator and gentle Lord. And yet, what is all natural love of God in comparison with the supernatural, holy love which is infused into hearts—that love which flows immediately from God as a spark, a flame of the divine love in which He Himself is consumed? It is the blossom and fruit of divine happiness. Compared to this, all natural love is as no love at all; it is as a fire without flame, as a plant without life.

It is of this supernatural love that the blessed Thomas à Kempis wrote: "Nothing is sweeter than love, nothing stronger, nothing higher, nothing wider, nothing more pleasant, nothing fuller or better in Heaven or on earth; for love is born of God, and cannot rest but in God, above all created things. . .Whosoever loveth, knoweth the cry of his voice. A loud cry in the ears of God is that ardent affection of the soul which saith: 'O my God, my Love, Thou art all mine and I am all Thine.' " (*Imit. of Christ,* Bk. 3, Chap. 5).

It is this love to which the Apostle gives such splendid praise when he exhorts us that, ". . . rooted and founded in charity, you may be able to comprehend, with all the Saints, what is the breadth, and length, and height, and depth: to know also the charity of Christ, which surpasseth all knowledge, that you may be filled unto all the fulness of God." (*Eph.* 3:17-19).

It is love, as St. Bernard says, that forgets guilty fear and the submission of a creature and raises itself boldly to God with the guilelessness of a child and the trust of a bride, to embrace Him as Father, Brother, Friend and Spouse. (*In. Cant. Cant.*, hom. 83:3).

Since it is only through this infused charity that we love God as He loves Himself, it is only through it also that God becomes truly ours. Through it, we receive God as our Father, as He through grace receives us as His children; through it we become more and more like Him, until finally, we are changed into His image and see Him face to face. (Cf. *2 Cor.* 3:18). Through it, we are made one spirit with God, as two flames merge into one, as two glowing metals flow into one and form one body. For since the Divine Nature is pure fire and a glowing stream of love, it must, if it finds in us a similar flame of love, form with us such an intimate union that its like is not to be found among creatures. When two loves are joined together, the union is perfect.

What earthly love forms such a strong bond between the lover and the beloved? What love can immerse one so completely in another? What love can receive its object in so intimate a way and possess it so securely?

O heart of man, little, miserable heart that always wishes to love and yet is never satisfied with it; heart that is always torn and divided by its love, while it seeks its life in you and finds only death; heart that always burns with the fire of love and yet is not warmed or softened by its flame, but becomes harder and more brittle! How can you close yourself to this grace of divine love that would satiate you with the stream of divine bliss, that would call forth in you an ever-blooming life and would set you aglow with a heavenly flame! How can you refuse to God, who draws near to you in such great love, the golden ring with which He wills to bind you to Him and Himself to you! How can you give yourself to another love, how can you still seek another love, when the purest, highest, sweetest and most powerful love is offered to you!

Oh, if you knew the gift of God, you would ask, as the Samaritan woman, for the living water of His love, that not only can satisfy the thirst of your heart for love, but gives you far more than you need to be satisfied. For grace does not only direct your natural love to the true Good, it is likewise the source of a new, heavenly love, of which heretofore you did not have even the faintest idea.

Hasten to fill yourself with divine love and to immerse every other love in it. Tear yourself loose from self-love, the great hindrance to true, unselfish love; subordinate every natural and earthly love so that it will be guided and transformed by the holy love of God. Then you will soon experience its heavenly sweetness, as so many saints have experienced of that which faith teaches on this point.

But since we live among men, we must also love them as God wills. And here the grace of God works another wonder. It penetrates our inner self so that its fire grasps all that we do and changes it into itself. Even earthly love is so great a power that nothing can stand in the heart beside it without feeling its influence, and often in a very disturbing way. However, divine love fills the heart so entirely that it either embraces whatever else may enter, and is then nourished by it as by new fuel, or, if this is impossible, is itself choked and driven out. For love will share its dominion over the heart with no other power.

Consequently, divine love grasps also the love of one's neighbor—presupposing that it is a righteous love that can coexist with charity—and changes it into itself, so that the supernatural love of neighbor is not a special type of love distinct from the love of God, but is of the same nature. Therefore, St. John makes all the beautiful and sublime things that he says of the love of God apply also without distinction to the love of neighbor.

Grace makes us embrace our neighbor with the same love that we have for God. We must love our neighbor in God as a child, a friend, a spouse of God. Divine love thus binds us with our neighbor so intimately, so firmly, so delightfully and holily that nature can neither effect nor imagine it.

Certainly the natural bonds of a common nature, of relationship and marriage, are strong and intimate. And Christian love is far from destroying that which is based on nature. On the contrary, it elevates and ennobles it without destroying its natural character. While love of neighbor without supernatural love of God is good in itself, when united with love of God, it possesses double value and strength. For just as the Christian loves God more than father or mother, so does he consider the bonds which unite him to his fellow-Christians to be more sublime than any natural bonds. Christians mean more to us than those who are related to us by nature. The latter are blood relations; the former are relatives in God. They remind us of the covenant God has made with us, of the Divine Nature that He has shared with us, of the union with Christ, whose members and brothers He has made us. These bonds are incomparably more intimate, because we consider our neighbor as one with us in God; they are more firm because God is their indestructible goal. Even death cannot break them, but only perfects and confirms them. They are holier and more sublime, of a Divine Nature, and therefore inexpressibly more delightful, because the sweetness of God Himself flavors and penetrates them.

Great and wonderful is the grace of divine love also in this effect. Here again it is a golden chain, which, hanging down from Heaven, links together most intimately, not only some individuals, but all who possess or are destined to possess the sonship of God. It acts as a heavenly cement, which forms us all into one great body and unites us so gently and firmly that an inexpressible, heavenly harmony and the peace of Christ reign over us all.

Here we recognize how true it is that the law of God is not a burden, but an honor and a source of delight. The law of God is united with grace, and grace with love. But love makes the fulfilling of the law easy and sweet, because the one who loves sees in the law a welcome occasion to give proof of his love for God.

When we have love, we have all that is necessary for our salvation and happiness, namely, obedience, justice and service of God. When we practice love, we practice all the virtues, and in such a way that the fulfillment of their various tasks is not only no burden but even a consolation.

Let us then esteem love more highly—not only far more highly than mere natural goods, but even [than] all other supernatural graces and virtues. For it is thus that St. Paul teaches: "If I speak with the tongues of men, and of angels, and have not charity, I am become as sounding brass, or a tinkling cymbal. And if I should have prophecy and should know all mysteries, and all knowledge, and if I should have all faith, so that I could remove mountains, and have not charity, I am nothing. And if I should distribute all my goods to feed the poor, and if I should deliver my body to be burned, and have not charity, it profiteth me nothing." (*1 Cor.* 13:1-3).

Having love, we have all things; losing it, we lose all. Where love is had, the other supernatural virtues are also had; where it is wanting, all the other virtues lose their vitality and their power and can no longer lead us to life everlasting. It is true that we do not lose faith and hope through every mortal sin, but we do lose charity, and with it, Sanctifying Grace. But without charity, faith and hope are lifeless and can hardly be named virtues, since they no longer enable us to merit Heaven and to live as children of God. Only grace and love make us children of God. Only faith, says St. Augustine, distinguishes the children of God from the children of the devil—only when it is made active through love. (*Ad. Bonif. contra duas Epist. Pelag.* 1. 3, c. 3, n. 5).

We must, therefore, acquire and defend charity at any price: we must give our life for it, for without the life of love we should be, with all our deeds, destined to eternal death.

Chapter 33

THE SUPERNATURAL MORAL VIRTUES

TOGETHER WITH Divine Charity, Sanctifying Grace brings into our soul a whole series of other supernatural virtues with which it adorns charity as with a crown of heavenly flowers. And that is only to be expected. For when eternal Wisdom unites itself as a spouse to our soul, the whole fullness of the divine splendor is received by the soul, as Holy Scripture says of wisdom: "All good things came to me together with her, and innumerable riches [of virtue] through her hands." (*Wis.* 7:11).

Through grace we become new creatures; we enter into a new position; we are true children and friends of God, and we strive after the highest and most sublime goal, the vision of God. Now since God gives to all His creatures, in view of the position and destiny of each one, the power and the means to live according to their calling and to be able to strive after their goal, He must also give to His children the sublime, heavenly virtues that correspond with their sublime task. He must give them the endowment without which they could not reach their supernatural destination. He must give them that wedding garment without which they will not be admitted to union with God.

But the children of God should be perfect as their heavenly Father is perfect. They should have divine manners and should reflect the image of God in all their features, ways and actions. Therefore, grace must give to us not only the Theological Virtues—Faith, Hope and Charity, by which we are united with God—but also all the others, through which we live according to our state as children of God and thus make our actions correspond to our high position.

There is a great difference between these supernatural

moral virtues and the natural or acquired moral virtues, which may be known and had also by men of the world and [by] unbelievers.

Indeed, we can also serve God by means of the natural virtues. For, through the light of our reason, we recognize Him as Our Lord, whom we love above all things and whom we should serve with all our strength. Hence, abstracting from God's revelation, we are obliged as rational creatures to have and practice religion, and through religious blessings, to change all our earthly deeds into religious doings.

But although from this standpoint we are capable of honoring God through naturally good acts, the first of which is the exercise of religion, nevertheless, these virtues are limited to our honoring God as Our Lord and Creator and serving Him as His slaves. But by the practice of the same virtues with supernatural motives, we become a kingly priesthood, as St. Peter says. (Cf. *1 Ptr.* 2:9). For thus we love and honor God in union with His only-begotten Son, the eternal High Priest, in a heavenly way, and we offer Him a spiritual sacrifice which has been sanctified by the Holy Ghost.

The virtues that we exercise by reason of supernatural grace are, according to their external aspect, not different from the virtues of the natural order. But that which makes a difference in the moral order is not the external act, but the inner spirit. Therefore, it makes a great difference whether one performs an act as the fulfillment of his obligation toward his supreme Lord, or in order to show himself to his Father as a faithful child, and, not content with having offered a sacrifice, places himself on the altar as victim. The first is good, the second is evidently far better.

From this appears the difference between natural and supernatural moral virtues. Through the natural moral virtues, we live together with our neighbor as citizens of an earthly kingdom, founded on right and morality, and we respect and support him as a rational being and a natural image of God, destined to serve God in accordance with the voice of his conscience. Through the supernatural virtues, on the other hand, we live together and help one another as brothers in God and Christ, according to the word of the Apostle, as "citizens with the saints, and the domestics of God" (*Eph.* 2:19), as confreres and heirs of a heavenly kingdom.

Through the natural virtues, we live in relation to ourselves as rational men, according to the dignity of our nature and of our destiny, in justice, decency, temperance, chastity, fear and service of God. Through the supernatural virtues, on the other hand, our spiritual life is far more sublime than our natural life. We walk, not according to our understanding and our spirit, but according to the inspiration of the Holy Ghost, who produces the fruits of a heavenly love, mildness, temperance, chastity and purity and moves us to imitate, not merely the devotion and purity of the Angels, but the holiness of God Himself.

In a word, as grace elevates and transforms our nature, so does it also affect all our faculties and deeds, enabling us to acquire virtues of so noble a kind that their fruits are far more beautiful and precious than all the natural power of men and angels can produce. We do not thereby detract in the least from the natural virtues. We say only that the supernatural virtues, for the sake of the soul that they enliven interiorly, are higher. Precisely because we esteem the natural virtues so highly, we have a still higher estimate of the supernatural virtues.

These glorious virtues, the basis of which is placed in us by grace, are members which surround the grace; they are the strong and fruitful branches which proceed from grace and overshadow our soul on all sides. They are the rich decoration on the royal robe with which God clothes His spouse, as the Psalmist sings: "The queen stood on thy right hand, in gilded clothing; surrounded with variety." (*Ps.* 44:10). They are those precious crowns that God places on the heads of His children, which the Prophet admired in holy rapture on the angel of light before he had lost grace through his pride. "Thou wast," he says to him—and in him to all the just—"the seal of resemblance, full of wisdom, and perfect in beauty. Thou wast in the pleasures of the paradise of God; every precious stone was thy covering: the sardius, the topaz, and the jasper, the chrysolite, and the onyx, and the beryl, the sapphire, and the carbuncle, and the emerald." (*Ezech.* 28:12-13).

If these precious stones in their manifold brilliance of color are a fit adornment for the brow of a queen, grace, together with the varied heavenly brilliance of the supernatural virtues, is a far more precious ornament for our soul, and makes it an object of delight for the choirs of angels and the heart of God.

If even the natural virtues so ennoble and adorn a man that we can see nothing more beautiful and lovely on earth than an innocent countenance, which is the mirror of a virtuous soul, how wonderfully must the lines of the heavenly virtues—which God Himself sketches in our heart with the Holy Ghost, *the finger of His right hand*—how wonderfully these must adorn our soul! What nobility, what splendor, what grace and beauty they add to the soul! If the ancient philosophers considered virtue as the highest good on this earth, for which everything else should be sacrificed, how much more should we Christians, having the light of faith, appreciate and love these supernatural virtues and be most intent on acquiring, increasing and preserving them!

Moreover, the supernatural virtues have, besides their sublime nature and in virtue of it, this other advantage over the natural virtues, that they may be acquired in a moment without great labor. This ought to endear them to us still more. The natural virtues are the fruit of our own labor, and we must devote much time and effort to their acquisition. But the supernatural virtues are the fruit of the Holy Ghost, whose grace, as St. Ambrose says (*In Lucam* 1. 2, n. 19), knows no tardiness in action. Through their infusion there comes into our heart the disposition and the power to exercise them. This takes place at the moment of justification, when we receive grace and love.

Their exercise, it is true, does not suddenly become easy and pleasant for us, because our evil inclinations and habits remain for a long time opposed to them. And since, on the other hand, they impose on us greater obligations and demand a more perfect exercise than the merely natural virtues, while, on the other hand, our nature, weakened by Original Sin and by our own faults, offers no small impediment, we must not wonder that there are so many weaknesses among Christians, precisely in the exercise of the virtues—weaknesses that often call forth wonder and severe censures against the truth of the Christian teaching.

Already for this reason, in order that the name of God be not blasphemed among the unbelievers (cf. *Rom.* 2:24), we Christians must strive so that no one surpass us in faithfulness and conscientiousness whenever there is question of fulfilling the obligations of the moral virtues. It is not necessary to repeat here that as Christians we have far higher motives.

Besides, we have more strength through grace, and precisely through those faculties of which we are here speaking, which are infused into the soul with grace. They give us light and power to overcome these impediments and to clear them out of the way; and to self-denial they give an indescribable charm, which we soon make use of to perform easily and joyfully what they demand of us.

But as they are inseparably united with Sanctifying Grace and love, acting as their royal attendants, they are likewise lost with these through every mortal sin. A moment is sufficient to destroy them all. Faith and hope can remain in the sinner without charity, but all other supernatural virtues stand or fall with charity, which is their root and motive power. For when we give up the high position afforded us by grace, we lose all the capability of living according to this position and of acting through those sublime virtues that correspond to the dignity and height of grace.

Thus is explained the terrible spectacle, not seldom witnessed, that through one sin there is destroyed the entire building of a life of virtue that was constructed with so much trouble. This fall can be so complete that one may say he is sorry that heretofore he lived a virtuous life. Such a one may mock that which was formerly dear to him; yes, he may be angry with himself and despise himself for having once been pious and faithful. Nothing can prove better than such an experience that in the supernatural life all the virtues, from the highest to the lowest, are inseparably connected by divine grace. What a calamity when a Christian has the fearful misfortune to lose forever his goal in the life to come!

O frightful power of sin, which, like a terrible flash of lightning, withers in one moment all these beautiful blossoms of heavenly virtue in our soul and mercilessly destroys even their roots! O sorrowful change of the soul which, suddenly robbed of all its charms and cast down from the summit of its exalted position, is covered with vices and animal lusts! O sad desolation, more lamentable than the destruction of the glories of Jerusalem, which the Prophet Jeremias so deeply bewails!

The lamentations of the Prophet rightly deserve to be repeated when we see a soul lose Sanctifying Grace. "How is the gold become dim, the finest color is changed, the stones of the sanctuary are scattered in the top of every street? The noble sons of Sion, and they that were clothed with the best gold: how are they esteemed as earthen vessels, the work of the potter's hands? . . . They that were fed delicately have died in the streets; they that were brought up in scarlet have embraced the dung. . . . Her Nazarites were whiter than snow, purer than milk, more ruddy than the old ivory, fairer than the sapphire. Their face is now made blacker than coals, and they are not known in the streets: their skin hath stuck to their bones, it is withered, and is become like wood." (*Lam.* 4:1-2, 5, 7-8).

This sad picture of the destroyed city of Jerusalem is only a weak image of the soul that has lost grace, after having been—by reason of grace—the spiritual city of God. Whereas the soul had been a holy temple of God, constructed from heavenly virtues, in which the glory of God was reflected, sin, as a terrible windstorm, has torn asunder and destroyed all the precious stones. Whereas formerly the soul was nourished with costly fruits of virtue and with the splendid pearls of holy sentiments, now it seeks to satisfy itself with the food of beasts, yes, perhaps even wallows in the mire of beastly lust. Whereas formerly the soul stood erect in the full vigor of youth, now its marrow is dried up; it lies weak and powerless, the joy and mockery of its enemies, as the captured Samson.

We are angry at the foolish man who betrays the secret of his great strength to the curiosity of a frivolous woman. But why are we not angry with ourselves when we betray the great power of our soul to our most bitter enemy, and even extend our arms that he may cut them off, and our sinews that he may bind them, leaving us unable to fight with him or to flee from him? But do we not do this when through sin we open the door of our soul so that he can destroy its supernatural power and then bind it in chains?

And if we did not fully betray ourselves, it would still be bad enough that we hold hidden as in a box this nervous system of our supernatural life, this source of endless merit, this heavenly treasure from which we can obtain all blessings and fruits in time of peace, all means of help in time of war.

Our generous God has not given us this rich treasure that we might bury it, but that we may reap profit and restore it to Him with much interest. Therefore, let us be prudent; let us cultivate by the practice of all the Christian virtues the treasures put into our soul by God, that they may bring profit and glory to their Author.

Chapter 34

THROUGH GRACE WE RECEIVE THE SEVEN GIFTS OF THE HOLY GHOST

THOUGH THE supernatural virtues, which are given to us along with grace, are great and glorious, yet they are not all and they are not the greatest gift that we receive with grace from the Holy Ghost. Indeed, these are gifts of the Holy Ghost, and very special gifts, for they make us partakers of the Divine Nature and similar to God. But there are other gifts that are ascribed to the Holy Ghost and are distinguished from all others by being called "the Gifts of the Holy Ghost."

The virtues, indeed, give us the power to perform good works and to lead a supernatural life. But the way to Heaven is so steep that it is not enough that the Holy Ghost give us those virtues by which we may ascend to our supernatural destination; He Himself must raise us up and carry us.

The virtues are the rudder with which we guide the ship of our soul through the stormy sea of time into the port of eternity; they are the wings on which we are to rise above all created nature to Heaven and to God. But we are too weak to move this powerful rudder and these strong wings. And even if we were able to do this, Heaven is so far distant from the earth and so high above it that, left to ourselves, we would certainly be overcome by fatigue and other difficulties. Hence, the Holy Ghost, who has given us the rudder and the wings, must also give us sails, which He Himself, as a powerful wind, must swell. As a strong wind that comes from Heaven and strives to return there, He must support our flight, as He gave Himself on Pentecost to the Apostles amidst the bluster of wind.

These sails—or the talents given to our soul through grace, in virtue of which it can be moved by the Holy Ghost easily and to the most sublime actions—are, according to the teaching of St. Thomas, what we call the "Seven Gifts of the Holy Ghost." There are seven because there are principally seven supernatural virtues, three Theological and four Cardinal Virtues, which must be developed in us and set in motion by the Holy Ghost.

The gift of Wisdom corresponds to supernatural love, for wisdom is, according to the explanation of theologians, the delightful knowledge of the highest Good, which permits us to taste His divine sweetness and lovableness, and thus enkindles love in us.

The gift of Understanding enlightens faith and produces in us so bright a light that, already in this life, we experience a foretaste of the future vision. It teaches us to understand the mysteries that we believe and to penetrate them as deeply as though we saw them with our eyes. It shows us the divine truth in bright light and urges us to attach ourselves to it more firmly.

The gift of Counsel is related to the virtue of hope. Through it, the Holy Ghost comes to us as the best counselor, helper and consoler, as our Saviour has promised us. He advises us to desire only eternal and heavenly goods. He "asketh for us with unspeakable groanings" (*Rom.* 8:26), in order to help us. He gives us for our consolation the power to put an unchanging and unshaken confidence in God and to embrace and hold Him as a pledge and surety of our hope.

The gift of Fortitude assists and quickens the virtues of fortitude and patience, that even in the greatest dangers it may not fail. It animates our courage in order that we may, out of love for God, undertake ever greater and more difficult works and never relax or despair in our high endeavors.

The gift of Knowledge joins with the virtue of prudence and gives a greater clearness and security in judging what we should do or permit. It is a holy instinct of the Holy Ghost through which He lets us know, when all the means of prudence have been exhausted, what God will have us do.

The gift of Piety furthers and perfects in us the virtue of justice toward God, as well as toward our neighbor. It makes our will pliant, devout, and yielding to all the demands of justice, so that we satisfy them, not only as the severity of the law commands, but with deep devotion and sincere affection, and we give our neighbor not only what belongs to him but more than that.

The gift of Fear, finally, strengthens the virtue of temperance. It inspires us with a holy reverence for the infinite majesty of God and [with] a deep conviction of our own lowliness, and thus effects that we never raise ourselves through pride above the place that becomes us. And since the fear of the Lord pierces our flesh, as the Psalmist says (cf. *Ps.* 118:120), it bridles and restrains the motions of concupiscence, preventing them from transgressing the bounds of modesty and holy propriety which this virtue imposes on us.

Thus the Seven Gifts of the Holy Ghost are the motive power among the supernatural virtues, giving a greater docility for the illuminations and greater mobility for the inner aspirations of the Holy Ghost. Moreover, they increase our energy and elasticity so that we correspond better to these supernatural impulses.

They form our soul into a pliable tool of the Holy Ghost by means of which He produces the most splendid works. They make the soul an instrument, strong with golden chords, from which the Holy Ghost elicits the sweetest tones, which ascend even into Heaven and by their wonderful harmony delight the Angels and God Himself. They are the seven lamps upon the candlestick of seven branches that were kept burning alternately day and night before the Ark of the Covenant. They also burn partly by day, that is, during the accomplishment of our duty and good works, and partly during the night of temptation, to preserve us from the snares of sin and to expose the delusions of the devil. As the cups of these lamps in the temple are explained by some learned interpreters to have been wrought in the shape of an ear, so the gifts of the Holy Ghost furnish our soul with spiritual ears, that it may hear the divine aspirations and be deeply impressed by them.

On the other hand, the soul receives through these gifts of the Holy Ghost—which, like the supernatural virtues, are given to us together with Sanctifying Grace—a powerful impulse to do everything that serves for the furthering of the supernatural life. Even the natural virtues are not static, purely passive capabilities, but they contain a certain inclination—which often cannot be grasped even by us—to develop externally. One can see this in a child and can thus usually determine for what the child is capable and destined. So one cannot imagine a supernatural virtue without an inner force that exercises itself in the deed for which it makes us capable. The Holy Ghost is so closely united to us through the grace that He cannot look indifferently on that which we do with the power that has been given us, but He is forced, so to say, to look to our salvation with His love and activity and to give us zeal and courage and spiritual clarity, that we may not leave such great gifts lying idle or misused. And that He does through His so-called Gifts.

Oh, how rich and beautiful does Sanctifying Grace appear also under this aspect, making us similar to the incarnate Son of God! The words of the Prophet Isaias may be applied also to us: "And the spirit of the Lord shall rest upon him: the spirit of wisdom, and of understanding, the spirit of counsel, and of fortitude, the spirit of knowledge, and of godliness. And he shall be filled with the spirit of the fear of the Lord." (*Is.* 11:2-3).

The same Holy Ghost who rested upon the humanity of the Son of God comes likewise to us when we are in the state of grace—not indeed transiently, but to remain with us and to impart to us His Seven Gifts. He hovers continually over our soul, fructifies it with His heavenly power, enlightens it with His divine light and spurs it on as a strong wind.

How much, how very much we lose when we lose grace! The ship of our soul, which heretofore hastened under full sail through the stormy sea of time to the port of eternity, is suddenly robbed of all its sails and lies in frightful calm in the middle of the ocean of this world, or becomes in the storm a helpless plaything of the whirling waves, that draw it down into the deep.

Whereas before the soul was a precious implement in the hands of the Holy Ghost and was used for the most excellent works—a beautiful instrument producing the most pleasing melodies—it is now cast away. Its strength is gone; its chords are broken; it is a frail, dried piece of wood that can serve no other purpose except to be thrown into the fire.

As these Seven Gifts of the Holy Ghost animate, they strengthen the seven principal virtues; they also ward off from the soul and conquer the seven-headed monster of capital sin and of temptation to sin.

Filial fear of the greatness of God conquers the capital sin of pride. Piety, by which we guilelessly render and wish everyone his due, dispels envy and malice. The gift of Knowledge, that gives to our spirit clarity, consideration and discretion, preserves us from the dangerous madness that anger produces in us. Fortitude destroys sloth and that laziness of soul which makes it incapable of withstanding the assaults of sin. The gift of Counsel heals us of covetousness, teaching us true prudence by which we know how to treasure things that are truly good and to despise all other things. By esteeming things only insofar as they aid us in gaining eternal good, we use them rightly, and thus not only are they not lost, but they bring forth fruit a hundredfold. The gift of Understanding, which gives us a taste for divine things, takes away our appetite for earthly things and protects us from gluttony by teaching us to prefer the sweetness of spiritual food (the knowledge of heavenly things) to all sense enjoyment. Wisdom, finally, which raises us far above the earth and draws us very close to God, keeps us from impurity, filling our heart with pure, heavenly love, and thus choking all impure, animal affection in the soul.

The fact that all these gifts are lost, together with grace, explains why evil begins to reign so quickly and so powerfully. Many find the Catholic teaching—that sin causes such a thorough ruin in man—difficult to accept, and they think that this is an exaggeration. But there is no exaggeration here. Only the sinner, says the Holy Ghost, can be indifferent to the fact that he has been cast down to the depth of misery. (Cf. *Prov.* 18:3).

When along with the Holy Ghost these Seven Gifts depart from us, sin raises its sevenfold head in our soul, subjects it to its power and lacerates it in a most cruel manner with the violent stings of passion, as the serpent attacks and wounds a helpless bird whose wings are broken. But we alone are to be blamed for this inestimable misfortune. For by committing the first grievous sin, we have torn ourselves loose from the hand of the Holy Spirit, who wished to bear us up to Heaven, and we have freely cast ourselves into a bottomless abyss.

Let us rather give ourselves entirely to the eternal Spirit of Love, so that He may, through His wonderful gifts and powerful hand, raise us ever higher and give us, already in this life, a foretaste of that sweetness which he has prepared for us in Heaven. This foretaste belongs likewise to the effects of supernatural grace. For through the acts of the seven virtues that we perform, following the impulse and with the help of the Seven Gifts of the Holy Ghost, we gain the happiness that our Saviour promised us in the Sermon on the Mount.

These beatitudes are also really seven in number, for the eighth, *the kingdom of Heaven,* is none other than the first. Besides, the conditions for acquiring these beatitudes which our Saviour named are, according to St. Augustine, seven; whereas, the eighth, "to suffer persecution for justice sake," contains in itself and crowns all the different degrees and parts of justice. Thus, according to the holy Doctor, they correspond in number and order to the gifts of the Holy Ghost and to the supernatural virtues, of which they are the fruit.

The gift of Fear and the virtue of temperance make us truly poor in spirit by mortifying our self-conceit and our desire for earthly goods, and thus they secure for us the kingdom of God with its sublime sovereignty and abundant riches. By the gift of Piety and the virtue of justice, we practice true meekness, live in peace and harmony with our fellow men and thus deserve undisturbed possession of the land of promise. By the gift of Knowledge and the virtue of prudence we acquire holy sorrow, and perceiving the vanity of earthly things and of human means, we seek our consolation and tranquility in God. The gift of Fortitude and the virtue of fortitude create in us a growing hunger and thirst after justice, which will hereafter be satisfied by God with all heavenly blessings. The gift of Counsel induces us above all to practice mercy toward our neighbor—keeping in mind the promise that it will be meted out to us in the same measure in which we give to others—that we may obtain mercy with God, and this increases and confirms the virtue of hope. The gift of Understanding and the virtue of faith plunge our heart into the divine light, purify it ever more from sensual attachment and thus procure for us that purity of heart which makes us worthy to see God in Heaven face to face. The gift of Wisdom, finally, and the virtue of charity, tend to unite us ever more intimately with God and with our neighbor in the enjoyment of the highest Good, giving us that peace which makes us true and perfect children of God.

And these beatitudes, which we are to expect in the life to come and to merit by a zealous application of the gifts of the Holy Ghost and of the supernatural virtues—these we may, according to St. Thomas, enjoy already in this life to a certain extent. Even now we may esteem ourselves heirs of Heaven, sovereigns over the earth, and children of God. Even now we are consoled by the Holy Ghost in our sorrow; our hunger and thirst are satisfied; even now we experience sweet consciousness of God's mercy toward us; we behold God with the eyes of a pure heart, though it be in the dim light of faith only, and we may thus possess Heaven already on earth. We must only be more generous toward God; we must do violence to our slothful and soft nature; we must turn to God with greater earnestness in prayer; then we shall soon experience how generous God can be.

Therefore does the Apostle speak not merely of blossoms that will ripen at harvest time, and whose fruit can be gathered only after some time, but also of the Fruits of the Holy Ghost, whose sweetness and loveliness we may enjoy already in this life. The fruits, however, that he designates are nothing else than the exercise and application of the supernatural virtues and of the gifts of the Holy Ghost. "The fruit of the Spirit is: charity, joy, peace, patience, benignity, goodness. . . . faith, modesty, continency, chastity ." (*Gal.* 5:22-23). The very name of these glorious fruits proclaims not only their heavenly beauty, but also their precious flavor and sweet fragrance, which delight and refresh the heart. This is especially true of the first three, which are, so to say, the life of the others; for charity is the mother and root of all other acts of virtue and communicates to them that heavenly joy and ineffable peace which it receives itself from the Holy Ghost, who is eternal charity.

Well may we apply, therefore, to the Holy Ghost and His gifts those beautiful words which He speaks of Himself in Holy Scripture—for the spirit of truth and wisdom is His highest and most precious gift—"I took root in an honourable people, and in the portion of my God his inheritance, and my abode is in the full assembly of saints. I was exalted like a cedar in Libanus, and as a cypress tree on mount Sion . . . like a palm tree in Cades . . . as a fair olive tree in the plains . . . I gave a sweet smell like cinnamon, and aromatical balm: I yielded a sweet odour like the best myrrh: . . . I have stretched out my branches as the turpentine tree, and my branches are of honour and grace. As the vine I have brought forth a pleasant odour: and my flowers are the fruit of honour and riches. I am the mother of fair love, and of fear, and of knowledge, and of holy hope. In me is all grace of the way and of truth, in me is all hope of life and of virtue. Come over to me, all ye that desire me, and be filled with my fruits. For my spirit is sweet above honey, and my inheritance above honey and the honeycomb . . . They that eat me, shall yet hunger: and they that drink me, shall yet thirst. He that hearkeneth to me, shall not be confounded: and they that work by me, shall not sin. They that explain me shall have life everlasting." (*Ecclus.* 24:16-31).

How can you hesitate, then, even for a moment, to follow this delightful invitation of the Holy Ghost and His grace, which promises you such sweet fruit and heavenly enjoyment? But if the testimony of divine truth is not sufficient for you, come and learn from experience how great is the sweetness of the Holy Ghost. "Oh taste, and see, that the Lord is sweet," cries the Psalmist. Certainly you would not throw away a fruit which you had heard praised very highly, without having first tasted it. Come then, likewise, to the grace of the Holy Ghost and taste the divine fruit. Receive grace within you, cultivate and cherish it, and let it operate within you. You will experience a peace and joy that the world cannot give, as soon as you turn from your sins to God in sincere contrition. You will learn for yourself how sweet the Lord and His grace are, and you will not be so easily deceived again by the vain joys of the world.

It would be unpardonable if we lost the grace and the Gifts of the Holy Ghost, or if we did not at least zealously endeavor to recover them as soon as possible. It would be equally unpardonable if, while in the state of grace, we placed obstacles to the work of the Holy Ghost, or if we did not faithfully and zealously cooperate with His grace. The Holy Ghost desires to make us an image of God that will become more and more like its model. He wishes to raise the structure of the temple of God higher and higher, until it reaches Heaven. How ungrateful, wicked and foolish it would be to restrain the master hand of this Divine Artist in this wonderful work!

In an ancient city it was decreed that anyone who cut off the hand of the sculptor who had adorned the city with very beautiful statues and works of art would be considered a traitor to his country. Yet what was such an artist, who from lifeless stones sculptured images of false gods and of mortal men, in comparison with the Holy Ghost, who, by His infinite power, forms out of men living images of the true, living God? And yet we restrain His hand, which we cannot cut off, when we resist grace; we wrest from the divine hand its wonderful instrument when we trifle with God's gifts; we destroy the work of God's master hand, which He has begun to trace in us. Must He not finally grow tired and discard as useless stones the very ones whom He had intended to be ornaments in Heaven? Indeed, we have deserved such treatment, and our loss will be so much the more lamentable the higher the honor to which we were destined. We should refrain from placing hindrances in the way of the Holy Ghost and no longer grieve Him by our stubbornness. Let us rather endeavor to offer Him a soft and pliable heart, which He can shape as He pleases. Let us entreat Him to melt our heart with His holy fire so that it may become soft as wax and may not require the chisel, but only a seal to receive the perfect image of God. And even if He does use the chisel to crush the hardness of our heart, so that we tremble under His powerful blows, we must not draw back nor be afraid. The pain that we feel in this process will soon change into the sweetest joy, and our very trembling is only a prelude to the delight and joy that will fill our heart when once it is made a perfect image of God. Then the Divine Artist, the Holy Ghost, who has worked so faithfully on it, will take away the veil in order to manifest its beauty before the Angels and Saints and before God Himself.

Chapter 35

SANCTIFYING GRACE BRINGS WITH IT SUPERNATURAL ACTUAL GRACE

IT IS evident from what has been said that Sanctifying Grace is, in a certain sense, actual or active, insofar as it not only makes the soul capable of performing supernatural acts, but also gives it an impulse toward such acts. As a permanent glorification of the soul, to which it gives an habitual capacity for the supernatural life of virtue and a continuous impulse toward this life, it has a more lasting and greater actuality than the so-called actual graces, which are merely transitory sparks of life and incitements to action. But this is not to be understood as though Sanctifying Grace itself calls forth the supernatural activity; it only sets the stage. It is either the foundation or the goal of that activity and inspiration through which the Holy Ghost excites and guides the activity of the free will.

These influences are in a stricter sense called actual because they consist of perceptible, inner illuminations and inspirations; whereas, Sanctifying Grace itself is not immediately perceptible, but only through *actual grace* and its accompanying inspirations.

While we are saying so much about the glories and the power of Sanctifying Grace, we must not forget or set aside the so-called *actual grace* of God. Without this [actual grace], Sanctifying Grace would not be sufficient to live the supernatural life, which it establishes in us, and to attain the goal that God has set for it.

It is Sanctifying Grace, of course, on which our salvation depends. It is the life-principle of supernatural acts; it gives the soul spiritual life and pours into it its supernatural activity, just as the soul does to the body as regards our nat-

228

ural life. Indeed, God can give actual graces to one who is not in the state of Sanctifying Grace. There is no one, no matter how far estranged from God, who does not receive such grace hundreds and thousands of times. But here also, God always has Sanctifying Grace in view. When He gives actual graces to sinners, He always purposes to draw them to the state of [Sanctifying] grace; and when He gives such [actual] grace to the just, He wishes to confirm them in the state of [Sanctifying] grace.

Moreover, actual grace is absolutely necessary for those who are in the state of grace, for without it no one can perform a work that is meritorious for life everlasting, not even the one who has Sanctifying Grace. Above all, we wish to show here how necessary actual grace is, and, on the other hand, how intimately it is bound up with Sanctifying Grace. Even when we are in the state of grace, we need for every single supernatural, good and meritorious work a special help of the Holy Ghost.

In the supernatural virtues and the gifts of the Holy Ghost, we have the power and the impulse to perform such acts, just as we have in our bodily health and in the various faculties and members of our body the capability of fulfilling our earthly duties. But as these faculties of the body must be moved by our free will in order that they may become active, so must the Holy Ghost, by a special act, stir up and set in motion the powers which are in Sanctifying Grace.

Even in its natural faculties, our soul needs an impulse from without in order to become active, an impulse that wakes it out of its sleep and excites it to action. All these activities—the prevenient, concomitant and subsequent helps of the divine omnipotence and love—are called the natural or general concursus, or aid of God. Since a supernatural power cannot be awakened by natural things, or set in motion by mere natural aid, and since, on the other hand, it [Sanctifying Grace in our souls] is much less our own and stands much less in our power than the natural faculties, the Holy Ghost Himself, who has given it to us, must work on it in order that it unfold and develop, and this activity of the Holy Ghost is called *actual grace*.

Plants, even in the fullness of their vitality, need nourishment, light and warmth. Moreover, the atmosphere and the climate must be adapted to them. The more delicate the plant, the purer must the atmosphere be and the milder the climate, to furnish it with the requisite nourishment and the proper degree of light and heat. In like manner, the germ of supernatural life cannot develop in our soul, except under the influence of a supernatural atmosphere that supplies it with heavenly dew and rain and a supernatural sun that gives it heavenly light and warmth. This seed can develop only under the constant influence of God, in whom we live, move and have our being. For, as in the natural order, God has not created things and then left them to their own laws, but remains in each and every being as the first mover and the last disposer, so also in the supernatural sphere, the Holy Ghost must awaken the seed of the supernatural virtues with His own breath, give it His own light, permeate it with His own warmth. Only thus can the divine life develop.

Moreover, by the acts of virtue we perform while in the state of grace, we must raise ourselves ever higher, that is, always ascend to a higher degree of grace. But this we cannot do of ourselves, even though we are in the state of grace, because no one can become greater than he is, except with the aid of a higher being. Therefore, the Holy Ghost must again give us His hand to draw us up and must incite us to strive for a higher degree of grace and raise us to this [higher level] through His aid.

The Seven Gifts of the Holy Ghost are not sufficient for this [prompting activity]. Because, although they spur us on to supernatural action more than the infused virtues, nevertheless, they too are static powers—of themselves only inactive qualities of the soul—which likewise demand a special movement of the Holy Ghost to pass into action. They are the sails with which the ship of our soul should move into the harbor of Heaven. But these sails must be filled and moved by the powerful breath of the Holy Ghost. Through them our soul becomes a pliant and easily movable tool of the Holy Ghost. But a tool must be actually set in motion and used by the master in order to produce its effects. This is done through actual grace.

Finally, actual grace is also necessary for every just soul, not only for every supernatural good work, but especially when temptation places one in danger of sinning. For if God did not watch constantly over His own and hasten to help them as soon as danger threatened, it would be unthinkable that they would avoid sin, into which so many occasions and dangers and their own frailty threaten to plunge them at every moment.

Briefly, *actual grace is for the supernatural life that we have in us through Sanctifying Grace what light and nourishment are for the life of the body and what medicine is for weakness and sickness.*

What has been said shows us—abstracting entirely from the misery into which sin has plunged us—our entire dependence on God. So great is this dependence that God must hasten to aid us in a special way every moment—even after He has raised us above our nature. This is necessary unless He take away, once [and] for all, our fragile being— which, out of consideration for His own honor and our good, He does not do.

For if we were in a condition to help ourselves, furthering our life of grace without additional help, what man would not be a victim of false confidence and self-complacency and thus come to ruin? Now, men are so dependent on a thousand needs and given over to so many dangers that one would think that he should not need to be warned not to trust himself too much and not to forget God. And yet, what does reality show us? The same would certainly be the case also in the spiritual realm, where the dangers are greater still, if God had left us fully free and, to use the common expression, on our own feet. On the other hand, the truth that we have just considered must give us great consolation. For Sanctifying Grace, as long as we retain it, makes us always worthy of this active help, that is, of the actual grace of the Holy Ghost.

Sanctifying Grace makes us children of God. As such, we deserve that our Father foster and preserve our heavenly life, that He strengthen us, enlighten us and accompany us on all our paths and that He never desert us, unless we first desert Him.

Through grace, we become living members of Christ. "But Christ," says the holy Council of Trent, "pours His power unintermittently into the just—as the head into the members and the vine into the branches—a power that always precedes their good works, accompanies them, and follows after them and gives that value without which they can in no way be pleasing and serviceable to God." (Sess. 6, chap. 16).

Through grace, the aid of the Holy Ghost becomes natural to us, because Sanctifying Grace clothes us with a heavenly nature. It is given as a staff in our hand that will never be taken away from us, unless we ourselves cast it away. It surrounds us always as the light of the sun surrounds our eye and never withdraws itself from us, except when we close our eyes or tear them out. It knocks continually at the door of our heart in order to stir us on to good; it speaks to us in order to lead us to all truth; it inclines us to all good and restrains us and holds us back from sin; it strengthens us in the hour of danger and holds us upright when we are about to stagger and fall. That which Moses sang of Israel holds also in regard to us: "He led him about and taught him: and he kept him as the apple of his eye. As the eagle, enticing her young to fly, and hovering over them, he spread his wings, and hath taken him and carried him on his shoulders." (*Deut.* 32:10-11).

Oh, how happy we are in the state of grace! How easy is it for us to do good! How secure we are against the dangers of sin and the temptations of Hell! We can cry out with the Apostle, "If God be for us, who is against us? . . . Who shall separate us from the love of Christ?" (*Rom.* 8:31, 35). How securely we can walk on God's paths, having no fear of stumbling over a stone! How easily we can run on the way of perfection and climb to its very peak!

But how unfortunate we are when, through sin, we fall away from God's grace. Then our need of help from the Holy Ghost is far greater, and at the same time our claim to this aid is much less—or rather, non-existent. But even then, God will not desert us entirely. As long as we live here on earth, God never forsakes us, and He never gives up the attempt to save us, since in His great mercy He does not will the death of the sinner, but rather that he be converted and live. But we do not deserve this help; we have nothing that makes us worthy of it, though we have very much that makes us unworthy of it and impedes its reception.

Without Sanctifying Grace, we have only the rights of our own human nature. But how could these give us the least claim to the help of the Holy Ghost, which is a free gift of God? Nature can give us this no more than it can give us a right to the grace of adoption as God's children. By nature, we are only servants of God; whereas, the gifts of the Holy Ghost are given only to him who is a child of God through grace and has been made partaker of the Divine Nature.

Now besides our lack of worthiness by reason of our nature, there is also our positive unworthiness. For through sin we despise, through our own fault, all the treasure of dignity and power which grace has given to us. By sin we cruelly and forcefully drive away the Holy Ghost, who so graciously and gladly dwells in our soul. Through sin, finally, we stain our nature in so lamentable a way that it not only ceases to be a useful instrument, but becomes the greatest impediment to grace.

The condition of our soul must be thoroughly frightful when, after we have separated ourselves through sin from the source of living water, the special mercy of God allows just a few drops to flow to us; or when, after we have closed the door of our house to the Divine Sun, only by a miracle, as it were, do a few weak rays of light come in. Then the heavenly dew no longer falls on earth that is fructified with living seed; then the rays of the sun of grace fall on swampy earth, which only gives off the more poisonous fumes the more it is warmed by those rays; then the Holy Ghost no longer finds a pliant tool that He can use and move as He wills. The result of all this can only be that we go farther and farther away from good and fall deeper and deeper into sin, until finally we are almost incapable of heavenly assistance.

For if the Holy Ghost withdraws His assistance from you and leaves you to your own resources, how will you cling to the rugged cliff on which you find yourself? How will you withstand the whirling torrent that has seized you? How will you break the chains by which Hell is dragging you into its abyss? How will you prevent yourself from being daily fettered with new chains? Though the Holy Ghost still grants you some assistance, unless you use it to regain grace, you make yourself unworthy even of this assistance and increase your guilt still more. Suppose, in order to punish you, the Holy Ghost would withdraw Himself and leave you to your own fate. What can you expect from yourself, since you are nothing but weakness and misery? How will you, alone, be able to cope, not only with your own passions and concupiscence, but with all the powers of Hell? Does not St. Paul say: "For our wrestling is not against flesh and blood; but against the rulers of the world of this darkness, against the spirits of wickedness in the high places." (*Eph.* 6:12). Resistance to such a terrible and supernatural enemy demands great power, and you cannot promise this to yourself for any length of time, unless you recover grace.

Return, therefore, speedily into the bosom of God; seek refuge under His wings; and conceal yourself in the recesses of His tent, where you will be secure against all enemies. And lest in the future you again become a prey to sin, make a good use, while possessing grace, of the many gifts and aids which the Holy Ghost offers you. Remember that all those who lose grace by mortal sin have brought themselves to this by neglect or contempt of the assistance so abundantly proffered them before. For God permits no one to fall into grave sin who has not first rejected His powerful assistance; He forsakes no one who has not first forsaken Him.

But that, precisely, is our misfortune: while we are in the state of grace, we stifle the inspirations of the Holy Ghost with thoughtlessness and ingratitude; we refuse to heed His counsel; we rebel against His wholesome restraint; we oppose His holy impulses; we do not trouble ourselves to follow His illuminations; and we allow His grace to go unused. By this ingratitude, we make ourselves unworthy of further grace, of that greater, extraordinary grace that we need in time of trouble. For how can God permit us to treat so slightingly and contemptuously that which He so generously and lovingly grants us? How can He allow us to cast away the graces that have cost Him the Blood of His only-begotten Son, both of which are of infinite value? How can He suffer us to trifle with them and thus to trample underfoot the Precious Blood of Christ? He will do with us as with the foolish virgins. They would not provide the necessary oil for their lamps when there was still time, and when they needed it, they could not obtain it. Consequently, they were excluded from the marriage feast.

That we may escape this great misfortune, let us not be deaf to the inspirations of the Holy Ghost. If we do not close our eyes to His light nor render vain His powerful assistance, we shall experience that grace not only strengthens our nature and heals our infirmities, but that it also makes us capable of all good works and of heavenly merit. We shall also feel how it makes the service of God such a source of consolation and joy to us that we must consider ourselves here below as being very fortunate and be consequently unwilling to exchange our lot with anyone in the world.

Chapter 36

THE INESTIMABLE VALUE
THAT GRACE GIVES TO OUR WORKS
AS A SOURCE OF MERIT

G RACE LEADS us to heavenly glory because by it we are made children of God and thus heirs of His divine happiness. But it does this especially by giving an extraordinarily high—yes, a divine value—to the works that proceed from it. Consequently, we can merit and purchase Heaven in the strict sense so that God must give us eternal glory, not out of His generosity nor out of His fidelity in fulfilling His promises, but out of justice, as the reward of our works.

Indeed, God does not have to reward any of our works, since as our Creator and Father He can demand with right all our service—yes, He deserves this already by reason of His infinite excellence and lovableness. Therefore, Heaven always remains a grace for us, and this so much the more because Sanctifying Grace, through which we become heirs of Heaven, and all the powers through which we perform supernatural works, are free gifts of God.

St. John, speaking of eternal glory, uses the expression *"grace for grace."* (*John* 1:16). Thus he wishes to say, according to many commentators, including St. Augustine, that the glory of Heaven is a grace that we receive in exchange for having rightly used the preceding grace; it is a second grace, of which we become truly worthy, through the first grace, a greater grace that we merit through the lesser.

For by reason of Sanctifying Grace, which makes us partakers of the Divine Nature, we are true sons of God, and the works that we perform in virtue of this grace are divine, heavenly works. Thus, we stand in a relation of equality to

236

heavenly glory, and when God actually promises this to us, He promises it as an inheritance and as a reward that is not above the dignity of our person and the value of our works.

A king is not obliged to reward either the service of his subordinates or that of his children. If he wills to grant a part of his kingdom to one of his subjects in view of faithful service rendered to him, this would be a very great favor, rather than a just and equitable reward. But if he decides to reward the fidelity and love of his children by giving them a part of his kingdom or a high position in his government, this would be less a matter of wonder. For it would be said that a small, ordinary gift that would satisfy an ordinary subject, would be too little as a public recognition of the service of his children. Nevertheless, this remains for them an unearned favor. Since they are obliged to serve their father, they have no claim to a reward.

We may draw the same conclusion concerning our Heavenly King and the reward He gives. For all the good works that we perform through our nature as servants of God, He not only has promised no heavenly [supernatural] reward, but according to strict justice, He could not do so, because there is not the least proportion between these works and the excellence of the happiness of Heaven. To have promised Heaven as a reward for such works would have been to lower the infinite value of Heaven. But when we are children of God, by reason of Sanctifying Grace, and serve Him with childlike love, all the good works that we perform with the help of grace are works of children, which God, if He wishes to give us a reward (and He does), cannot reward with mere earthly blessings.

Indeed, eternal happiness remains for us an undeserved favor. For, in addition to the fact that God is not obliged to reward our service, our very condition as children of God, in virtue of which He can give us nothing less than a place in His kingdom—that is, if He wishes to reward us at all—is a pure gift of His divine mercy.

How is it, then, that we can speak of merit, and indeed of merit in the sense of strict justice? Here we begin to realize the full import of the truths that we have already learned.

If we were nothing more than a child of God—each one for himself—then this claim to Heaven could not be justified. Not every child of the king has a just claim to the kingdom. One only is the heir, namely, the firstborn. In the kingdom of God, one only has a just claim to the possession of glory, namely, the only-begotten Son of God. But we have been received by Him as co-heirs. We are one with Him as the members are one with the head, and consequently, all that He has is ours. Hence, after He has made us by grace what He is by nature, all that He has is due to us out of justice. One can say most truly that Christ, not we, has merited the kingdom of God for us, and that we can merit it only through Christ. But again, one can say that we merit it.

Through grace, which the only-begotten Son of God has merited for us, we become like Him and receive a share in His divine dignity. As Christ gained infinite merit through the smallest deed that He performed in the service of His Father—through every drop of His holy sweat and Blood—because He is the true Son of God, so we possess, through the grace received from Him, the dignity of adopted children of God, and for this reason all our good works have an exceedingly high value in the sight of the Father.

The difference between Christ and us is only in this: that Christ gained His merit through His own worth and in a measure that suffices for all men (for there is no grace or merit in any man, in the Church, in the whole redeemed human race, that is not found in Christ and distributed by Him, the Head, over the whole body and its members); while on the other hand, we received our dignity through Him, and we can, by reason of our littleness, receive it only in small measure. It is, however, great enough to merit our happiness.

By reason of grace, we are living members of Christ. But every action of a member has the same value as if it proceeded from the head. Whatever the members suffer is considered the same as though suffered by the head. In view of this, every work that we perform in the state of grace is a work of Christ, who lives and acts in His Mystical Body.

By reason of grace, moreover, we are temples of the Holy

Ghost. The children of God are, according to the teaching of St. Paul (cf. *Rom.* 8:14), led by the Spirit of God, who dwells in them as in His temple. (*1 Cor.* 3:16). The Divine Spirit is as the soul of their life, and they are as instruments that operate in virtue of His power. "The Holy Ghost," says St. Francis de Sales, "acts in us, through us and for us so admirably, that though our actions are our own, they belong more to Him than to us. We perform them in Him and by His direction, while He performs them in us. We act for Him while He acts for us, and we cooperate with Him while He cooperates with us." (*Treatise On the Love of God,* Book II, Chap. 6).

Accordingly, the value and merit of our deeds is, according to St. Thomas (*S. Th.* I, 2, q. 114, a. 3), not to be measured according to our natural power and dignity, but according to the infinite power of the Holy Ghost, who is in us. This is also one of the reasons why the Apostle calls the Holy Ghost the Spirit of promise, the pledge of our inheritance (cf. *Eph.* 1:14), and us, the children of promise. (Cf. *Rom.* 9:8).

O incomprehensible dignity! O inexhaustible wealth of divine grace! It is not only a great good in itself, but it is a source of numberless supernatural, heavenly gifts. It weighs so much in God's scales that we miserable, earthly men can, with our insignificant works, balance the whole Heaven. "For that which is at present momentary and light of our tribulation," says St. Paul, "worketh for us above measure exceedingly an eternal weight of glory." (*2 Cor.* 4:17). What can give such an immense value to our troubles and sufferings, which are in themselves but trifles? All that we are capable of is like chaff, and "the sufferings of this time are not worthy to be compared with the glory to come." (*Rom.* 8:18).

The answer is easily found. One side of a scale that contains only a straw or a feather can never balance the other, which holds a bar of gold, unless one add to the straw or feather a weight that is equal to or greater than the bar of gold. That weight, then, must be without limit that so strengthens our insignificant powers and sufferings that we not only counterbalance the weight of glory, but even out-weigh it. Such, now, is the weight of grace, such is its great-ness and majesty, that through it the light chaff of our deeds balances the eternal, infinite glory of Heaven, that is, the highest and most perfect Good, eternal and heavenly blessedness.

Without grace, we can do great and sublime works. We can make whole nations happy; we can succor the poor, devote our whole life to the service of a beautiful ideal. God would certainly not let this go unrewarded, but He cannot reward it with heavenly glory. We may suffer all that the martyrs underwent, practice all the fasts and mortification of the holy monks and hermits—but without grace, all that is too little, or rather, nothing, as far as the reward of even the smallest drop of heavenly sweetness is concerned. With grace, however, we need not perform such great things or endure great sufferings; we need only pronounce the blessed name of Jesus with devotion, or give our neighbor a cup of water to drink, or say a short prayer, or offer up to God a momentary, insignificant suffering, and we have already merited Heaven. Doubting human wisdom cannot grasp this. It sees here a poetic exaggeration, even an injus-tice attributed to God.

But where grace is concerned, nothing is unimportant, because all these works and sufferings are those of God's children. Dipped in grace, the chaff becomes gold; filled with its rays, the drop of water becomes the brightest pearl. Thus, every good work, though little in itself, becomes, through grace, of very great value, capable of purchasing for us the greatest treasure, Heaven and God Himself.

The reason for this is that it is not the human act itself which is the basis for its supernatural value, but the basis for all supernatural merit is the work of Jesus Christ Him-self. For how could a natural act merit a supernatural reward? How could an act performed in time gain eternal merit? Our works are planted in Christ, as the tree has its roots in the earth. Our works come to Christ as to their com-plement, so that one may rightly say that justice is not pre-cisely in the just, but the just are in justice, that is, in the justice of Christ. Hence, the Prophet Daniel prays: "It is not for our justifications that we present our prayers before thy face, but for the multitude of thy tender mercies." (*Dan.* 9:18).

If, then, it is grace that makes our works meritorious before God, we may say that the higher the degree of grace we possess, the more meritorious will be our works. This is true for three reasons. The closer we are to God by reason of grace, the more our person is esteemed by Him, and this dignity of person flows into our works. Even among men, the works of a more distinguished person are more highly esteemed than the works of others. A similar arrangement obtains in relation to souls, according to their various degrees of grace. Hence, those who have a higher position according to grace merit more by their works than others. Thus, it can happen that two just men give alms in equal measure or practice the same mortification, and yet one may merit more than the other.

Secondly, the Christian offers to God, along with his meritorious works, himself also. If he appears more worthy before God and is more loved by Him by reason of his greater degree of grace, he consequently offers himself to God as a gift that is more pleasing than would be that of one having little grace. Such a one ultimately gives more than the other, even if the actions of both, considered in themselves, are equal.

Thirdly, the intrinsic value of the action itself is enhanced by the greater love and greater fervor of the one who acts, because his more perfect inner disposition has not only an external influence on the act, but an internal influence as well, and gives it greater intrinsic merit. Of itself, the heart of man is but barren soil, but by the grace of God it is made fertile. It is evident that a field which is better cultivated and receives more rain brings forth better and more beautiful fruit than another that is not so well cared for. Likewise, the supernatural virtues must bring forth better and sweeter fruit in a heart that is well watered with the rain of grace than in another that is less blessed. When two persons make an act of love of God with equal exertion, the act of one may be far more perfect and more worthy than that of the other, because with grace his power of loving is greater than that of the other. And so, two persons may give equal alms to the poor, with the same good intentions and under the same external circumstances, and yet these acts, so similar in appearance, may in regard to their intrinsic value be as different as two coins of the same size and impression, one of which is gold, the other silver. The value of our works is determined less by the external act than by the intention that clothes itself, as it were, in the external act. Hence, the Prophet says: "O Lord, thy eyes are upon truth" (*Jer.* 5:3), that is, on the intention. And God Himself says to Samuel: "Man seeth those things that appear, but the Lord beholdeth the heart." (*1 Kgs.* 16:7).

How much greater, then, dear Christians, must your admiration for grace be when you see that it not only makes your works meritorious, but can increase this merit without limit! Who, then, would not esteem and love grace, since it grants to us so readily what otherwise we could never obtain, even with the greatest effort! We ought to burn with a holy desire to acquire and preserve this grace. Who can be satisfied with a small amount of grace? Should we not hasten to increase it as soon and as much as possible by cooperating faithfully and zealously with that which we already have? We have so much the more reason to do this since God gives grace in order that we may unite ourselves ever more closely to Him and since He Himself exhorts and urges us to do this.

"Arise, my love, my beautiful one, and come," calls the just soul in the Canticle of Canticles. (*Cant.* 2:13). Yes, we should indeed hasten, and not only run but fly as the dove, in order to attain the crown prepared for us. "He that is just, let him be justified still; and he that is holy, let him be sanctified still," says our Saviour. (*Apoc.* 22:11). "Blessed is the man," sings the Psalmist, "whose help is from thee: in his heart he hath disposed to ascend by steps." (*Ps.* 83:6). That we "in all things grow up" (*Eph.* 4:15) is the continual exhortation of the Apostle of the Gentiles. On many other pages of Holy Scripture, God exhorts us that we be clever and zealous merchants and that we neglect not the precious opportunities for such an advantageous bargain. Yes, He even obliges us strictly to make the talent of grace that He has given us grow and multiply, and He threatens us with punishment if we fail to use it. How foolish we are to let opportunities go by daily and hourly, when we could increase our merit.

What damage we do to ourselves through laziness! Even if we do not sin by praying only seldom, by living comfortably, by avoiding mortification, by not doing violence to ourselves, by doing but few good works, nevertheless, by this negligence we suffer an inestimable loss. If we made an act of love of God three times a day, we should acquire, as it were, a hundred more degrees of grace in one month; a thousand in a year; and in a few years, we should be immensely enriched with grace, for which we could expect in Heaven a corresponding degree of glory. If you fail to make these three acts of love, how can you consider it a trifling loss?

But how much do they gain who, with the Apostle, mortify themselves the whole day, who constantly sing the praises of God, bear His love in their heart and accomplish His will in their deeds! With what great and wonderful splendor they will be introduced into the possession of the kingdom of their Father! Who, then, can be content with a few prayers only, a few mortifications and good works when we are able to fill every hour and minute with holy and meritorious works?

The loss, however, that you suffer through your negligence appears double and threefold when you consider that your present negligence in acquiring merit deprives also your future works of a part of their value and even leads you into the danger of losing again what you have already acquired.

For since the merit of our works depends principally on the degree of grace that we have, our future works will be evidently less meritorious if we have a lower degree of grace. Since by every good wrok we can acquire a higher degree of grace, it follows that, if we fail to make use of an opportunity, our negligence and sloth in the practice of virtue must deprive all our future works of a part of their value, thus causing an incalculable and irreparable loss.

Moreover, the negligent merchant endangers that which he already possesses. We are placed with our treasures, as it were, on a rapid stream. If we do not tend upwards against the stream and struggle against the current, we shall be carried away by the torrent, together with our treasures.

Finally, God Himself holds in high esteem the gifts of grace and glory that He offers us, and He cannot permit anyone to despise them. But this we do when we are so negligent in seeking them. We thus lessen both our desire to obtain them and God's readiness to give them to us.

Would that we might take to heart that so consoling and at the same time so terrible word of the Lord: ". . . the kingdom of heaven suffereth violence, and the violent bear it away." (*Matt.* 11:12). And likewise this saying: "But I say to you, that to every one that hath shall be given, and he shall abound: and from him that hath not, even that which he hath, shall be taken from him." (*Luke* 19:26).

Besides, it is not necessary in order to gather merit for Heaven that we do extraordinary works which are not commanded by any law. Even if we only fulfill the law and do that which we cannot omit without sin, we acquire merit with God, and our merit is the greater the more zealously and solicitously we perform our duty in great things and in small. Thus by suppressing an inordinate motion, by combating a temptation, we may acquire the greatest merit there where the devil intended to do us the greatest damage.

We can increase our merit precisely through that which superficiality and pride consider so worthless, namely, the little sacrifices and self-denials for which we daily have opportunities. Let us admire again the power of grace and the liberality of God. But let us likewise be astonished at our own incomprehensible folly when we so easily lose a good as great as is merit for Heaven and bring upon ourselves the great evil of sin and all its consequences.

What shall we think of the one who by mortal sin loses, not only the merits he might have acquired by overcoming the temptation, but also all he had hitherto acquired, and renders himself incapable, as long as he remains in sin, of gaining any further merit? How sad it is when one hears sinners saying: "What does it matter if I sin? I can confess and make all things good again!"

O man, I will say nothing of the hideousness of sin itself, which offends the highest Good and dishonors your own soul; I will say nothing of the uncertainty as to whether or not you can convert and avoid eternal damnation. But is it a little thing that you lose in a moment all those precious treasures of merit, gathered perhaps through many years with much labor and effort? Is it a mere trifle that during all the time that you remain in sin, you are unable, even with all possible labor and pain, to acquire the slightest merit for Heaven? Without grace, all the works that you do are dead with regard to eternal life. Your sufferings, your prayers, your works of mercy are of no use in regard to eternity; whereas, if you had remained in the state of grace, they would have brought you great profit. For the Prophet tells us: "If the just man shall turn away from his justice, and shall commit iniquity: . . . his justices which he hath done, shall not be remembered." (*Ezech.* 3:20).

If a rich banker should cast into the sea a large sum of money—which had been bringing him daily interest of a thousand dollars—with the hope that in a month or so he might draw it up again, would you not consider him a great fool, especially if he pretended to have lost only a trifle? Without doubt you would, not only because his loss was great, but also because it could most probably never be recovered. But is the loss of the merit that you might have acquired in the state of grace less great and irreparable? Even though the merits acquired before and lost by mortal sin revive again when grace is recovered—which depends, according to some theologians, on conditions that you perhaps cannot so easily fulfill—or even though you compensate in the future for lost time by redoubled fervor, the time that you have spent in sin is certainly lost beyond recovery. Your redoubled zeal would have brought far greater fruit if you had always preserved and made use of grace.

If it were possible to have sorrow in Heaven, there would

be no more just cause for it than the neglect of grace upon earth and the subsequent loss of a higher degree of glory. Give vent now to holy grief and endeavor in the future, at least, not to be guilty of this neglect.

We should here call attention to the fact that the necessity of Sanctifying Grace for heavenly merit must not prevent us from doing all possible good and supernatural works, even after we have had the misfortune to lose grace through sin. Though these works are not elevated by grace, and are consequently of no value for eternity, yet they restrain us from many other sins; they dispose our heart for receiving charity again and also move the goodness of God to grant us soon the grace of perfect conversion. If we omitted these works also, we should withdraw even more from grace and finally lose almost entirely the hope and likewise the power of regaining it.

This also must be noted, that the merit of good work depends principally upon the grace that we possess, but that the act itself, and especially the intention, must be taken into consideration. We must not think that any and every act we perform in the state of grace, even when we have but natural motives, is meritorious in God's sight, provided of course that it is not sinful. Only those acts that we perform with supernatural motives under the inspiration of the Holy Ghost and the influence of Jesus Christ, only those which are rooted in grace and correspond to its high dignity are borne aloft by grace to the throne of God and are pleasing and meritorious in His eyes. And they are so much the more meritorious the purer our motive is and the more we make use of all the fervor of our grace in doing them—in other words, the more they are accomplished with the full strength and in the spirit of grace. As a man, therefore, who has more grace may with the same effect and in the same work gain more merit than one who has less grace, so, on the other hand, the latter, if he acts with all his fervor and with a more noble motive, may merit more than the former, who would have a less noble motive and be less fervent in this particular act. If, then, we would merit much, very much before God, we must not only seek by all possible means to acquire grace, and in its highest possible degree, but we must also seek to perform our works entirely in the spirit of grace and with its full strength, with the greatest effort and with the highest motives. The manner in which we must do this will be shown in Part 5, which treats of the practice and exercise of the supernatural virtues.

Chapter 37

GRACE ENABLES US TO MAKE SATISFACTION FOR THE PUNISHMENT DESERVED FOR SIN

THE MERIT of a higher degree of eternal glory in Heaven is not the only fruit of the supernatural works that we perform in the state of grace. They have this other incalculable advantage, that they remove the obstacle which after death may delay for a long time our entrance into Heaven, namely, the sufferings of Purgatory. We may draw this conclusion from the fact that grace entirely wipes away the guilt of mortal sin. If grace is able to destroy the guilt, which is a far greater evil than its punishment (of which it is the cause), it must be able to take away the punishment also. Although it generally leaves a part of the temporal punishment to be paid, it enables us to make worthy satisfaction for our offense.

As it makes the good works of the children and friends of God very pleasing to Him and worthy of a heavenly reward, so it likewise makes all their sufferings exceedingly valuable and offers them up to God as a worthy satisfaction. We need only joyfully accept the difficulty and labor connected with the performance of good works or bear inevitable sufferings patiently, and God will, in consideration for the high dignity [which] grace has given us and the supernatural charity of which it makes us capable, appreciate these little sufferings more than if, without grace, we had suffered far more. As the satisfaction of Christ receives its infinite value far more from the dignity of His Person than from the greatness of His sufferings, so the sufferings of His living members receive from grace an ineffably high value, which they could not have of themselves. These sufferings are considered by His Father and

248

Our Father as a part of His sufferings.

We could better appreciate this great blessing of grace if we had a clear notion of the terrible sufferings of Purgatory. Many theologians affirm that they are more frightful than the most excruciating sufferings of the martyrs, greater than any sufferings one can undergo during this life. St. Thomas teaches that they are more painful than the sufferings of Christ. (*S. Th.* III, q. 46, a.6, ad 3). According to the opinion of many theologians, the fire of Purgatory is of the same kind as that of Hell. In this case, the sufferings of the soul in Purgatory would differ from the sufferings of those in Hell only because they are not eternal and do not exclude [the] certainty of salvation and the hope of one day being freed.

What a treasure we possess in grace, since by it we may alleviate so many and such great torments by insignificant and trifling sufferings! If a king would decree, by a special privilege, that every penny possessed by a certain subject that was burdened with a heavy debt should be accepted and valued at a thousand gold pieces, how willingly such a one would give over all his pennies in order to free himself of debt! How he would hasten to help his relatives and friends and to leave to his posterity a large treasure! In the same way, while you are in the state of grace, you can by an insignificant suffering and a slight effort make satisfaction for the debt of sufferings much more terrible and lasting. That which would otherwise be of scarcely any profit to you is now estimated by God at an exceedingly great value because of grace. The hundredfold fruit which Christ has promised for our good works (cf. *Matt.* 19:29) certainly has reference, not only to the earthly addition to the heavenly reward, but also to the expiation of merited punishment. Grace is really a token in view of which God accepts all our pennies at a thousand times their actual worth.

Grace makes us so rich that we can, with little effort, make satisfaction, not only for our own sins, but also for those of others. How poor and miserable we are, on the other hand, when we have lost grace. While we have grace, the endurance of all pain, even of that which could not be avoided, brings us the greatest profit; whereas, without grace, all voluntary suffering can do nothing toward the remission of the punishment of sin. We may suffer grave diseases, hunger, poverty, insult, offenses, the loss of earthly goods, the most cruel pains in soul and body—anything that a man can suffer in this life: Without grace, all is without fruit for eternity. And even if we would suffer all these things till the last day, we would not redeem, without grace, the slightest offense against God. For divine justice can accept no satisfaction from an enemy whilst remaining still an enemy.

Learn therefore to do penance and strive to possess a spirit of penance. It is something holy, salutary and very necessary. Without the spirit of penance, no one would persevere in good; no one could overcome his own weakness, the temptations of the enemy, the enticements of the flesh and of the world. But out of the spirit of penance we obtain the incitement to satisfy for our former sins by works of virtue and to placate God for all our former offenses through greater fidelity.

The Saints would soon have quit the way of perfection without the spirit of penance. This it was that strengthened them and made them capable of heroic deeds and sacrifices. It is certain that there is no one in Heaven who did not have the spirit of penance, and one can say of most of the citizens of Heaven that they owe their heavenly reward more to penance than to their other works. What shall we say, then, we who know that there are only two ways to happiness, that of innocence and that of penance—we who have long ago left the way of innocence!

Let us therefore be eager for penance—we who have more reason for penance than the Saints. And if sometimes, conscious of our weakness, we wonder if we are doing all that is fitting as children of God, let this be an admonition for us to do penance so much the more zealously, as becomes sinners. Then we shall not have to fear that we may fail to attain our sublime goal.

Chapter 38

GRACE MAKES US SHARE IN THE GOODS OF CHRIST AND OF THE SAINTS

THE WONDERFUL power of grace is not exhausted by enabling us personally to gain merits for Heaven and to make satisfaction to divine justice for our sins. It also makes us participate in the merits and satisfactions of all the Saints and of Christ Himself. In this sense, we may understand the Psalmist when he says: "I am a partaker with all them that fear thee, and that keep thy commandments." (*Ps.* 118:63).

Through grace, we enter into the closest and most living union with Christ and all the Saints, for we are bound together with them into one Mystical Body, whose soul is the Holy Ghost. But if in this union there prevails the most perfect communion in goods, then the entire treasure of merits and satisfaction that Christ and the Saints have accumulated by their good works and sufferings belongs to all who are bound together by grace.

In regard to merit, it is indeed certain that Christ died for sinners and wishes to apply His merits to them. Through Him are offered to every sinner graces in the richest measure. All these remain fruitless in regard to the spiritual life if they do not lead the sinner to Sanctifying Grace and reconciliation with God. One actually becomes a partaker of the merits of Christ and gains access to eternal life, which Christ has gained for us, when through Sanctifying Grace he is changed from an enemy to a child of God. Therefore, except through grace, no one draws advantage from the merits of Christ, though they are so richly offered.

Grace makes us living members of Christ. Now it is evident that a living, healthy member draws much nourishment and power from its connection with the heart and the head. To a dead or half-living member, this is not possible. Thus, the justified, in virtue of their living union with Christ, receive a great wealth of actual graces to practice virtue and avoid sin, from which sinners are excluded.

The just alone have access to the Sacraments of the Living, by which the merit of Christ is applied to us and grace is increased in us far more than it could be done by our merit. For the Sacraments are channels through which streams of grace flow to us from the infinite treasure of the merits of Christ. Yes, the most holy Sacrament of the Altar is the source of grace itself, so that we need only to approach with devotion and to draw from it in order to make our treasure of grace ever greater and more perfect.

The merit of the Saints is, on the one hand, personal. However, we are so closely united with them through grace that their merit gains also for us an increase of Sanctifying Grace. Moreover, the great merit of the Saints gives a greater power to their prayer, so that they can obtain many and great graces for us, thus keeping us from losing Sanctifying Grace and urging us to acquire ever greater merit for ourselves. Where our prayers would not be sufficient, the Saints come to our aid and by their prayer make possible for us an increase in grace that we alone could never attain.

On the other hand, they are members of the same body to which we belong. As the health and the power of one member profits the whole, and as the whole body has but one health and one power, the merits of the Saints are accordingly ours. (Cf. *1 Cor.* 12:12ff).

All these treasures are lost when one is not in the state of grace. While others are favored with a golden stream of grace from Heaven, while others are filled and blessed by the abundant sufferings of the martyrs, by the charitable works of the patriarchs, by the ardent desires of the prophets, by the zealous labors of the Apostles, by the austere life of confessors and virgins and by the infinite treasure of the merits of the ever Blessed Virgin and the King of Saints, Christ Jesus Himself, you alone are left empty-handed.

What an unspeakable misfortune! While others are

immersed in the stream of divine grace and enjoy the Bread of Eternal Life in the most holy Sacrament of the Altar, you must perish miserably from hunger and thirst. More than that, you are forbidden under grave and just penalty to approach the Table of Life, while others have free access thereto. If you should approach sacrilegiously, you would receive deadly poison and a consuming fire that would burn you forever, whilst others derive therefrom imperishable riches and eternal life.

You are spiritually, so to say, excommunicated, that is, cut off from living union with Christ and His members, even though you may belong externally to the body of Christ. If the public, juridical excommunication of the Church is so terrible and is rightly dreaded by the faithful, how much more terrible is sin, which deprives you of the fellowship of the Saints and blots out your name from the number of children of God!

On the other hand, when you are in the state of grace, you can appropriate to yourself the superfluous satisfaction of others in whatever measure you wish. Every one of your friends, every Saint can turn over to you his satisfactions, which benefit you just as well as him. The Church itself can shower you with blessings and indulgences from its inexhaustible treasure of the satisfactions and merits of Christ and its chosen ones. Indeed, if you make yourself worthy, the Church can so enrich you with grace that, free from punishment and guilt, you can enter Heaven without being touched by the fires of Purgatory. So great is the dignity which grace confers upon you, so intimate the union in which it associates you with Christ and the Saints!

How easy grace renders growth in merit, as well as the paying of the awful penalties of sin! It even makes easier for us that proportionately small personal effort and labor by which we may satisfy in this life for the punishment of Purgatory. Yet we, who usually are bent upon acquiring the greatest amount of good in the easiest and most comfortable way possible, are in this case so foolish that we trouble ourselves little when we lose grace and the society of the Saints and thus cut ourselves off from the more convenient way.

May we not have to repent—then too late—at the hour of our death that we have done so little, that we have not made use of the help of the Saints, that we have not moderated the fire of Purgatory, that we have not shortened the time that separates us from the beatifying vision of God?

When in the state of grace, we are bound to Christ and His Saints, forming one living body and able to perform all good works in union with theirs. By reason of their great perfection, their works can offset what is lacking in ours and thus make our poor efforts pleasing to God. Therefore, God wishes that His children unite with one another and with His only-begotten Son in their service and praise of Him. Christ Himself has said in this regard: "For where there are two or three gathered together in my name, there am I in the midst of them." (*Matt.* 18:20).

How pleasing must our service and praise be to Him when we are united in one spirit, not only with one or the other, but with all the Saints! How sweet and consoling for ourselves and what incitement to zeal there is in knowing that we do good and serve God, not alone and isolated, but in union with so many holy souls who are burning with love of God, offering themselves as sacrifices of praise and intoning with us the same hymn of praise!

Likewise, our works are worthless, our prayers are fruitless, our condition is without consolation when, not in the state of grace, we are separated from Christ and all the just. We must fear, consequently, to depart from God, for then we can no longer attach ourselves to the crowd of holy souls which formerly took us into their midst.

Then may rightly be applied to us the frightening words which God once spoke to the sinful people of Israel: "To what purpose do you offer me the multitude of your victims, saith the Lord? I am full, I desire not holocausts of rams, and fat of fatlings, and blood of calves, and lambs, and buck goats . . . Who required these things at your hands, that you should walk in my courts? Offer sacrifice no more in vain; incense is an abomination to me. The new moons and sabbaths, and the other festivals I will not abide, your assemblies are wicked. My soul hateth your new moons, and your solemnities: they are become troublesome to me; I am weary of bearing them. And when you stretch forth your hands, I will turn away my eyes from you." (*Is.* 1:11ff).

Hasten, therefore, O sinner, hasten back to the grace of God and the society of the Saints. God and His Saints will gladly help you that you may regain grace. What a consoling figure was used by our Divine Saviour in the Gospel— the figure of the poor woman who swept out the whole house for the lost groat and then called together all her friends that they might rejoice with her when she had found it!

If Christ and His friends, namely our brothers and sisters and the Saints in Heaven, have such great joy when we again enter their company and can take part again in their merits, what joy must fill their hearts over the fact that we are made worthy of this society through grace. Here below a man considers himself fortunate when he has access to a group of noble men among whom he can learn noble manners and acquire a higher education. What an honor, what a consolation, what a stimulus to strive after perfection when through grace we enter into union with the Saints, the most noble ornaments of humanity, who draw us to virtue by their example and place all their possessions at our disposal. Truly, the man who has grace can hardly imagine the ocean of blessings in which he lives.

Chapter 39

THE WONDERFUL POWER WHICH
GRACE MANIFESTS IN THE WEAKNESS
OF OUR NATURE

BEFORE WE conclude this Part on the effects of grace in the soul, we must call particular attention to the wonderful power of grace in comparison with the weakness and infirmity of our nature.

The high, supernatural value which grace gives to our actions is certainly in itself a most sublime effect of grace. But as long as we are on this earth, it is visible only to God and the Saints. Because we perceive it only through faith, it is not such a great matter for wonder. But when Sanctifying Grace, together with the actual graces that go with it, breaks the chains of our passions and of our bad habits, when it overcomes the weakness and infirmity of our nature, or at least gives our nature power to practice self-denial, just as much as we have heretofore felt the hard yoke of our passions and the misery of our nature, then we shall have occasion to experience its wonderful power directly.

"Come and behold ye the works of the Lord: what wonders he hath done upon earth," sings the royal Psalmist. (*Ps.* 45:9). Cassian applies these words to the work of grace. "Come and see," he says, "how it converts a hard-hearted usurer to liberality, how it makes a spendthrift and debauchee continent, a proud man humble, a soft and delicate person severe and penitent, embracing voluntary poverty and mortifications. These are truly works of God; these are truly miracles, which in a moment convert, as in the case of Matthew, a publican into an Apostle, and as with St. Paul, a raving persecutor into a most zealous preacher of the Gospel. These are the works of God, which the Son of God, as He said, performs every day, together with the Father.

"Who would not admire the power of grace when he sees the attraction to gluttony and the love for sensual pleasure so mortified in himself that he is content with vile and insipid food and takes even this sparingly and unwillingly; when he perceives the fire of concupiscence and of carnal lust, which he considered inextinguishable, so cooled within him that he scarcely notices the slightest motion of it; when he beholds irritated and impatient men, who were incited to anger even by marks of great tenderness, made so meek and mild that they are no longer moved by gross insults, but, on the contrary, enjoy them?" (*Coll.* 12:12).

St. Bernard teaches us the same thing, saying that the omnipotence of the Eternal Word is manifested in nothing more than in the fact that it makes those who trust in Him omnipotent through grace. (*In Cant. Cant., Sermo* 85, n. 5). St. Paul remarks that he can do all things with this strength. (Cf. *Phil.* 4:13). Grace makes us all-powerful through the courage of enthusiasm which it pours into us and of which the Psalmist sings: "Who hath made my feet like the feet of harts: and who setteth me upon high places. Who teaches my hands to war; and thou hast made my arms like a brazen bow." (*Ps.* 17:34ff).

Remembrance of these words drove out of the heart of the Blessed Andrew Spinola fear of the mortifications of monastic life, which held him back from entering the Society of Jesus. This remembrance made such an impression on him, accustomed as he had been to the pleasures and comforts of the court, that he later found the greatest joy precisely in those things which had caused him to tremble. He was enabled, finally, to undergo cruel death by fire as a missionary in Japan.

Everyone experiences this, though perhaps not in such a high degree. According to the words of the Prophet Isaias, "they shall take wings as eagles." (*Is.* 40:31). They fly without effort or weariness on the way of perfection, for the grace of God supports in a wonderful way the awkwardness of the body and the weakness of the soul, and it seasons with heavenly balsam this bitterness of all labor.

Though seeming to be an exaggeration, the saying of St. Augustine is very true, viz., that the soul which gives itself to God and faithfully uses its weapons, especially prayer, has from the assistance of divine grace more power to subdue the flesh than the flesh has in kindling the fire of concupiscence. (*Sermo* 155, n. 2). Then is fulfilled that word of Holy Scripture: "The lust thereof shall be under thee, and thou shalt have dominion over it." (*Gen.* 4:7). St. Augustine spoke not without experience; he only repeated for the instruction of others what he had experienced in himself. Long and laboriously he had battled with the vanities of this world, with his evil habits and passions, but they had held him strongly enslaved, and he could not break their chains. But when grace had suddenly burst these chains asunder, he exclaimed: "How sweet on a sudden was it to become to me to be without the sweets of those toys! And what I was before so much afraid to lose, I now cast from me with joy. For Thou, O my God, didst expel them from me and didst come Thyself instead of them, sweeter than any pleasure whatever." (St. Aug. *Conf.* 9,1).

St. Cyprian had a similar experience, of which he tells us in these words: "As I was held enslaved by the innumerable errors of my former life and did not believe that I could free myself from them, so attached was I to the vices that adhered to me, that, despairing of a better life, I loved my evils as if they were already my bondsmen and my property. But after the power of the waters of regeneration had washed away the stains of my former life and had infused a light from above into my cleansed and purified heart, after I had been imbued with the Spirit from Heaven and had by a second birth been transformed into a new man, then I felt, suddenly and wonderfully, all doubts dispelled, all hidden things clear, all obscure things plain, and what before seemed difficult to me appeared now very easy." (*Ad. Donat. De Gratia Dei*, c. 4)

St. Gregory the Great applies to the grace of the Christian the promise made to Saul: "The spirit of the Lord shall come upon thee, and thou shalt prophesy with them, and shalt be changed into another man." (*1 Kgs.* 10:6). (*In Lib. 1 Reg.* 1. 4, c. 5, n. 18). As Saul was changed through the Spirit of the Lord from a poor shepherd into a powerful king, before whom the enemies of Israel were to tremble, so the same Spirit through grace makes you a strong ruler over concupiscence, a king victorious over your flesh. He changes you into another man, to whom that which formerly was feared and avoided is now sweet and pleasant. "This is the change of the right hand of the most High" (*Ps.* 76:11), which the Psalmist admires. That is a supernatural deed which only grace can effect, a wonder of which Holy Scripture says: "God is wonderful in his saints." (*Ps.* 67:36).

In order to make this appear less wonderful and supernatural, one might wish, perhaps, to object: but does it not belong to the nature of our spiritual soul to rule over the flesh, to subdue its lusts and to love the beauty of virtue and justice more than all goods and pleasure of the senses? True as this may be, inasmuch as the spirit fights against the flesh and strives to rule over it, it is also true that the spirit is the slave of the flesh and it cannot free itself from its dominion. Therefore, it groans under the heavy yoke imposed on it. The Apostle himself cries out: "Who shall deliver me from the body of this death?" (*Rom.* 7:24). It is only grace that frees the soul from this sad slavery, clothes it with supernatural strength and gives it its fitting place above the flesh and concupiscence.

It is still more wonderful that grace not only orders the flesh back into its natural position of subjection to the spirit, but it gives the spirit power to hate the flesh, that is, to deny it many things which it could licitly desire, and to impose on it things that are not to its liking—yes, even to have it consumed as a holocaust for the honor of God.

Is it not wonderful that delicate virgins and children, as St. Agnes, St. Eulalia, St. Pancratius and innumerable others, have triumphed over the rage of tyrants, who with most exquisite cruelty, ordered all possible torments to make them give in? But the Saints in holy joy only made light of these pains and torments. What shall we say of the holy hermits, the fathers of the desert, and so many other Saints who voluntarily lived for many years in the greatest seclusion and poverty, denied themselves all gratification of the flesh, labored by fasts and chastisements to overcome concupiscence and lived here on earth as angels in Heaven, not having any flesh? Whence came to them this power, if not from the inexhaustible source of grace?

Grace is more powerful than nature. It arms nature against itself so that it is able to renounce itself and to do holy violence to self. Grace makes us capable of that superhuman mortification and perfection which the Saviour demands of us when He instructs us to renounce all, even what nature holds dearest—yes, even to "hate" and sacrifice [the powers of] our own soul.

This is one of the greatest wonders for which we have grace to thank, one of the greatest mysteries which enkindles our love for God, that for the salvation of our soul it induces our spirit not only to mortify the flesh, but to deny and mortify itself. To renounce its own will and its own judgment and to offer itself in unconditional obedience to God as a perfect holocaust—that demands the greatest strength.

This great power of grace over nature appears at first sight as unnatural, for which reason nature strives against it and does not even wish to hear of the necessity of penance and mortification. But the obligation of penance remains, and precisely because of nature's opposition, it cannot be emphasized often enough or earnestly enough.

Softened, wounded nature, moreover, makes difficulties greater than they really are. Grace does not wish to destroy nature, but only to elevate it, that is, to drive out the evil that makes it sick and then to introduce a new and better life. By taking away all that nature loves to its own detriment, and thus wounding it in its innermost depth, it at the same time pours such a healthful balsam into this wound that it is a delight to be wounded in this way. Ask the Saints if they have ever experienced any greater delight than in those moments when they offered themselves, body and soul, as a victim to God. St. Francis Xavier will answer in the name of all, that he knows nothing more delightful than to overcome and deny oneself for love of God.

Ask yourself if you have ever enjoyed a deeper or more genuine delight than when you suppressed a violent desire of proud, angry nature, or performed any other act of heroic mortification with the help of grace.

If, then, grace could give the Saints such a wonderful, superhuman and heroic courage as to elevate them above themselves and make them lead an angelic life already in the flesh, can it not enable you to live at least as a man, in harmony with your natural dignity, and not as a slave of the flesh, of the passions, of your own will and opinion?

As man, left to your own reason and natural strength, you might indeed tremble before this task, although you have certainly done, and can do much that belongs to it. But conceding that you cannot effect it perfectly with your natural powers only, you can indeed do it through grace. Believe me, you can do all things. You yourself will cry out with the Apostle, when you experience the power of grace (and this you will do when you cooperate with it), "I can do all things in him who strengtheneth me." (*Phil.* 4:13). Yes, with grace I can tame my insolent flesh. I can restrain my passions, I can crush evil desires, root out bad habits, cut off sinful inclinations and affections, even though the operation should draw blood; and if I do not do these things, I am myself at fault. Yes, I can humble myself and subject myself to all for God's sake; I can die with Christ and for Christ, die a slow death, not in the body, but what is more, in ambition, in vanity, in touchiness, in wrangling—and all that with steadfastness, calm and joy.

O heavenly power! O wonder of grace, which changes this frail reed, this soap bubble of our nature, into a brazen column, an impregnable wall and makes it strong, not only against its external enemies, but also against itself! Oh, that we would make better use of this power! We should soon experience how strong it makes us.

Yes, grace manifests its strength, preferably not in making the strong stronger, but in uniting itself with the greatest weakness. Thus, the Apostle says: " '. . . power is made

perfect in infirmity.' Gladly therefore will I glory in my infirmities, that the power of Christ may dwell in me. For which
cause I please myself in my infirmities, in reproaches, in
necessities, in persecutions, in distresses, for Christ. For
when I am weak, then am I powerful." (2 Cor. 12:9-10). Precisely when we are weak, the wonderful power of grace
reveals itself in us, and just for this reason—that we are
weak.

God could have given us a strong and healthy nature, as
He did to our first parents in Paradise, so that grace would
need only to elevate and glorify it. It would have been easy
for Him then to take away through grace—which makes us
His children—the weaknesses and miseries that we have
with our fallen nature. But that would not be so glorious, neither for His grace nor for ourselves, and it would not reveal,
as it does now, the wonderful power that grace gives us, by
which we can triumph over our weaknesses and infirmities.

Let us thank God, therefore, with our whole heart for the
wonder that He works in us through grace; and let us prove
our gratitude by never doubting the word of God, but by
holding it fast in spite of all our misery, for His grace is sufficient for us, as He spoke to St. Paul: "My grace is sufficient
for thee, for power is made perfect in infirmity." (2 Cor.
12:9).

We must not consider it as a heavy burden, but rather as
an honor and a sublime work, that we are pressed by our
conscience and put in position by grace to mortify our
nature. Let us not make use of grace for empty words or
fruitless wishes or unmanly sighs, but let us earnestly practice the necessary and so neglected duty of mortification.

We should not complain so much when the devil and the
flesh besiege us with strong temptations, in which we think
that we must surely be overcome. We must only, by watching over our internal and external senses and by thinking
of the presence of God, avoid whatever can give him [the
devil] an occasion thereto and whatever can give him the
advantage. Let us be humble, fearful of ourselves, seeking
our strength in prayer and in the exercise of mortification,
and then we shall fight more effectively against our ene-

mies without weariness and without allowing ourselves to lose hope because of past failures. And though it is not forbidden us to wish for the removal of these temptations and to ask for this, yet let us bear them patiently until God deigns to take them away. For precisely when God sends us struggles, we are sure that He will give us a rich measure of grace to purify us from our faults, to free us from our false trust and self-love and to give to grace freer access to our heart, that it may find the occasion to give proof of its splendor by its glowing victory over our weakness.

—Part 4—

THE EFFECTS OF GRACE

Chapter 40

GRACE MAKES US WORTHY
OF GOD'S PROTECTION

THE SUPERNATURAL effects which grace produces in our souls are just as splendid and sublime as the mysterious union with God to which it leads us. Grace is a divine light that pours into our soul in a higher way and in a fuller measure all those blessings and benefits which the light of the sun spreads over the earth. It destroys with one blow the worst of all evils, mortal sin. It plants in us the seed of divine virtues, through which we take part in the life of God and merit heavenly happiness. It brings us the precious Seven Gifts of the Holy Ghost and a whole chain of other gifts which we need on the road to Heaven. It makes us partakers of the merits and satisfactions of Christ and of all the Saints. Finally, it overcomes in a wonderful way all the weaknesses and infirmities of our nature.

But the treasury of grace is not exhausted by these many and great goods that we have briefly listed here. We still have many to name, many that are worthy of notice, and these form the object of this fourth Part.

Since grace makes us children of God, whom He, in His ineffable tenderness, embraces in our Brother, His only-begotten Son, we are certain that God will watch over us with fatherly care in all our needs. Accordingly, we can entrust to Him with full security all our cares and desires, and we may expect that He will give to us, not only His heavenly kingdom, but all else that is necessary insofar as it is useful to us.

"Seek ye therefore first the kingdom of God, and his justice, and all these things shall be added unto you, says our Saviour. (*Matt.* 6:33). The kingdom of God is grace, through which God rules in us. The justice of the kingdom of God is the sum of all the virtues, which belongs to the children of God, the coheirs of Christ, the citizens of God's kingdom.

We must incite ourselves especially—or rather, only—in regard to the retaining and increasing of grace, for we may fully trust that God will fulfill His promises and take care of us in all things. Consider under what easy and beneficial conditions God makes this contract with us! All is ours if we only adhere to Christ and God. "All things are yours," says the Apostle to us, as to the faithful at Corinth, "whether it be Paul, or Apollo, or Cephas, or the world, or life, or death, or things present or things to come; for all are yours; and you are Christ's; and Christ is God's." (*1 Cor.* 3:22-23).

The Saints are ours, in order to help us; suffering and temptations, in order to free us from imperfections; trials are ours, in order to strengthen us in virtue; the world, in order to give us the means to serve God and to lighten our goal; life is ours in order to make us happy in God; death, in order to lead us to God.

O happy and secure position! Only adhere to God, and you will be lord over all things; for the Lord, the Friend, the Father, cannot permit anything to be wanting to His servant, friend and child.

God does not merely compare His fatherly care with that of a mother for her child, He shows that His care is still greater than this: "Can a woman forget her infant . . . ? and if she should forget, yet will I not forget thee." "Hearken unto me, O house of Jacob," He calls out, "all the remnant of the house of Israel, who are carried by my bowels . . . even to your old age . . . and to your grey hairs . . . I will carry and will save." (*Is.* 46:3-4). And again, He says through the prophet Zacharias: "He that toucheth you, toucheth the apple of my eye." (*Zach.* 2:8). Therefore the Psalmist consoles himself with the words: "For he hath hidden me in his tabernacle; in the day of evils, he hath protected me in the secret place of his tabernacle." (*Ps.* 26:5).

Since God loves us so much and cares for us so zealously, because through grace we have become His children, what can be wanting to us in body or soul, provided that it is really useful for us and will make us truly happy? If God feeds the animals and supports the flowers of the field, how much more will He care for us men, His children!

Hence our Saviour says: "Therefore I say to you, be not solicitous for your life, what you shall eat, nor for your body, what you shall put on. Is not the life more than the meat: and the body more than the raiment? Behold the birds of the air, for they neither sow, nor do they reap, nor gather into barns: and your heavenly Father feedeth them. Are not you of much more value than they? And which of you by taking thought, can add to his stature one cubit? And for raiment why are you solicitous? Consider the lilies of the field, how they grow: they labour not, neither do they spin. But I say to you, that not even Solomon in all his glory was arrayed as one of these. And if the grass of the field, which is to day, and to morrow is cast into the oven, God doth so clothe: how much more you, "O ye of little faith?" (*Matt.* 6:25-30).

What can make us worry if we are in the state of grace? Eternity belongs to us as heirs of Heaven, and here on earth God cares for all that we need for attaining our inheritance. On Him we can cast all cares as St. Peter admonishes, for He has care of us. (Cf. *1 Ptr.* 5:7). We do not need to fear any enemy since God stands by us. We need not tremble before any misfortune since He covers us with His wings. We need not be anxious about food and clothing since our heavenly Father takes better care of this need than we ourselves or an earthly father could do.

But, you will say, why do the children of God suffer? Why do they often suffer such great need here on earth, sometimes more than the children of the world and sinners? Why are they visited by so many sorrows, so that it sometimes appears that God has deserted them more than the rest of men?

It is easy to answer these questions. None of these evils can affect you without special permission from God. As long as you remain a true child of your God, who loves you so much, He cannot permit any evil to befall you, unless it be for your good. Hence, all these trials are special gifts of the fatherly love of God.

"God deals with you as with sons," says the Apostle, "For what son is there, whom the father doth not correct? But if you be without chastisement, whereof all are made partakers, then are you bastards, and not sons. Moreover we have had fathers of our flesh, for instructors, and we reverenced them: shall we not much more obey the Father of spirits, and live? And they indeed for a few days, according to their own pleasure, instructed us: but he, for our profit, that we might receive his sanctification." (*Heb.* 12:7-10).

These words of the Apostle are much more penetrating when we remember that God wishes to make us similar to His only-begotten Son, who likewise had to enter into His glory through suffering. (Cf. *Luke* 24:26). If God has not spared His own Son, His beloved, innocent Son (Cf. *Rom.* 8:32), are we going to complain that we are put on the same level with Him?

And what shall we say when we recall the reward that will be received for patient suffering! "And we know that to them that love God, all things work together unto good, to such as, according to his purpose, are called to be saints." (*Rom.* 8:28). These sufferings receive through grace a supernatural, a holy consecration, insofar as they consume our nature as a holocaust that is seasoned with the celestial incense of grace, for the honor of our heavenly Father. They should, moreover, awaken in the children of God a longing for their heavenly country, so that they may not become too attached to this land of exile, nor allow their heart to be drawn away from heavenly joy by an abundance of earthly goods.

As children of God we are made for eternity, and we already have a right to life everlasting. All temporal things should be but a means for attaining the eternal. Now the more certainly something leads to this goal—be it sweet or bitter, difficult or pleasant—the more valuable it must be to us, the more we must admire in it the temporal providence of our heavenly Father. Let the pagans run after the passing goods of this earth; let them weep over unfruitful years and watch anxiously over the weather; since they have nothing higher to hope for. For us temporal things are nothing more than aids to be used for a moment only, that we may attain the Highest Good in eternity. Likewise all our needs and sorrows are but means, that through them we may be freed from all hindrances on the way to our goal.

Oh, that we might rightly esteem our own sublime dignity and the wonderful providence of God toward us! We would then consider it below our dignity to concern ourselves so eagerly with temporal things and to attach our hearts to these earthly trifles.

Let us imprint deep in our souls the words of St. Peter Chrysologus: "After the Lord has been so generous to us and has given us His grace in so great a measure, He commands us that since we are destined to a royal inheritance, we throw away the miserable and insignificant possessions of our state of servitude. 'Sell what you possess and give alms.' (*Luke* 12:33). Royal dignity does not permit a common ornament; for such a sublime elevation a diadem and purple are required. Accordingly, whoever believes that he has been made a king by God must lay aside the clothing of his state of servitude. Hence, when that supreme King sees such a one daring to come to the feast with a garment unworthy of his dignity, he has him put out, for the unbecoming appearance of the guest brings about the disgrace of the host. And whoever retains the poor possessions of his earlier servitude, after he has been showered with royal riches"—that is, whoever is not satisfied with the heavenly treasures to which he has been called, but clings to earthly goods with inordinate tenacity—"such a one, caught in his earthly misery, does not know how happy he can be with God." (*Hom.* 23).

Far from desiring temporal things with inordinate solicitude, we should rather gladly give them up when it is necessary in order to gain Heaven. We should seek at any price only heavenly goods, and all other things, if truly useful, will be given us. But without grace, these can only be harmful and dangerous.

"Why do you spend money for that which is not bread," the Prophet calls to us, "and your labour for that which doth not satisfy you?" (*Is.* 55:2).

Let us buy Christ; He costs us neither gold nor effort. He will quicken us, His grace will become in us a fountain of living water, springing up into life everlasting (cf. *John* 4:14; 7:28), and will call forth a sweet hunger and thirst in our soul for heavenly goods, which is more pleasant and beneficial than any earthly satisfaction.

Chapter 41

GRACE OBTAINS SPECIAL PROTECTION FROM THE ANGELS

IN HIS PROVIDENCE, God takes care of the just, not only by Himself, but He also sends the hosts of heavenly spirits to guard and serve them. The woman clothed with the sun in the mysterious *Apocalypse*—which is a figure of the soul that is ornamented with grace—has the Archangel Michael and a host of other angels at her side for her protection. (Cf. *Apoc.* 12:7).

Jacob, God's favored one, on his return to his fatherland, was astonished at the Angels that came to meet him, and he recognized them as the soldiers of God.

Eliseus saw them standing ready in arms as powerful auxiliary troops for him and his disciples. (Cf. *4 Kgs.* 6:16). To Abbot Moses, who was much troubled with serious temptations, Abbot Isidore showed the well-ordered ranks of the holy spirits, saying: "All these the Lord of hosts sends as aids to His servants, and a greater number stands, as you see, on our side than on that of our enemies." (*Vitae Patrum* 3, 10; 5, 18, 12). Thus is fulfilled the prophecy of the Psalmist: "The angel of the Lord shall encamp round about them that fear him." (*Ps.* 33:8).

But what can move God to send His own court, the heavenly spirits who stand about His throne to serve and praise Him—what can move Him to send His most faithful watchmen from Heaven to earth that they may serve us poor and wretched men? And what can cause the Angels, who gaze upon the face of the heavenly Father without ceasing, to offer us citizens of earth their services and to accompany us as faithful comrades?

What dignity do we possess that we deserve so sublime a

service and companionship, and what great things can the Angels do with us that would be worth their zealous effort and care?

Indeed, according to our nature we should rather serve the Angels than they us. But grace gives us such a high rank that even the highest angels do not consider it below their dignity, but rather think themselves fortunate to be able to lend us their aid. They know better than we that grace has raised us to be true children and brides of our King, and that it has given us a dignity which they themselves do not possess by nature. They recognize in us the supernatural image of God and honor and serve God Himself in us.

What wonder that they come to us and that God sends them to us, when the Holy Ghost and the entire Holy Trinity comes into the soul in order to dwell in it as in a temple? If the King of the Angels comes into our soul and with joy remains with it and cannot be separated from it, how can His followers remain behind and not hasten to surround and watch the resting place of their King in closed ranks?

Who can grasp the honor that comes to our soul when, as the bride of God, it is surrounded by the heavenly court and receives from it service and homage? Human pride knows nothing higher than the splendor of a powerful king whom a whole country acknowledges, whom numberless splendidly dressed servants stand ready to serve, who has acquired for himself a distinguished following of the princes and nobles of his country. But who can grasp the splendor of the soul of a just man, who is surrounded and honored, not by men but by angels, not by the princes of this world but by the princes of Heaven, and indeed not with forced devotion but with the deepest reverence and upright love? This office and the service bound with it is so sublime that the Angels themselves treasure it with ineffable delight.

The work of grace and salvation is so sublime that God Himself cannot confer anything greater on a pure creature. Now are the Angels not "ministering spirits, sent to minister for them, who shall receive the inheritance of salvation?" (*Heb*. 1:14). The more they recognize the greatness of grace and salvation, the more they realize how great God's goodness is who has given these blessings to us as well as to them, the more faithfully they enter into the designs of God, the more clearly they see how greatly these divine gifts are required by us poor beings, [and] with so much the more joy do they serve God by helping His children to attain salvation, their heavenly inheritance.

It would be a task unworthy of the Angels to help us to gain only earthly goods and human wisdom or to protect us from merely temporal or bodily evils. Only grace and our heavenly inheritance are precious enough to bring them down from Heaven to support us in acquiring and increasing these and to keep us from losing them. But they put all their solicitude on grace and devote all their efforts to safeguarding this precious treasure in our fragile vases.

Indeed, as our heavenly Father, they extend their care to acquiring also earthly goods for us and to keeping us from bodily evils. But they do this only because, through grace, we are children of God and only insofar as our pilgrimage in time can be useful for our eternal salvation.

They desire nothing else but our true happiness. For this they work with a zeal the world does not know, a zeal that can sprout only from heavenly love. Their solicitude is surpassed only by the zeal and love of God for us.

What can be more pleasant and desirable to us than such a willing service and such a powerful solicitude, which God, as the Psalmist assures us (*Ps.* 90:11), has sent for the protection of His children, giving them "charge over thee; to keep thee in all thy ways. In their hands they shall bear thee up: lest thou dash thy foot against a stone." With what trust we can continue on our way, convinced, as the Psalmist says, that we shall "walk upon the asp and the basilisk: and . . . trample under foot the lion and the dragon." (*Ps.* 90:13).

And what else shall we fear? Certainly we shall not believe that the heavenly spirits are not a match for the demons of Hell. Why do we need to complain that we are left alone when we have so many and such faithful and powerful comrades? If only we do not hand ourselves over to our enemy and stretch out our hands that they may be bound with chains, we shall not only come out of the battle unscathed, but we shall also defeat our enemies, thanks to the support of the heavenly spirits.

Moses, through his prayer, Josue and Judas Machabeus, through their heroic fighting, broke the power of the enemies of Israel. And should we be doubtful about victory when the Angels fight for us here on earth, and in Heaven above the Seraphim pray for us? Only let us not forget what they do for us, namely their fighting and praying, and let us not make ourselves unworthy of the help which they offer us so readily and joyfully.

We are indeed, according to the words of our Saviour, like weak lambs that are surrounded by ravenous wolves. It would be fatal to such a lamb to be left alone and exposed to such enemies. But when watched by a faithful shepherd, there is no danger.

Surrounded by a hundred hellish wolves, we would have to give up if stronger protectors did not come to our aid. Now, however, not only are the shepherds of the Church here on earth destined by God to watch over us, but the forces of Heaven are also sent to help us.

How much we should thank them, how willingly and joyfully we should accept their help and make use of it! And what an effort we should make that we may be worthy of their companionship and remain worthy of their help! Let us lead a life that pleases them, a life that they may hold before the eye of God without any shame. Let us cultivate heavenly manners, as is becoming for God's children who dwell in the heavenly court. Let our mind be turned away from earthly things and be with the Angels in Heaven, where they stand before the face of God. Let our heart be attentive to their counsel and docile to their suggestions. But above all, let us hold fast to grace, which already here on earth makes us fellow-citizens and brothers of the Angels and through which, alone, we are worthy of their companionship and service.

The high esteem for grace brings with it greater honor to the holy Angels. Through grace we enter into a special relationship with them, since they possess the same grace. The more we learn to treasure grace, so much the higher will be our esteem for the Angels, since in them we honor spirits who are blessed with grace in a far higher degree than we. Moreover, they are confirmed in it forever.

The more we in our weakness have to fear the loss of grace, so much the more fervently must we recommend ourselves to their care and defense. The more we keep our heart from sin and from attachment to this earth, the more we become like them, whose purity and heavenly mind is an encouraging example for us. It can easily be seen, therefore, that an increase in grace increases our love for the Angels, and vice versa, devotion to the holy Angels is not the least means for obtaining an increase of grace.

Chapter 42

WITHOUT GRACE THERE IS NO TRUE HAPPINESS

SINCE GRACE contains so much good in itself, as we have seen so far, and since it places us in a special way under the protection of Divine Providence and of all the Angels, we can easily imagine what happiness and good fortune it brings to us even during this life. Let us add that, without grace, there is no true happiness on this earth and it will be apparent that we are forced, if we wish to be happy, to seek our good fortune in the grace of God.

We need only call on our own heart and daily experience as witnesses in order to make clear that the three outstanding things in which the world seeks happiness, namely, sensual pleasure, riches and human honors, only torture us and make us unhappy.

If happiness consists in the full possession and enjoyment of all good things, especially of the Highest Good, how can it be in sensual pleasure, which soils the nobility of our rational soul, darkens its spiritual eye and draws it down to the irrational animals. How can true happiness be in pleasure that robs the soul of its personal freedom, pushes it down into the most disgraceful slavery of the flesh and drives it on to innumerable foolish and senseless deeds? Yes, sensual pleasure even takes away the strength of the body, and precisely at the moment when it is being most fully enjoyed. Then, as a field loses its fertility and is ruined by swampy water which remains standing on the surface, so is the body corrupted by lust and plagued with incurable and disgusting diseases. It decays while it still lives, and its life is more miserable than a manifold death.

Riches, which are only a means by which we acquire sensual pleasures or human honor, evidently cannot contain true happiness. For then riches would not be desired as means, but for their own sake, and would by themselves satisfy all our desires. Temporal goods, however, do just the opposite in our soul.

Rightly, Holy Scripture calls riches and sensual pleasures prickly thorns. (Cf. *Luke* 8:14). For like a thorn in the heart, the desire to gain riches torments us; like a thorn is the care and the fear with which their possession is coupled; like a thorn is the pain caused by their loss. They prick and wound, whether we press them to our heart or whether they are torn away from it. They awaken only desire for more, and since we cannot have all that we wish, they make us poor and unhappy. Only when we consider them as nothing do they leave our heart at rest. Hence, our Saviour praised as happy only those who are poor in spirit.

What shall we say of human honor? Who does not know how vain, ambiguous, how unstable and uncertain this type of goods is! St. Anselm portrays the ambitious very well when he compares them to children chasing butterflies and being deceived every moment by their ever-changing flight. With great haste the children run after them and close their empty hands, rejoicing as though they had caught their booty—whereas, it has escaped them. Meanwhile, they strike their head on a tree, fall to the ground or perhaps break a bone. If they have once succeeded in catching a butterfly, coming home, covered with perspiration, as soon as they open their hands, they find that they have nothing but a pitiful worm, robbed of all its beauty. Thus do the ambitious plague and trouble themselves; thus do they ever hasten after fleeing fame; and if they succeed in acquiring a drop of it, they have nothing but deceit, because then they see for the first time how vain their catch is.

All these earthly pleasures together cannot satisfy our soul. They are too poor to fill our heart, too difficult to obtain, at least in the quantity desired. They are too transitory for us not to fear their quick loss, too small to keep us from desiring always more. They are too dangerous for us to give ourselves fully to their enjoyment without fear and reserve, too uncertain to allow us to find in them true peace.

"Our heart is created for Thee, O God, and it is restless until it rests in Thee," says St. Augustine. (*Conf.* 1, 1). By its very nature, our soul is too noble to be satisfied with sensible and external goods. It is immortal and demands a lasting and immortal happiness. Where the hope of such happiness is not had, the soul cannot have even a moment of true happiness. And how much less can our soul find peace here on earth when it realizes to what high destiny it is called by grace.

A man of humble condition can be happy in his state and can be satisfied with the goods and pleasures that it offers him. But when such a one is adopted by a king, or if he had fallen into this condition through misfortune, knowing himself to be of royal ancestry, he would find his lot unbearable and would not rest until he had recovered his royal dignity.

The case is similar with us. Even if the goods of this earth could make a man happy, they could not satisfy the heart of him who knows that he is called to Heaven and is destined to the dignity of the children of God. This heart is so sublime that the whole world lies at its feet; it is so large and spacious that all created things cannot fill it, and even God cannot satisfy it except by giving Himself with all His glory and happiness.

Do you think that you can drive your sublime calling out of your mind and thus attain happiness by becoming attached to the world? But would not this cruel insensibility to the Highest Good be itself the greatest misfortune and the most degrading shame? But no, you would not succeed in trying to be satisfied in your baseness. You may strive against grace, you may close your heart to it, but it will always be pressing against it, if not to fill it, at least to let it feel its infinite emptiness. Grace makes the soul need the infinite and Heaven, and it never allows to it a restful and full enjoyment of earthly goods. The more your heart wishes to satisfy itself with earthly goods, so much the more does grace excite its hunger and thirst for those of Heaven. And woe to you if you wish to satisfy your hunger and thirst otherwise than with full draughts of eternal goods! Grace and your own nature will take revenge: grace, insofar as God will make it a torment for the heart that will not let itself be made happy by it; your nature in that it will rise up against him who cruelly and criminally wishes to deprive it of its highest good and eternal happiness.

"O ye sons of men, how long will you be dull of heart? Why do you love vanity, and seek after lying? Know ye also that the Lord hath made his holy one wonderful." (*Ps.* 4:3-4). Thus the Psalmist cries to all who here on earth seek their happiness outside of grace. For they find everywhere, as Solomon, nothing but "vanity of vanities, and all is vanity," and they must finally admit with him that "all is vanity and vexation of spirit." (*Eccles.* 1:2, 14).

Grace, however, gives us the one and only and the highest happiness that one can have here on earth. I do not speak here of that happiness which will be ours in Heaven through grace, but only of that which it gives us here below. To this belongs hope in the heavenly happiness to come. If we had nothing else here on earth, this hope alone would give more joy to our heart than the full enjoyment of earthly goods. The mere consciousness that we have made our lot secure for all eternity, the certainty that the joys of Heaven surpass all the ideas and imaginations of the human soul, and the knowledge that they will be given to us by God with infallible certitude, all that is enough to comfort and quiet our heart perfectly.

Moreover, through grace, we possess God, the highest and infinite Good, not only in hope, but we really and truly have Him in us; we can embrace Him now already and taste His sweetness. Through grace, we bear God in us; with every right we call Him our own and hold Him so fast that no power in Heaven or on earth can rob us of Him against our will. Through grace, we receive Him with the arms of holy love; we enclose Him in our heart and unite Him so closely to us that we are one heart and one soul with Him.

Through grace, therefore, we enjoy even now the highest joy in union with God, who gives it to us—joy that so far surpasses all pleasures of the senses as Heaven is above the earth. Through grace, we possess the greatest riches, since

we have in us Him who has created all things, whose greatness knows no shrinking. Through grace, we enjoy the highest honor, since we really appear great to the eyes of the
infinite God and of the Angels and we are honored and
esteemed most highly.

But above all, grace gives us that sweet, heavenly peace
which the Son of God brought to earth, the peace of Christ,
which the Apostle says surpasses all understanding. (Cf.
Col. 3:15). The outstanding fruit of grace, this peace, is also
the primary condition of true and perfect happiness.

Indeed, peace is something so heavenly that the world
dares not even to pretend to be able to give it to us. The
world promises its children glamour, pleasures and enjoyment, but not peace. It rather seeks to convince its children
that true happiness is not in the quiet of peace but in constant change and in perpetual variety.

What a deceiver the world is! For what else is happiness
but the quieting of desire, and where do we find this quiet
if not in peace? If grace promises us happiness, we should
believe it for this reason alone, because it places true happiness in peace. And in reality it gives us this peace, uniting
our heart permanently with God.

Nothing in the world can rob us of this divine peace, as
long as we hold fast to grace. Though we lose everything
else, though all that the world calls evil and misfortune
come upon us, as long as we possess God, we have all. He
suffices for us, He alone; He alone fills our heart completely
so that it needs nothing else.

All suffering and misfortune become not only bearable to
the children of grace through its heavenly balsam, but are
made even sweet and lovable. They consider themselves
happy to be able to suffer something for God and for
Heaven: for God in order to show their gratitude and devotion; for Heaven, in order to purchase it in some way, at
least, that it may not seem to be in no way deserved by us.

Grace sanctifies and glorifies, not only the good that it
finds in nature, but also, with the exception of sin, all the
imperfections and defects of nature, giving to them an infinitely high value, which makes them so lovable and honor-

able that the Saints desire nothing more from God than to be showered with sufferings and sorrows.

But if grace changes all bitterness into sweetness, all suffering into gems, all sorrow into joy, giving us that peace which the world cannot give; if it enables us to enjoy God on this earth, and adds, besides, the pleasant hope of eternal blessedness, is it not true that it makes us really happy already here on earth? Why then do we still hesitate to throw ourselves into its arms and to seek in it the only true peace and perfect happiness?

Let us not be deceived by the vain appearances with which the world seeks to repress and put to sleep the deep longing of our heart for true beatitude. Let us listen to the strong cry of the ardent, intimate and infinite longing which grace itself elicits from our heart; let us listen to the unutterable sighs that the Holy Ghost calls forth in our heart, and let us follow them to the source from which they spring. Then we shall not stray from the true path, and already here below we shall enjoy the peace of Heaven, insofar as it is possible in this valley of tears.

Now it is hardly necessary, my dear Christian, that I tell you how miserable and unfortunate you are made by the loss of grace through sin. The misery of sin corresponds in exact proportion to the happiness that grace brings to you. The sinner loses the certain prospect of eternal happiness and must fear, instead, the dreadful punishment which God threatens to inflict on those who despise His grace and His Heaven. He loses the sweet peace with God and with himself and falls into the most wretched discord, that makes bitter all his joys and pleasures. As the supernatural, heavenly peace of grace preserves one in delightful quiet, the discord of sin casts one into the most tormenting disquietude. Blessing has become a curse to the sinner. He is ejected from the face of God and dares not look up trustingly to His angry Judge.

His heart is disturbed and agitated. His own nature rises up against him and torments him with uneasiness. And if all creatures do not rise up against him to destroy him as the despiser of their loving Creator, that is but another proof of the forbearance and patience of God, who awaits his repentance.

You yourself, my dear Christian, if you were ever in this awful condition, have experienced how empty and disconsolate your heart was, how it was depressed by the curse of God and tortured by the sting of conscience. And if you did not experience it, that is a sign that you had lost every idea of true happiness and that in extreme blindness you held death for life and misery for happiness. That is precisely the greatest misfortune, not even to know true happiness; and it is the fullness of misery to love misery itself and not even to desire to escape from it.

Thank God, therefore, that He has let you see your misery and has enkindled in you a desire to be freed from it and has led you back to Him. Now you can measure the bitterness of sin from the opposite state and see how graciously God rewards service done to Him. Remain faithful to Him and daily seek to serve Him more zealously. If He so richly rewards your first steps on the way to Him, what do you think you will receive when you have once attained your goal?

Chapter 43

GRACE MAKES US HAPPIER THAN THE FAVOR OF MEN

SINCE MOST men here on earth seek their happiness not so much in the grace of God as in the favor of men, especially of the great and rich, we must condescend, though the comparison appears very unworthy, to place the grace of God and that of men side by side in order to see which of the two gives greater happiness on this earth.

If we understand correctly what we possess in God's grace, we must admit that it makes us richer, more secure, more independent than any other creature on earth. Whosoever understands in faith and feels that he is a child of God will ask what he has to expect from the favor of men or to fear from man's threats. Therefore, the Wise Man says: "He that feareth the Lord shall tremble at nothing, and shall not be afraid." (*Ecclus.* 34:16).

By this we do not mean that the man who has God's grace does not need men for earthly things, or need not fear them. But there is a greater difference between those who fear God and those who do not fear God in their heart. Whereas the latter change their views like the moon and sacrifice their conviction and conscience, the former are ready, rather, to give their life than to be unfaithful to a fellow man.

And while the former are almost dying out of fear that an enemy may hurt them, the latter stand as a rock in the fire, firmly convinced that no power on earth can harm them, unless their Father permits it, and that God can protect us by His grace in all dangers and will protect us from all harm.

On the other hand, without the grace of God, the favor of

all men cannot help us; it cannot obtain this grace for us, much less protect us from the terrible consequences of God's disfavor. When this human favor is courted and unduly esteemed, it is only too often the cause of our falling into disgrace with God. For men require, as a condition for their favor, things which we cannot reconcile with our conscience and the obedience we owe to God. Woe to us if we fear men more than God! "God hath scattered the bones of them that please men." (*Ps.* 52:6). We shall perish together with them, and we shall see too late that we have based our hope on a weak and fragile reed rather than on an immovable rock.

Moreover, the desire for human favor awakens in our soul all our passions. There is nothing that alienates our heart more from virtue and induces it to all wickedness than the inordinate desire to please men. It leads to the practice of cunning and deceit, of flattery and hypocrisy. It begets bitter envy and the most ardent jealousy, implacable hatred and perpetual enmity among rivals.

What can the favor of men give us that is truly great and good and that could make us truly happy? It can give us external flattery, riches and honor, but it cannot enrich our inner being. It cannot give us greater gifts of the mind, more perfect knowledge, a better and more excellent will; in one word, it cannot make us interiorly any better than we are.

The grace of God, on the other hand, transforms, beautifies and perfects our soul. It gives it an internal splendor and improves all its faculties. It will never furnish an occasion for sin or any other evil. On the contrary, it infuses all the virtues into our heart and awakens in us a holy zeal to please God through progress in all virtues.

Since it is offered so gratuitously by God, we need have recourse to no artifice or intrigue to obtain it. But every sin and every injustice is an impediment to its acquisition, and we enjoy it the more, the more we wish others to share it with us and the more we seek to lead others to it.

Moreover, it is not in the power of men to let us enjoy, truly and permanently, the goods that they offer us. A king may offer his friends riches and pleasures in abundance; he is unable, however, to grant them also enduring health and vigor of life, without which they must perish in the midst of abundance. He may shower them with honors and influence and command his subjects to serve them, but he cannot compel a sincere respect and an interior love, and that reverence which is affected and merely external is in the end more bitter than to have been entirely ignored. But if a king were capable even of this, how could he give his courtiers that interior peace and the pleasant quiet of the heart that is the kernel of all true happiness?

In the hand of God, however, is health and life. In His hand are the hearts of men, and He inclines them to whomsoever He will. In His hand is the heavenly peace that fills our heart to its very depth. Is not this reason enough to esteem the grace of God infinitely higher than the favor of men and of kings?

But we have yet another reason. The favor of men is as uncertain and changeable as the wind; the grace of God is secure and stable. Who would not admire the high favor in which David stood with Saul, being his armor-bearer and remaining constantly in his presence to soothe and calm him in his evil moods? And yet, in the short time that David was absent from the court, he was so forgotten by Saul that not even his name was remembered, nor his family, nor his rank, and upon being aroused by the heroic victory over Goliath, Saul inquired who this David might be. (Cf. *1 Kgs.* 17:55). And the courtiers, who formerly had been unfriendly toward David, now, when they saw that he had found favor with the king, acted as though they had never dealt with him before. This is the result of the services that one wastes on men.

Assuerus was indebted for his life to Mardochai, who had averted from him the swords of the conspirators. But how long did he wait until he again remembered his deliverer? And this finally happened only through the special providence of God, or as men say, through pure chance.

But Thou, my God, dost not turn Thine eye from those who seek and treasure Thy grace. With care and unfailing accuracy, Thou dost examine all the deeds and works which may render them more worthy of Thy favor. Thou dost never forget either them or any of their merits. Thy grace, Thy favor, extends even beyond the limits of time; it lasts forever.

What an injustice we do Thee when, besides Thy grace, or in place of it, we seek and esteem the favor of men! Do not permit us in the future to prefer men to Thee, nor to consider them as Thy equal, lest we be worthy of the awful sentence: "Cursed be the man that trusteth in man" (*Jer.* 17:5), but that we may rather hear the consoling words: "Blessed are they that hope in the Lord: their hope will not be confounded."

Chapter 44

In Grace We Find the Highest Enlightenment, the Truest Liberty, the Greatest Progress

ENLIGHTENMENT, liberty, progress—these are the powerful catchwords with which the spirit of the times designates the principal goods of mankind. Splendid words are these, full of deep meaning; therefore, they kindle a flame in every heart that is concerned with the dignity and fortune of mankind. But it is a lie when the world claims for itself the possession of the things which these words signify, and pretends that it is the first to proclaim them. The joyful message of divine grace that Christ brought down upon earth proclaims nothing else than enlightenment, liberty and progress.

"I am the light of the world," said our Saviour. (*John* 8:12). "The night is passed, and the day is at hand" (*Rom.* 13:12); "you were heretofore darkness, but now light in the Lord" (*Eph.* 5:8), cries His Apostle. "If therefore the son shall make you free, you shall be free indeed" (*John* 8:36), says Christ, and the Apostle teaches us that this freedom is "the liberty of the glory of the children of God." (*Rom.* 8:21).

"Be you therefore perfect, as also your heavenly Father is perfect" (*Matt.* 5:48), the Son of God says to us. "Grow in grace, and in the knowledge of our Lord and Saviour Jesus Christ" (*2 Ptr.* 3:18), that "you may be able to comprehend . . . what is the breadth, and length, and height, and depth . . . that you may be filled unto all the fullness of God." (*Eph.* 3:18-19). Thus the princes of the Apostles admonish us. The highest enlightenment, true freedom, and the ~~greatest~~ progress are given to mankind through nothing ~~e~~ the grace of God which God has brought to earth.

The world wishes enlightenment, freedom and progress without God and in spite of God, through itself alone and for itself alone. But such an enlightenment is only darkness, such a freedom is only slavery, and such progress is only retrogression and decay. "Every best gift, and every perfect gift, is from above, coming down from the Father of lights" (*James* 1:17), says St. James. The enlightenment, liberty and progress which mankind can work out by himself cannot at best transcend the narrow limits of human nature and its natural faculties.

Grace gives us a supernatural and divine enlightenment and freedom; it raises us up above our nature to God and thus makes possible for us a progress that knows no stopping point and no decrease. For what is enlightenment and culture? An illuminating and ennobling of our soul; not just the mediocre, but a true, useful perfection that raises us out of our former condition and transfers us to a higher state. The greatest enlightenment is evidently that which gives us light concerning the most sublime truths; the highest culture is that which raises us to the greatest perfection or gives us the means to attain it.

What great illumination can we attain without grace? When we do not possess grace, we have nothing but our own natural reason and that of our fellow men, or at most, the wisdom of that hellish serpent who promised to enlighten our first parents in Paradise and cast them, [instead], into the greatest misery. Our reason can, at its best, enlighten us about sensuous things, about our natural dignity and destiny, and even this it can do only with great difficulty and seldom without error.

Unfortunately, those who call themselves apostles of enlightenment often do not even try to cultivate the mind in the right way. They consider it great wisdom to lower man to the level of the brute, to deny the immortality of his soul, the freedom of his will and his eternal destiny. They put the sensuous in the place of the understanding; they belittle faith in spiritual things as darkness and desire that we limit ourselves in study and in enjoyment to the world of the senses. They wish to free us from the authority of the

Church, of conscience, even of God Himself. Instead of the authority of the Church, they would place us under the tutelage of a flippant, ever-changing public opinion, of the boasting of other men, who make their foolish notions and vagaries the measure of all truth and wisdom.

On the contrary, grace does indeed put us under obedience to God because it makes us children of God. But as it is no disgrace, but rather the greatest honor and happiness for us to be children of God, we must esteem ourselves happy to be under His tutelage and to be able to attend His school. For here truth is revealed to us in all its glory. Here we are enlightened by a supernatural light that destroys all doubts by its infallibility, broadens our view without limit and raises us high above all that is earthly.

Grace shows us our true dignity, by which we are children of God. It reveals to us our supernatural destiny that we should attain in the vision of God. It shows us clearly and certainly the way that leads to heavenly happiness. It perfects not only the light of reason but also adds a new, infinitely higher light. It frees us from all prejudices with which our senses blind us; yes, grace alone frees us from the slavery of human respect and so-called public opinion and lets us judge infallibly of all the important things, of the world itself and of its doings.

"But the spiritual man," says the Apostle, "judgeth all things; and he himself is judged of no man." (1 Cor. 2:15). Who will dare to say that the grace of Christ impedes enlightenment and not, rather, that it alone truly enlightens us? How can we allow ourselves to be intimidated by the world when it mocks and insults us as obscurantists? Like the first Christians, we should with holy pride call ourselves "the enlightened and illuminated," since we have had the great good fortune to be freed from the darkness of the world and to be called by God into His wonderful light.

How weak has our faith become that we are ashamed of the divine light, as though it were inferior to the light of human knowledge, and think that we do something great when we silence the teaching of Revelation and seek to make it more like human wisdom by mixing it with present-day opinions and errors! What is all knowledge—I do not say of the worldly wise, but even of the Doctors of Divinity and interpreters of Holy Scripture—in comparison with a glimpse into the depths of the sense of Holy Scripture, into the ways of Divine Providence, into the holy intentions of God regarding infliction of punishment and the permitting of evil, as we find it in wholly simple souls who meditate on the word of God in silence and solitude!

As the Christian is truly enlightened through grace alone, likewise, he alone is truly cultured, provided that he realizes in his inmost heart that he is a Christian, a child of God, a brother and disciple of Jesus Christ and acts in a way corresponding with this dignity.

What the world calls culture is only an external polish in manner and behavior, at best a certain development of the natural faculties of the mind, which appear great and splendid in the eyes of men but very often vanish into nothingness before the eyes of God. The highest and truest culture, on the other hand, is that which impresses on our soul the image of God and puts us in position to lead a heavenly life here on earth as members of God's family and fellow citizens of the Angels.

Where the belief in God and in our supernatural value has perfectly permeated our thinking; where the love of God and its inseparable companion, the love of neighbor, has truly filled the heart; where the fear of God has made our whole being tender, mild and earnest; where a true, deep piety has penetrated the inner as well as the outer man; there one finds in ordinary men a tenderness and fineness of soul, a carriage of one's exterior, a consideration in dealing with others which the most polished manners of the highest society cannot offer. If Christians only strive to become Christians in the fullest sense of the word, they will acquire this gift without even thinking of it. That is a culture that causes astonishment in the minds of the children of the world, astonishment that they cannot deny. They revile it only because they feel its superiority and because they hope that we, being weak in faith, will be intimidated by their mockery and will esteem it as being of little worth.

The second gift, which the world promises but which can be really and perfectly obtained only through grace, is liberty. There is no word more abused and misinterpreted than this. At first glance, it might seem that grace would be the last thing that could give us liberty. But a closer consideration will show us the truth.

Liberty is a good only when it is freedom from evil and from the impediments to good, or in other words, when it is a freedom *for good*. The freedom to be able to choose the good and the evil is a good and perfect faculty only insofar as we may thereby determine ourselves with so much the greater decision and service to do good. Therefore, once we are in Heaven, we lose this type of freedom, for there we can only will the good.

But now, it is precisely grace that gives us the capability of being free from evil and the freedom to do good. For it gives to us the power to free our spirit from the great weight of sensual desires, which tend to draw it down from its height to the level of the brutes. It gives us the power, not merely to practice the natural virtues, but to perform acts that are supernaturally good, through which we are able to merit heavenly happiness.

In one word, grace frees us from all that disturbs or hinders our highest happiness and makes us capable of doing whatever can further it. Consequently, it makes us free in the way in which God is free. That is what our Divine Saviour meant with the words: "The truth shall make you free." (*John* 8:32).

It is only from dependence on God that it cannot and will not free us, for since it is only through God and His grace that we are able to triumph over all impediments and enemies of our happiness, we must be subject to Him and remain dependent on Him. But this dependence also becomes for us the most perfect freedom, for it is nothing else than the closest union with God. As the child is subject to its father, the wife to her husband (but in a very different way from the subjection of a slave to his master—in a way, namely, that both make one person), so are we, through grace, one with God. His freedom is our freedom, His dominion is our dominion, His possessions are our possessions. And when we serve Him, we do it, not with the love of a servant, but with the free and noble love of a child for its father, of a bride for her husband.

Christianity promises to all men this high and heavenly freedom of the children of God; this freedom of grace is offered to all who will accept and make use of the power that is given them of becoming children of God. All men without exception, from the most powerful ruler to his most wretched slave, from the richest to the poorest, from the master to the servant, can attain this freedom, all have a claim thereto.

No earthly power can rob us of it; we carry it with us even when we are in chains or when we must do the work of slaves. In this freedom the servant is as much as the master, for each is a king. When one of them serves the other, he does it out of free love of God, who has willed the difference of conditions and knows that the servant, when he surpasses his master in grace and virtue, stands higher and freer in the eyes of God.

Where now are the apostles of liberty, who promise us freedom without the grace of God? How shamefully they abuse the sublime word in order to cover up the most wretched slavery! For without God, as there is no true good, there is likewise no true liberty, for this is a peculiar quality of the Godhead.

To wish to be free without God is the same as wishing to exist without God. When man wishes to be like God and to make himself another god, it is precisely then that he falls back into his nothingness and into the lowest slavery.

Freedom without God is not freedom from evil and for good, but rather, freedom from good and consequently slavery to evil and wickedness. Whoever seeks freedom in casting off the sweet yoke of grace and justice takes upon himself the heavy burden of sin and its punishment and becomes a slave to sin. Such a one loses the sublime dignity of a child of God and lowers himself so far that, so long as he does not turn again to God and submit himself, he even loses the strength to arise from sin and to raise himself up toward Heaven. He loses control over his passions and is carried away by them with irresistible power.

May the grace of God protect us from this terrible freedom. May it enlighten us that we may recognize our true Saviour and seek only the freedom that He has brought from Heaven.

Then we shall know how to value every other liberty, which the spirit of our times makes so much of. We shall not overestimate them, and we shall seek first of all to acquire and maintain the freedom of spirit and of conscience, freedom from a crippling consideration of human judgment, freedom from servile fear of men, freedom from an unbecoming striving after favors and honor and advantages. We shall seek freedom from the pressure caused by the annoying thought that it might hurt us to break once and for all with dangerous things and strive after the means of salvation, as our better outlook advised us for a long time.

As the world clamors for enlightenment and culture, so likewise, it clamors for progress. Restless, unimpeded progress is the password, especially in these days. But we may justly ask to what are we to make progress? The friends of progress have no answer for this. They say only that all that is standing must be torn down that something new may be built in its place. They feel that nothing on earth is sufficient for them, nothing satisfies them. But can they raise themselves up above the earth and soar up to Heaven? Certainly not. But this is precisely the progress that we must make; this is the only progress that we must make; this is the only progress that will lead us to our goal; the only progress that will satisfy us and lead us to happiness—this progress that we make through grace. It is a progress guided by the hand of God, who leads and bears us on, a progress that raises us above the earth and above ourselves, that draws us up to Heaven, our true home, yes, even up to God Himself. It is a progress that oversteps the immeasurable distance between the finite and the infinite and unites us with God, a progress that never stands still but always pushes forward, that may increase indefinitely as grace itself. It is a progress that does not improve the health of our body or the natural faculties of the mind, but it transforms soul and body from glory to glory into the image of God.

On the other hand the progress which the world seeks by its own powers is not to be underestimated, but it is proportionately very small, as the slow crawling of a worm that drags itself along and cannot rise from the earth. How we would laugh if this worm would boast to an eagle of its great progress, after it had crawled over a short space of earth! Must not God in Heaven with His Angels smile, if we may so speak, or rather must He not be justly angered at the foolish boasting of men who have done something seemingly superhuman and consequently think they can get along without God?

Let us look at the progress which the world demands with the same eyes as do God and the Angels, and let us be little concerned if the world calls us men of retrogression. The world does not know what it wants nor [even] what it says. We, however, do know what we desire.

We know that we are borne aloft on the pinions of God and can thus ascend from earth to Heaven. We know that God will finish the work which He has begun in us. (Cf. *Phil.* 1:6). We know that the whole of Christian teaching is nothing else than an invitation to ceaseless growth and progress.

It was only for this reason that the Son of God descended from Heaven, namely, to make a bridge thither for us, to take us upon His shoulders as the eagle takes its young, and to carry us heavenward.

Let us show the world, then, that we are as earnest about true progress as it is about its own type. Let us at least command the respect and reverence of the world by not being slothful and negligent on the way that we follow, for it is precisely this indolence of the Christian that exposes him to the just derision of the world. Let us be solicitous to make progress, especially in those things in which progress is our holy duty, and we shall then receive the grace of God to advance also in earthly things insofar as they are the sphere of our work. For here also Christ's saying holds: "Seek ye therefore first the kingdom of God, and his justice, and all these things shall be added unto you." (*Matt.* 6:33).

Chapter 45

HOW MUCH THE ANGELS ESTEEM GRACE

ALTHOUGH WE have by no means enumerated and described all the glories and advantages of grace, yet those already mentioned are certainly great and numerous enough to induce us to esteem, love and appreciate it above all other things as the highest good that God has granted us. In order to strengthen us still more, however, in this love and esteem, we wish to mention some examples which should light the way for us. We have already considered God's estimation of grace. Next to God, however, no one knows its value better than the blessed Angels and Saints: the latter because they already possess glory, the perfect fruit of grace, the former, because they know that they owe everything to grace.

The Angels manifest their love and esteem for grace by descending from Heaven for its sake, in order to assist us in acquiring and preserving it. The great zeal that they manifest, their anxious solicitude to guard and protect this treasure, not for themselves, but for others, ought to be a stimulus for us to use at least the same zeal and diligence, since it is a question of our own good, of our eternal salvation.

We learn of this great esteem from the ineffable joy that the Angels experience when we obtain grace or make progress in it. This great joy of the Angels is described to us by their King, the Son of God, saying: "There shall be joy in heaven upon one sinner that doth penance, more than upon ninety-nine just who need not penance." (*Luke* 15:7). The Angels rejoice over all the elect here on earth, but they rejoice still more over the sinner who has again acquired the grace that he had lost.

How great and glorious, then, must this good be which fills

with such great delight and excites so much sympathy in the Angels, even though they are inebriated with the stream of highest happiness! Men acquire immense wealth, attain high positions of honor, ascend thrones, found flourishing kingdoms, acquire fame through brilliant victories throughout the world and by works of science and art, and yet at all this the Saints of Heaven are silent. They appear not even to notice these acquirements; much less do they wish these things to their friends and relatives. But if a wretched beggar, a person forgotten and deserted by all, is led back again to grace, there is a feast of joy and the Angels hasten to offer congratulations to a soul that has been so despised.

A rich merchant who always deals with large quantities of gold and money and is accustomed to great profits considers a small gain as nothing; he scarcely takes notice of it, and what others would consider as a very worthwhile possession appears to him as loss and detriment. Those glittering trifles which give small children the greatest joy scarcely draw a compassionate smile from grown persons. How great then must be the riches and splendor of grace, which gives such rapture to spirits who are so rich, so glorious and so wise.

Let us then at least imitate the Angels, who are certainly richer and wiser than men. Let us leave to the children of this world the joy of acquiring earthly things and to complain of the loss of brilliant vanities, and let us realize that then alone do we lose something when we lose grace, and then only do we truly gain something when we acquire grace, or merit its increase. Let us rejoice at the saying of our Saviour that our "names are written in heaven" (*Luke* 10:20), that is, in the book of the children of God and of the heirs of Heaven. This joy alone is entirely pure, and it alone is entirely capable of driving away all sadness from our heart.

Hence, let us say with the Prophet: "I will greatly rejoice in the Lord, and my soul shall be joyful in my God: for he hath clothed me with the garments of salvation: and with the robe of justice he hath covered me, as a bridegroom decked with a crown, and as a bride adorned with her jewels" (*Is.* 61:10), that is, with the grace, the virtues and the gifts of the Holy Ghost.

The joy that the Angels experience when grace introduces us into the friendship of God appears to have especially three motives: the first is God, the second is the Angels themselves, the third is we ourselves.

In the first place, the Angels rejoice on account of God, for they know how much He desires to reconcile us with Himself, to find us again and to take us into His bosom. The Son of God compares Himself to a shepherd who, with eager desire, seeks us as lost sheep in the desert, rejoicing, takes us upon His shoulders, takes us home and then calls together His neighbors and friends, saying: "Rejoice with me, because I have found my sheep that was lost." (*Luke* 15:6). How ready the Angels must be to follow this imitation of their King! How enraptured they must be by His indescribable love for us, and how they must hasten to share His joy and to congratulate Him!

Secondly, the Angels rejoice for their own sake, because through grace we become their brothers and fellow citizens. Far from being filled with jealousy (because, though by nature we are far below them, in grace we are made their equals), they have no greater desire than to share their blessedness with us. They wish to see the pride of their fallen brethren avenged and humbled by the fact that we, notwithstanding the lowliness of our nature, receive glory as great as theirs. This reason should also incite us to esteem grace highly, since by its possession we attain to the glory of the Angels. By its loss, however, we become like the devil and are associated with his great fall.

Finally, the Angels rejoice for our sake because, through grace, we become sharers in the greatest good, being reborn as children and heirs of their King. How great is the joy at the court of an earthly king when a crown-prince is born! What rejoicing fills every heart, what great celebrations take place! But of all this rejoicing, the newborn heir can experience nothing when he first sees the light of day. We, however, know what great joy exists in the heavenly court when through the Sacrament of Penance we are again made children of God, or when by good works we merit an increase of grace. And should we—who are the object of it all—alone remain cold and indifferent to all this joy that surrounds us and to all the felicitations that are showered on us? "We made the angels rejoice," says St. Bernard, "when we turned to repentance; let us hasten to make their joy over us complete." (*Serm. 2 in Vig. Nat. Dom. M. 6*). But what am I saying—the joy of the Angels? No, but that of the whole heavenly court, the joy of its most holy Queen, the joy of the adorable Trinity Itself. It is such a joy that the whole Heaven congratulates us at the restoration of our friendship with God.

O inestimable gift of grace! O primary and principal object of God's care and of the congratulations of Saints and Angels! Let us hasten to be the joy of God and of His Angels by growing in grace through good works and by keeping it unstained until death, that we may then really be received into the society of the Angels and, in union with them, praise God forever.

Chapter 46

WE MUST HAVE A GREATER ESTEEM FOR GRACE IN US THAN THE ANGELS AND SAINTS OF THE OLD LAW

FROM THE fact that the Angels esteem grace in us so highly, we may infer how much they love it in themselves and hold it in honor. They have proved this by the fact that they have so faithfully kept grace, and in order to defend it, they engaged in a terrible battle with their rebellious brothers.

For the Angels, also, grace is an entirely unmerited, free gift of God. Hence, their gratitude and their high esteem for it. We men have the same grace as they, the same Gifts of the Holy Ghost, the same fruit of the supernatural endowment, that is, the same vision of God in Heaven. According to its nature, neither grace nor happiness is greater for them than for us, nor is it more supernatural for us than for them. Therefore, we are justified in saying that we should treasure our grace much more than the Angels theirs, because ours is more valuable for us than theirs for them.

First, the grace of the Angels has not cost God anything. God has given it without making any sacrifice, purely out of His generosity, by a simple act of His omnipotence. But for us this pearl has been bought by the sweat, the suffering, the Blood and the death of the Son of God. Therefore, we must be more thankful to God for the smallest degree of grace, that cost Him so much, than the Angels are for the abundance of grace that was showered upon them.

Every degree of grace in us is especially dear and valuable also to the heart of God, as the child whom she has borne with the greatest pain is to a mother. Thus, the Patriarch Jacob loved especially Benjamin, the son of the suffering of his dear Rachel; thus also, King David loved Mt. Sion more than his native city because he had taken it in a bloody battle. How precious and holy, then, the smallest degree of grace ought to be to us since we enjoy the benefit of it!

If the fall of Lucifer, who lost grace as quickly and easily as he had obtained it, was immediately followed by so great a commotion in Heaven that he and his associates were at once cast into the deepest abyss, how much should he lament his fall who is made a traitor, not only to his Creator, but also to his loving Redeemer, by so frivolously risking the grace bought so dearly and laboriously? Such a one insults the Precious Blood, the adorable suffering and death of the Son of God—a thing which no angel did—and therefore has more reason to lament his fall than the reprobate angels have to mourn theirs. How can a man be blind to the greatness of this loss and look at it with indifference?

Moreover, grace was given to the Angels but once, and once having lost it, they were never to be offered it again. We, on the other hand, have all lost it in Adam, and we still frequently lose it by our personal sins, and nevertheless, we receive it back again and again.

A thing is prized more highly by its owner when, after having lost it, he gets it back again. Thus, the shepherd rejoices over the sheep that he had found again, a father rejoices over the return of his lost son, the widow over the coin she has recovered—they rejoice more over the recovered good than over the things that have never been lost. Hence, our Saviour and the Angels, as He Himself says, have greater joy over a sinner who does penance than over ninety-nine just who do not need penance. (Cf. *Luke* 15:7). Should we not then esteem the treasure of grace more now that we have, without any merit on our part, recovered it, after having lost it so frivolously? And should we in the future be equally careless about preserving it, or so abuse the hope of recovering it again by risking its loss with even greater carelessness?

Be that far from us! Rather, we should, after having had the misfortune of losing it once, preserve it henceforth with greater care, if possible, than the Angels who never lost it, lest perhaps otherwise we lose it forever.

Our grace appears still more precious compared with the grace of the Angels when we consider that the Angels are indeed children of God, but not as we are, members of Christ. By grace, however, we are made living members of the [Mystical] Body of Christ, who has taken on our nature. As the dignity of our Head is reflected upon us, a new luster is added to our grace; indeed, our nature has a certain claim to grace itself. For God must love us more than the Angels since His Son stands in our midst and He has raised our nature higher since He made it one with His. In Christ, our nature has been raised above all the choirs of Angels, and through this nature we shall share the honor of our Head.

Truly, if the Angels were capable of envy, they would be tempted to it because God has so greatly favored us, notwithstanding the lowliness of our nature. Who then could be so foolish as to esteem the grace of Christ so little and to prefer something else to it? Let us emulate the holy Angels in their high estimate of grace. If they have more light and strength for this, we have more motives. Though they can preserve it easily and without effort, we ought to account it a special honor to be able to suffer something and to make some sacrifice for its sake. God in Heaven will behold this emulation with great pleasure, and the Angels themselves will gladly assist us therein.

The Saints of the Old Testament were indeed, through the merits of Christ, given the same grace that is given to us. They lived under the shadow of a strict law and did not enjoy that wonderful familiarity with God, which Christ has given us, as is evident from His words, "All things whatsoever I have heard of my Father, I have made known to you." (*John* 15:15). In the Old Testament the just were not given that fullness of the Holy Ghost, that sweet and strong love, that spiritual and heavenly mind that Christ, after His Resurrection, gives to His members. Therefore, the observance of the divine law was not for the faithful such a light and pleasant yoke as it has become for us through the merits and example of our Saviour.

Moreover, the Saints of the Old Testament did not have the good fortune of being able to unite themselves so intimately with Christ, the Fount of grace, as we may do in the most holy Sacrament of the altar. They could not truly enjoy the heavenly bread of the children of God, nor could they drink the grace-stream of Christ's Blood in the other Sacraments, with which we daily refresh and rejuvenate our souls.

Finally, in the Old Testament grace did not have the power to lead the children of God after death into the inheritance of their Father, but they had to languish in Limbo until the death and Ascension of Christ. And yet, how great was their hunger and thirst for justice! How carefully they walked in the fear of the Lord that they might not lose His grace! How great were the sacrifices they made! They preferred to suffer all things rather than lose the grace of God through one sin. How they will put us to shame on the Day of Judgment, because we who have received such greater gifts and graces remain so cold and tepid! Yes, we even show to God the greatest ingratitude. How we shall tremble in their presence before God's judgment seat, unable to make an answer or an excuse—we whom God has honored more than them, yes, even more than the Angels!

Let us remember, then, that we are more obligated toward God than Abraham and Moses, more than the Prophets, more even than the Angels, and let us therefore make an effort to retain grace as faithfully as they did and to make the talent entrusted to us bring forth fruit.

Indeed, we have a difficult task before us if we wish to equal in faith, hope, chastity, love and patience the champions of these virtues, Moses, Abraham, Joseph, Isaias, Job and Tobias. And we should not merely equal them, but surpass them, surpass them in the same proportion in which the excellence of the New Testament surpasses that of the Old Testament.

Chapter 47

HOW HIGHLY THE SAINTS VALUED GRACE AND HOW MUCH THEY DID FOR ITS SAKE

I F ANY MEN have esteemed grace according to its true worth, insofar as this is possible here on earth, without doubt it has been the Saints of the New Law. If we wish, therefore, to realize the true value of grace, we shall do best to follow these Saints.

In order to defend and to preserve grace, the Saints have spared neither their honor, their property, their limbs nor their lives. Rather, they believed, after having sacrificed all these things for grace, that they had gained great profit in the loss of all earthly and natural goods, and they thought that grace was given to them gratis, even though they had paid such a great price.

They thought of the words of our Divine Saviour which teach us to tear out our eye, to cut off hand or foot, daily to carry our cross and even to give our life, in order to keep from losing grace and Heaven.

Following these words of our Saviour, the holy martyr Quirinus allowed his hands and feet to be cut off; St. Serapion permitted his body to be hacked into pieces; St. Nicephorus allowed himself to be burned on the gridiron and afterwards to have his whole body crushed and torn to pieces. But why do we consider individuals only, since innumerable martyrs suffered the same and even greater tortures. All that the rage of Hell and wicked men could devise was not painful enough but that the martyrs would have endured still more for the sake of grace.

Other Saints did not even wait until an enemy's hand inflicted such cruelties. In order to escape or lessen the danger of losing grace, they freely became their own tyrants and considered themselves fortunate to be able to buy perseverance in grace by means of the greatest suffering, mortifications and sacrifices. St. John Bonus stuck sharp splinters under his fingernails, that he might be able to overcome a difficult temptation against holy purity. The Blessed Martinian made a slow fire of brushwood and then allowed his limbs to be burnt on it, asking himself meanwhile how insignificant was this pain when compared to the eternal fire of Hell, of which he would make himself deserving by losing grace. St. Francis rolled his bare body at one time on cold snow, at another on thorns, in order to make himself strong against the dangers of the flesh.

All of these torments seemed trivial to the Saints if they could, by means of them, avoid a sin. They were not stones, as Job says (cf. *Job* 6:12), so as to be insensible to pleasure or pain. But the perception of the heavenly sweetness of grace and the desire of its preservation overcame all pain and gave them the wonderful courage that we can only behold with mute admiration. They preferred to sacrifice the fragile vessel of their body than to lose the precious treasure of grace from their soul.

Others, again, to whom all the joys, honors and riches of the world were offered, wished rather to leave all these and to pass their whole life in suffering, poverty and contempt, than to expose themselves to the many dangers with which the world makes the preservation of grace difficult. Thousands and millions have done this, and very many still do it daily before our eyes.

The world is astounded and makes fun of such a queer step, but those who take such a step know what is good for them. With a lively faith they have recognized the infinite value of grace and the vanity of the world; they have put both on the balance, and the world has been found wanting. They sought and found in the grace of God the heavenly peace which their hearts longed for, and therefore, they are so jealous of it that they will let no other good, no other pleasure, rob them of its possession or disturb them from its enjoyment.

How ashamed we must be, in view of these sublime examples, that we do so little to keep grace! We avoid the least sacrifice that might ward off a danger of sin or help us to remain faithful to the commandments of our heavenly Father. We find every little suffering too great to undergo for the sake of grace. Indeed, we increase our weakness by fleeing from self-denial; by our effeminacy we increase the flames of evil desires.

This should not be. Let us rather sacrifice health and body, honor and life, let us give up all things without exception, rather than expose ourselves to the danger of losing grace. Let us willingly receive every temptation and trial from God and take upon ourselves every act of self-denial and burdensome thing, rather than risk the loss of grace.

Still more are we put to shame when we see how much the Saints have done and suffered, not only to retain grace and to escape His anger, with its terrible effects, but also to increase grace in themselves and to make others partakers of it.

St. Bridget begged God that she might lose her extraordinary beauty and be disfigured in countenance that she might more easily remain a virgin and be able to serve God more freely. She had obtained for a pious nun the restoration of her sight. Later on, when this nun had made more progress in virtue, through the prayers of St. Bridget, it was granted to her again to become blind, that she might thus pray without disturbance, and through the practice of patience, increase in the grace of God and in merit.

St. Mandet, son of a king of Ireland, asked and obtained as a favor from God an awful disease that disfigured his whole body and spread a pestilential odor about him, that he might not be obliged to marry, but by virginity might preserve the flower of grace more pure and splendid.

When St. Sabas, while still a boy, had allowed himself while working in the garden to be overcome by a temptation to take an apple from a tree, he immediately threw it on the ground and trampled it under foot, and as a punishment, he denied himself for the rest of his life the pleasure of eating apples.

The world becomes impatient at such deeds and calls

them foolish and superfluous. The Saints, with the Apostle, have also called them foolishness—foolishness, however, for the sake of Christ (cf. *1 Cor.* 4:10), a foolishness in God, who is wiser than all that passes for wisdom among men. (Cf. *1 Cor.* 1:25). But they did not consider their strict life worthless. If they had not been convinced that all this effort was advantageous, and sometimes even necessary, for preserving grace and increasing in holiness, they would not have made the way to Heaven so difficult.

How do we dare to blame the Saints because their rigor condemns our tepidity? Would we not do better to say to ourselves that, if they found such effort necessary in fighting for grace, we must make still greater effort because of our weakness?

We must blush when we glance at the practice of virtues, the humiliations, the self-denial and mortification which the Fathers of the Desert and so many Saints practiced for years in order to grow daily in merit and grace and to become more pleasing to God.

Never did human ambition or human avarice seek the goods of this world with such zeal and perseverance as the Saints have sought the increase of the grace given them. The ardent desire for it left them no rest day or night; there was in them a burning thirst that could never be entirely satiated with the heavenly dew of grace. They let no moment pass in which they did not raise their thirsting heart to the fountain of grace and open their mouth, begging God to fill them with His grace. They passed the day in labor for the glory of God and the welfare of their fellow man in order to amass ever greater merits, and the night they devoted to prayer to draw down upon themselves additional graces.

Therefore, it is not to be wondered at that the Saints, who sought grace for themselves so zealously, strove with such care and effort to obtain it also for others. Behold the Apostles and the other missionaries, who leave family and country to proclaim the blessings of grace to the most savage nations, to spread its light to the most distant parts of the earth, notwithstanding countless troubles and difficulties. See how ready and happy they are to seal the truth of their glad tidings with their blood, and even to shed the last drop of their blood in imitation of their Saviour, that it may become a fruitful seed of grace and salvation for their executioners.

Many Saints have gladly risked honor and even life itself to deliver one sinner from the state of sin. Others spent whole nights in prayer and scourged themselves to blood to obtain the grace of conversion for sinners. No labor, no sacrifice was too great when there was a question of leading a stray sheep back into the bosom of grace.

How can we remain idle in view of such examples, and how can we esteem as little that which the Saints, who were enlightened from above, valued so highly! Indeed, we can never answer for it if, in the face of such sublime models, we are still so indolent in gathering heavenly treasures for eternity. What account can we give of ourselves if, instead of cooperating in the sanctification of others, we help to confirm them in their tepidity and if we deal with grace as with some earthly trifle?

The sublime enthusiasm of the Saints for grace sprang from a deep consideration and thorough knowledge of its inestimable value. Hence, they could not find words to express its excellence and to reveal its inexhaustible riches, to impress its value on us and to admonish us to treasure and preserve it carefully.

Let us hear, in the name of all the others, the enthusiastic admonition of St. Ephrem: "Take care," he says, "always to hold fast divine grace in your hearts, that you may not be deceived. Honor grace as your guardian, that it may not be offended by you and depart from you. Heed it as your invisible teacher, so that you may not have to wander about in darkness, as you will have to do if it departs from you. Without it, begin no struggle, lest you be ignominiously overcome. Without its companionship, do not enter on the path of virtue, for the roaring lion prepares snares for you. Without its counsel, undertake nothing with regard to your spiritual welfare, for there are many whose heart has been disturbed by the appearance of good.

"Obey grace with a ready will, and it will enlighten you concerning all things. It will make you a child of the Most High if you will adopt it as a sister. As a mother, grace will offer you her breasts and protect you as a child from your persecutors; trust in its love and favor, for it is the queen of all creatures.

"You have not seen the love that grace bears you. But neither do infants recognize the care that their mother has for them. Be patient and submit to the direction of grace, and you will receive its fruits and blessings. Neither do infants know how they are nourished, but when they have grown up and have become men, they admire the power of nature in themselves. So shall you attain perfection if you persevere in divine grace." (*De gratia, ed. Vossius,* 76s).

—Part 5—

HOW TO GROW IN GRACE

Chapter 48

THE ACQUISITION OF GRACE

IF FROM THE previous Parts you have been convinced of the glories and of the inestimable worth of divine grace and if you now esteem it at its true value, you will desire nothing more earnestly than to know how to acquire, increase and retain it and how to regulate your life in accordance with it. It is of this that this fifth Part will treat.

The first and most important question, therefore, is how we may acquire Divine grace. Through our own power or merit, it cannot be acquired. "And if by grace, it is not now by works," says the Apostle; "otherwise grace is no more grace." (*Rom.* 11:6). "Now to him who works, the reward is not credited as a favor, but as something due." The word *grace* designates, first of all, a free, unmerited love or gift. But the grace of God is a very special gift, as has often been said already. It is such a sublime, heavenly good that not even the purest and most excellent creature can merit it by its own power of works, even in the remotest way. (Cf. *Rom.* 3:24).

Only the incarnate Son of God, who by nature possesses grace in an infinite measure, can, in the strict sense, merit it for us. (*S. Th.* 1, 2, q. 114, a. 6). Indeed, we can by no means acquire grace for ourselves through our own efforts. No more than we could call ourselves out of nothingness and give to ourselves natural being or existence could we bring forth in ourselves supernatural life. For grace does not grow out of our natural powers, as plants from their roots, but it comes to our nature from without. It is poured into us from above, as a branch is grafted onto a wild tree.

The same God who has given us being must create us also supernaturally through His wonderful power, or rather, He

315

must beget us again through His Spirit, in order to make us His children. What then, we may ask, remains for us to do in regard to the acquisition of grace? Much, very much! Though we cannot merit grace nor produce it of ourselves, we may, led by it, prepare ourselves for it and make ourselves capable of receiving it, for in our supernatural life also we remain free.

We can and should seek grace from God. We must remove the obstacles that stand in its way and so dispose our wills that grace may find a welcome there, and though we are not worthy to receive it, we should not be entirely unworthy. We can and should strive for a disposition that is pleasing to God and befits the high state into which grace leads us. Inspired by grace, we can and should open our arms to it. God will then, according to His promise, come to us with it.

Of course, we cannot do all this through our own power alone. It is one of the errors expressly condemned by the Church which holds that man by his own natural power can effectually desire grace or prepare himself for it. Much less, then, can he be said to merit it. For, since grace is infinitely above our nature, at every step toward it, our nature would have to raise itself above itself and exceed its natural sphere of activity. But this it can no more do than it can, by its own power, raise itself to the state of grace, just as a stone not only cannot give life, but cannot even produce in itself the first beginnings of life. Nothing remains, therefore, than that the same Spirit of God who infuses into us Sanctifying Grace should also, by His actual grace, move us toward it, or rather, draw and bear us up to it. "No man can come to me," says the Son of God, that is, no one can be united to Me through grace, "except the Father, who hath sent me, draw him. . ." (*John* 6:44).

Indeed, St. Paul teaches that we cannot even think effectually and in a way useful to salvation on that which is related to grace: "Not that we are sufficient to think any thing of ourselves, as of ourselves: but our sufficiency is from God." (*2 Cor.* 3:5).

By its nature, iron cannot make itself red hot; therefore, neither can it create in itself the first degree of warmth that would dispose and lead it to intense heat. Rather, the fire that makes it glowing hot must also gradually warm it up. As fire makes iron red hot, God, through grace, makes a created spirit like Himself. Consequently, He alone can prepare, by other supernatural gifts of grace, the entrance of creatures into this supernatural state.

The bright light of day, and the morning dawn that precedes it, are of the same species and flow from the same source. Hence, if through grace the daylight of divine holiness and justice is to shine in our souls (and the preparation for justification is nothing else than the dawn of that day), such a preparation must be a ray of the same Divine Sun of which we partake through justification.

We must, indeed, in order to prepare ourselves for justification, practice the same virtues and have the same dispositions as after justification—though in a less perfect degree. We must believe in God, hope in Him, and love Him in a supernatural way, or we must at least earnestly long for the fulfillment of His supernatural law. But this can only take place if God draws us supernaturally by a special actual grace, or already before the reception of Sanctifying Grace, makes us conscious to a certain degree of the beginnings of the supernatural virtues.

Indeed, these supernatural virtues have their root in grace alone. But as light and heat have their origin in the flame of fire and yet may, in the object to be heated, precede the fire itself, so may God, before justification, infuse the supernatural virtues, which are the light and warmth of grace, at least in an imperfect form, in order to lead us gradually to grace.

Preparation, therefore, for Sanctifying Grace is an anticipation of its effects. It is the first breathing of the Holy Ghost, through which He makes us feel His gracious nearness, announces His coming and invites us to open the door of our heart to Him and to accept the proffered grace. It is a supernatural magnetism by which our soul is drawn to God as to its supernatural good, although it has not yet attained union with Him through Sanctifying Grace.

Our part, therefore, in justification can consist only in

this, that we faithfully cooperate with the graces that are given us as the forerunners and beginning of Sanctifying Grace. We must open our eyes to the light that dawns upon our soul and makes our heart responsive to the mysterious impulse that grips us. We must actually accept with our free will, elevated and strengthened by God's prevenient grace, the holy disposition that God infuses into us; that is indispensable for the reception of Sanctifying Grace.

But even by this cooperation with the prevenient grace, we do not in a true and strict sense merit Sanctifying Grace. For through this cooperation, we do not prepare ourselves to receive a reward, but rather, a gift, and this we receive, not because we have merited it, but because, out of His free love, God gives it to us.

Would you say that someone merits a gift that you offer him out of love because he stretches forth his hand with your help and invitation? And if a king would promise one of his subjects that he would take him as his child under the condition that he would put on the royal clothing furnished by the king and strive to wear it in a way becoming the promised dignity—would such a one merit, through the fulfillment of such a condition, that the king adopt him for his child? By no means!

So it is also with Sanctifying Grace. God has destined it for us out of pure love, on account of the merit of His Son; whereas, we were not only not worthy of it, but through sin we were positively unworthy. Even after it was offered to us, we could not even stretch out our hand for it, much less adopt the holy sentiments that are becoming a child of God. Even if we had been capable of this, grace would still have been a free gift of God, that He would have been obliged to give us only in view of His gracious promises. But now, since God Himself gives us our first desire for grace, since He not only lays it before us but also leads us to it, can we in any way boast of our merits? Must we not be doubly thankful for this twofold love of God?

Indeed, if we faithfully cooperate with His prevenient grace, God will not withhold Sanctifying Grace from us. But whence is He obligated? Not by our cooperation, but rather because, being God, He must remain faithful to Himself and must perfect the work that He has begun. He is bound by the fact that, once He has led us to grace, He cannot leave this first act fruitless and without a purpose, but He must carry it through to its final goal.

From what has been said, we see that the acquisition of grace is an extremely delicate and difficult affair. Grace itself must do so much that the little that remains to be done by us almost disappears in comparison with it. We must, of course, do our part. But the smaller this part is, the more careful we must be not to omit it. For, when it is a question of such little things, the neglect of the smallest detail can cause very great loss.

If we wish, therefore, to acquire Sanctifying Grace, we must faithfully correspond to all the illuminations, warnings and inspirations of God's preventive [prevenient] grace. This grace God gives to all. It is present to us without our seeking it. Even against our will, it knocks at the door of our heart, that admittance may be accorded to the Holy Ghost. If we follow the first motions of grace, God will undoubtedly give us new and more powerful inspirations, and if we make use of these, He will lead us on step by step until He has made us His children.

Here we understand the earnestness of the admonition: "Today if you shall hear his voice, harden not your hearts." (*Ps.* 94:8). All depends on our acceptance of the grace that knocks for the first time at our heart's door. For what will become of us if, as a punishment for our lingering, that grace departs from us? All depends on our doing our part today; for we have *today,* but who guarantees that we shall have *tomorrow?* All depends on our faithful perseverance, as long as there is a *today* for us. For what good is there in having begun well yesterday, if today we interrupt what we have begun?

Oh, how serious is the way to life! Only when we do all that we can on our part shall we reach our goal. When grace gives us everything and does all our works in us, only then can we begin, only then can we make progress and end well. Only when enlightened by the light of God and borne by His own power can we climb from the first step to the last the mysterious ladder that leads from the lowliness of our nature and the abyss of sin to the throne of God.

But first of all, it is a question, not of attaining our goal, but of the first dispositions and beginnings. Here also we have that same cooperation between grace and our activity. Here also the beginning belongs to grace; fidelity in cooperating is our affair. Only with the help of God can we acquire that supernatural preparation for grace which, according to the holy Council of Trent, consists of faith, fear, hope, love and contrition. Of these we shall now treat singly.

Chapter 49

SUPERNATURAL FAITH AS THE
FIRST PREPARATION FOR THE
RECEPTION OF GRACE

IN THE THIRD Part, we have already spoken of supernatural faith, as well as of supernatural hope and love,
but only insofar as these virtues, by reason of their inner
splendor, form the royal retinue of Sanctifying Grace. And
toward the end of this book we must again speak of faith,
since it is necessary to show how the whole Christian life
must be permeated and guided by the spirit of faith, if it is
to correspond to its task.

Faith has a threefold work to fulfill. First of all, through
it we must dispose ourselves for the reception of supernatural grace. God's actual grace helps us in this. Sanctifying
Grace, which is given to us after actual grace, cannot give
us habitual faith, since we do not possess this Sanctifying
Grace itself. It works in an anticipated way insofar as the
actual grace that is given us to make faith possible is given
in view of Sanctifying Grace, that is, in order to make us
capable of receiving this latter. When, then, habitual Sanctifying Grace is poured into us, we receive with it the habitual, supernatural gifts. Among these are the supernatural
habits, that is, permanent faculties for the exercise of the
so-called Theological Virtues [faith, hope and charity],
among which faith holds first place. But there is a great difference between the more or less frequent use of these
virtues and the spirit of faith that should permeate all our
thinking and acting. All our progress toward perfection
depends on the fervor of this spirit. Hence, we must deal
with this in a special way later on.

We are considering faith here as the preparation for justification. The first condition for the reception of grace—and at the same time the beginning, the foundation and the root of all other conditions, and therefore also, according to the holy Council of Trent (Sess. 6, c. 8), of justification itself—is supernatural faith.

Faith, itself already a gift of God, is the first step on the way to grace. (Cf. St. Aug., *De praed. Sanct.* c. 3, n. 7). Without it we cannot take another step. It is the cornerstone, on which all other salutary acts must build. (Cf. *St. Aug. ep.* 194, c. 3, n. 9). It is the living and powerful root out of which all else that is necessary for the attainment of grace sprouts of itself, as it were, and receives strength and life. "The first word of him who recognizes himself as a Christian," says the great Cardinal Hosius (*Confessio cath. fidei* c. 1), "is the word, *I believe.*" Faith makes a man a Christian, even when it is not yet living through love," says another great theologian. (Soto, *Natura et gratia* 1, 2, c. 8, prop. 2). In one word, faith is the first and most essential preparation for grace because it alone enables us to know, to seek and to receive grace. (*S. Th.* 1, 2, q. 113, a. 4).

For, if we wish to acquire grace, we must first of all recognize its splendor and its inestimable value, in order to desire and to seek it. Secondly, we must know where and how to seek and find it, in order that we may actually seek it there, insofar as this is possible to us, and with God's help find it.

In all this, faith must help us, not only in knowing but also in seeking and finding grace. Let this be said very clearly from the beginning that we may avoid every fatal error that would limit the faith to a merely rational activity.

Faith is indeed a work of man's intellect. This also must be emphasized. For we live in times when not a few wish to reduce it to mere trust. The intellect, they say, is completely free and can bend under no authority, except the command of its own vision. Therefore, [this error claims that] one must distinguish well between faith of the intellect and faith of the heart. No one can demand of us faith of the intellect. That we must give of ourselves. But we can give it of ourselves only if we have vision of that which it requires of us. Moreover, we have no reason to worry if we cannot give this intellectual assent. For true faith is that of the heart. That alone is important; that alone is required by God. Even when our reason cannot assent to a truth of faith, we may still have the faith that is necessary for salvation if we only embrace with our heart that which the dogmatic formula wishes to express—even though our intellect has every reason to doubt the literal correctness of the formula itself.

This error has been expressly condemned by the Church, and whoever dares to affirm that the obligation of faith cannot be imposed on the intellect is considered as having deviated from Christian truth. (*Conc. Vat.*, sess. 3, c. 3, 1). And it is considered heretical to say that the assent which the intellect can and should give is nothing more than the necessary conclusion of the premises grasped by reason. (*Conc. Vat.*, chap. 3).

Faith is above all an act of the intellect. It is, moreover, a subjection of the intellect to God's word. It must be that—even when it is capable of a greater or lesser insight into the truths of revelation. (*Conc. Vat.*, can. 3, 5).

Precisely in this lies the importance of faith as preparation for the supernatural life. Grace, it is true, makes us children of God; whereas, by nature we would be merely His servants. But this makes no change in the natural obligation of men to consecrate themselves to God in complete subjection. The Christian remains a man, just as God remains the Lord, even when He condescends to become our Father. When a servant is adopted as a child, far from losing his obligations toward his lord, he is now bound by them in a much higher way. For us, however, whom God makes partakers of His nature without undergoing any change in Himself, there is added a second, far more weighty, obligation of giving ourselves entirely to God.

It is evidently an indispensable presupposition for adoption among the children of God that we declare that we wish to use this distinction not as a pretext for withdrawing ourselves from this service of God, but rather as a summons to give ourselves to Him more completely than we have done heretofore.

Now we easily understand why faith is demanded of us precisely as a sacrifice of reason. A man may give up everything; he may reject even his own will, if necessary; only one thing does he retain for himself, namely, his own opinion, the right to think for himself (at least in his heart) concerning what he agrees with or what does not please him. Thus, he can deceive men, but not God, who sees man's inner self. This is precisely the sacrifice that God demands above all, the sacrifice of the most noble gift that He has given us. Truly it is to reject God contemptuously to declare that we are ready to give Him everything else—only our best, our reason, must be refused. In the Old Testament God forbade with serious threats the offering to Him of a defective sacrifice. And we, the children of promise, dare—what even the obstinate Jews did not dare—to drag a victim before the altar from which we have previously cut off the head!

Though the subjection of reason is the most important part of the sacrifice that God desires of us, it is not the whole of it. God does not accept a partial sacrifice. He desires the whole man for Himself, not that He has need of him, but in order to reform the whole man and thus to restore him to Himself.

That is one of the reasons why He has so created man in such a way that not one of his constituent parts can by itself fulfill his task. The will cannot perform a truly human act, unless the intellect cooperates and leads the way. And the intellect will never be convinced, even in matters that are most evident, unless the will permits. A perfect act, in which God can find pleasure and man true satisfaction, must be of such a kind that the understanding shows the right way to the will and the will supports the understanding, that it may do its duty—an act in which the heart cooperates, that the result may not be the mere fulfilling of an obligation, but may be done with warmth and enthusiasm, not merely as the fulfilling of a law, but as a joyful effluence of the whole inner man.

If this holds in regard to the ordinary acts of life, it is so in a very special way when there is a question of our salvation, and God Himself takes this in His hands. The works of God are perfect. With Him there is no half-way measure or piecemeal work. God does not leave men with only one half, but He comes to their help in regard to the whole.

Concerning mere intellectual faith and faith of the heart, to have one without the other is indeed possible, if a man gives a purely human assent, because the deeds of men have the sad privilege of being able to be imperfect and contradictory. But this is not so in the supernatural sphere. A one-sided intellectual faith is not divine faith, and the same is to be said of one-sided faith of the heart.

That it be true faith, having value in God's sight, all the constituent elements must work together in unison. Hence the teaching of the Church that the act of faith is a free act (*Conc. Vat.*, sess. 3, can. 3, 5), in other words, that it is not merely a necessary conviction of the intellect through its own insight, but that it is rather a subjection of the understanding through the will, in obedience, as the Apostle says (Cf. *2 Cor.* 10:5).

The will must move the intellect to consider the reasons for believing. And after the intellect is convinced and has informed the will that it is not unreasonable, but rather entirely justifiable to accept the proffered proofs of the Divine veracity, the will must again move the intellect to go through with the act. And thus finally the act of faith is produced through the mutual cooperation of intellect and will, whose union, so to say, the heart blesses.

No one comes to faith by research alone. One may be thoroughly convinced of the truth and yet not be able to make the act of faith. If a man does not wish to believe, no reason will convince him; or if he is convinced, no conviction will bring him to true faith. Therefore, one must want to believe; then he can, provided, of course, that he is aided by grace. But one must not doubt this, for it is precisely grace that has pushed him thus far, that manifests itself to him through the unrest in his heart, that does not leave him even if he turns away from it.

For the faith that should make us children of God is a supernatural act. Therefore, all one's thinking and all one's willing is not of itself sufficient. The Church, with very deep insight, speaks of the pious desires to believe as the best disposition for faith. The act of faith is far from being an empty activity of the intellect; it is rather an act of piety.

This was very well expressed by that man mentioned in the Gospel who, with an apparent contradiction, cried out: "I do believe, Lord: help my unbelief." (*Mark* 9:23). "As far as it lies in me," he wished to say, "I have done all that belongs to the act of faith. I am convinced, I wish to believe. But I see well that that is not yet faith, as it should be. Therefore, help me with Thy grace in order that it may really become perfect."

O happy man, who has thus shown us the last decisive step. Since grace is essentially supernatural, we cannot produce it, but God must give it to us. Since faith is a human act, a virtue, we must also do our part. Since faith is both human and divine, a union of the natural and supernatural, God must bow down to us with the gift of faith, and we must raise ourselves up to God through prayer for faith. This prayer is the best thing that we can and must do in order to obtain faith. In this, the Holy Ghost certainly aids us, without our even knowing for what we must ask. (Cf. *Rom.* 8:25).

We see from what has been said how many factors enter in before one possesses the faith that is necessary for salvation. Perhaps many a one thinks he has faith, when it is in reality far from him. In this affair, the beginning of our salvation, deception is not at all difficult.

How little is faith understood by those who think that it is a thing for weak minds and hardly worth the time of men who have more important things to think of. As though there could be something more important and of more worth for one's supernatural and eternal life! As though there were something that contains more in itself and demands more effort in the right direction than faith!

Much more belongs to faith, and there is much more in faith than many think. On faith is based the entire substance of the Christian religion. To believe is not merely to accept some truth—for example, the existence of God. Faith does not merely consist in the fact that one accepts some truth in view of God's testimony. We speak of *believing in God,* and this expression has a deep meaning. That is more, far more, than simply to give faith to God. To believe in God is to direct one's whole soul, understanding, will and heart to God as to one's goal; it is to place oneself entirely in God's service: it is to seek God with all one's powers. To believe in God is to give one's whole being that orientation whose end is perfect love. Faith in God turns the soul to God; love actually attains God. Faith is the beginning; love is the completion.

Therefore, it is not to be wondered at if in Holy Scripture the acquisition of grace and justification are so expressly ascribed to faith that it almost appears that nothing else is needed thereto. It is a great mistake, likewise, and a dangerous narrowing of the way of salvation to consider faith as the only preparatory element for justification. (*Conc. Trid.,* sess. 6, cap. 5, 6 can. 9).

Indeed, if justification is nothing else than a mere imputation of the merits of Christ, in a purely external justice by which the inner wickedness and sinfulness of our souls is covered over, but in which the soul is not renewed and reformed interiorly, then faith in Christ might by itself be sufficient. (*Conc. Trid.,* cap. 9, can. 12).

But in reality, faith is only the beginning of justification, which goes far beyond this first step. It would be a strange honor for God if we would refer to Him only faith—a part of the work of grace—and deny Him the other elements. Justifying faith is not only faith in the cause, but also in the effect, and indeed the whole effect of grace.

The effect of the love of God and of redemption through Christ is the expulsion of sin, the inner change of a sinner into a child of God, and the pouring in of God's holiness. In short, it is the raising of the soul to a condition of supernatural glorification by the Holy Ghost, who dwells in it.

From this it follows that it cannot be enough if we impart to ourselves through faith the merits of Christ and at the same time are unwilling to move a hand to make His virtues our own and to receive His gifts into our heart and to cultivate what He has planted there. Therefore, faith must be accompanied by many other preparations that dispose us to receive that wonderful gift.

These other preparatory elements, however, are all included in some way in faith and only through it have an effective influence in the acquisition of grace. For through faith we receive from God the movements of grace that are necessary for salutary fear, hope and contrition. Moreover, through faith we are moved to fear the anger of God, to hate sin, to hope in God, to love justice and to seek after grace.

Through faith we consecrate all other preparatory acts, draw down on them the blessing of God and unite them with Sanctifying Grace. For since we cannot merit these in the strict sense, we must expect them from the omnipotence and goodness of God through the merits of Christ.

Through faith, finally, we make fruitful the grace that we have received and bring its fruit to maturity. All the virtues, as well as the highest degrees of Christian perfection, have their root in faith and draw their strength from it. (S. Th. 2, 2, q. 4, a. 7). Such are, for example: contrition, the spirit of penance, love of mortification, the spirit of prayer, the imitation of Christ, the love of God. Devotion in prayer is nothing else than lively faith; as our faith in the presence and majesty of God is, so will our recollection and fervor be. Our subjection to God's providence and our submission to His holy Will correspond to the measure of our faith. The measure of our love of God, our spirit of sacrifice, our striving to be like God—all these will be as strong and fervent as our faith.

Hence, faith must also follow the other preparatory elements, as well as preceding them, in order, through submission to God, to impress His seal on them and to make them acceptable to Him. We wish merely to mention this here, since we are to consider it more thoroughly later. Here, it is only a question of preparation for grace.

Among all the dispositions for grace, it has been clearly proven that faith is the first, both as regards time and importance. One must not, however, understand the word "disposition" as though faith were only necessary at the beginning and lost its importance later. That would be the error—condemned by the Church—which holds that faith corresponds only to the first steps of a child in Christian life, and cedes its role to other higher factors when one progresses in this same life.

No, faith is indispensable in the beginning, indispensable for progress, indispensable for perfection. Faith is necessary as preparation for justification, as well as for preserving and using the grace obtained in justification. Faith is so necessary that God has made the activity of the means of grace dependent on it. As Christ has joined the activity of His miraculous power to faith, we are likewise justified by faith, even when we receive grace in the Sacraments. Not as though our faith gives its strength to the Sacraments, as one pours water into a basin when he wishes to wash his hands. They operate, as is said, *ex opere operato,* that is, they themselves hold the water of grace that flows out of the heart of our Saviour. But they can exercise their power only when those who receive them, on the one hand, open the canals through which grace flows to us from God and Christ, and on the other hand, hold their heart underneath so that the stream of water does not flow away. (*S. Th.* 3, q. 62; q. 69, a. 9. a. 9).

It is perfectly true that we find grace only through supernatural faith, just as we can seek it only through faith. Therefore, the Apostle says: "By whom [Christ] also we have access through faith into this grace, wherein we stand, and glory in the hope of the glory of the sons of God." (*Rom.* 5:2).

One sees from what has been said that it is hardly possible to exhaust the full meaning and importance of faith. To repeat once more, it is precisely the contents of the whole Christian life. It is also faith, therefore, that impresses on the Christian life its own peculiar character.

Our Christian faith is the direct opposite of that Pharisaical self-justification which thinks it can purchase the favor of God with some poor human deeds. It is equally opposed to that worldly gentlemanliness that is looked upon as holiness if no wrong is done, though it considers itself high above faith and its requirements.

"But without faith it is impossible to please God. For he that cometh to God, must believe that he is, and is a rewarder to them that seek him," says St. Paul. (*Heb.* 11:6). Therefore, he scolds the Jews because they thought that they had merited God's grace through the works of their law, and therefore they refused to submit to Christ in humble faith. Even of Abraham he says: "For if Abraham were justified by works, he hath whereof to glory, but not before God." (*Rom.* 4:2). How much more would he condemn in us a hypocritical, human justice and deny to it any value in God's sight! How much more sharply would he scold us Christians if we did not seek above all things to secure God's favor through purity of faith and the joyful exercise of the same! On the other hand, our faith also contains the condemnation of that opinion that consoles itself with the thought that it can possess the kingdom of God through faith alone, without living according to our belief. Our faith differs from that of the demons only in this, that it makes our heart clean and our hands fruitful in good works; whereas, it merely makes them the more culpable. (*St. Aug.* serm. 53 n. 10). Without works, says St. James, our faith is dead. (Cf. *James* 2:17). It is living, however, when we perform deeds that are a testimony to the power of faith, a testimony that we seek grace from God alone and expect it only from His goodness by reason of the merits of Christ.

Place your trust, therefore, in these words alone, or rather in their root, the humble but great and mighty submission of faith, through which you glory not in yourself but in God. Sink this supernatural root deep into your soul, that it may grow together with you. The more deeply faith is rooted in you, the more quickly and powerfully will the tree of grace grow up with the riches of its heavenly blossoms and fruits.

Chapter 50

FEAR OF GOD AS THE SECOND PREPARATION FOR GRACE

IT MAY BE that the gracious light of faith that shows us the glories of grace is sufficient in its very beginning to subject the heart of the sinner completely to God. Sometimes God effects wonderful things in a moment. His holy intentions and reasons are above our comprehension. Ordinarily, however, the supernatural life imitates the course of our natural life and progresses slowly, step by step, from the first beginnings to the conclusion of the whole work. This is seen also in the activities that faith calls forth.

The first thing faith unveils, after its entrance into the soul of man, is the infinite splendor of the majesty and holiness of God, the depth of the misery into which sin has thrust us and the frightful disproportion that exists between God and us.

Nothing is more natural than the fear that affects a man at the moment when he first deals earnestly with God, as represented to him by faith. It would be unnatural, or a proof that one was lacking in knowledge of God or in true earnestness, if he was not seized by a deep feeling of holy fear of God.

The ordinary way in which a sinner is led back to God is the way of holy fear. It is rightly called "fear of God." It is the majesty of God, the holiness of God with all its properties, one after another, of which is manifested to us the horror God has for all evil, the impossibility of union between His excellence and purity and the lowness of sin, His all-seeing eye, His incorruptible veracity, His justice—that it is which begets the fear of God and which makes it holy fear.

The effects of these divine attributes, His disfavor toward

331

sinners, the punishments that His justice demands, may be the first things that frighten the sinner. But if he is filled with the spirit of faith, he rises from this fear, to God. Faith shows its activity in this, that it leads the sinner to fear, not punishment as such, but eternal punishment, insofar as it proceeds from God and shuts him out from the possession of God, for whom he already longs. There lies also in fear of God's punishment, as begotten by our faith, fear of God's greatness and holiness. (*Conc. Trid,* sess. 6, c. 6).

Any other fear of merely natural evils, of temporal punishments, of loss of health or honor, has nothing to do with the acquisition of grace and cannot easily impel us to seek it. Such a purely natural fear is not entirely without effect, but it cannot lead us into the realm of grace. (*S. Th.* 2, 2, q. 19, a. 4, 5, 6).

Fear of God's disfavor and of its consequence is, on the other hand, a supernatural fear, for it presupposes supernatural faith in the order of grace. Moreover, it is awakened by the fact that the Holy Ghost draws us in a supernatural way to grace and makes us realize that we lose everything with [the loss of] grace and that God will punish terribly those who despise it. (*S. Th.* 2, 2, q. 19, a. 7).

This fear is, according to the holy Council of Trent (*Sess.* 14, c. 4), a gift of the Holy Ghost, a precious and mighty gift that pierces our inner being as a powerful sword and cuts through with holy violence all the bounds that bind us to the object of our sinful love. It constantly hangs over our head until we have taken refuge under the cloak of grace and hidden ourselves in the bosom of God.

If we do not perceive in ourselves the activity of this gift of the Holy Ghost, but continue to live carelessly and boldly, that is because we do not listen to the warning of the Holy Ghost and do not earnestly consider with lively faith the truth that Revelation discovers to us concerning God and ourselves.

The seriousness of these truths, however, concerns not only the so-called great sinners, nor is it intended to affect only beginners in the spiritual life; rather, this holy fear of God is a virtuous practice that should fill our whole life. The

Old Testament cannot find words enough to make us aware of the necessity and utility of the fear of God. If less is said in the New Testament, that is because it is all presupposed, for as our Divine Saviour says, He does not wish to change one iota of the law. (*Cf. Matt.* 5:18). Yes, according to the teaching of the Church, the fear of God remains even in life everlasting.

That can easily be understood. If the basis on which holy fear rests is the majesty and holiness of God, it must be even in those who do not strictly have to be concerned about the rigor of divine justice. A noble soul has a far more potent motive to tremble and to be contrite when it compares its imperfection with the divine purity, when it weighs its own unworthiness in view of the divine benefits, when it thinks of the responsibility the divine love places on it and with what earnestness love is demanded in return.

Only too true are the words that God has spoken through His inspired writer: "He is mighty to forgive and to pour out indignation." (*Ecclus.* 16:12). As sublime, generous and unfathomable as the mercy of God shows itself in making us His children through grace, so frightful and unfathomable also must be the strictness of His justice that will be shown to those who despise His grace. Through grace God pours into us the fullness of His blessings, as an abundant rain; He is filled with love for us and wills to unite Himself to us; He promises to pour over us the stream of His happiness. But the severity of His offended love is equally great; hence, Holy Scripture tells us that He will rain down His war upon the sinner and that He will accomplish His indignation upon them. (Cf. *Job* 20:23; *Ezech.* 6:12).

Nothing is more sensitive than despised love; the greater, the more tender and gracious the love was, so much more powerful, bitter, and frightful will be the anger into which it changes when it is insulted and rejected. Hence, Holy Scripture goes so far as to say, "As the Lord rejoiced upon you before, doing good to you and multiplying you; so he shall rejoice, destroying and bringing you to naught." (*Deut.* 28:63).

God is a pure fire of infinite power and strength—and

likewise a fire of love and anger. As beneficient and pleasant as this powerful fire is when in grace it lovingly penetrates, warms, transforms and glorifies us, it must be equally cruel and terrible when it pierces, consumes, harasses and tortures those who were hardened against its gentle blessings.

As the sin of a child against its father is more detestable and deserving of greater punishment than that of a servant against his master, so the sin we commit as the chosen children of God against our heavenly Father is incomparably greater and more deserving of punishment than that which we might commit as mere servants of God. We must not think, then, that we need fear only those punishments which are threatened in general for any offense against God, though even these are certainly great enough to make every reflecting person tremble with fear. No, in case we have abused grace, we have something very different to expect, of which we have as little an idea as of the heavenly happiness which God has promised us through grace. God opens for us another abyss of infinite depth, as immeasurably deep as the dignity of His children is inestimably high and sublime. And as He expends all His power in order, through His mercy—greater than all miracles—to make us sharers of His nature and happiness, so He employs the same omnipotence to give full rein to His avenging justice against our ingratitude.

We should scarcely believe that God would punish our sins and the contempt of His grace so rigorously had we not seen that His only-begotten Son was obliged to suffer so much—far more than any man has ever suffered—in order to atone for our sins and to regain grace for us. "For if in the green wood they do these things, what shall be done in the dry?" (*Luke* 23:31).

Our imagination is too weak to picture to ourselves such a terrible punishment; our heart is too wretched to sufficiently appreciate such a mysterious evil and to tremble in view of it. Let us therefore ask the Holy Ghost that by the supernatural life of faith He may allow us to glance into the abyss of Hell, and then, by His supernatural grace, awaken a great and holy fear in us. May He pierce our heart and marrow with this fear so that we may dread nothing more than the anger of God and may hasten to escape its terrible judgment by an immediate and determined return to grace. Indeed, it is good for us to place sometimes before our eyes the misery out of which the grace of God has snatched us and what dangers threaten us in the midst of such grace if we do not correspond to our vocation. It was very useful to St. Teresa that God allowed her to see what place would have been hers in Hell if she did not earnestly make use of her excellent qualities. How useful it would be likewise for us, in order to spur us on to greater earnestness in striving after perfection, if we would sometimes consider the dangers that follow the abuse of grace.

We are so afraid of temporal and natural evils that happen to us here below, and in order to escape them, we are often induced to cast away grace or put off regaining it. How much more should we tremble at the eternal and supernatural evils, precisely because we do not see or experience them now and cannot even comprehend them! For this incomprehensibility is a proof of their inestimable greatness and of their inexpressible bitterness; it is a proof that all the natural evils cannot even be compared to them.

Let us often think how awful it is to fall into the hands of the living God (cf. *Heb.* 10:31); following the advice of the Holy Ghost, let us think of our last end and we shall never sin. (Cf. *Ecclus.* 7:40). But if we have sinned, the same holy fear must move us to repent of our sins without delay and to seek again the grace of God, which alone can preserve us from His frightful anger.

Fear of God's wrath suffers no delay; it allows us not a moment's rest until we have escaped the danger. Every moment the sound of God's vengeance is suspended over our head; we may die at any moment, and then we are given up forever to our Judge.

Moreover, we do not know, even if we do live for a long time, whether we shall afterwards regain the grace of God with such ease and certainty. For this depends more on the supernatural help of God, which is not in our hands, than on our free will, and hence we can make no calculations concerning the certainty of our future conversion. Every moment that we pass in the state of sin, we make ourselves less worthy of His grace, insofar as we despise and neglect it all the longer. What if the thread of God's mercy, that holds us back, would break? What if God would withdraw His grace and allow us to sink? How many in Hell now lament, too late, that they despised and neglected so long the rich graces that were offered them and postponed their conversion to a later date!

Let us tremble at the inscrutable judgments of Divine Providence! It is full of goodness and blessing when we hold ourselves by its hand, but it is terrible and unfathomable if we withdraw ourselves and mock and deride it. According to the warning of the Apostle, let us work out our salvation with fear and trembling while there is yet time. Let us tremble before the frightful punishments of eternity, before the inscrutable ways of God, before our own levity and unfaithfulness. This holy fear is, along with faith, the surest foundation for the love of God and the greatest assurance that we shall not lightly cast off the grace we have acquired.

Chapter 51

SUPERNATURAL HOPE AS THE THIRD PREPARATION FOR GRACE

IN VIEW OF the majesty and holiness of God, especially of His offended majesty, and in view of our own weakness, fear would crush us and lead us to despair if it were not for confidence in the infinite goodness and power of God to reopen to us the way to grace and to give us firm hope that with God's help we can acquire it again and keep it until the end.

In the work of salvation, the virtue of hope has a very important role to play. Whosoever has learned through faith to know God and himself thoroughly and does not throw out the anchor of hope at the right time is in great danger of being lost. Faith and fear alone do not make a man better. On the contrary, one not seldom finds men who murmur and even blaspheme against the pretended rigor of God and the undeserved fate of mankind, souls that reject with bitterness and scorn every word concerning improvement, perfection, and salvation—though they are not without faith. Generally they are shipwrecked souls who have not the support of hope, nor indeed that of humility.

Usually, the greatest enemies of faith are those who once possessed it but who cast it away because they did not find the way to climb out of the misery of their nature, and of all its accompanying defects, to the confidence of the children of God. Pressed down by the feeling of God's greatness and their own misery, they threatened at first to fall into despair. But soon they began to consider their wretchedness as invincible and as a right of nature. Finally, they rejected thoughts about God because these weighed heavily on their souls as an unbearable burden. If they had learned to know the virtue of hope, they would have borne their weakness with humility and patience; they could have fought confidently and would have climbed up to higher virtues.

From this it follows that hope has a twofold task. On the one hand, it must lead timid souls to true humility. An abashed, timid man, who has no hope of improvement or forgiveness, always stands on the threshold of impudence or even of revolt. But whereas, on the one hand, hope softens human nature, on the other hand, it raises it up by referring to supernatural help and thus forms, in a certain sense, a bridge to the supernatural world into which the sinner should be led.

Consequently, hope must bear in itself a supernatural character. It can be based on nothing else than the infinite mercy of God, which alone forgives our sins, and on the omnipotence of God, which alone can so strengthen us that in spite of our natural weakness and inconsistency, the highest of all goods rushes upon us.

But this presupposes that we hold fast with supernatural and living faith to two truths: We must be deeply convinced that without God's help our power is of no avail, and that all our wretchedness can offer no impediment to God, provided that we wish to be helped by Him according to His good pleasure. Presupposing this, there is no difficulty in holding fast that God does not cease to call us to His grace, even when we are sinners, and that He places the whole treasure of His omnipotence at our command, in order to lead us to grace. (S. Th. 2, 2, q. 17, a. 7).

Indeed, such confidence is possible only where faith has already struck its roots deep in one's heart. If our faith is weak and wavering, as is often the case, and if we look more at our own sins and weaknesses and at our supposed strength and independence, rather than on the ineffable love of God and the merits of Christ, our hope of regaining grace will likewise be weak and powerless.

But let us with a lively faith look at the undeniable generosity of God and listen to the inspirations of the Holy Ghost, who promises to us forgiveness of our sins and the restoration of grace and so much the more strength from

God the more we give up all false trust in self. Then our trust cannot fail, and with holy confidence the soul goes before the throne of Divine mercy, where it hopes to find forgiveness and mercy and infallibly finds them there.

God has expressly told us in Holy Scripture that He wishes all men to be saved and does not wish the death of the sinner, but rather that he be converted and live. (Cf. *Ez.* 18:23, 32; *1 Tim.* 2:4; *2 Ptr.* 3:9). God might have been more sparing in dispensing His grace and might have ordained that it be imparted only to those who sought it most zealously, and that it might belong to those only who, having received it once, had never lost it. But no: He wished that it rise like the sun on the just and unjust, the pious and the sinners, that all might at all times bask in its light and receive its blessings as soon as they wish to open their eyes. Instead of waiting for us to seek grace from Him, He offers it to us freely and generously at every hour. He Himself knocks constantly at the door of our heart and leaves us no rest until we open to Him. Therefore, the holy Fathers and all theologians teach that God will deny Sanctifying Grace to no one who, with the aid of prevenient grace, does what lies in his power. (*S. Th.* 1, 2, q. 112, a. 3).

Only one thing is necessary on our part: that we have a good will and sincerely desire to receive God's grace and mercy, that we humble ourselves in the consciousness of our helpless and that we raise ourselves to God in faith and trust. All the rest God Himself will do. In His love, He will take away our sins and will give such power to our will that we shall be able to overcome and remove all the impediments of grace.

No matter how severe the justice of God, and though our sins be as numerous as the grains of sand on the seashore and as great as mountains, infinite mercy stands beside justice and stays its avenging arm, as soon as we sincerely wish to escape. The mildness and indulgence of mercy outweigh the severity and zeal of justice, for "His tender mercies are over all His works." (*Ps.* 144:9). God cannot punish us unless we compel Him to do so, but He offers us spontaneously His forgiveness and blessings, and He is deeply grieved if we reject them. He has not shed a drop of sweat to punish us; but in order to give us grace, He has offered up His sweat, His Blood and His life, amidst the most cruel sufferings. He has by no means exhausted His power in punishing sinners, but to reconcile sinners with Himself, He has expended the whole treasure of His omnipotence and wisdom and has wrought the greatest of works—an infinite work—the Incarnation of His own Son. Accordingly, if we have reason to fear His avenging justice because of our sins, we have far more reason to trust in His mercy and hope for the forgiveness of our sins.

In order to strengthen us in this hope, our Saviour has proposed to us the touching Parable of the Prodigal Son. The sin of this son was just like our own. With base ingratitude he had left his father's house, had taken along his inheritance and in a strange country had squandered it in the most irresponsible way. Who would not have expected that, returning home later in his misery, he would have been mercilessly rejected from his father's door? And yet he was lovingly received by his father, accepted again as a child and welcomed with such joy that the elder brother, who had remained faithful, was moved to jealousy.

In like manner, we have left the house of our heavenly Father through sin and have wasted most ungratefully the inheritance of grace. We are no longer worthy to appear before His face, much less to regain the squandered inheritance. Nevertheless, we need only acknowledge our misery and our ingratitude and earnestly desire the grace of our heavenly Father in order that He hasten to us with joy, take us again into His house, kiss us with the kiss of peace and pardon, adopt us again as children and give back to us our whole lost inheritance. Indeed, He receives us with such affection that, if His faithful children, the Angels and Saints, were capable of envy, they would have to envy our good fortune.

What an injustice we would do to God, if after all these proofs of His infinite mercy, we should still remain pusillanimous and despondent, instead of courageously breaking the fetters of sin and casting ourselves confidently into His parental bosom. How can we still fear our enemies, our bad habits and ourselves when God stands ready to humble our enemies by His omnipotence and to break the yoke that we have welded through our sins and to endow our will with a superhuman strength? Why do we not dare to take the one step necessary, that is, to climb into the lifeboat that God holds ready for us, since He sends His angels to help us and even offers us His own hand to save us? Why do we hesitate to stretch out our hand to our Liberator that He may grasp it? Do we fear His reproaches? But how can we think of such a thing when we see the preparations that He makes for our salvation and when we see how He even gives His only Son in order to free us?

Let us approach God, therefore, with full confidence, and take His hand, that He may save us. How quickly the unfortunate one who has fallen into a well grasps at the saving rope that is cast to him; how he clings to it, forgetting everything except the fear that it might break! This care is for us superfluous. "A threefold cord is not easily broken." (*Eccles.* 4:12). The life-rope that is thrown to us is made up of the mercy of the Father, the sacrifice of the Son, and the love of the Holy Ghost. Let us grasp it with faith, cling to it with hope, hold fast to it with perseverance and we are saved. But let us not think that the task of hope is already finished when we have once cast ourselves into the hands of divine mercy, that it may draw us out of the sea of our sinfulness. No, we need this virtue on all the paths of our life. And who knows but that, later on, we may need it still more than in the beginning!

It is certain that lassitude on the way to perfection, delay after a good beginning and even regress is often due to the lack of the practice of this virtue. God does not easily place the greater struggles and the more difficult trials in the beginning, but in the later stages of the spiritual life. Usually, He allows our enemy to try our resistance thoroughly, only when we earnestly seek to pass from the state of beginners to that of those making progress. And when one strives earnestly for the state of perfection, he should know that the way leads through terrible trials, which St. John of the

Cross calls *the dark night.* The mystics call it the *purgatio passiva* (a painful purification), while other Saints who have passed through it say that no idea and no name of it can be given.

Hence, teachers of the spiritual life say that progress in the virtue of hope is indispensable and that no one attains perfection without reaching an heroic degree of hope.

Chapter 52

CONTRITION AS THE FOURTH AND LAST PREPARATION FOR GRACE

ONE THING still remains for us to do, with the help of God, if our hope of regaining grace is to be realized. We must sincerely detest sin and be earnestly resolved to live and act accordingly to the laws and directions of grace.

If with a lively faith we desire the grace of God, we must also endeavor to adopt those sentiments which grace requires of us. And what are these sentiments? First and above all, we must have the earnest will to fulfill all the duties which we take upon ourselves when entering the state of grace, that is, we must have the firm resolution to commit no grave sin [mortal sin] in the future, but rather to live as true children of God. This resolution, if sincere and efficacious, is a supernatural act, because it is the beginning of supernatural life in us. We can elicit this act only by following the impulse of the Holy Ghost, who wishes to lead us to supernatural life, and by declaring ourselves ready to preserve and nourish this life within us. How we are to accomplish this will be shown in later chapters.

Since, however, before we have Sanctifying Grace, we are in the state of sin and have grievous sins on our souls, which make us unworthy of God's grace and exclude it from us, we must not only make a good resolution for the future, but also seek to make good the past, as far as lies in our power. We must be sorry for having committed those sins, for having so greatly offended God by them, and if we are truly sorry, we must endeavor to render such satisfaction to God for these offenses as He requires and of which we are capable. In a word, we must sincerely repent of our sins and do penance for them.

In order that this sorrow be salutary for us and pave the way for God's grace, it must be supernatural. Otherwise, it would have no proportion to the supernatural state of grace for which it must prepare us. (*Conc. Trid.*, sess. 6, c. 3). But when is this sorrow supernatural? When in the light of faith and under the influence of the Holy Ghost we detest sin as a supernatural evil, or better, as that evil that robs us of all supernatural goods, as a violation of God's supernatural law, through which we lose grace and God's supernatural love.

It follows from this explanation that sorrow may be of two kinds, perfect or imperfect. If we repent only because sin, in robbing us of grace, deprives us of the greatest happiness and consequently makes us fear the greatest evil and punishment, such sorrow is imperfect. In such sorrow, we consider grace only insofar as it is a good *for us*, and sin only insofar as it is an evil *for us*. This contrition does not yet contain the pure and perfect disposition of God's children, which consists in love of Him. Nevertheless, even imperfect contrition implies a sincere desire for grace and all that goes with it, and consequently also for the love of God. Hence, although it does not yet render us worthy of the immediate infusion of grace, it prepares us sufficiently to receive it in the Sacrament of Penance.

If, on the other hand, we consider how great a good grace is for God Himself, how much He is glorified by it and how by sin we offend Him and withdraw from our dutiful, filial love, our contrition then is perfect. Such includes filial love of God. Then we no longer merely have a desire for the grace of the children of God; we already act as His children; we already embrace Him in the arms of love. Then He can no longer hesitate: He embraces us with His paternal love, receives us into His bosom, presses the kiss of reconciliation on our forehead and restores to us at once the grace of children [of God].

Imperfect contrition is good and valuable; it has great power and ought to be very dear and precious to us, because it qualifies us for the reception of grace. But its power cannot be compared with that of perfect contrition, which does not merely qualify us for grace but immediately brings it to us. We should therefore not be content with the former, but endeavor always to make progress to that which is perfect. We should be ashamed to make only the least possible effort or to omit anything in our power to regain grace. For thus we show that we do not esteem grace as it deserves, and if we do not consider it important, we place ourselves in danger of not desiring to recover it.

Let us recognize with lively faith and with the help of the Holy Ghost the great evil of sin, which robs us of grace. Then we shall immediately detest it with all the power of our soul and banish it from our heart. We shall detest it because, in depriving us of grace, it deprives us of the highest good and of the possession of God and make us worthy of the most severe punishment from His hands. We shall detest it still more because by sin we commit the greatest wrong and the greatest offense against the Author of Grace.

For after we have been called through grace to be children of God, we offend Him not merely as our Supreme Lord and Master, to whom we owe unlimited service and respect, but as our most loving Father, our best Friend, the most tender Spouse of our soul. We despise the ineffable love with which He embraces us and return the basest ingratitude for His inestimable gifts and blessings. We disgrace Him and insult His name by dishonoring the name of His children and by showing ourselves unworthy of Him. We tear loose from His bosom the soul that He loved as the apple of His eye and considered as the jewel and joy of His heart. We rend the heavenly robe of innocence and sanctity with which He had clothed us and presented us to the whole Heaven. Like Judas, we desert Our Lord and Saviour, who by grace has numbered us among His friends and loved ones.

What pain we inflict on the tender heart of our heavenly Father, how deeply we offend and wound it! Must He not utter the same complaint about us that He spoke of Judas through the mouth of the Psalmist: "If my enemy had reviled me, I would verily have borne with it . . . but thou, a man of one mind, my guide and my familiar, who didst take sweet meats together with me? (*Ps.* 54:13-15). And should we be so inhuman and devoid of feeling as not to be moved, or to think only of the harm which accrues to us from such a terrible sin?

The offense of a son against his father is more wicked and abominable than the offense of a servant. But it would be far more wicked still if a servant, whom the special kindness of his master had adopted as a son, would not hesitate in base ingratitude to grieve and offend him. But this is the case with us who have been made children of God by His grace and who are thus far more indebted to Him than if we were His children by nature. That we should even now dare to refuse Him our love and requite His tenderness by mean disobedience! What a crime! What ingratitude!

But how great must be our sorrow when we consider what God has sacrificed for us in order to make us His children, how He gave His only-begotten Son for us, in order that He might, by His Blood, purchase grace for us! If our heart still retains a feeling of humanity and gratitude, it must dissolve in unbounded sorrow. For by sin we have trampled under foot the precious Blood of the Son of God, frustrated its efficacy in us, rejected the dearest pledge of the love of the Eternal Father. He seeks our friendship at any price, and to secure it, sacrifices the best He has to offer. How must He be pained if, in spite of this, we despise and reject His friendship!

Oh, if we will have no mercy on ourselves, let us at least have mercy on our tender Father, whom we have grieved so greatly! Let us feel with Him the gravity of our sin, the greatness of our ingratitude and let us instantly relieve His paternal heart by sincere repentance and deep contrition. Let us hasten to ask His pardon, to wash away the stains of sin with our tears and to make it good, as far as possible, by most fervent love!

Let us never be content with our sorrow, for it can never be great enough to outweigh such a sin; for if the infinite merit of Christ did not come to our assistance, we should never be able to render perfect satisfaction to God, and all our effort would avail nothing, unless the grace of the Holy Ghost rendered it precious and valuable. Let us never cease to weep and to be indignant at ourselves; let us humble ourselves in the sight of our heavenly Father and, in humble confusion, confess to Him that we are not worthy to be called His children. Thus, we shall soon regain His grace and experience in our sorrow that sweet joy which is the privilege of the child who finally returns home after a long exile.

True contrition must continue even after reconciliation with God and precisely in this prove its sincerity. A child that has grievously offended its father will not forget him after its fault has been forgiven, but will always be sorry for having done such a great wrong. It will be more careful in the future not to offend its father again, to whose indulgence it is doubly indebted. From the remembrance of its fault, it will find motives to make good its failing and to supply what has been omitted. We, likewise, after God has cast our sins into the depths of the sea, dare not forget them, the more so because, precisely in the forgiveness of our sins, the ineffable love of God was made known to us.

The consciousness of reconciliation should fill us with peace and holy joy. But we shall truly experience this peace and joy only if we continue to lament our sins and to do penance for them. Thus, we become ever more worthy of the grace of God and ever more certain that He has truly forgiven our sins. The enduring sorrow for our former calamity and the remembrance of our past wickedness will alone prevent us from relapsing into the same sins and repeating the same crimes.

Chapter 53

THE SUPERNATURAL LIFE THAT WE MUST LEAD WHEN IN THE STATE OF GRACE

L ET US give thanks to God if by His mercy He has delivered us from our sins and received us again in His Grace. But now we have the obligation of living and acting in accordance with the high dignity we hold, and of turning the talent received to the best account.

"For you were heretofore darkness," the Apostle cries to us, "but now light in the Lord. Walk then as children of the light. For the fruit of the light is in all goodness, and justice, and truth." (*Eph.* 5:8-9). "Therefore," he says in another place, "if you be risen with Christ, seek the things that are above; where Christ is sitting at the right hand of God: Mind the things that are above, not the things that are upon the earth. For you are dead; and your life is hid with Christ in God." (*Col.* 3:1-3).

Yes, dear Christian, when you are freed from the death of sin, born again to a new life, and from a servant and an enemy have been made a child of God, you must deem it your honor, pride and highest happiness to fulfill the duties which your new state imposes on you. You are estranged from the world, the devil, and the flesh, freed from their tyranny, made a citizen of Heaven, a domestic of God and a temple of the Holy Ghost. It behooves you, therefore, to renounce the laws of the world, the devil, and the flesh to live and labor henceforth according to the Will of your heavenly Father, the example of His only-begotten Son, and the inspirations of the Holy Ghost.

This new life must be a heavenly, spiritual, holy and divine life and therefore a mysterious life, as Holy Scripture itself expresses it. (Cf. *1 Cor.* 15:49f). It must be heavenly

348

because by grace you are raised from earth to Heaven; you have the right and duty to stand like the Angels before the throne of God and to praise Him. It must be spiritual because it is inspired in you by the Holy Ghost, who guides and vivifies the children of God, frees them from the slavery of the flesh and teaches them to walk in the flesh as angels of Heaven. It must be holy; for if God is holy, His children must likewise be so: holy in their sentiments, in their words, in their conduct. It must even be a Divine life, because by grace we have been made partakers of the Divine nature, so that it is no longer we who live but God lives in us, acts in us, and fills us with His infinite power.

For this very reason, it is a mysterious and hidden life, a life that remains hidden from the eyes of the world and cannot be known in all its depth and sublimity even by us. The world does not recognize in us the sublime dignity of God's children, nor the sublime and intimate union with God that grace effects, and therefore it scorns our modest, quiet life, which is hidden in God, as idle, meaningless hypocrisy.

Let us not thereby be deceived! Let us adhere to our holy faith that leads us beyond the world to invisible, mysterious regions, where our natural eye cannot penetrate. Let us allow God to develop His mysterious operations in our soul; let us surrender ourselves to the direction of the Holy Ghost, who dwells in our heart and fills it with the fullness of the Divinity. Let us remember that the life of the Son of God here on earth was also a hidden life and that, according to the words of the Apostle, when Christ our Life shall appear, we also shall appear with Him in glory. (Cf. *1 Col.* 3:4).

The more mysterious and sublime this life of grace is, the more do we need a visible pattern according to which we may form it in us. This model for all the children of God is the only-begotten and first-born Son of God, Jesus Christ. He and only He could give us a worthy example as to how we should behave as children of God. He and He alone is a worthy model of our sublime state and calling. If grace did not raise us so high above our nature, it would have been unworthy of Him to come down from Heaven to earth. Merely to teach us how we should live as men, He need not have come at all. But if from earthly men we were to become children and domestics of God, only the Son of God could teach us heavenly, divine manners and by His example show us what corresponds to this new calling.

A man of the common people who had never seen the court of a king, if suddenly adopted as son of the king, naturally could not know how to act in his new position, nor could he learn it from his equals. He must at once take the king's children as his models. Likewise, we can learn neither from reason nor from the example of other men the manners and life which become us as adopted children of God. But since on earth we cannot see the only-begotten Son in the divine glory which He enjoys with the Father, He had to descend to earth to walk visibly among us, to unfold before our eyes His divine life and the splendor of His holiness and thus become our teacher and model.

We must imitate Him if we would be children of God; Him we must put on; to Him we must conform. We must bear His image, we must appropriate His spirit, we must study and express His inclinations and virtues, that His heavenly Father be honored by us as by Him and take pleasure in us as in Him.

What an honor for us that we may imitate the only-begotten Son as His brethren and members of His Body! We admire the heroic virtues and noble qualities of many men and would consider ourselves happy if we could acquire them to some extent, thereby elevating ourselves above the narrow limits of the great multitude and of daily life. How honorable it must be, then, for us to be called to imitate and to express in us the divine and heavenly virtues of the Son of God, which are an object of admiration for the whole heavens!

How disgraceful it would be for us if, on the contrary, in our high state we should be content with the empty phantom which the world calls the virtue of a righteous man. Of course, a Christian does not despise this; he must possess it, but he is bound also to strive for the higher virtue. For if a natural human righteousness can adorn a man, provided it is genuine, it suffices for a Christian as little as the manners and education of a civilian would do honor to a king.

We are, as St. Peter says, "a chosen generation, a kingly priesthood, a holy nation." (*1 Ptr.* 2:9). Through Baptism and grace we have become members of Christ and have been raised to a royal dignity, and with Christ as our head we must serve the King of kings as His children and share with Him His kingdom and happiness.

We are Christians, that is, members of Christ, brothers of Christ. We are Christians, that is, sanctified and consecrated by the anointing of the Holy Ghost. As Christians we must lead a Christian life, a life of following the example of Christ, a life which Christ lives in us as in His members and that we live in Him as our head.

Christians themselves understand only too little the sublime nature and divine character of this Christian life. Usually they have a very confused and indistinct idea of it. Let us endeavor to clarify this idea. In man we distinguish—with reference to his nature—a twofold, and if we take grace into consideration, a threefold life: sensuous, spiritual and divine life. In each life, we find a proper principle, law, light, end and motives.

The principle of sensuous life is the soul, with those powers and activities which it has in common with animal souls. In the sensuous nature of man there is a natural law, the law of flesh, that moves one to seek sensuous goods and to promote one's bodily life. The light that directs one in following the law is the light of the five senses, which proposes to him this good. Corresponding to this law, bodily life has for its end the preservation and propagation of bodily life. The proximate motive is the sensuous pleasure which it finds in material goods; the ultimate motive is the retaining of one's earthly health and life.

If a man would give himself entirely to this sensuous life, he would evidently renounce his noble, spiritual nature and the natural likeness of God in his soul and would degrade himself to the level of the brute—and even beneath this level. The animal leads a sensuous life because it cannot do otherwise; it is called and qualified for no other. By such a life, however, man drags into the mire all the high and noble qualities with which God endowed him. By throwing himself with his greater strength into the sensuous, he does not confine himself to the limits which nature has placed for the brute, but sinks deeper than that level. Therefore, our nobler nature struggles against such conduct. The spirit opposes the flesh, says the Apostle, and the shame that covers our cheeks is witness thereto. (Cf. *Gal.* 5:17).

Following nature, therefore, our sensuous life must be subordinate to our spiritual life, whose principle is the soul, with its spiritual faculties, reason and will. Its law consists in the natural striving after spiritual goods that correspond to our spiritual nature and in the natural relations which, as rational creatures, we have toward God and our fellowmen. Its light is therefore our natural reason. Its end is the attainment of natural happiness and such glorification of God as He may expect and demand of His servants. Its motives, finally, lie in the affinity and conformity of spiritual goods with our spiritual nature and in the reverence for the imperious law of our mighty Lord and Creator.

This spiritual life may be good and true, or it may be just the opposite. It is true and good if we follow the true tendency which our Creator has implanted in our nature (and which in reality is nothing else than the law of our Creator Himself), if we tend to those goods which can render our nature truly perfect and happy and if, above all, we seek knowledge and love of our Creator.

It is a false life, on the other hand, if we seek a merely apparent good, as the honor of men, or if instead of following the highest good and seeking happiness in it, we would be satisfied with a finite, created good, and if, instead of referring the knowledge and love of creatures to the knowledge and love of the Creator, we would be satisfied with the former alone.

This false spiritual life is that of most men of the world who do not rush headlong into the whirl of sensual lust. It is the life of the more honorable among them who have only the education of the world and follow it. This life is usually described as upright, honorable, scientific, cultured and humane. There is no doubt that this life does not satisfy man completely. It is less disgraceful and humiliating than animal life, yet equally vain and foolish, equally unworthy of man, and incapable of giving him happiness, as is animal life itself.

Even the truly natural spiritual life that we have described, even if pure, would be far from satisfying us as Christians. It is worthy of the natural man, and if God had given us no higher dignity and destiny, we might and ought to be content with it, and God would likewise be satisfied.* But if God has given us a higher dignity and destiny—as He actually has done—He can find no pleasure in such a natural life on our part, and we must not be satisfied with it.

Since we have been elevated far above our nature by the grace of Christ and are more than mere men, having been made partakers of the Divine nature and children of God, we must live a supernatural life, a life that is not only far above the sensuous, not only above the vain and false spiritual life, but above the purest and most perfect spiritual life—in a word, we must lead a life that is infinitely above all natural life.

The principles of this supernatural life are the spiritual faculties of the soul, as elevated by grace, the supernatural virtues infused by the Holy Ghost and especially the Theological Virtues [faith, hope and charity]. Its law is a supernatural law, not naturally implanted in us, but supernaturally written and impressed on our soul by the finger of God, and which we know neither by our senses nor by reason but by supernatural faith in the light of the Holy Ghost. Its end is the possession and enjoyment of the highest and most sublime gifts which God Himself possesses and enjoys and that glorification of God which He can expect and demand as a Father from His children. Its motives finally lie in that supernatural and mysterious relationship with God into which we enter by grace and in the wonderful power of attraction which God and His supernatural gifts exercise in consequence of this relationship.

---

*In the concrete, "natural man" is man turned away from God by original and actual sin; there is no neutral natural state that a person can choose. —*Publisher*, 2000.

Then only do we live as Christians, when our life is from grace, directed by the light of faith and by the law revealed to us by the Holy Ghost, when it tends toward the heavenly happiness promised us by God and when its acts are determined by supernatural motives. Then only is our life in harmony with the heavenly nature of grace when it is a supernatural life. For the supernatural life, and it alone, is becoming to the man who has been elevated by grace above all the boundaries of nature. The supernatural life ceases, as it were, to be supernatural for him, since it becomes his second nature, and he would act against his higher nature if he would lead a merely human, natural life.

He would act as contrary to his nature as when a man in the natural state would not live conformably to the nobler part of his nature, namely, reason, but to the lower part, sensuality. It is natural for a worm to crawl upon the earth, and it would be unreasonable to demand of it that it fly. But if God's omnipotence had changed it into a bird and had given it wings, this demand would no longer be unreasonable, and the worm would act contrary to its new nature if it would continue to crawl on the earth. Likewise, it would be unreasonable to demand of the earthly man that he lead a divine and heavenly life. But after he has put off, by grace, the lowliness of his nature and has been clothed with a divine nature, he would belie himself if he continued his former way of life and refused to move in a higher sphere.

Let us not think that only the great Saints can and should lead a supernatural life. This life does not consist in those extraordinary revelations, ecstasies and miracles with which the Saints are favored by God, but rather in the intimate union with God which grace renders possible for us all and in that holy consecration which the unction of the Holy Ghost communicates to all the action of true Christians. The common dignity and destiny of all Christians is the foundation upon which the Saints constructed the tall edifice of their virtues and graces; it is the root which in the Saints is developed in all its richness, in all its fullness. We have, then, the same foundation, the same root of sanctity, and if in us it does not attain such splendid development, usually this is because we do not sufficiently cooperate with the work of grace, or perhaps we even place many obstacles in its way.

"God is wonderful in his Saints" (*Ps.* 67:36), says Holy Scripture, wonderful in the high degree of perfection to which He leads them, wonderful in the supernatural favors which He bestows upon them, wonderful, finally, in the works which He does through them. But God is wonderful also in every Christian who tries to preserve and develop the sanctity received in Baptism. Every supernatural act we elicit, every act of faith, hope or charity is a wonder that God works in us, a greater wonder than the external signs that God works through His Saints, a more beneficial wonder than the sensible, heavenly illuminations and emotions which He often grants the Saints.

For ultimately, there can be nothing greater on earth than the acts of the Divine virtues by which we share in God's own life. These special favors should be only means by which the Saints are drawn to unite themselves to God even more intimately in faith, hope and love and are to invite others to a supernatural union with God.

How is it possible that there are still so many men who are unmindful of their high calling and who rather cling to the earth than allow themselves to be borne to Heaven by God—Christians who prefer to move within the limits of their poor nature than to transcend these limits and with the Angels lead a heavenly life.

I do not speak of those who give themselves to the lust of the flesh and lower themselves to the level of the beasts, nor of those who cling to the vanities, if not to the filth, of this earth, but to those who at least profess to practice natural, reasonable virtue and piety, and who despise and ridicule all that goes beyond this as mysticism, bigotry and hypocrisy. What greater insult can they offer to God than to despise His noblest gifts? What greater disgrace can they bring on themselves than to forget their heavenly dignity and with narrow stupidity close their heart to God's grace?

Be this far from you, dear Christian, if you know the meaning of the Christian name and glory in it! Embrace with your noble heart the grace of God, and as a true child of God, endeavor to become more and more like Christ, your Heavenly Model. Be not guided by the laws of a perverted world, but by the law of grace and of the Holy Ghost. By constant striving after every virtue, keep yourself on the lofty height to which grace has raised you. Soar above the earth and above your own nature through intimate communion with God, your Father. Keep yourself, as much as possible, through constant prayer, in the vestibule of Heaven. This [type of] life alone offers an occupation worthy of your high dignity; in it alone is the realization of the supernatural, Divine life that the children of God should lead.

Chapter 54

THE EXERCISE OF
SUPERNATURAL LOVE OF GOD

FOR HIM who has been regenerated by the grace of Christ, the most peculiar, natural and sublime act is that of supernatural love of God. This love is the breath that vivifies the child of God, it is the pulsation of his heart and the motive power of all his actions.

The communication of grace is the most complete proof of the intimate love of God for His creature. What better and more pleasant thing could the soul do to repay this love, through which God approaches it so closely, than to love Him as it is loved by Him.

If love in general calls for a return of love, this holds especially in Divine love, which is shown us in grace. For when God bestows His grace upon us, He makes us worthy of His love and gives us the power to love Him, a thing that no other lover can do. Moreover, He unites Himself so intimately to the soul that He not only is and remains substantially present in its interior, but forms, as it were, one whole, one spirit with it.

What is more natural than that the soul which sees itself so indescribably loved by God, animated and attracted by Him, should burn with fervent love for Him? Nothing is more natural to fire than to give light and warmth. Now, grace is the heat coming out of the Divine nature which makes the soul like God and transforms it into the image of His Divine Being, which is the purest, spiritual fire. Hence, nothing is more natural for grace than to enlighten and warm, to enlighten through the sharing of knowledge, to warm through the love of God. Grace will perfectly enlighten only when it has passed over into glory and lets us all see God face to face. Until then, it must develop chiefly its warmth here below. As in Heaven the vision of God is the natural and principal act of the elect, on earth love of God is the most natural and important act of the just. Hence, Our Lord says: "I am come to cast fire on the earth: and what will I, but that it be kindled?" (*Luke* 12:49). Oh, that we might suffer it to be kindled and to burn in us, that we also may inflame our soul with the fire of grace that transforms and beautifies it and that our will might be changed into a living fire of love, in order to live and act only in love!

The love of God is not only the most natural and appropriate, but also the most sublime activity of the just soul. Or rather, the love of God is so appropriate and natural for the child of God because it is so sublime, because it is peculiarly divine. God Himself has no greater or more sublime occupation than the vision and love of Himself. This occupation alone is worthy of His infinite greatness and calls into action all His power. Through all eternity He does nothing else and has no other need than to behold and love His infinite beauty and goodness. The whole immense work of His Creation does not occupy Him so much as one of His own perfections that calls forth His immeasurable love. The world claims His activity only insofar as it is an image of His glory and an effluence of His love and a means to manifest this to others. For Heaven and earth are only a little spark, sent up from the fiery ocean of Divine love, to reveal something of its infinite fullness and glory. What greater thing could the creature do, what greater proof could it give of its participation in the Divine nature and its similarity to God, than to love Him, and especially to love Him as He loves Himself? If all Creation is nothing in comparison to the Divine love from which it proceeds, how much less are all the works of a creature in comparison with one act of Divine love?

An act is perfect according to the sublimity of its object and according to the intimacy of the union it effects between us and the object. But can there be a more sublime object than God, the Infinite Good, and can we be united with Him more intimately, at least here on earth, than by love? And if this is true of natural love of God, how much more is it true of supernatural love, that God pours into our heart as a drop out of the ocean of His holiness, in order that we may become as much like Him as possible by sharing in His activity! Indeed, as the love of His infinite goodness is the only love worthy of God, so also Divine love of God is the only occupation worthy of His children. This love alone ought to satisfy us, even if we had nothing else on earth. It alone makes us more like God than all other works, be they ever so great.

In this love we should take the greatest pride, for it is truly a just reason for holy pride to believe that through grace God has made us to share in His nature, and that through love we take part in His activity. This love is so great and so sublime that theologians and spiritual writers say that it deifies us and changes us into God. Grace transforms our nature into God by the greatest possible likening to and union with His nature. Supernatural love, however, transforms our affection into a divine affection by likening and uniting it, as far as possible, to the Divine love and goodness. St. Augustine expressed this idea thus: "As the love, so the man." (*Serm.* 96, n. 1). Through love of God you ascend on high; through love of the world you descend into the abyss. (St. Aug., *Enarr. in Ps.* 126, n. 1). If you love God, you draw close to God. (St. Aug., *Enarr. in Ps.* 85. n. 6). The more your love increases, the closer you approach to God. (St. Aug., *Enarr. in Ps.* 83, n. 10). If you love God, you shall become God. (St. Aug., *Enarr. in Ps.* 121, n. 1).

Let us endeavor to explain this mystery more fully. As long as we consider ourselves according to our nature, we may love ourselves for our own sake; we are the first object of our love. Even though we must love and respect God as our Creator infinitely more than ourselves, we still are the object that so draws our love in reality that God could easily be neglected. At best, love of self and love of God would be two courses that run alongside of one another, but are with difficulty joined together.

By grace, however, we are so intimately joined to God that

we are in a wonderful way made His members, one with Him as the member is part of the body, and we live more by Him than of ourselves. Hence God must be the first and only object of our love, because we live in God as well as dependently on Him and for Him.

Furthermore, our supernatural love is a participation of that love which God has for Himself. Our love, then, must resemble in a manner the love of God, that is, we must embrace in the first place only God by this love and every other thing only insofar as it is like unto God, is united to Him or belongs to Him. By this love we can no longer even love ourselves outside of God but only through and in Him. From that it follows that the supernatural love of our fellow men and of ourselves is not only an outflowing of the love of God, but is of one nature with it. (*S. Th.* 2:2, q. 25, a. 1).

As by grace, therefore, we cast off the lowliness of our nature and transcend its narrow limits, we must through supernatural love broaden our narrow natural love and go beyond the narrow limits of our natural life, in order to live only for God and in God, as though we were but one being and one person with Him. If we truly love ourselves with supernatural love, we cannot separate love for ourselves from love for God—and love ourselves and creatures with one love and God with another—but as God loves Himself for His own sake, we must love Him and ourselves in Him for His own sake.

"O chaste and holy love!" exclaims St. Bernard. (*De dilig. Deo,* c. 10). A sweet and pleasant sensation! O pure and hallowed tendency of the will! So much purer and holier because there is no longer any admixture of self-love; so much sweeter and more agreeable because all that is felt is divine. To be thus affected is to be deified, as a drop of water poured into a large quantity of wine is lost therein and receives the color and taste of wine. As the iron glowing with heat loses its own previous form and is made like the fire, as the air, pervaded by the light of the sun, is changed into the same luminous splendor to the extent that it seems not only to be illuminated, but to be the light itself, so all human affection of the Saints must one day be dissolved in a certain wonderful way and must entirely pass over into the Will of God. Otherwise, how could God be All in all, if in man there remains anything of man.

Behold, dear Christian, how glorious and sublime is the perfection of love to which you have been called by grace and which is contained in grace as its germ, so that you need only, with the help of God, to develop it. Do not shudder when you hear of mortification, of self-denial and renunciation of self, or rather of self-love. You must surrender yourself only to find yourself again, better and more beautiful in God. You must cease to love yourself with a natural human love, in order to embrace yourself in God and for God with a holy and divine love. Mortification, as anyone may learn from experience, is so much the sweeter and more pleasant, the purer and more perfect it is, and as grace does not destroy our nature but glorifies it, so the divine love that proceeds from grace only changes your love, making it nobler and holier.

But as on this earth grace does not so change our nature that all its frailties and miseries disappear, but only in Heaven unites it entirely with God and transforms it into His image, so it is impossible on this earth for our love and affection to be entirely deified, that is, that we love God alone and all else in and for Him. Only in eternity, where God is All in all, will we enjoy this indescribable happiness. But this does not prevent us from striving after such perfection already on earth and to attain it here to a certain extent. For by grace we are born for Heaven, and the love which has its source in grace can and must be at least of the same nature, if not of the same perfection, as the love of the Blessed in Heaven.

If we cannot, therefore, banish from our heart all natural love of self and of creatures, it is still possible to love ourselves and them with a supernatural, divine love and to take care that the natural love does not oppose the supernatural. That is as far as the law of charity goes, as God has imposed it on us for this life.

But noble souls are not content with this. They wish to share, already here on earth, the lot of the Saints in

Heaven, and hence they endeavor to renounce completely nature and natural love, to be immersed evermore in the abyss of grace and to cultivate and foster in themselves only supernatural love. Hence their mortification, their prayer life and their striving for virtue.

They do not crush their natural impulses and inclinations, but they take care not to allow them to operate alone, even where they do not oppose grace, because these weaken their intimate union with God and render it more difficult. If they cannot attach all their faculties and inclinations to God and give them a divine orientation, they at least strive to keep their free will fixed upon God and united with Him. They try to change both into God through holy love, that, penetrated by divine fire, they may seek and love only what God loves, as He loves it and because He loves it. Thus, they live in God, as far as that is possible here, and God lives in them, and they can say with the Apostle: "And I live, now not I; but Christ liveth in me." (*Gal.* 2:20).

This is the life of grace; this is uniting oneself to God through love as He unites Himself to us through grace. If here below we cannot acquire that perfection which the Saints possess, we should seek it in some measure; otherwise, we are faithless to the grace given us, not making its power our own nor developing its seed. Otherwise, we bury this sacred fire beneath its ashes, and we are in danger of extinguishing the glowing coals even under the ashes.

Grace abhors inactivity more than nature abhors a vacuum. Whoever does not permit grace to work in him despises it and God Himself, who gives it only to inflame us. Who does not consider a gift wasted that he has given to an ungrateful man? And who is not grieved to see his gifts go unused? It is right, therefore, that we be grateful to God and zealously use His grace, if we wish to keep it.

Let us therefore endeavor to cultivate and develop that holy love which the Holy Ghost has infused into our soul and let all our activities and desires be penetrated by it. Let us clear away the ashes of sinful and earthly inclinations under which this holy fire is smoldering, and let us simply permit God to act in us. He Himself will inflame and increase it; He will draw us ever more to Himself and unite us ever more closely to Himself, so that we too may exclaim with St. Paul: "And I live, now not I; but Christ liveth in me." (*Gal.* 2:20).

Chapter 55

THE EXERCISE OF
SUPERNATURAL LOVE OF OUR NEIGHBOR

BESIDES GOD, we must also love our neighbor in a supernatural way, or rather, we must realize the love of God in the love of our neighbor. For the supernatural love of neighbor is, as has been said, essentially one and the same virtue as the supernatural love of God.

When we love our fellowmen with natural love, we love them because they are of the same nature as we, because they are like us, because they have certain natural qualities and are related to us by near or remote bonds of beneficence or society. Thus, the child loves its father, the brother his sister, the friend his friend, the citizen his fellow citizen. This love is not only unobjectionable, but it is of obligation and therefore good, so long as it is not contrary to the love of God or does not violate other obligations. But it is always a mere human and natural, not a divine and supernatural, love and therefore is not meritorious for eternal life.

The Christian is indeed obliged to love his neighbor for natural reasons, because considerations of relationship, of gratitude and of the common life do not cease even though one has higher obligations to fulfill. But it does not follow that the world has reason—on account of this virtue, to which the simplest natural considerations move us—to boast [of this natural virtue] as it does or to consider it as more glorious and beautiful than Christian love, which springs from grace and supernatural motives.

As Christians we must love our neighbor also according to nature, but still more according to grace, that is, insofar as he is bound to us by grace. We must love him because he also has been made a partaker of the Divine nature and has been raised above his own [nature], or at least [has been] destined to such elevation and glory.

The motive of our love must not be his human nature, but the divine nature, which impresses its own image on him; not so much he himself, but rather God, who is united to Him by grace, must be our motive, and therefore we must embrace him with that same supernatural love that we have for God Himself. Indeed, is not our neighbor a child of God by grace, begotten and born of God, the supernatural likeness of God? Must not, therefore, the same love that embraces God also extend to him as a child of God?

Is not our neighbor by grace our brother, and what is more, a living member of Jesus Christ? Was he not bought at the price of a divine life, and accordingly, in the eyes of God, so to say, worth as much as the Lord Jesus Christ Himself? Can we love Christ without at the same time loving His brothers and members in Him and with Him? Is he not by grace a temple in which the Holy Ghost truly and personally dwells—not merely as a man in his house, but as the soul in the body? Can we think of separating in our affection what the divine love has so naturally and inseparably united?

We can and must love our fellow men in God and on account of God. This does not exclude, as said before, the special connections that we have with certain ones by reason of relationship or society. But we should consider these bonds only in relation to God, who has made them, and thus lend them a heavenly consecration and a Divine nobility.

In God and through grace only does our neighbor truly draw close to us, much closer than all natural relations can bring him. In grace we are all one with God and therefore one among ourselves, because God, as [does] a mother of twins, bears us all in His bosom and in His heart. Hence, supernatural, Christian love is called the love of neighbor *par excellence.* By nature, one person is nearer to us, another more distant, and many stand in almost no relationship whatever to us. But grace brings all wonderfully together in a spiritual way. We are all children of God, brothers in Christ, stones of the same divine temple and members of the same Mystical Body of Christ. All are our neighbors, and hence we also can and should embrace all with the wide arms of divine love. Thus, Christian love of neighbor has its special supernatural motive in this, that our neighbor through grace has attained a supernatural lovableness.

But the grace that we ourselves have received must also impel us to this love. He who is loved, as we have said above, must love in return. He who receives a favor must be grateful and make as great a return as he can. But we can give God nothing that will perfect Him and that is not His already. Therefore, He requires that, as we have been loved and favored by Him, we must love our neighbor. At the same time, He promises us that He will accept all we do for His children as if we had done it for Him. "My dearest," says St. John, "if God hath so loved us; we also ought to love one another." "And be ye kind one to another," the Apostle admonishes, "merciful, forgiving one another, even as God hath forgiven you in Christ." (*1 John* 4:11; *Eph.* 4:32).

The greater the grace that God has given us [and] the more generous His liberality by which He gives us Himself in grace, the more charitable, liberal and merciful must we be to those whom we may help and assist. We should be boundlessly good and merciful toward our neighbor, as God has been infinitely good and merciful toward us. We should devote ourselves to our neighbor and sacrifice our life for his salvation, as God has given Himself entirely to us in grace and has offered His own life to obtain grace for us. Only thus shall we give proof that we truly and perfectly acknowledge His favor and show ourselves worthy of it.

These reasons have infused into the first Christians and into all the Saints of Christian charity that sublime lofti-ness of spirit, that superhuman enthusiasm. It is under-standable that this new love appeared as a phenomenon of the other world, astonishing all and making the pagans cry out: "See how they love one another." (*Tert.* Apol. 39). Yes, he alone can love as the Saints loved who knows how much he, as well as his neighbor, is loved by God. How grateful he must be for the grace received from God, and how much the neighbor, as a child of God and a brother of Christ, deserves the same love and respect as God who lives in him and to whom he belongs!

But now, dear Christian Reader, you also are aware of it, since you have considered and understood the glories of grace. Will you remain behind on the path of love and not hasten to follow in the footsteps of the Saints? Will you still be indifferent toward your neighbor and despise him who by grace is a child of God and heir of Heaven, a member of Christ and a temple of the Holy Ghost? Will you in the future close your heart and your hand and deny him your help and your service when God has poured out upon you the fullness of His infinite love and has enriched you with all His treasures?

No, I know that with the Angels you will henceforth serve God in His children. You will be happy to return, in some measure at least, God's unbounded love for you through the benefits which you render your neighbor. You will love your neighbor as God has loved him, who came down upon earth for his sake, shed His Precious Blood and loved him to the end, unto death. You will love him, as the Apostle admonishes, not in word nor with the tongue only, but in deed and from your heart.

But by what deeds will you manifest your love for your neighbor? With what gifts will you enrich him? First of all, with those supernatural gifts of grace with which God has so lovingly endowed you and which are the most sublime and glorious gifts that He Himself wishes to your neighbor above all others. If you truly love God, you will desire that your neighbor be united to Him by the same love. If you love your neighbor and are zealous for his happiness, your first care will be to make him partake of the same happiness of grace which has fallen to your lot.

Above all and in all circumstances, you may pray for the salvation of souls. Pray for the infidels, that the heavenly dawn of faith, the harbinger of grace, may illumine their souls. Pray for sinners, that God may lead them by a sincere conversion back into the bosom of grace. Pray for the just, that they may persevere in it to the end and ever grow in it toward the highest perfection.

You may let your example shine before men, that they may learn how sweet and pleasant it is to adhere to God and how easy it is, with the help of grace, to overcome sin and practice virtue, with the assistance of His grace. You may instruct the erring, confirm the wearied, encourage the indolent, warn the incautious and rescue those who are in danger of being seduced. Your charity will find a thousand other occasions and means of activity, for love is inventive, and the more fervent and zealous it is, the more inventive it will be.

Do not ask how you can do something for your neighbor, but love and be zealous for souls. The occasions to give proof of your love will quickly present themselves. Heavenly charity seeks, in the first place, to give heavenly gifts. But as the Son of God came down not only to give us heavenly goods, but also to alleviate the bodily and temporal miseries of man, as He went about doing good and marked His every step with wonderful blessings, so the Divine love which a Christian has for his neighbor passes from the soul to the body of the neighbor, without denying its heavenly origin and character.

The whole man is sanctified by grace. The body is also made a temple of the Holy Ghost and is incorporated into the Mystical Body of Christ. It also is destined to partake one day of the glorification of the soul by grace and to enjoy the glories of Christ with it. Is this not sufficient reason for the Christian to embrace it with the same holy charity with which he embraces the soul?

This is well understood by those enlightened souls who devote themselves to the service of the poor and [the] sick with greater zeal and more tender charity than mothers show to their children. Such souls joyfully offer their possessions, their labor, their health and even their life in order to feed the hungry, to clothe the naked, to nurse the sick. If they do not miraculously heal the sick and multiply the loaves as our Saviour did, they do indeed perform miracles of devotion, of self-sacrifice, of self-denial and [of] charity— miracles which can proceed only from the wonderful power of grace.

This spirit of charity, which always lives in the Church of Christ, breathes with greater vigor in our own days—a sign that we do wrong when we look at the Church with little faith. No, God has not forgotten His kingdom. Though much may have grown weak in it, at least the number of hearts which are seized and moved with love increases from day to day. Will you, dear Christian, also follow this impulse? Will you not also renew within yourself the earthly life and works of our Divine Saviour? God calls you; the grace of Christ presses you. Do but open the eye of your soul and body. They will show you the boundless misery which envelopes and overwhelms so many of your fellowmen, who lose their high dignity through which they merit all your love—and merit it the more the greater their need is.

If you do not feel moved to help and console them as much as you can, you bear the name of Christian in vain, and you are not worthy of possessing God's grace, for grace is love, and love inclines toward mercy. How can you expect, then, that God will still generously give you grace in the future?

"Blessed are the merciful, for they shall obtain mercy." (*Matt.* 5:7). "Give and it shall be given to you." (*Luke* 6:38). The mercy and charity that we show others is so pleasing to God and so meritorious that, on the day of judgment, Our Lord, in accounting the works to be rewarded, will mention only those of mercy, and in the case of the reprobates, will only assign the neglect of these works as the cause of their damnation. In the dispensation of grace, God generally follows the same rule as in the dispensation of the eternal reward. He will be generous to us in this dispensation in proportion to our generosity toward our neighbor. For we deny God what we deny our fellow men, since they are the children and members and temples of God. We give God what we give them, for He accepts it as if we had given it to Him.

In order that God may accept our gifts, it is necessary that we intend them for Him, that is, that we see God in our neighbor and serve our neighbor for God's sake. If we give alms out of other motives, if we give them without a spirit of faith, we give them to our neighbor only and not to God, and He will not acknowledge them as given to Him and will not reward them with the supernatural gifts of grace.

Let us then be animated with the spirit of faith and Divine charity, and let us dispense blessing and consolation whenever possible, and the blessing of Divine grace will follow our every step.

Chapter 56

THE EXERCISE OF
SUPERNATURAL HUMILITY AND CHASTITY

WE HAVE seen how the glories of grace are the basis and occasion of a supernatural union of charity with God and our fellowmen. The world does not know this love because it proceeds from the Holy Ghost and not from nature, because it is a heavenly, divine thing and therefore peculiar to the Christian order of grace. From this love spring all the other holy acts and exercises which distinguish the life of the Christian from that of the man of the world. At least these actions must be in some manner connected with charity, which is the soul of all virtues. If they do not proceed from charity, they must at least lead to it, or be directed in some manner to the same supernatural end with which charity unites us.

We might now review all the virtues and show how the Christian, in the state of grace, ought to practice them in a supernatural manner. But this is hardly necessary. For if the divine virtues of faith and love are alive in us and rule over us completely, we shall perfectly understand and practice all the supernatural virtues.

Indeed, whoever has great charity does everything out of love and is taught by this same virtue how to do it. If then we lovingly embrace God with an ardent supernatural charity, this will be the motive and end of all our actions and will give these actions the highest supernatural value. This charity, which the Holy Ghost diffuses in our soul, is the unction of God, and St. John says of it: "And as for you, let the unction [anointing], which you have received from him, abide in you. And you have no need that any man teach you; but as his unction teacheth you of all things, and is truth,

and is no lie. And as it hath taught you, abide in him."
(*1 John* 2:27).

He who loves knows how it is to act out of love, and he
knows this far better than words can express. If you wish,
therefore, to practice the supernatural virtues, there is no
shorter and better way than that you exercise yourself in
love.

If it appears too difficult for you to acquire in a short time
this fervent love of God, at least enliven your faith. This you
can do by meditation. Think of God, of your neighbor, of
yourself, of your relations to others and of all your duties, in
the light of faith. Look on God as your Father through grace,
your neighbor as your brother, yourself as a child of God, a
member of Christ and a temple of the Holy Ghost. Then you
will worship God, not with servile fear, but with childlike
reverence. Then you will honor your neighbor as your fellow
citizen in the kingdom of Heaven and as a domestic of God.
Then you will esteem yourself holy, not merely as a rational
creature, but as the supernatural likeness of God, as a great
and holy temple. Thus, all the rights that you must respect
will appear to you in a supernatural light, hallowed with an
additional claim to respect; and all your duties will receive
a new and holy sanction, which will be imparted to all your
actions and will give them a supernatural character.

Although, as stated above, the general principles must
suffice, we shall nevertheless, select two moral virtues,
Christian humility and chastity, and by means of these
describe more in detail the character and spirit of the life of
grace. These two virtues are the rarest and most beautiful
blossoms of the tree of Christian grace and outside the
Christian world are least known and understood. They are,
more than all the others, closely connected with all the mysteries of grace and supernatural love. For as grace raises us
up to God, it frees us from the proud selfishness of our spirit
and the filth of the flesh. As by supernatural charity our
soul is absorbed in God and finds its greatest pleasure in
Him alone, so it also learns from charity its own value and
the meanness of sensual indulgence. Moreover, these
virtues render our self-love supernatural, and it is right

that we should speak of the supernatural love of ourselves after having spoken of the supernatural love of God and of our neighbor.

Humility, in its proper sense, is scarcely known, even in name, outside of Christianity, and even among Christians its inestimable supernatural value is but little understood. It would even seem, at first glance, that Christian grace, by raising our nature so high, would by no means further the practice of humility. But the very opposite is true.

If God so elevated us to make us sharers in His own nature, He does this out of pure condescension and gratuitous love. The more we understand the glory and sublimity of grace, the more we recognize our inability and lack of merit. We shall readily perceive and acknowledge how little is the value of our nature, how insignificant its perfections when compared with the countless gifts and perfections of grace, which nature cannot of itself possess or acquire. We see how little is its resemblance to God and how unworthy of His love and pleasure. We are confounded at the condescending, gracious love of God, who deigns to stoop so low to raise us up to Himself, and we exclaim with the holy Job: "What is a man that thou shouldst magnify him? Or why dost thou set thy heart upon him?" (*Job* 7:17).

Indeed, we may take it as a general rule that the more the creature is elevated by God, the more it may and ought to despise itself. This does not mean that we must deny any of the gifts that God has given us or any of the success that He has allowed us to attain through Him. That would be contrary to truth and gratitude. But it is seldom that inordinate self-love does not creep in to exaggerate our own advantages to the harm of others, or to ascribe them entirely to ourselves. Since the true estimation of our own advantages must be bound together with a repression of the false evaluation of self, a man hardly comes to a true reckoning of his worth without contempt for self.

Who was greater and more favored by God than His holy Mother? And yet who was more humble than she? How is this possible? Because she well knows that all her prerogatives were gifts of God, that to Him was due all honor for

them and that she of herself did not deserve them. Therefore, she chanted: "My soul magnifies the Lord . . . because
He has regarded the lowliness of His handmaid . . . because
He who is mighty has done great things for me." The higher
she was raised, the more she recognized the infinite distance between her natural lowliness and the glories with
which God has honored her and which she of herself could
neither merit nor repay. Thus, as Mother of God, she was
the most humble of His servants.

As the greatness of Divine grace ought especially to
excite and foster humility and self-contempt, so God, on the
other hand, requires nothing so much as humility in dispensing His grace. Nothing disposes us so well to receive
the gifts of God with respect and gratitude than the
acknowledgment of our lack of merit and ability before God
and the giving of all honor to Him. The deep conviction and
sincere confession of our unworthiness and lack of merit is
the best disposition we can have for the reception of grace.
If then, as Christians, we wish to render ourselves worthy
of the supreme grace of God, first and above all, God
demands that we humble ourselves before Him and confess
our lowliness, and that we seek in grace, like the Mother of
God, not so much our own as His glorification. As Mary,
when about to become the Mother of God, confessed that
she was His humble handmaid and accepted maternal dignity, not out of pride, but in obedient and grateful submission to the gracious Will of God, so must we, in deepest
humility, accept the dignity of children of God which He
offers us.

Moreover, grace so raises us up to God that we recognize
Him in the whole immeasurable depth of His gifts and love
Him alone as the highest good for His own sake. But the
better we know God, the more we ourselves disappear
before the splendor of His glory, as the mist before the
brightness of the sun. The more we love Him, and by love
are immersed and changed into Him, the more we will stifle and destroy self-love, and the more we will desire that
God alone be loved and honored and be All in all. We shall
no longer think of seeking our own honor and greatness, but

we shall rather long to be despised and scorned, if only God be honored and glorified thereby.

The more progress we make in the knowledge and love of God, the more we shall perceive how little our love—be it ever so supernatural and sublime—corresponds to the infinite greatness of God and His grace. We shall see also how little our gratitude is, and this will stir up our love to desire a constant increase. We shall never boast of the virtues and good works that we possess, but rather despise ourselves for having loved God so little and having profited so little from His grace.

If by sin we have offended the infinite and immeasurably generous goodness of God, we shall despise ourselves far more and desire to be despised by others. If we had offended God outside of the order of grace—when we were not so near Him and not so indebted to Him—this would suffice to humble us completely and to consider ourselves as worthy of eternal contempt. But now we have offended Him as our most loving Father; we have despised His tender love and trampled underfoot His most precious gifts; now we have violated the seal of His own sanctity, which He impressed upon us. What contempt do we not deserve? What humiliation and neglect is now so great that we should not gladly take it upon ourselves? And especially, if we again embrace God with fervent supernatural love, shall we not hate and detest ourselves as offenders of God in the same measure in which we now love Him, namely, above all things? Indeed, if we had never committed grave sins, but only venial sins, and these almost unconsciously, or if we had only neglected some inspirations of God, we ought never to forget it, but sincerely detest it.

When we consider all this, we cannot be surprised at seeing that the greatest Saints and the most favored souls were also the most humble. Those who were raised above all creatures humbled themselves beneath all. They considered their smallest failings and imperfections as great and terrible, and hence they performed the severest penances in atonement for them, considering themselves even far worse than the greatest sinners. They recognized the abundance of graces that God had given them and believed that they had corresponded less zealously and less gratefully with them than the sinners had corresponded to the grace given them. In the brightness of the light of faith that illumined their souls and in the fervent charity which consumed them, they noticed every mote, every small defect that still clung to them, and these faults appeared so terrible to them that they did not notice the former grievous faults of others and thought themselves worse than all other sinners. How much greater reason have we, who have committed so many and such grievous sins, to humble ourselves before God and our fellowmen and to esteem all others more than ourselves!

Grace, then, is the source of supernatural humility in us, since, by revealing its supernatural glory, it removes every pretext for taking pride in our nature or person and because, the higher it raises us, the more it humbles us. As, on the one hand, it dispels all self-conceit and pride, on the other hand, it tends to destroy in us the esteem of human honor and vain ambition.

To see the good qualities we really possess recognized by men and to be honored and esteemed for them is not in itself an evil, but rather a positive good. The desire for this honor, if not exaggerated and abused, is a noble inclination given by God and sanctioned by reason. It can even be useful in acquiring virtue, provided only that we esteem virtue more highly than the honor due to it. (S. Th., 2, 2, q. 131, a. 1). But grace obtains for us a supernatural dignity and the highest honor in the sight of God Himself, of His holy Angels and of all the Saints of Heaven. Compared to this, all honor that we can enjoy among men, and especially for natural good qualities, is vain and empty.

Grace, therefore, makes human honor loathsome and detestable to us, and we ought to despise it, even if it were deserved and void of danger for us. We ought to despise and avoid it because it is apt to draw our mind from the esteem of the invisible, divine honor that we have through grace and puts us in danger of losing it.

If we have appreciated the glories of grace and are jealous

of its possession, let us imitate the example of the Saints and say with the Psalmist: "I have chosen to be an abject in the house of my God, rather than to dwell in the tabernacles of sinners." (*Ps.* 83:11). With joy, the Saints trampled underfoot crown and scepter to acquire the heavenly crown of grace. Thus, unassuming Christian humility is one of the most sublime virtues, a supernatural virtue, that can proceed only from grace (*S. Th.*, 2, 2, q. 161, a. 5) and from pure love of God. This is evident with respect to the contempt for human honors, because only a heart filled with the glories of grace and borne aloft by its power can raise itself so far above the noble attractions of this earth. It is equally evident with regard to contempt of self, because true joy presupposes a clear knowledge of the nothingness of our nature in comparison with grace; it presupposes an intimate love of God, which makes us lose our being, as it were, in Him and forget self in the sight of His majesty. This very self-humiliation is the starting point and aim of the highest flights of our soul and the truest and noblest magnanimity.

Equally glorious and beautiful as humility is Christian chastity; and therefore it is equally an offspring and fruit of grace. There is a natural chastity, a virtue that would be a necessary adornment of man, though not elevated by grace. On the one hand, our soul is naturally a spiritual being and an image of God, and therefore can never be carried away by the animal passions of the flesh without debasing itself. On the other hand, although our flesh is in itself similar to that of the animals, it has nevertheless, by its substantial union with the rational soul, received a higher dignity and therefore must no longer follow its own impulses and lusts, but must be subject to the guidance of the spirit and made subservient to higher, nobler ends. Man must, then, for the sake of his human nature, preserve the natural nobility of his soul and live pure and unspotted. This he will easily do if, with the help of God, he keeps his eye steadily fixed on the beauty of virtue and other spiritual gifts and esteems them more highly than all lusts of the flesh. From a natural viewpoint, also, chastity is possible and obligatory, and every violation of it is a sin.

But the injury that through sin has affected our nature shows itself especially in the lusts of the flesh. Hence, it has come so far that the world explains the commandment of chastity as unnatural and impossible to observe. Indeed, we cannot deny that without the aid of supernatural grace it is most difficult to observe and is seldom met with.

Grace, therefore, has a great problem in regard to chastity—that is, Christian, supernatural chastity. But it solves this [problem] splendidly, for the honor of God and of His institution, Christianity. Grace invests our soul and body with an incomparably higher dignity than they both possess by nature. From the state of a mere creature, it raises our soul to that of a daughter, a friend and a spouse of God. It dedicates our body, which by nature is merely the dwelling of our soul, as the living temple of the Holy Spirit, a temple in which the Holy Ghost is to dwell with the fullness of His divinity as the pledge of its future glory and immortality. What reverence and respect do we Christians owe to our soul? With what solicitude must we not preserve this pure mirror of the Divinity from the smallest stain, to say nothing of the filthy mire of sensual lust! With how much zeal must we guard this daughter and spouse of the purest and holiest King, lest, forgetting its own dignity and that of its Spouse, it dishonors itself and Him and from the heights of Heaven casts itself down into the abyss of the lowest and meanest sensuality, of which by its very nature it should be ashamed.

And how holy and unspotted we should keep our body, this temple of the Holy Ghost, this member of Christ, this bone of His bone and flesh of His Flesh, this body which was so often nourished with the purest Flesh and Blood of the Son of God! How carefully we should guard it against all impurity and uncleanness. "He that committeth fornication sinneth against his own body." (*1 Cor.* 6:18). He sins against his body because it is the dwelling of the rational, immortal soul. How much more does he sin against it when by grace it has become the temple of the Holy Ghost? Rightly does the Apostle say that uncleanness must not even be mentioned among Christians, so foreign must it be to them, since chastity is so intimately connected with Christianity and grace.

Hence we understand why Christianity, from the very beginning, brought with it a certain emphasis on the practice of this virtue in a perfect degree—not that marriage was belittled or considered as something imperfect. In marriage, Christianity sees that means provided by God for spreading His kingdom on earth. To this end, marriage was made a holy Sacrament, a figure of the sacred union which unites Christ with His Church. (Cf. *Eph.* 5:32).

Grace, however, joins the human soul so intimately with Christ that it excludes any other love. Hence, the Christian who is full of grace shudders at the thought of sharing his heart with a creature and of living to please such a one (cf. *1 Cor.* 7:33), and the thought comes naturally to consecrate himself body and soul to God in perfect purity and to preserve the blossom of virginity.

Indeed, this is not an obligation, because the use of Matrimony dishonors neither soul nor body, but it is a holy and urgent counsel, not only to preserve soul and body from dishonor, but to preserve them in the highest honor. Such chastity is above the capacity of the rational man, and when he sees it in others, he necessarily admires it as something heavenly and divine. But such virtues are precisely the special fruits of grace, which not only raises man to a supernatural dignity and destiny, but gives him at the same time the power to live in harmony with the dignity.

For grace is accompanied by supernatural love, which the Holy Ghost breathes into the soul. This holy love frees the soul from the fetters of sensuality and gives it a heavenly sense. This love, which finds its peace in God alone and binds us inseparably to Him, expels all sensual love and smothers the flame of concupiscence. It preserves to the Christian command over the flesh; it enables him to sanctify his whole life; it directs his thinking and striving to the highest goal. When this love is fervent, there is no need of a law against unchastity, not even a counsel of virginity. When the soul is so mysteriously attracted by its Heavenly Spouse, so bound by His holy ties, so charmed and overcome by His beauty, His sweetness and delight, then it is of itself estranged from the world and the flesh; then it scorns every pleasure, despises every sensual indulgence and desires only to adhere to its Divine Spouse in all that it feels and does. The more the soul loves Him [and] the more it desires to possess Him alone, the more it will avoid every interference in this possession and enjoyment from contact and dealings with earthly things—[also], the more it will belong wholly and exclusively to Him and dedicate soul and body to His service. Love teaches it to understand and practice that which, according to the words of our Saviour, not all can understand. (Cf. *Matt.* 19:11). Such a soul does not find mortification of the flesh and its lusts [a] hard sacrifice, but accounts it rather a holy joy, a natural consequence of intimate union with Christ—who has become its all—with Christ, in whom it finds all that it has left in the world in a better, purer and richer way.

Thus, Christian chastity, as well as humility, is rooted in the mystery of grace. In this mystery, both virtues have their foundation, their law and their vitality, and their relation to this mystery is similar to their relation to the divine maternity in the case of the Blessed Virgin Mary.

Humility and virginal chastity were the practical and most proper virtues of the Mother of God. Through these, she had to prepare herself for her sublime dignity of [divine] motherhood, and her divine maternity had to nourish and increase them. The Blessed Virgin is now the model of the children of God. As these resemble her in her supernatural dignity, they must also resemble her in those supernatural virtues; and as Mary was incited to the practice of these virtues by her exalted vocation, we also ought to be animated to the same practice by the recollection of our high vocation.

As these virtues were never perfectly practiced by anyone on earth before the Mother of God, so they flourished after her only where, by faith in Christ, the mystery of grace was known and glorified. Where grace is not known, Christ is forgotten, and where Christ is not present, holiness must fall away and die out. Only where grace is esteemed in all its splendor, can one understand the supernatural virtues, and only where Christ is loved, can one worthily and enthusiastically practice perfection. If, then, you wish to acquire and cherish these virtues, you can do nothing better than to consider attentively the glories of grace which effect such resemblance between you and the Mother of God, and by this consideration be inflamed with a holy love and admiration for grace. And on the other hand, if you will conform your life to the high dignity of the state of grace, practice especially, besides the supernatural love of God and your neighbor, Christian humility and chastity, or rather, practice by Christian humility and chastity supernatural self-love.

With regard to love of self, we have received no special law because by nature we love ourselves. Therefore, we are only required to keep this love within due bounds, lest it clash with the love of God, so that we no longer love ourselves, but God—or at least love ourselves in and for God alone. If we wish to know exactly how natural self-love is made supernatural, the answer is [this]: by loving ourselves, not according to our natural goodness, but according to what we have become by grace and desiring for ourselves supernatural gifts rather than the natural. We love God and our neighbor supernaturally only when we consider how God has become by grace our Father, Friend and Spouse and the object of our supernatural happiness, and when we consider in our neighbor what grace has made him for himself, for God and for us, namely, a supernatural likeness of the Divine nature, a child of God and our brother in Christ.

If we love ourselves according to grace, we must despise all that we possess outside of grace. We must be solicitous, above all things, to preserve in us pure and unstained the heavenly splendor of grace, and this is done precisely by Christian humility and chastity. Although at first sight these two virtues seem to indicate only mortification and renunciation of self-love, they are in reality nothing less than the most beautiful and sublime expression of the purest and most perfect supernatural self-love, and nothing is more true than that the humble and chaste man loves himself truly and perfectly.

The whole supernatural law of grace is expressed in the threefold command: to love God, our neighbor and ourselves according to grace. But since grace, the splendor of the Divine nature and the bond of union with God, can be loved perfectly in God only, that threefold command is resolved into the one: to love God as the source and end of grace. This love of God is itself the first and highest law of grace.

Let us then love God, our neighbor and ourself in grace. Love is life, supernatural love is supernatural life, love according to grace and proceeding from grace is the life of grace. All else will take care of itself. Then we are truly Christian, then we honor our name and in turn count this name an honor.

Before we close this chapter, it will not be superfluous to observe how the doctrine of grace is the foundation of the three evangelical counsels [poverty, chastity and obedience]. Since their observance is partly a means for attaining the highest perfection and partly a fruit of such perfection, they must evidently have a common foundation in grace.

In regard to virginal chastity, this has already been shown. Voluntary obedience to men for the sake of God has its root in Christian humility, which, in order to give itself entirely to God, submits itself also to men and allows itself to be led by God through men, who take His place in order to do God's Will in all things and self-will in nothing. Evangelical poverty consists in renouncing the external means which may serve to gratify our ambition, pride and sensual lust. The same foundation, therefore, which supports obedience and chastity, must also support poverty. Here also, grace manifests the sublime dignity of the children of God, of whom the mean goods of the earth are entirely unworthy, and it shows us a rich treasure of heavenly goods, in view of which it cannot be difficult to despise the whole world and all its treasures and to trample them underfoot.

The children of God should be free from all servile bonds, free also, if possible, from all those fine cares which fasten them to the world and even entangle them in it to some extent and which may be a hindrance to their free intercourse with their heavenly Father, a hindrance to their life in God, of God and for God. Therefore, those who are called to be perfect children of God receive from Him the wise inspiration to renounce their own will perfectly, their temporal possessions, their sensual enjoyments. Through grace, they are so estranged from the world that they find no peace until they have bidden farewell to it.

Chapter 57

FAITH, THE SOUL OF THE LIFE OF GRACE

IT IS impossible to speak here of all the practices of piety and virtue that belong to the life of grace, for this would require a complete treatise on asceticism and mysticism. This we can the more easily omit because, thanks to the grace of God, there are so many excellent works of introduction to Christian perfection. We must, however, counsel anyone who seriously desires progress in virtue to study these works thoroughly. Just as one will not become perfect without practicing every virtue, neither will he travel on this difficult and dangerous way without erring, unless he obtains advice from those who are masters in this life, the spiritual writers and teachers. Here we wish to give the general principles, or rather, the dogmatic principles of the spiritual life.

To this end, we must come back to the first and deepest foundation of grace, namely, faith. For faith is not only the beginning of the life of grace (as we have already shown), but also the permanent driving-power of its development—for the life of grace and according to grace, and indeed for this life in its fullness, that is, for all the virtues and exercises that the life of grace embraces. [sic]

By this we do not mean to exclude love, the most excellent of all the virtues. We cannot esteem love highly enough nor strive after it earnestly enough. Our Divine Saviour has not commanded us to be perfect, but He has commanded us to strive after perfection, an obligation that is to be understood in the strict sense, that holds for all Christians, not merely for priests and religious. Now perfection consists essentially in love. The perfection of a Christian is nothing else than the perfection of love, and as is self-evident, not

384

merely of infused but of actual love. By that we are obliged, at least always to be ready to fulfill any obligation of love toward God, or for His sake, toward our neighbor. This holds for temporal as well as spiritual things, in matters of our own salvation and also in those that pertain more or less closely to our vocation.

But the higher the edifice of Christian perfection that love has to build, the deeper must the foundation be. But the foundation is faith. Precisely the necessity of love, of a strong, active, sacrificing love, shows us the necessity of faith for the carrying out of our task.

Love not only presupposes faith in order to be born in our heart, but it lives on it and works through it. A strong and lively faith must rule the soul, that it may be able to fulfill its great task; a faith that gives it fervent enthusiasm, so that it may reach the highest goal; a faith that makes it capable of every sacrifice, that it may overcome all internal and external impediments; a faith that allows no self-denial to appear too great when it is a question of obeying God in difficult things and being faithful to Him in little things and of matching our generosity with His.

Faith must do all that and much more for love, and as for love, so for every virtue that belongs to the life of grace. Hence, we are right in saying that faith is the soul, the driving-power, the nourishment of the whole spiritual life.

Faith is not only the light by which we must find the lost drachma of Divine grace, not only the morning star that is going to lead us to the Sun of Justice, as the star led the Wise Men, not only the gate through which the Lord of life enters into our soul, not only the firstborn of the supernatural virtues, but it is also the light in which we must walk in order to find our way; it is the firewood that nourishes the flames of love; it is the breeze that fans the flames of enthusiasm and zeal; it is the salve for those who fight and the healing oil for all the wounded in battle; it is the pillar of fire and the cloud in which God goes before us on the way; it is the last as well as the first of all virtues. If one has the misfortune of driving all the other supernatural virtues out of the soul, one at least remains, faith; and as long as this remains, there is for grace and all the other virtues a connecting link. Only when faith also is cast away is the last bond broken that binds us with God.

According to the measure of faith, so will be the measure of doing, of energy, of the spirit of prayer, of sacrifice, of love, of the supernatural life. This ineffable truth cannot be repeated often enough. That is the sense of the words: "My just man liveth by faith." (*Heb.* 10:38). Faith is the basis of supernatural life and the promotion of all its manifestations, of all works of penance, of all prayer, sacrifices, of the fulfilling of one's duty, of all perfection and holiness.

From this we see that faith, although essentially always the same in the justified, is capable of very different degrees, and its fervor and power can increase indefinitely. In fact, it must grow constantly if we are to make progress in our supernatural life. Progress in virtue also, as well as the highest perfection, depends on the measure of faith, so much so that spiritual writers are accustomed to call the highest form of prayer, *the prayer of faith or of pure faith.*

What damage is done by those unfortunate ones who, I do not say bury faith, but who do not hesitate to weaken the spirit and the joy of faith, those who make it their business through their perpetual criticizing, through the coldness with which they deal with holy things, to cool their reverence for the supernatural and enthusiasm for the Faith out of fear that it could turn into fanaticism. Of such damage only those can come near having an idea who see in the teachers of mysticism and in the lives of the Saints to what purity of life, to what union with God, to what heroic practice of every virtue the spirit of faith can lead.

The Saints themselves had other ideas of the importance of faith, because from their own experience they recognized the influence of faith on one's life. St. Ignatius emphasizes that, if we wish to fulfill our duty, it is not enough to believe what the Church commands us to believe, but we must strive to think and feel with the Church. And St. Teresa, who could never thank God enough that He destined her to be born as a child of the holy Catholic Church, affirmed that she was willing to suffer martyrdom, not only for every letter of the Church's doctrine, but even for every ceremony. This being so, it is of great importance for us to know how it stands with us in regard to the spirit of faith, not merely for the sake of believing, but in order to make progress in the path of virtue.

From what has been said, it cannot be difficult to see clearly our condition. If we find reverence for God, fear of sin, striving after mortification, devotion, humility, self-denial, constant practice of the presence of God and of inner recollection increase in us, then our spirit of faith is also certainly on the increase. But if we are going backwards in fidelity to our religious duties and in striving for holiness, our faith is also suffering.

We deceive ourselves if we point to the Church's teaching and say: "Yes, I could live more fervently, but the teaching is that faith, on that account, is not lost, and mine at least has suffered no harm." So we live on, consoled in our laxity, till we eventually come to imagine that the spirit of faith has become pure and strong and virile in us only since we have cast off the childlike—or, as we prefer to say, the childish—practices of piety and the estimation of emotional devotion in which only feminine narrowmindedness places value.

That is certainly not the mind of the Church. It teaches us that the gift of faith, the infused faculty of believing, is not destroyed by sin. But it is by no means affirmed that the virtue of faith, the vitality, power, fervor of the spirit, is not injured by laxity. Nor is it said that the external practices of piety and the sentiments of devotion are without meaning for the spiritual life. On the contrary, we may conclude to a loss of the fervor of faith after every neglect of fervent prayer and of striving after virtue. How could we be so tepid regarding the dishonoring of God through our coldness and thoughtlessness in prayer if we were deeply penetrated by faith in the presence and in the majesty of God? How could we judge as simple scrupulosity and ridicule the tender conscience of pious souls who tremble at an evil thought, if fervent faith placed before our eyes the holiness of God, the greatness of sin and unfaithfulness? From all this, it follows that our progress in good depends on the increase of the spirit of faith.

We must go forward; the Holy Ghost tells us that expressly. (Cf. *Apoc.* 22:11). The saying of St. Bernard, "Not to wish to go forward is to go backward" (*Ep.* 254, 3, 4), is a winged word in the mouth of all Christians. Then we must constantly increase in the spirit of faith, as the Apostle says: "Try your own selves if you be in the faith; prove ye yourselves." (*2 Cor.* 13:5).

Faith and life have one and the same destiny. Hence, the Church has condemned the teaching of those who doubt about the faith and think they can take away from it whatever no longer agrees with the times and the world without endangering their salvation. On the contrary, the Church has expressly declared that there is but one faith, common to the learned and to the common people, that is taught in the schools and preached from the pulpit, and this is the same faith by which we are justified and should become holy. (*Conc. Vat., sess.* 3, *de fide,* c. 3).

As the sanctification of man proceeds gradually and must be continued through our whole life, and [as] we never dare to be too sure of our faith and never be satisfied with it, so we must ever strive to know it better, to practice it more perfectly and to take greater joy in it.

Now the way of salvation—according to the Fathers, theologians and spiritual writers—runs through three stages, that are usually named the way of purification, of enlightenment and of union, or the way of beginners, of those making progress and of the perfect. A more detailed explanation of these three stages and of the practice of the works proper to each one must be sought in the ascetical books to which we have referred above. Unfortunately, many of the recent books on Christian piety pay little attention to this division; whereas, those written in the spirit of the ancient Catholic times place much weight on it. The bad effects that have followed the neglect of this division show how well the ancients have done. For he does wrong who is scarcely able to take a few steps in the spiritual life and yet attempts to do wonderful things that the Saints have seldom accomplished. Without having laid a solid foundation, some wish to see God, to enjoy God's sweetness before having placated Him, before having tasted the bitterness of penance. Such a one stops in the middle of the way because of lack of order, of discipline and earnestness.

This order must be directed by faith, or better, faith must prepare the way and make sure that one holds it. It can lead only to evil when the Christian neglects this teaching as unimportant, or despises it because of impatience. Why is it that so many good, well-meant beginnings in virtue end so quickly in laxity or go wrong through little exaggerations? How is it to be explained that precisely those who have begun with the greatest energy later often lose all piety— sometimes even their faith? It is said that they lacked order of enlightenment or cleverness. This indeed! But faith gives supernatural enlightenment. And they allowed it to fail in food and strength. Either they have from the beginning dared to attempt works of a higher stage, for which this faith and spiritual strength did not suffice, or they sought to make progress in the life of virtue, but failed to further their spirit of faith at the same time by reading and study, by listening and obeying, by prayer and meditation. Hence their failure!

To obviate this mistake, the Holy Ghost reminds us with so many words that the spirit of faith must be nourished and cultivated. The justice of God, He says, is revealed to us from faith to faith (cf. *Rom.* 1:17), in other words, always according to the measure in which our faith progresses from one step to another. Faith must first of all cleanse our heart. (Cf. *Acts* 15:5). Then comes the illumination through this heavenly gift. (Cf. *Heb.* 6:4). Finally follows the faith of the Saints, which, however, the word of God joins with the patience of the Saints to teach and warn us. (Cf. *Apoc.* 13:10). Evidently, it wishes to tell us that we must act according to the measure of our faith. If this is too small, we must try to merit an increase, with the help of God's grace, until it corresponds with our desire for action. As we never reach a goal without patience and perseverance (cf. *Luke* 21:19), so we reach this high degree of faith only through that persevering practice through which the Saints attained their goal.

If we weigh all this, we may well say that the sad condition the life of Christendom so often exhibits is more often to be traced to lack of a spirit of faith than to other reasons. Good will is often not lacking, but an enlightened will, that is, the enlightenment of faith, often fails. And when earnestness is wanting, the ultimate reason will certainly be lack of lively faith.

Let us seek, therefore, with all our power to further the spirit of faith; then certainly striving after a life that becomes the children of God—after true perfection—will increase among Christians. We may feel ever so weak, we may tremble at the height of the goal to which we must climb, but yet the word of our Saviour holds here: if you can believe, you will be helped.

Chapter 58

GRACE AND VENIAL SIN

IN A BUILDING, all depends on the foundation. If this is placed negligently, the result cannot be good. The higher the building rises, the more cracks and fissures appear, frames and walls sink, and finally the whole structure collapses. The greater the building, the better must the ground walls be. When it is a question of a building like that of the life of grace, which must reach from earth to Heaven and last for eternity, the foundation must be more carefully laid than for any earthly building.

God Himself has laid the foundation of this spiritual edifice through His grace. But He demands that we cooperate in the construction of our own building. For we are not only God's building, but also His cooperators. Hence, as wise builders (cf. *1 Cor.* 3:9-10), we must lay the foundation so that the whole will be a success and will stand forever.

The foundation of this spiritual building, as far as our work is concerned, is the so-called "way of purification." To neglect this would be to make all our work useless. As it would be effort wasted to plant a tree on a rock, or a vineyard on a pile of stones, or to place a house in a swamp, so too, all our later work would be wasted if we did not beforehand dry the swamp of its bad inclinations, remove the stones of bad habits and the rocky ground of laziness and hard-heartedness.

This is a tiresome work that demands much knowledge and yet more action. The great masters of the spiritual life take the greatest care in teaching of the purgative way because they know that the result of our supernatural life depends on the difficult and painful work that must be done here.

There are especially three practices that constitute the task of this first step. The first is *the putting off of sin,* as well as the habit and inclination thereto. The second is *mortification,* in the widest sense of the word, not only outward rigor of the body and its lusts, but also the difficult correction of the senses, of the eyes and tongue especially, and yet more of the internal faculties, especially of the self-will and the imagination and finally the bridling of the passions. The third task is the persevering use of the great means of salvation, *prayer,* without which no hope of success can be had.

Mortification must not be practiced out of self-will; otherwise, it easily opens false paths. It is merely a means of purifying the soul, and only when thus understood does it lead to the true goal. But then it is of the highest importance and cannot be too earnestly recommended and practiced. And even prayer must not be practiced in this or in a higher stage out of self-will, that is, because in it we find consolation, but rather as a service to God and as a means of strength against our faults and for the practice of virtue.

Of all those important things we cannot deal here. We wish to mention again, however, the persevering reading of spiritual books, one of the most important means for successfully leading a spiritual life. It must suffice us here to speak of the chief task of beginnings, the struggle against sin.

We do not intend to deal with mortal sin. Certainly we may conclude that those who have been freed from sin by grace and intend to live a life of virtue would rather die than knowingly commit a mortal sin. We even presuppose the intention not even to commit deliberately a venial sin. For whoever does not wish to do this much will hardly be able to make progress. But since human weakness is so great that we only too easily fall into such faults, and since we so gladly count these as insignificant because of their number and of custom, we feel bound to arm ourselves through a special meditation against these small but efficient enemies of grace.

Many think that a sure means to arm ourselves with proper fear of venial sins is to consider them [to be] as grave as possible, yes, rather as too great than as too small. Hence the usual saying that grace, destroyed by mortal sin, is also lessened by venial sin, so that we would always lose a certain amount of grace that we had merited through God's generosity. This would certainly be the strongest motive to avoid venial sin. No doubt it was this consideration that gained entrance for this opinion in ascetical literature. But it is not necessary that we have recourse to this view, for there is reason enough to fear venial sin in the manifold and great harm it effects. But according to the very common teaching of theologians, we may hold that venial sins, neither singly nor collectively, lessen in us essentially either Sanctifying Grace or the supernatural virtues. (*S. Th.*, 2, 2, q. 24, a. 10).

Natural virtues are indeed lessened not only by grave sins but also by light faults. For as they are acquired and increased by persevering practice, so are they weakened by neglect and yet more so by sins, and finally are driven out entirely when one constantly works against them. A thing is destroyed in the same way in which it is acquired. Therefore, what is acquired by purely natural activity may also be destroyed by the same.

The supernatural virtues have this in common with the natural virtues, that a certain ease in performing acts of virtue, which has been acquired by earnest practice, is weakened and lessened by venial sins. But since this ease effects only the external completion of the act, not the inner essence, this weakening cannot touch the essence of the virtue. They [the supernatural virtues] are rather like pure gold, that can be covered with dust but is not injured in its essence and does not lose its inner beauty and purity. They are like a powerful fire that, when covered with material that will not burn, cannot blaze forth so freely, but nevertheless is not robbed of its inner glow.

Neither is the grace, the corresponding love of God, nor the merit of our works essentially lessened by venial sins, because the supernatural virtues cannot be lessened. By venial sins we offend God as our highest and best friend, we become displeasing in His sight and deserve great punishment. This displeasure in God's sight can, however, exist alongside of grace. The punishment for that offense will certainly be great enough. We do not wish to speak of the fact that God will send various sufferings for them and will delay our admission to the blessed vision of His face. For him who knows the value of grace and divine friendship, it has more weight to realize that every venial sin, even the least, saddens the heart of God, calls forth His displeasure and robs us of many favors that He had destined for us.

Without doubt, venial sins deprive us of many actual graces. But we need not believe that it deprives us of a part of the Sanctifying Grace that we possess. (*S. Th.* 1, q. 89, a. 1). Though one commits many venial sins, he still retains, in spite of the punishment he deserves, at least the title to heavenly beatitude. The splendor of grace will be dimmed, as St. Thomas says (*ibid.*), but in its essence it remains untarnished. The gold of grace is always precious, even when it is covered with such dust and mixed with much dross. The dust must be washed away with tears of penance; the dross must be burned away in the fire. But then we stand before God with all the riches of grace that we gathered before the venial sins or between the committing of them.

From this we learn two things. First, what an awful evil mortal sin is. Venial sin is truly a great misfortune, but it cannot be compared with the evil that grave sin causes. On the other hand, we see here how high in the eyes of God grace places us, how closely it has bound itself with our soul, so closely that a great infidelity does not succeed in driving it out, as long as the infidelity remains a half-measure and does not attain to a full turning away from God. Precisely this shows us clearly that grace is not our work, but the fruit of the Divine love and activity.

Although we need not fear that venial sin will destroy our treasure of grace, nor even lessen it, yet we must not be less careful to avoid it. Precisely here we must admire the infinite love of God, who does not withdraw His grace, even though we soil it. And we must admire His power, that does not allow His works to be so easily disturbed by us. Moreover, here we first understand rightly the costliness of holiness and grace. For if it were not so pure in its essence, if it were not the purest divine gold and a ray of the heavenly light, it would be removed by sin. That it is not removed is not to be laid to the insignificance of sin, but to the indestructibility of its own nature.

Grace is the purity and holiness of God shared with us. It cannot exist together with mortal sin, for this is the cessation of obedience, the conscious and willing turning from God's holiness and the giving of oneself to lying and impurity. Venial sin stains and dishonors the soul through shameful flirting with the wicked, through tepidity and mediocrity toward God, through indecisive wavering between Him and His enemies. But since it does not wish to break entirely with Him, He holds fast the covenant that in His fidelity He made with the soul and even strengthens His grace against this foolish play of blindness and indifference in order to shame our infidelity.

The more divinely grace stands here before our eyes, the more frivolous the sinner appears. The dull spirit of the ungrateful man says indeed: "Of what importance is venial sin since it does not touch grace itself!" This is a way of thinking that finds excuses only in human blindness. For should not one rather believe that frivolity, coldness, mediocrity of the creature toward its Lord, lukewarmness, and the so-called imperfection, are so serious precisely because they are related to such holiness and are committed while trusting in the unchanging fidelity of God?

All this teaches us to avoid venial sins most carefully. As the eye rejects the smallest object that enters it, and if this is not possible, feels pain and sheds tears, so should our soul reject every venial sin and never rest until it has loosed itself from it. Hence the Saints warn us to imitate doves, which take the greatest care to keep their feathers clean, and to this end avoid every place and every thing by which they might be soiled. For the soul adorned with grace is, according to the Psalmist, a dove with silver plumage, resplendent as pure gold in the bright sun. (Cf. *Ps.* 67:14).

Let us not attach ourselves to earthly things, but rather

tear ourselves loose from them whenever we can, being as careful as the dove not to soil ourselves when it is necessary to deal with them. And when some stain has become attached to our wings through negligence or oversight, let us shake the dust off and hasten to wash our souls clean again in the brook of Christ's Blood.

Besides the stain, there are still two great disadvantages for grace that result from venial sin. If this sin does not lessen grace essentially, it weakens its fervor and fruitfulness and leads to its complete loss. We can and must consider grace under a twofold figure—either under the figure of light and fire, or under the figure of a supernatural seed. From both viewpoints we easily see the damage done by venial sin.

He who commits many venial sins weakens the activity of grace in himself, he even works against it, presses it back, lessens its fervor and prevents it from breaking forth into a full flame. On the other hand, venial sins are like brambles and thorns that hinder the joyful blooming of the life of grace. The heavenly seed of grace cannot flourish where so many poisonous plants grow up beside it. Their proximity ruins the ground and poisons the atmosphere. They ruin the ground because their multitude saps its strength; they poison the atmosphere because the Holy Ghost withdraws from the field sowed with weeds the light and dew of His grace in order not to pour them out in vain.

Thus, on the one hand, the increase of grace is hindered in many ways by venial sins. On the other hand, venial sins increase the tendency toward evil and therefore lessen one's inclination to good; they lead to thoughtlessness and abuse of grace, as well as indifference toward offenses against God, and thus prepare for the loss of grace.

That is indeed a great harm, sufficient to fill us with fear for these so-called small sins. Hence, the Wise Man says: "He that contemneth small things shall fall by little and little." (*Ecclus.* 19:1). And the Apostle likewise warns: "Know you not that a little leaven corrupteth the whole lump?" (*1 Cor.* 5:6). What is still worse, venial sins undermine and loosen the roots of grace and push the fertile ground away, so that it can easily be torn out. For although only mortal sin cuts the roots of grace as with a sharp knife, such a terrible cutting instrument could not so easily penetrate the earth if the venial sins had not prepared the way.

As sickness precedes death, so venial sins precede mortal. Not as though grace itself could grow sick (that is as impossible as [its] being corrupted or lessened) but because through venial sins the activity of grace is crippled and weakened—just as in bodily sickness the soul itself is not injured, but the body, through the disturbance of its organs, becomes a useless instrument of the soul. What the organs of the body are for the soul, the natural powers and inclinations of the soul are for grace. As a disturbance of the bodily organs, if not impeded from the beginning, or removed, gradually makes it impossible for the soul to remain united with the body, so here venial sins gradually estrange our nature from grace because they lead our natural powers in the wrong direction, turning them away from God and toward creatures and thus withdrawing them from the governing influence of grace. And then there is needed only a small blow to tear the last bond that has heretofore bound nature to grace. And we wonder that often a very slight occasion can draw after it a terrible fall!

Indeed, only grave sin [mortal sin] drives away Sanctifying Grace, but venial sins are truly sins and are related and bound with mortal sin. Even though weak, they storm against the temple of God that grace has built in us. Against it they can do nothing; they can only soil it and shake the foundation. But they are the messengers of a more powerful enemy that follows on their heels and can then more easily complete the work of destruction.

Is that not enough, Christian soul, to make you also avoid venial sins as the most dangerous enemies of grace? Is that not much worse than if they robbed you of only some degrees of grace? Yes, indeed, much worse! Oh, how useful it would be sometimes if God would let you suddenly commit a grave fault. You would certainly rouse yourself up and, like the Prodigal Son, return to Him more earnestly and more carefully. But you live from year to year in tepidity and console yourself with the thought that you are not going too far, while the Holy Ghost says: "I would thou wert cold, or hot. But because thou art lukewarm, and neither cold, nor hot, I will begin to vomit thee out of my mouth." (*Apoc.* 3:15-16).

Since this is so, how can you be so friendly with these deceitful enemies who, though pretending to take nothing from you, wish ultimately to take all? The less important they seem, the more dangerous they are, for the less they are feared, the more undisturbed they can carry on their destroying game. Therefore, hate them, flee from them, fear them, and beware of them as your greatest enemies.

Let us omit the question concerning the essence of venial sin, which is so difficult to fathom. Let us rather try to see clearly how they affect God and what we do through them. When we do this, we shall understand why we should carefully avoid them, because through them, we offend our best Father, our most lovable Friend, our dearest Spouse.

In the state of grace you are more obliged than ever to love Him and to cause Him joy. For you are so intimately bound with Him and so overwhelmed with signs of His favor that your heart should breathe only love and thankfulness toward Him.

What grief you cause Him when, though you do not fully put an end to your friendship with Him, you deny Him on every occasion the simplest services of love. You do not wish to leave your Father's house altogether, but you do not hesitate to refuse Him childlike obedience and reverence and thus to fail in the obligation that your dwelling in His palace places on you. You say that you do not wish to be unfaithful to your Spouse, and yet you do not hesitate to deal with His enemies and to look amorously at them. You do not wish to renounce His grace, but you act with it as tepidly and as wastefully as possible, as long as you reckon that it will not be entirely withdrawn from you.

O man, when will you see the inexpressible wickedness that is in every venial sin? When will you begin to serve God more zealously and faithfully and to please Him in all your actions? If you will not do it out of love and gratitude toward Him, do it at least out of fear for the awful punishment that He has ordained for such ingratitude and lack of love. These punishments are great—and must be great—because the sins also are incomprehensibly great.

The holy fire of grace that you have covered through sin, without extinguishing it, will naturally seek an exit wherever possible. Venial sins hinder the fire from reaching up to God. Instead, they pile brambles and straw in great quantities all around. Thus, the holy fire must change into an avenging fire. This the whole created nature no more knows nor is able to produce than the fire of grace. It is a fire that only the glowing and powerful love of God is capable of making in order to cleanse the soul of its stains.

How frightfully will this fire of grace torture you if God does not admit you immediately after death to the blessed vision of His face. Then there will be such a longing, such a burning thirst for this vision, which is the natural goal of grace, that, by reason of this pain, you will forget all others. And the nearer you think you are to your goal and the greater the degree of glory that awaits you in Heaven, the greater the suffering will be. (*Collet., De purgat.,* c. 3a. 7).

Therefore, hasten to extinguish this awful fire with the tears of true penance, and in the future gather no more chaff in your soul that could furnish new material for it. Hasten to enkindle in yourself that lovable fire of grace and of Divine love and with it delay not to wipe out all stains. Thus, you will not only keep grace pure, unspotted and intact, but you will constantly increase its fruits without delay.

Chapter 59

THE OBLIGATION AND FACILITY OF CONTINUAL PROGRESS IN THE LIFE OF GRACE

IF OUR life is to be worthy of God and His grace, it is not enough that we acquire grace and do away with everything in us that is contrary to it. We must also strive to promote and increase the life of grace in us according to the desire of the Apostle who prays "That you may walk worthy of God, in all things pleasing; being fruitful in every good work, and increasing in the knowledge of God: strengthened . . . according to the power of the glory, in all patience and longsuffering with joy." (*Col.* 1:10-11). To accomplish this is the task of the second stage in the spiritual life, that is, the way of enlightenment. The four chief duties that we have to fulfill in this stage are: the acquiring of the Christian virtues; meditative prayer with its nourishment, spiritual reading; the following of Christ, the most perfect model of Christian perfection; and the fight against temptations and deceitful suggestions of the evil one, that are much stronger now than at the beginning. We say nothing more in detail about prayer, because it is a common task on all the steps of the spiritual life and it is understood that the higher one goes, the more necessary prayer is.

In the spiritual life, it is customary to call the persons who are on this step the ones making progress. The most important obligation that binds such persons is to make progress in all good, in that which is proper to the present one. Progress, new efforts, greater zeal, deeper penetration, enthusiasm, demand all the practices of the purgative way—the more so because the light of faith, which has now become stronger, sees their importance more clearly than

400

before. Hence, care must be taken for the purification of the soul, the ruling of the senses, the bridling of the passions; sanctification and prayer must not be lessened, but rather increased. It goes without saying that the practices of the new stage are bound by the same laws and that we must constantly increase in them.

All life, in time, strives to develop according to its nature and to perfect itself more and more. When this effort ceases or no longer succeeds, we can conclude that it has run its course, that its power is broken, that its resources are exhausted and that death has already begun to find its mark.

Now the life of grace can never be exhausted. On this earth we never reach an end of love or of perfection. The heavenly plant of grace, rooted in the bosom of God, can never cease to grow, until it has passed from the vicissitudes of time into the quiet of eternity. Therefore, if we cease growing, the fault cannot be with grace, but only with us. Either we fail by not esteeming the life of grace highly enough, or we neglect it through laziness by leaving unused its inexhaustible fertility and do not trouble ourselves to contribute with all our strength to its development. God must then consider us rather dead than alive, in spite of all the powerful [physical] vitality in us, because we allow the grain of seed [of His grace] to lie dormant in the earth and do not cultivate it, that it may grow up into a mighty tree.

Grace should grow as the grain of mustard seed in the Gospel, for it contains an abundance of vitality and power, though appearing small and insignificant, like the seed. "The path of the just," says the Wise Man, "as a shining light goeth forwards and increaseth even to perfect day." (*Prov.* 4:18). We must grow as members of the Mystical Body of Christ, until we are strong and perfect, or as the Apostle says, "Until we all meet into the unity of faith, and of the knowledge of the Son of God, unto a perfect man, unto the measure of the age of the fullness of Christ." (*Eph.* 4:13).

But how are we to acquire this growth in grace and perfection? You think, perhaps, in the same way as we make progress in natural virtue or in the acquisition of knowledge, with this difference only, that there we apply our natural faculties of intellect and will, but here the already acquired supernatural faculty of grace. This is only partially true. If we wish to make the intellect capable of a quicker and more perfect understanding and the will more capable of a resolute tendency toward good, we need only call into action the dormant faculties of the soul and by practice develop and strengthen them. But we cannot increase grace and the supernatural virtues by our own activity any more than we can thus produce them. It is true that the acts that we perform while in the state of grace are supernatural acts and have far greater efficacy than natural acts or those performed without grace; they help, therefore, to make easier an increase in the supernatural virtues. But in this easing of their practice, there is merely an external, not an inner or essential, increase of the supernatural virtues. This intrinsic increase consists in greater fruitfulness which the soul acquires and in the greater merit and value of its activity. This increase takes place only when God raises us to a higher degree of grace, as He has before raised us to the first degree of grace and of the supernatural virtues; when He now glorifies our soul in a higher measure, as He previously glorified it to a certain extent by the first rays of His light; when, finally, He now infuses a larger measure of supernatural vitality into our soul, as He before infused its first degree.

God alone is the immediate and efficient cause of the increase of grace and the life of grace in us; of Him alone we must ask and expect it. But since He has deposited the treasury of His grace in the holy Sacraments, we can do nothing better than receive these very frequently and with the best possible disposition. In the Sacraments we have the stream of grace, rising in the Sacred Heart of the Son of God and flowing to us in inexhaustible abundance. We need only approach the stream and draw from it in order to be filled with new grace and new supernatural vitality. We receive more of course, the more we approach, the more we enlarge the vessel of our heart through firm hope and make it receptive of holy grace through fear of sin and purity of intention.

Above all the other Sacraments, however, ranks Holy Communion, which has been especially instituted to increase in us grace and the life of grace. In the other Sacraments we find channels of grace; in this one the fountain itself of grace, with all its abundance. In it we eat the Bread of Life, which contains the fullness of the Divinity, and we drink the same Blood which vivified the humanity of the Son of God. As often as we receive it, we, the branches, grow deeper in Christ, who is the heavenly Vine, and grace, the divine sap of this Vine, flows ever more abundantly into us for the increase and nourishment of supernatural life. If then you have at heart the increase of grace, be nourished and strengthened very often with this Heavenly Food; hasten to your Saviour and with ardent desire and a lively faith receive this Divine Bread and living water that springs up into eternal life.

"But," you may ask, "can I not by my own works, by the practice of supernatural virtues, increase these virtues and grace?" In a certain way you can. Though you cannot of your own power raise yourself to a higher degree of grace, nor by your own activity increase the measure of grace and virtue which you already possess, you may by your good works merit and obtain from God that He increase His grace in you. Insofar as you move God by your merit, you become also a cause of the increase of grace.

The power of supernatural good works comes from the merits of our Saviour. The merit that we gain when we cooperate with the merits of Christ obtains an increase of grace and a share of heavenly glory out of the same source. Hence, the Council of Trent condemns all who say "that the justified, by good works he performs, does not truly merit an increase of grace and eternal life" (*Sess.* 6, *de justif.*, can. 32), and consequently those who say, "that good works are merely the fruits and signs of justification, but not a cause of the increase thereof." (*Sess.* 6, can. 24).

Precisely because good works are fruits of grace, they are not merely signs of existing grace, and not only give us a claim to a heavenly reward, but a claim also to a higher degree of grace. For by using the grace which we already possess, we are made ever more pleasing and acceptable to God, and that in the same measure in which we cooperate faithfully and zealously with grace and produce good and beautiful fruit. And since God's pleasure cannot remain without fruit, He will, for every good work, infuse a higher degree of grace and raise us to a higher state of virtue. Ultimately, however, it is not we, but God who gives us this higher degree of grace, and He alone can do it because grace is an effluence of His divine holiness.

Here we see how God and man must work together and how we can live and grow and merit through union with Christ. The branch of a tree receives new sap from the trunk in order to use it for bringing forth blossoms and fruit. In like manner God, who is the root of our supernatural life of grace, infuses new grace into us in the proportion in which we have allowed the previous power to develop into the blossom and fruit of good works. There is this difference, however, that the branch of the tree consumes its strength by using it, while the soul retains and increases it. Consequently, it grows greater and stronger by the new influx of vital power.

The plant exhausts itself in producing its fruits; the just soul, however, nourishes itself and grows by its fruit, for it nourishes itself with that with which it delights and pleases God. Good works are beautiful blossoms and fruits of grace which belong to God. Hence, the spouse in the *Canticle of Canticles* sings, "Let my beloved come into his garden, and eat the fruits of his apple trees." (*Cant.* 5:1). If we delight the eye of God and comfort His heart by our good works, new light must stream upon us from His eyes and new life from His heart. The treasure of our good works sends a sweet fragrance to Heaven, which descends again upon our soul from the bosom of God as a fruitful shower of grace and increases its treasure of grace in the same proportion in which it bore fruit.

The consoling element of this gracious institution of God is increased by the consciousness that we, through that supernatural practice of virtue, acquire an increase, not only of one, but of all the virtues. By the practice of one virtue, a person increases naturally only that particular virtue. When, for example, one fasts, and the practice of fasting becomes through these acts easy, he does not thereby find easy the practice of generosity to the poor or the controlling of his tongue, because these virtues have different objects. By the acts of supernatural virtues, however, we acquire an increase of Sanctifying Grace. But since this is the root of all supernatural virtue and feeds all equally with supernatural vital force, it must imply the increase of the other supernatural virtues. This holds only when we practice the virtue frequently and as perfectly as possible. When we think of the tepidity with which we usually fulfill our duties, we shall readily understand that many theologians find difficulty in applying this teaching to our ordinary actions.

If then, being in the state of grace, you earnestly practice mortification, you not only strengthen the virtues of temperance and abstinence, but also those of love of God and of your neighbor, of mercy, of holy silence; and when in the future you perform an act of one of these virtues, that act will be more perfect, more valuable and more pleasing to God than if you had omitted the first act of mortification.

It is, of course, self-evident that this increase in grace and all virtues is quicker and greater in proportion to the dignity and value of the virtue and to one's zeal and effort in placing the act. Since the love of God is the most noble and precious of all the virtues, the increase of grace must depend chiefly upon it. The life of God consists principally in this love, which may be called its barometer. For in the same measure in which we love God, we are loved in turn by Him and filled with His grace. Love is moreover the mother, the root, the perfection of all the other virtues. It is the mother because it produces all the other virtues in the soul; the root, because it feeds, vivifies, and actuates all; the perfection, because it directs all to the highest end and gives them their final sanction. The growth of love must therefore, in a special way, promote the growth of grace and all the supernatural virtues and is evidently the shortest and surest way to find the greatest wealth of grace and virtue.

The greater and speedier increase in grace, however, depends, not only on the noble quality of its fruits of virtue, but also upon their number and greatness—that is, upon the frequency of our acts and [their] supernatural value (and especially acts of love) and upon the greatest possible exertion and zeal in performing them. The greater our zeal is in the practice of virtue, the greater and more numerous will be the fruits produced by grace, and the more grace itself will be nourished and increased. This will be the case especially when we apply our zeal to the noblest virtue, to acts of love, and endeavor to make them as frequently and as perfectly as possible.

Fortunately, the practice of no other virtue is so easy and agreeable as that of love. We often lack the necessary means and occasions for the practice of other virtues. Thus, we cannot always practice a high degree of patience because we have not always to endure great suffering; not all persons can practice rigorous fasts or give large alms. But we are always able to love, to love frequently and to love ever more. Love requires no great labor or effort, for love is purest sweetness and heavenly delight, so pleasant and agreeable that it makes us forget all troubles and bitterness which may be met with in the practice of the other virtues.

See then, Christian soul, what wonderful power and fruitfulness God has granted you, that you may incessantly and indefinitely increase in His grace and in all the virtues! And should you leave this capability unused? Should you sit idle and not labor with the greatest zeal to build up this temple of God within you? You might make some excuse if the increase of grace cost great labor and trouble, if you were obliged to storm Heaven in order to secure it—though even then you ought to avoid no sacrifice to obtain so great a good. But when I point out a way to you that is very easy, without any steep ascent, without thorns, almost without any difficulty, a way that you need only to enter upon with the foot of good will, then certainly you are no longer excusable.

In the first place, you may obtain a constant increase of grace simply by offering to God your daily actions, even the most trifling and insignificant, and sanctifying them by a holy intention. To this end you need not perform any great, extraordinary labors, but only the ordinary things in a good and holy manner.

We have already mentioned that in our good works the external work is of less importance than the good intention and the inner spirit with which it is done. This truth is of importance here also, when we ask how we can increase in virtue as much as possible. For it shows us that we do not need great and extraordinary deeds, but that through the simplest and most common things we can reach this goal, if we have the right supernatural intention.

Hence the Apostle says: "Therefore, whether you eat or drink, or whatsoever else you do, do all to the glory of God." (*1 Cor.* 10:31). Therefore, be of good heart, you who are striving for holiness. You do not need the greatest mortification nor the wonderful deeds that the Saints have done. Not only when you fast or give alms, but also when you eat, recreate yourself or rest, if you offer all these to God, you become more pleasing to Him and richer in grace.

This will be the case still more if in your actions you make not only one good intention but several. Thus, you practice at the same time several virtues and acquire a twofold or a threefold merit. Thus, you may offer up your daily prayers to God for His glory, in thanksgiving for His benefits, for the conversion of sinners, for the relief of the poor, and you will practice at the same time reverence and gratitude to God and the corporal and spiritual works of mercy. You may likewise labor with the intention of supporting your family and the poor, of doing penance for your sins and of suffering for the love of God and thus practice at the same time the virtues of parental and filial love, of mercy, penance and love of God. In this way, each of your good actions will be, not only one fruit, but a fruit-laden branch on the tree of grace, which is offered to God and in turn draws down upon you streams of Divine grace.

But not only those actions which we actually perform obtain for us an increase of grace, but those also which we *desire* to perform, though we are unable to do so. You say you cannot fast, you cannot chastise yourself, you cannot give alms. But God does not require impossibilities of you. Who hinders you from having a fervent desire to do these good works? God looks at the heart, not at the hand; at the good will, not at the work; at the interior, not at the exterior. Moreover, grace is an internal, spiritual good that must be acquired by internal, spiritual acts. In God's sight, the act is done when the desire to do it has been elicited by the will. As a sinful will displeases God and deprives us of His grace, even if it cannot be carried out, so the virtuous will renders us pleasing to God and obtains grace for us, even if the external act cannot be done.

But what am I saying? Not only the desire for new works renders you more pleasing to God, but also the joy you take in all the good works that you and others have done or that are still being done for the honor of God. If you had done something wrong—for example, an act of revenge—and would afterwards rejoice at the act, you would commit a new sin. Must it not then make you more acceptable to God if you rejoice at having performed some good act, provided this joy be rooted in the love of God?

If you rejoice at the sinful deed of another, you become accessory to his sin and with him incur the displeasure of God. May you not equally rejoice at all the good works performed in the world, at the missionary labors of apostolic men, at the holy zeal of so many priests, the self-sacrifice of religious persons in instructing others, in nursing the sick, and in doing penance for their fellowmen, and will not this be pleasing to God and merit an increase of grace, by this approbation of good works, by the joy at seeing God thus glorified?

This will be more abundantly so if, not content with this joy, you repeat your former good actions and endeavor to perform others. Hence, offer yourself again and again with all your thoughts and desires, renew your resolutions and promises, and as often as you do this, you will increase in grace. God is not like men, to whom you cannot offer the same gift twice. It is not so much the gift that matters, as the perseverance and constancy of will in the offering and in His service. It is His greatest delight to receive again and again the gifts already offered Him, and He accepts them each time as if they had never been presented to Him before.

He accepts even the good works of others when offered in our name, if we unite ourselves with them and rejoice that by them He is honored, and if we offer to Him the holy deeds of others with the fervent wish that we could do similar things. This is to say with the Psalmist: "I am a partaker with all them that fear thee, and that keep thy commandments." (*Ps.* 118:63).

Thus you may offer to God all the works which have been performed from the beginning of the world, not only by the Saints, Apostles, martyrs, confessors and virgins, not only by the Angels, but also by the Blessed Virgin Mary and by Jesus Christ Himself. You may adore God with the adoration of His own Incarnate Son and of all the Saints, praise Him with their praise, love Him with their love, render thanks to Him with their thanks, pray to Him with their petitions and suffer for Him with their patience. You need only rejoice unselfishly and with deep shame for your weakness that they have loved God with so much fervor and devotion and have thus supplied for your neglect and indolence. In like manner, you may participate in the fruits of all the numerous and perfect works and secure a higher degree of God's pleasure. What an inexhaustible treasure you have found for the increase of grace within you! How easy it is for you to be enriched with grace daily and hourly, without any other effort but the recollection that you may make this offering a hundred times every day, without neglecting in the least your business and daily labor.

Let us adore this Divine Providence, let us honor and embrace this infinite goodness which prepares so many and such easy means for our daily advancement in grace and perfection. We ought not to be numbered among those unfortunate ones who become so much the more negligent in acquiring grace, the easier God has made it.

This ingratitude would be aggravated by the fact that we could not excuse our negligence by pretending forgetfulness. For by His actual graces, God constantly arouses the soul from its torpor and urges it on to activity and progress. By these graces, He shows it how far it is still removed from its end, what a distance it has yet to traverse, what a height it still has to climb, and points out also the means by which it may approach this end. He even supports its foot, that it may hasten its step, directs and strengthens its hand, that it may seize His gifts. If we still hold back, if we still persist in our torpor and sluggishness, we indeed deserve to be deprived of all His gifts.

Instead of opposing our progress in grace so foolishly or so perversely, ought we not rather seek every means of furthering this progress and endeavor to obtain actual graces in ever greater abundance? Actual grace is for the growth of the soul what sunshine and rain are for the growth of the plant, with the difference that rain and sunshine influence the growth of the plant immediately, while the illuminations and inspirations of the Holy Ghost further the growth of grace only mediately. Actual grace leads us to produce good works as fruits of Sanctifying Grace, and by these fruits Sanctifying Grace is again fed and increased. Without actual grace our soul, though endowed with Sanctifying Grace, would remain cold, barren and fruitless, and could not even give a sign of life, much less grow and increase.

The Holy Ghost dispenses the rays of His heavenly light and the rain of His beneficent assistance among all the just, as the sun and the clouds let their blessings descend upon all living plants. But if we wish to progress in grace more easily and speedily, we must endeavor to secure not only His general aid and solicitude, but a very special and particular care. For as plants grow more quickly and luxuriously when, besides the rain, they are irrigated by the gardener and placed in a hothouse to receive a greater degree of heat, so will grace develop in the soul more beautifully and abundantly if we place it under the care of the Holy Ghost. This we can do by inviting the Holy Ghost in humble prayer to act as gardener in our soul. No prayer will be more certainly heard than this. The Holy Ghost will joyfully accept this position and will bestow a tender care on us in proportion as our prayer is ardent, confident and persevering. He Himself has the most earnest desire to further our prayers and waits only till we dispose ourselves by such prayer for His special assistance.

We cannot overemphasize the necessity of prayer. Without it, there is no salvation, because there is no grace. Without prayer, we are hardly disposed for grace, because we do not have a desire for it. Only in prayer do we open our soul in order to drink in the heavenly dew of the Holy Ghost and to absorb His blissful rays. Only in prayer do we open our mouth to take in the lifebreath of the Holy Ghost, according to the words of the Psalmist: I opened my mouth and breathed in the spirit. (Cf. *Ps.* 118:131). Hence the admonition of Our Lord that we should pray without ceasing. (Cf. *Luke* 18:1). We must pray as long as we need grace, pray that we grow in it, pray that we persevere in it, pray and pray always, not fainting, that we may obtain salvation.

The Saints are certainly right when they say that no one can be saved without prayer, and no one will be lost if he perseveres in the practice of prayer. Seize this means, therefore, dear Christian, that the good God offers thee, in order to make progress in grace and thus follow the Divine command: "He who is just, let him be just still." (*Apoc.* 22:11).

To encourage you in this progress, the Son of God, although from the beginning He possessed in His humanity the fullness of wisdom, sanctity and grace, wished nevertheless to reveal it only gradually, just as the sun, without increasing in light itself, develops its splendor gradually, from morning till midday. You do not of yourself possess the light of grace. Therefore, you must make progress in reality, as Our Lord did in appearance. Endeavor, then, with the assistance of God, to increase in wisdom, virtue and grace with God and man. God's blessing will not be wanting to you, if only you confide in Him.

"Blessed is the man," says the royal Psalmist (*Ps.* 83:6-8), "whose help is from thee: in his heart he hath disposed to ascend by steps . . . For the lawgiver shall give a blessing, they shall go from virtue to virtue: the God of gods shall be seen in Sion." That is, until after their assumption into Heaven, the vision of God will be the reward of their aspirations.

Chapter 60

PRESERVATION OF GRACE UNTIL THE END

AFTER THE way of enlightenment follows the third and highest stage of the spiritual life, the way of union. The practices that belong to this way, partly as preparation, partly as its proper task, form the principal contents of that which is usually called mysticism.

This way is so sublime that no one may travel it without a very special invitation and the very choice grace of God; grace that He does not always give, even to His outstanding servants. This stage of the practice of virtue embraces the so-called heroic virtues, which are possible also to him who is in the way of enlightenment and are to be recommended to him. Even though one has not reached the state of union, he may at least imitate the type of prayer that is proper to this degree by acquired contemplation. But no one can by his own efforts attain infused supernatural contemplation. Indeed, one may say that it is a kind of intemperance, at least that it is as fruitless as it is dangerous for anyone without a special call to strive after an extraordinary grace.

Of this rare and extraordinary degree of grace we have no reason to deal here. We speak only of that which everyone can and should do with the help of grace. Hence, concerning this stage of the spiritual life, we shall be silent. Fortunately, perfection, as well as holiness, does not depend on these extraordinary things. To become holy, it is sufficient that one undertake in the most perfect way the exercises of the purgative and illuminative way and that he persevere and progress herein until the end.

That which is absolutely necessary to a good end is that one persevere. Now indeed it is certain that perseverance to the end, that is, the retaining of grace to the very last, or the

413

recovery of grace at the moment of death, is a special grace that we cannot merit but must obtain as a pure gift from God. (*S. Th.* 1, 2, q. 109, a. 9). Nevertheless, we must do what we can in order to preserve the grace we have received, and we have every reason to hope that God will not withhold from us the last all-important grace when we have made ourselves, as far as it is possible to us, disposed for it. Of that we must speak more in detail.

All our efforts to obtain and treasure grace will be in vain unless we preserve it until the end of our life, so that we may appear with it before the throne of God. Then only is grace perfectly ours when it is ours forever; then only does grace perfectly make us children of God when we are no longer in danger of losing this dignity, when we return with it to the bosom of our heavenly Father, to possess Him and to be His forever. Then only will we derive salvation from grace and enjoy its most precious, eternal fruit when we can no longer destroy its living germ in us.

Let us be careful, therefore, to preserve this precious treasure with the greatest solicitude, especially since we bear it, as the Apostle says, "in earthen vessels." (*2 Cor.* 4:7). The earthen vessel of this treasure is our poor, weak, earthly nature, in which God has deposited His grace, and this vessel is as frail as the treasure which it contains is holy and precious.

As much as our nature in its nobler part—which is the natural image of God—is susceptible of grace and embraces it as its highest good and as the source of Divine happiness, so much is it in its lower elements foreign, even hostile, to grace and seeks to expel it from the soul, so that it may be undisturbed in the full gratification of self-love and sensual pleasure. The lower part, then, by seeking to draw down to its own level and to subject to itself our higher nature, draws the will away from grace, which then no longer finds a place where it may rest quietly and securely. Instead of being cherished with tender love, it is repelled, and its beneficent balsam is thrown away. Our nature, then, instead of uniting and concentrating all its faculties for the purpose of retaining grace, divides them in its attachment to earthly things, divides itself thereby and loses the precious treasure which it bore in its bosom. So it is no wonder that it is difficult to retain grace. So much the more is this the case since our vessel is not only weak and frail, but exposed to a thousand enemies who wish to snatch it from us, now by secret burglary, again by open robbery.

On the other hand, this treasure is itself its best protector. Grace is a heavenly balsam which heals the frailty of our nature: it hallows, purifies and strengthens the vessel that contains it. Like oil, it is easily spilled, but by its unction, it refreshes and strengthens us against our enemies, as well as against our own weakness and misery. Nevertheless, it is very necessary that we carefully guard our treasure and its vessel and have it watched by reliable custodians.

First of all, we must ourselves guard it with solicitude and caution and with all possible zeal; yes, with holy jealousy we must take care of it and ward off its enemies. With the greatest care we must keep it clean, lest anything impure might enter which would expel grace from it. We must carry it cautiously so that it strikes no stone that would shatter it to pieces. We must guard it from ourselves, from our inclinations and habits, which gradually infect our soul and dislodge grace from it. We must guard against the proximate and remote occasions of sin, lest we be suddenly surprised and overwhelmed by a superior force of the enemy, before we can make use of our weapons.

But if our enemy attacks us openly and with great force, if, notwithstanding our precaution, the concupiscence of the flesh bursts forth in a flame, if the world and its seductive charms have thrown their noose about our neck, we must courageously defend our treasure in open, heroic battle; then we must fear no sacrifice, no pain, no wound for its preservation. We must not hesitate to risk even our lives in defense of our Divine dignity, our crown, our throne, our heavenly kingdom. As the serpent exposes its whole body to save only its head, so must we be ready to expose everything, if only we save grace, because grace will one day make good a hundredfold all that we have sacrificed for its sake.

But our own watching will not suffice to guard and defend securely our precious treasure, considering the frailty of our nature and the power of our enemies. Hence, our Divine Saviour tells us: "Watch ye, and pray that you enter not into temptation." (Mark 14:38). By persevering, earnest and confident prayer, we must call other sentinels to our aid to assist our frailty, as well as to destroy the power of our enemy. We must beg them to place our treasure in some secure place. Let us first beseech the holy Angels, whom God has given to His children as a royal bodyguard, that they may bear us and our treasure in their hands, lest we dash our foot against a stone or be harmed by walking on the asp or basilisk. With the greatest readiness, they will come to our assistance. They are equal and even superior to the infernal lion that goes about seeking to devour us. They will undertake the fight for us and will gain for us a glorious victory. They will expose the secret snares of the enemy and will destroy them before we think of avoiding them. With flaming swords, they will station themselves before the door of our soul, as before Paradise, to guard in us the tree of life, which is grace, lest it be touched and robbed by unhallowed hands.

Let us also commend our soul and its treasure to the maternal bosom of the Mother of God, who is likewise the Mother of grace and of all God's children. Her bosom is the sealed fountain which was neither infested by the poison of human frailty nor accessible to the prince of darkness. In her our nature was restored to its original purity and strength; in her the power of Hell was crushed. If we have recourse to this sanctuary, if we hide in it, we shall without fail triumph over our frailty; we too shall place our foot on the head of the hellish dragon, and it will in vain lie in wait for our heel, as for hers. Mary will receive us into her bosom with truly maternal tenderness because we come to conceal in it that precious jewel for which she gave the priceless Blood of her Son—which had flowed in her own veins—and offered her heart to the Heavenly Father in flames of the most fervent love and of most cruel pain.

Still more should we commend our soul and its treasure

to the Sacred Heart of her Divine Son. For grace is nothing else than the price of that most Sacred Blood which flowed from this heart. Grace is, as it were, the blood of a Divine life, which we draw from the Divine Heart of the Son of God, by which we live in Him and through Him, or rather, we live no longer, but Christ lives in us. How tenderly and lovingly will the Divine Saviour, if we entreat Him, preserve in us that treasure for which He has paid so dearly! How lovingly will Christ receive our grace into His Heart and nurse and cherish it, since He has shed for it the last drop of His Heart's blood! And how secure we know our treasure will be in this holy and inviolable vessel! What enemy will dare to wrest it from this sanctuary? What cunning can gain entrance thereto? How can even the frailty of our own vessel harm us, as long as we keep it enclosed with our treasure in this holy tower which repairs and protects our frailty by its solidity and our weakness by its Divine power?

Finally, let us commend our treasure to the arms, to the bosom, to the heart of our Heavenly Father, who has presented it to us. As He has raised us with His arms from the depths of our nature, has regenerated us in His bosom and pressed us to His Heart as His children, so will He guard and preserve for us this grace of sonship, especially if we earnestly beg it of Him. Our treasure is His treasure. It is the fruit of His bosom, the price of the Blood of His only-begotten Son, the end of all His works. It is the most precious thing that He has given us and that He Himself possesses in us. Therefore, He will also preserve it with His infinite power, love and wisdom. He will guard us as the apple of His eye, as He has assured us through the Prophet Zacharias: "He that toucheth you toucheth the apple of my eye." (Zach. 2:8). But if we are so secure already in the hands of His Angels, in the bosom of His Spouse, in the heart of His Son, how secure shall we be in His own eye! How carefully will His all-seeing eye watch over us; how effectually will His omnipotent hand protect us; how tenderly will His love hold us embraced.

Let us therefore watch and pray without ceasing, watch in holy fear of our own weakness and of the power of the enemy, and pray with holy confidence in the watchful protection of the Angels, of Mary, of the Son of God, and of the Heavenly Father Himself.

"Wherefore he that thinketh himself to stand, let him take heed lest he fall," says the Apostle. (*1 Cor.* 10:12). And again: "With fear and trembling work out your salvation. For it is God who worketh in you, both to will and to accomplish, according to his good will." (*Phil.* 2:12-13). These words are very remarkable and express a great mystery. The reason which the Apostle indicates for our fear is at the same time the reason for our hope and firm confidence. We should work out our salvation with fear and trembling because the will and the accomplishment depend upon the grace of God. For this reason, we must endeavor always to cooperate faithfully with the grace of God, lest God withdraw it from us and leave us to ourselves. In which cause we could do nothing more for our salvation.

But we must also have confidence. Since it is God who effects in us, not only the willing, but also the accomplishing, since He who has begun the good work will perfect it unto the day of Jesus Christ (cf. *Phil.* 1:6), we need not doubt because of our weakness, for we are certain that, by faithful cooperation with God's help, we shall retain grace and reach our goal.

Indeed, we must tremble in the face of the mystery of predestination and pre-election. For as it is God who works salvation in us, so it is He who predestines us for its attainment. "You have not chosen me," says our Divine Saviour, "but I have chosen you." (*John* 15:16). Therefore, we must be extremely careful not to frustrate the intentions of God concerning us, not to depart from the ways by which He wills to lead us. Otherwise, we shall not attain our goal.

But on the other hand, we know that as God has called us to the grace of His sonship and to the inheritance of Heaven, so also, if we are not unfaithful to Him, we shall obtain this grace and be led to our inheritance. Since God wills to make all men happy (cf. *1 Tim.* 2:4) and has called all to salvation, it remains for us to correspond with His plans.

St. Peter admonishes us of this: "Wherefore, brethren, labour the more, that by good works you may make sure your calling and election . . ." (2 *Ptr.* 1:10). As long as through good works we allow grace to be fruitful in us, as long as we avoid sin, as long as we recommend ourselves into God's hands through earnest prayer, we may hope to belong to the elect, of whom the Apostle says that all things work out for their good and that God, as He has called and justified them, will also glorify them. In one word, as long as we try to remain faithful to God, He will remain faithful to us, according to the Apostle: ". . . And God is faithful, who will not suffer you to be tempted above that which you are able: but will make also with temptation issue, that you may be able to bear it." (*1 Cor.* 10:13). "For the gifts and the calling of God are without repentance" (*Rom.* 11:29), that is, the vocation and the grace that He has once given us, He never takes back, if we do not neglect it and refuse it.

So we may and should have the firmest hope that we shall keep grace to the very end and through it attain eternal glory. But let us not forget the words of the Apostle: "Know you not that they that run in the race, all run indeed, but one receiveth the prize? So run that you may obtain." (*1 Cor.* 9:24). Likewise, let us remember the words of admonition of the Son of God: "Hold fast that which thou hast, that no man take thy crown." (*Apoc.* 3:11).

If we lose grace just once again, we are in danger of dying in that condition. We then have to fear that God will remove our candlestick upon which we have extinguished the light of grace, as in the *Apocalypse* (cf. *Apoc.* 2:5) He threatened the Bishop of Ephesus. We must fear that He will forever take away our talent and give it to another who will preserve and invest it more faithfully.

God has no need of us; much less can we dictate to Him how to dispense His grace. As He rejected the people of Israel when they had made themselves unworthy, in spite of all His favors to them, and in their place He called the heathens into His kingdom of grace; as He chose the shepherd boy, David, in place of the disobedient Saul, the penitent thief in place of the traitor Judas, the unbelieving and worldly minded Augustine for the proud monk Pelagius, the poor Indians for the apostate nations of Europe, so He will perhaps reject us and give our place to another soul, which we perhaps considered as lost.

Oh, what confusion for us on the Day of Judgment if we behold others occupying the throne and wearing the crown that were intended for us and to which we had already acquired a claim by grace! This confusion alone would be a new Hell for us, especially if we would consider how many merits we had already acquired, how wantonly we had forfeited this treasure and how easily we might, with God's help, have preserved and increased it. Hence, "Hold fast that which thou hast, that no man take thy crown." (*Apoc.* 3:11). Preserve grace as a favor, as an unmerited, exceedingly precious gift of Divine goodness. Preserve it in humility, without becoming conceited, without boasting of your pre-eminence and despising others. Preserve it with humble gratitude toward God, for nothing makes you more unworthy of His grace than ingratitude. Preserve it with wholesome fear of your own weakness and faithlessness, but at the same time with lively confidence in the power and fidelity of God who has given it to you.

Let us in conclusion listen to the admonition of the Prince of the Apostles, as we have in the beginning learned most clearly from his explanation of nature and the great value of grace. "And do you all insinuate humility one to another, for *God resisteth the proud, but to the humble he giveth grace.* Be you humbled therefore under the mighty hand of God, that he may exalt you in the time of visitation: casting all your care upon him, for he hath care of you. Be sober and watch: because your adversary the devil, as a roaring lion, goeth about seeking whom he may devour. Whom resist ye, strong in faith: knowing that the same affliction befalls your brethren who are in the world. But the God of all grace, who hath called us unto his eternal glory in Christ Jesus, after you have suffered a little, will himself perfect you, and confirm you, and establish you. To him be glory, and empire for ever and ever. Amen." (*1 Ptr.* 5:5-11).

ABOUT THE AUTHOR

F R. Matthias Joseph Scheeben (1835-1888), one of the greatest
Catholic theologians of modern times, was born at Mecken-
heim near Bonn. He studied at the Gregorian University in Rome
under Passaglia and Perrone (1852-1859) and was ordained to the
priesthood in 1858, after which he taught dogmatic theology at
the diocesan seminary of Cologne (1860-1875).

Among Fr. Scheeben's writings, *The Mysteries of Christianity*
(1865-1897) has been called his masterpiece and "the greatest
synthesis of theology written in modern times." He also wrote
Nature and Grace (1861), *The Glories of Divine Grace* (1863), five
pamphlets in defense of Vatican Council I, directed against
Döllinger, Schulte and other Old Catholics, and a large work
called *Handbuch der Katholischen Dogmatik* (1873-1887). Fr.
Scheeben died before completing this work; it was finished by others and reduced to two handy volumes entitled *A Manual of
Catholic Theology Based on Scheeben's Dogmatik* (3rd edition,
1906). Fr. Scheeben founded and edited (1867-1888) the Cologne
Pastoralblatt and edited for 13 years *Das ökumenische Concil vom
Jahre 1869*, which was later entitled *Periodische Blätter zur wis-
senschaftlichen Besprechung der grossen religiösen Fragen der
Gegenwart*.

Fr. Scheeben held that a deeper understanding of Catholic
dogma should be available to all Catholics. As he wrote in his Pref-
ace to the first edition of *The Mysteries of Christianity*: "I cherish
the deep conviction that speculative theology is of supreme importance for the truest and highest formation of mind and heart, and
that under the guidance of the great doctors of the Church, secure
roads must be built, reaching to the very summits of divine truth,
roads that can be traveled without excessive hardship not only by
a few privileged spirits, but by anyone who combines courage and
energy with a sufficiently sound education. . . ."

In *The Glories of Divine Grace*, one sees Fr. Scheeben's remarkable talent for bringing out the amazing consequences of revealed
truths in a way accessible to all Catholics. This work is in itself a
lifetime accomplishment for any man; it is obviously a gift of
Divine Providence to the world.

Spread the Faith with . . .

TAN · BOOKS
A Division of Saint Benedict Press, LLC

TAN books are powerful tools for evangelization. They lift the mind to God and change lives. Millions of readers have found in TAN books and booklets an effective way to teach and defend the Faith, soften hearts, and grow in prayer and holiness of life.

Throughout history the faithful have distributed Catholic literature and sacramentals to save souls. St. Francis de Sales passed out his own pamphlets to win back those who had abandoned the Faith. Countless others have distributed the Miraculous Medal to prompt conversions and inspire deeper devotion to God. Our customers use TAN books in that same spirit.

If you have been helped by this or another TAN title, share it with others. Become a TAN Missionary and share our life changing books and booklets with your family, friends and community. We'll help by providing special discounts for books and booklets purchased in quantity for purposes of evangelization. Write or call us for additional details.

TAN Books
Attn: TAN Missionaries Department
PO Box 410487
Charlotte, NC 28241

Toll-free (800) 437-5876
missionaries@TANBooks.com

TAN·BOOKS

TAN Books was founded in 1967 to preserve the spiritual, intellectual and liturgical traditions of the Catholic Church. At a critical moment in history TAN kept alive the great classics of the Faith and drew many to the Church. In 2008 TAN was acquired by Saint Benedict Press. Today TAN continues its mission to a new generation of readers.

From its earliest days TAN has published a range of booklets that teach and defend the Faith. Through partnerships with organizations, apostolates, and mission-minded individuals, well over 10 million TAN booklets have been distributed.

More recently, TAN has expanded its publishing with the launch of Catholic calendars and daily planners—as well as Bibles, fiction, and multimedia products through its sister imprints Catholic Courses (CatholicCourses.com) and Saint Benedict Press (SaintBenedictPress.com). In 2015, TAN Homeschool became the latest addition to the TAN family, preserving the Faith for the next generation of Catholics (www.TANHomeschool.com).

Today TAN publishes over 500 titles in the areas of theology, prayer, devotions, doctrine, Church history, and the lives of the saints. TAN books are published in multiple languages and found throughout the world in schools, parishes, bookstores and homes.

For a free catalog, visit us online at
TANBooks.com

Or call us toll-free at
(800) 437-5876